The Romanian Revolution of December 1989

THE

Romanian Revolution
of December 1989

PETER SIANI-DAVIES

CORNELL UNIVERSITY PRESS

Ithaca and London

First published 2005 by Cornell University Press
First printing, Cornell Paperbacks, 2007

Printed in the United States of America

Library of Congress Cataloging-in-Publication Data

Siani-Davies, Peter.
  The Romanian revolution of December 1989 / Peter Siani-Davies.
     p. cm.
  Includes bibliographical references and index.
  ISBN-13: 978-0-8014-4245-2 (cloth : alk. paper)
  ISBN-13: 978-0-8014-7389-0 (pbk. : alk. paper)
  1. Romania—History—Revolution, 1989. 2. Romania—Politics and
government—1989- I. Title.
  DR269.5.S55 2005
  949.803'2—dc22   2004018923

Cornell University Press strives to use environmentally responsible
suppliers and materials to the fullest extent possible in the publishing
of its books. Such materials include vegetable-based, low-VOC inks
and acid-free papers that are recycled, totally chlorine-free, or partly
composed of nonwood fibers. For further information, visit our website
at www.cornellpress.cornell.edu.

Cloth printing   10 9 8 7 6 5 4 3 2 1
Paperback printing   10 9 8 7 6 5 4 3 2 1

For Mary and Michael

Contents

Acknowledgments

The research for this book involved a number of interviews with leading Romanian political figures. In keeping with the sensibilities surrounding the revolution, an early decision was made to free those interviewed from the danger of direct quotation by eschewing a tape recorder and keeping discussions informal. In consequence, although their words were often important in shaping my own interpretation of events, I have not directly cited these interview subjects in the text. Instead, I would like to record here that the following were kind enough to spare the time to talk to me, and to express my gratitude for their efforts that greatly improved the quality of this work and enriched my own understanding of Romania: Călin Anastasiu, Victor Babiuc, Ioana Brătianu, Silviu Brucan, Pavel Câmpeanu, Corneliu Coposu, Petre Datculescu, Caius Traian Dragomir, Dinu Giurescu, Andrei Muştescu, Dragoş Negrescu, Bogdan Niculescu Duvăz, Teodor Nicolaescu, Vladimir Pasti, Horia-Roman Patapievici, Dorel Şandor, Vasile Sccăreş, Adrian Severin, Ovidiu Şincai, Ştefana Steriade, and Stelian Tănase.

During the time I was conducting the research for this volume I was fortunate to make the acquaintance of a large number of Romanians. Any list of acknowledgments is bound to be incomplete, and I apologize for any unintentionally forgotten, but I thank in particular the past and present staff of the Nicolae Iorga Institute of History, and especially Şerban Papacostea, Paul Cernovodeanu, and Florin Constantiniu, for providing a friendly base for me in Romania. Yvonne Alexandrescu, Vlad Moga, Adrian Pop, Vasile Lăpăduşi and Simone Micălescu were all helpful at various times, as were the staff of the Romanian Embassy in London. Liviu

Ţărau valiantly coaxed a reluctant photocopier into action to provide me with a copy of a manuscript by Costel Neacşu. Paul Michelson and Larry Bush also provided important information. Judy Batt and Anita Prazmowska both made helpful suggestions. The Economic and Social Research Council generously funded part of the research, while the British Council and University of Bucharest sponsored my attendance at a Romanian language summer school. My colleagues at the School of Slavonic and East European Studies, University College London (SSEES), and, especially, the Centre for South-East European Studies have provided good company and valued support. I would particularly like to thank Wendy Bracewell for her incisive comments on an earlier version of this manuscript, George Kolankiewicz for his support, Dennis Deletant for sharing with me some important sources, and George Schöpflin, whose undergraduate courses first awakened my interest in Eastern Europe. The staff of SSEES library have also been helpful, especially Vlasta Gyenes, who tracked down some of the Romanian sources. Elena Manailescu of Rompres selected some of the photographs from their extensive archive. Brenda Walker kindly gave permission for the reproduction of the poem in Chapter 1. Finally, I would also like to thank John Ackerman at Cornell University Press, who has overseen this project through its long gestation, as well as Karen Laun and Eric Schramm for their sympathetic editing.

Several Romanians through their friendship have been particularly important in shaping my appreciation of their country. Vlad Niculescu's boundless enthusiasm for Romanian culture was truly infectious, while Dan Niculescu Duvăz over the years has proven to be an always unbiased and thoughtful observer. He diligently commented on an earlier version of the manuscript and, together with his family, over endless convivial lunches, has greatly increased not only my appreciation of Romanian cuisine but also my understanding of Romania as a whole. With his encyclopedic wisdom Nicolae Tanaşoca patiently guided me through the mazes of Romanian history; he and his wife, Anca, were ever welcoming. My deepest gratitude, however, remains to the Familia Nedelcu: Catrinel, Tudor, Ioana, and Ileana Baracu, for their kindness and hospitality over the years. Theirs was always a welcoming portal, and without their generosity of spirit Romania for me would have forever remained an alien land.

Finally, I am happy to acknowledge many years of support and encouragement from my father and mother and, most of all, my wife, Mary. She has been a constant companion during the research and writing of this work, bearing much with fortitude and understanding. As an always critical intellectual sparring partner, she has done much to help make sense of what at times seemed like a shapeless mass of ideas, and as a wife she has always been ready to give hope in times of doubt. It is to her that I owe the deepest debt of gratitude and to her that I dedicate this book.

Abbreviations

CFTUR	Confederation of Free Trade Unions in Romania
CNSF	Council of the National Salvation Front
CPSU	Communist Party of the Soviet Union
DCR	Democratic Convention of Romania
DNSF	Democratic National Salvation Front
DSS	Department of State Security
EMR	Ecological Movement of Romania
GTUFR	General Trade Union Federation of Romania
GSD	Group for Social Dialogue
HDUR	Hungarian Democratic Union of Romania
NEFM	New Economic and Financial Mechanism
NLP	National Liberal Party
NPP	National Peasant Party-Christian Democratic
NSF	National Salvation Front
PCNU	Provisional Council of National Unity
PEC	Political Executive Committee (of the Central Committee of the Romanian Communist Party)
PSDR	Party of Social Democracy in Romania
RCP	Romanian Communist Party
RFE	Radio Free Europe
RSDP	Romanian Social Democratic Party
SRI	Serviciul Român de Informaţii [Romanian Information Service]
USLA	Unităţii Speciale de Luptă Antiteroristă [Special Anti-Terrorist Combat Units]

Introduction

The Romanian revolution broke out on December 15, 1989, in the city of Timişoara. It started as a small-scale protest against a clumsy attempt by the authorities to evict a dissident priest, László Tőkés, from his residence but the ten days that followed were to shake Romania to the core. In Timişoara, Bucharest, and several other towns and cities, ragged street protests, which were violently suppressed by the security forces, were the prelude to huge mass demonstrations. In the face of these crowds, the longstanding head of the Romanian Communist Party (RCP), Nicolae Ceauşescu, fled by helicopter from the central committee building in Bucharest on December 22. Within hours of Ceauşescu's departure, a new governing group, the National Salvation Front (NSF), led by Ion Iliescu, had taken power, but the same evening violence again returned to the streets, as the army, aided by the civilian population, began to fire upon an enemy identified as terrorists. There followed a confusing swirl of events in which nearly 1,000 people died before the shooting began to peter out on December 25. On that day Ceauşescu, together with his wife Elena, was executed in the city of Târgovişte.

December 25, 1989, did not mark the end of the Romanian revolution. The coming months saw continued political strife as the NSF struggled to consolidate its hold on power and impose its political vision on Romania. Indeed, the end of any revolution is notoriously difficult to pin down, because, while it is essentially a political phenomenon, the term also bears connotations of wider cultural and socioeconomic change and this, by its very nature, tends to be a longer-term process. Within this wider revolutionary process, however, it is often possible to divine a shorter-term end point, built around the institutionalization of the new political order. Such an end point represents a process of accommodation culminating in "an arrangement . . . whereby . . . the main principles which the revolution has established cease to be matters of controversy."[1] This book ends its narrative on February 9, 1990. On that day convened a proto-parliament, the Provisional Council of National Unity, gathering together representatives from most of the political groups then extant in Romania. This represented a formal recognition of the wider anti-Ceaușescu coalition and, together with the disappearance of the NSF factory councils and the adoption of a territorially based politico-administrative system, laid the ground for a revolutionary settlement which broadly conformed to Western norms of democratic organization. Although it may be more visible in hindsight than it was at the time, even before the elections of May 1990 and the adoption of a new constitution in December 1991, the future institutional framework of Romanian politics had to a substantial degree ceased to be a matter of contention, save for the issue of the former king, whose return remained on the political agenda of some parties. On February 9, 1990, one significant political end point to the revolution was therefore reached, even if at this stage it still remained more revolutionary in form than in content.

The centrality of the revolution of December 1989 to recent Romanian history is indisputable. It provided a base for the subsequent postcommunist reforms and has remained a powerful political symbol within domestic discourses. In terms of the wider world, it brought Romania to international prominence, achieving some notoriety as the first so-called televised revolution. As the most violent of the events that transformed Eastern Europe in 1989, it also provided many of the defining images of the fall of communism in the region. At the time the events were subject to enormous media interest, and in the years after 1989 the overthrow of the Romanian leader and his death have come to be something of a metaphor for the fate of tyranny.[2] Subsequent to December 1989, a steady stream of books and, especially newspaper articles, has appeared about the revolution, mostly in Romanian but in other languages as well. Immediately after the events, these were mostly straightforward eyewitness accounts, together with some important documentary sources, including a transcript of the television broadcast on December 22. By the close of 1990, however, there had also begun to appear a parallel, more interpretative, literature which questioned the original story told about the events. Often written in French, these works soon spawned a host of Romanian imitators, with one significant subgroup within this genre seeking in the process to rehabilitate elements of the former regime, especially

---

1. Edwards quoted in Krejčí (1994), 5–6.
2. At the time of the 2003 Iraq war Saddam Hussein was frequently compared with Ceaușescu. See, for instance, *Guardian*, April 10, 2003; ibid., April 30, 2003.

the *securitate*. To this literature there can also be added the reports of a host of state bodies which investigated the revolution. These have included various senatorial and governmental commissions of inquiry, the Romanian Information Service, the military procurator, and the Romanian army, among others. Trials of those accused of crimes during the revolution have furnished even further details. Yet despite, or perhaps because of, this flood of information, since it can be argued that much of this literature was designed to peddle a certain line rather than offer clarification, so many questions still remain unanswered about December 1989 that one well-known Romanian historian has labeled the revolution "the greatest enigma of Romanian history."[3] Who exactly were the terrorists who wrought such havoc after the overthrow of Ceauşescu? What was the role of the *securitate* in December 1989? What part did the USSR play? Were Arabs involved? What was the extent of the plotting prior to 22 December 1989? Did the National Salvation Front exist prior to this date?

This book is entitled the "Romanian Revolution of December 1989" and at first sight the decision to term the events in Romania a "revolution" would seem straightforward. Elsewhere in Eastern Europe the events of 1989 had been so lacking in the violence and tumult usually associated with "true" revolutions that a whole new class of oxymoronic epithets was coined, such as "velvet" revolution and "negotiated" revolution.[4] Only in Romania was the blood and passion traditionally associated with the overthrow of an *ancien régime* seen together with classical revolutionary symbolism. The seizing of the central committee building in Bucharest could be equated with the storming of the Bastille. The flight of Ceauşescu by helicopter and car was merely a twentieth century equivalent of the headlong horse-drawn coach dash to Varennes, and in his subsequent execution the Romanian leader met the same fate as Louis XVI. Yet, despite this, many within Romania and the outside world have come to deny that the events should be termed a "revolution." A December 1992 domestic opinion poll found only 46 percent of respondents willing to call the events by this name; when a similar poll was held seven years later, this figure had risen only slightly to 49 percent.[5]

The doubts about what the events should be called did not just arise from the many questions which still remain unanswered about December 1989. They also have their roots in the fact that the revolutionary act of December 1989 and January 1990 was only a small segment of the wider revolutionary process which embroiled Romania in the 1990s. This process was characterized by protracted and occasionally bloody political confrontations, most notoriously during the descent of the Jiu Valley min-

3. Florin Constantiniu in the introduction to Domenico (1999) 7.
4. Bruszt (1990), 365–87.
5. Câmpeanu (1993), 181; Foreign Broadcast Information Service (hereafter FBIS)-EEU-1999-1223, December 23, 1999.

ers onto Bucharest in June 1990 and September 1991. In the circumstances it is hardly surprising that there arose a fierce polemic over the nature of the revolutionary act, as control of the official narrative and symbols of revolution, sometimes aided by the selective use of the judicial process, became central to the legitimization of power. In the immediate aftermath of December 1989, Ion Iliescu and the new leaders of the NSF had little choice but to proclaim the events "a revolution." As tribunes of the people, their very right to rule was based on the claim that they were the anointed of the revolutionary crowd on the street. Their opponents of all persuasions thought otherwise. Drawing upon the many inconsistencies in the Front's story, they charged that it had shadowy conspiratorial origins and that it had only assumed power through manipulation of the events, perhaps with foreign assistance. Instead of a revolution they called the events of December 1989 a coup d'état.

In the months after the revolution, how the events were perceived became something of a touchstone of political orientation not just at an elite but also at a popular level. An opinion poll from 1992 found a clear correlation between interpretations of December 1989 and voting behavior, with supporters of the Iliescu-oriented Democratic National Salvation Front (DNSF) understandably more likely to see it as a revolution than those of the National Peasant Party-Christian Democratic (NPP)-dominated Democratic Convention of Romania (DCR). After the 1992 elections, partly because of the continuing political domination of Iliescu, the DNSF and its successor, the Party of Social Democracy in Romania (PSDR), the revolution retained political charge. When, in September 1996, the report of the senatorial commission of inquiry into the revolution was finally passed to the president of the Senate it came in two forms: seven members of the commission, led by Sergiu Nicolaescu of the PSDR, had signed one document, while the other four, including the president of the commission, Valentin Gabrielescu of the NPP, had signed another. Instead of offering closure and an end to the controversy, the two reports merely served to reflect the continuing divisions within Romanian society. On the day the senatorial commission was due to present its report, 1,000 protesters, members of various associations of former revolutionaries, gathered outside the Senate chanting that Gabrielescu was nothing other than a second Ceaușescu. With presidential and parliamentary elections looming, its seems to have been judged politic to set the reports to one side, with the excuse that they could not be circulated to the senators as intended, because the Senate did not have sufficient funds to pay for the photocopying of the two documents, each of which was over 1,000 pages long.[6]

6. *Adevărul*, September 19, 1996, 1; ibid., September 24, 1996, 2; ibid., October 1, 1996, 2.

Each of the various narratives of revolution and coup d'état produced in Romania in the 1990s legitimized itself by claiming to possess the real truth about the events of December 1989. In the process the concept of the truth became highly politicized, and the search for justice for the crimes committed during the revolution obscured. At first sight President Emil Constantinescu in 1998 would seem to have been speaking for all when he declared "we must find out the truth and assume our recent history in all honesty and pass it down correctly to the next generations. . . . Romanian society must know that today we can state the truth about the 1989 December repression and the guilty people involved, that we have the political willingness to utter the entire truth."[7] Yet in his unspoken suggestion that the previous NSF/DNSF regime had deliberately obscured the truth about the events and that only the DCR government could put this right, Constantinescu was merely giving a further example of how politicized the question of the revolution had become. For him, the truth about December 1989 had been deliberately hidden for political ends. It was not lost, however, it could still be discovered through diligent and honest inquiry.

Constantinescu's expectation that the "entire truth" about the revolution could still be revealed was probably matched by most Romanians. But for this to happen the entire past has to be known and faithfully reproduced as history, because history is a record of that past. Yet not only can the whole past never be known, and this is especially true of an event as chaotic as a revolution, but the conjunction between the past and history is not and cannot be perfect. In this sense the Romanian revolution becomes just one highly politicized example of a more general problem, as the gap between referentiality and representation places into question the whole possibility of the existence of a unified narrative claiming to represent the truth about the events.[8] Instead of a single grand unified narrative, history consists of multiple conflicting interpretations, and this is not just a problem for an author engaged in writing a history of the Romanian revolution or for scholars trying to come to grips with other past events. As noted above, it has also been a problem for the Romanian people themselves as they have struggled to make sense of the competing claims about the revolution and tried to comprehend their recent past. In all three instances the issues are the same, as are the problems and processes.

The acceptance that it is not possible to encompass an entirely true reproduction of the revolution in a single metanarrative and that instead there will always be a plurality of truths is both liberating and unsettling. On the one hand, it is positive in that it allows for a better understanding

---

7. FBIS-EEU-98-099, April 9, 1998.
8. Berkhofer (1995).

of the mechanics behind the production of these various truths and the reasons why they have come to exist.[9] It can, for instance, allow us to understand why *securitate* apologists produce the narratives they do.[10] On the other hand, such an idea also raises the prospect that no version of the events will be seen as authoritative, consigning all the narratives to drift aimlessly in a sea of moral relativism; although to assume this is to take as absolute a position as that held by those who believe unquestioningly in the idea of reproducing a single objective representation of the world as it really exists outside of human subjectivity, and is, at least morally, equally dubious.[11] Even if the entire truth about the revolution cannot be known, nobody can fault Constantinescu for wanting to "assume our recent history in all honesty and pass it down correctly to the next generations."[12] The challenge therefore for scholars researching December 1989 and for the Romanian people themselves is to rescue the events from this sea of relativism and avoid their consignment alongside such exemplars of modern history as the assassination of John F. Kennedy, where "factual statements . . . cannot be founded and further research does not *reduce* but *enhances* the puzzlement about 'what really happened.' "[13]

It is against this background that this book has been written. Drawing on the mass of information released in the years after the events, its primary aim is to provide as accurate and as credible a narrative of the revolution as possible. In the process it also seeks to make a contribution to a number of wider debates that have relevance beyond Romania or Eastern European area studies in general, particularly as regards the nature of revolutions and of history itself. The first chapter examines the causes of the revolution through the required prerequisites for such an event: the mobilization of revolutionary challengers, a permissive international environment, and state breakdown. Although the figure of Nicolae Ceauşescu necessarily looms large, rather than concentrating on his character this chapter instead focuses on his relationship with key institutions such as the RCP and the security forces. The second chapter is a narrative of the events from December 15 until noon on December 22, when Ceauşescu departed by helicopter from the central committee building in Bucharest. The narrative chiefly focuses on events in Timişoara and Bucharest but also covers a number of other towns and cities. Particular attention is paid to the response of the authorities to the accelerating emergency, with Ceauşescu apparently being guided in his actions by a persistent but faulty

9. Selbin (1997, 123–36) argues collective memory and narrative construction are important in understanding revolutions but does not take the argument as far as it is developed in this book.
10. Hall (1999).
11. Appleby, Hunt, and Jacob (1994), 247.
12. FBIS-EEU-98-099, April 9, 1998.
13. Lorenz (1994), 315. A good discussion of this tendency in Romania is Hall (2002).

analogy with 1968, when he successfully rallied the nation to his side in his defiance of the Soviet Union at the time of the Warsaw Pact invasion of Czechoslovakia.

The third chapter offers an account of the second phase of the revolution from the overthrow of Ceaușescu to his execution along with his wife on December 25. The narrative seeks to clear the confusion surrounding the events by focusing on two key issues: the means by which the NSF seized and then consolidated power, and the nature of the violence that erupted in Bucharest and a number of other towns and cities. Far more people died in this period of the revolution than in the period prior to the departure of Ceaușescu from Bucharest, and so a central aim of this chapter is to shed some light on the circumstances surrounding these deaths. At the time of the revolution and since, it has frequently been charged that the violence at this time was a diversion deliberately created by terrorists, who are generally presumed to have belonged to the Department of State Security, better known as the *securitate*. The first part of the fourth chapter investigates this claim by considering the activities of the leading *securitate* units during the fighting. The second half of the chapter then considers the other great mystery of the revolution: the extent of the plotting prior to the overthrow of Ceaușescu. A myriad of conspiracy theories surrounds the events, with allegations that there was plotting inside the country as well as interference from outside states. In assessing these claims, the stress throughout is on placing any conspiracy in proper perspective and judging its direct impact on the unfolding events of December 1989.

The fifth chapter, after surveying the structures and composition of the new regime, turns to the question of the cultural matrix in which the NSF shaped its initial ideology and abortive political project of consensus. Although the latter was never clearly enunciated, it seems to have foreseen a continuation of something close to single-party rule in which differing factions and parties would be permitted, but only under the wider umbrella of the Council of the National Salvation Front. This chapter also suggests that alongside strong currents of reform socialism, the ideology of the NSF also included a number of broader strategies, such as "dialogue" and "competence," which were primarily aimed at raising the social status of displaced intellectuals and allowing them to once more occupy the center of the national stage. The end of the conflict brought no end to the confusion and strife in Romania, and the sixth chapter is concerned with the events of January 1990 during which the NSF, while attempting to consolidate its hold on power, came under challenge from important segments of the urban population. As the month progressed, this was increasingly centered on the newly reactivated traditional parties of pre-Second World War vintage, the National Peasant Party-Christian Democratic, National Liberal Party, and Romanian Social Democratic

Party. During this turbulent period, the NSF was forced to abandon its initial governing structure in favor of the more broadly based Provisional Council of National Unity. The final chapter revisits issues raised in this introduction. Measuring the idea of revolution against those of coup d'état and popular uprising, it once again considers the name that should be given to the events. Then, after exploring how the death toll came to be so exaggerated, it concludes by returning to consider how various popular narratives both shaped the events and perceptions of its outcome.

CHAPTER ONE

The Causes of the Revolution

Just before 3 o'clock in the afternoon of Christmas Day 1989, the newly deposed president of Romania, Nicolae Ceauşescu, together with his wife, Elena, was unceremoniously hauled in front of a wall at an army garrison in the city of Târgovişte. They had been in the barracks since their flight from Bucharest on the afternoon of December 22. Now, after a brief trial lasting only an hour, they were hurriedly executed by a small firing squad of paratroopers. In a year in which aging communist leaders had been swept from power throughout Eastern Europe, only the Ceauşescus were to meet such a brutal end. The decision to put them to death was largely taken in response to the exigencies of the revolution, but for many Romanians it was merely just retribution for years of despotic rule.[1]

The most visible aspect of Romania's plight to the outside visitor in the late 1980s was the struggle to find food. In towns and villages across the country musty shops with their decor stuck in some distant, more bountiful time were "stocked" with nothing more than rows of almost identical tins and bottles of pickled vegetables and usually inedible preserves. Food rationing had been selectively imposed in 1981, spreading two years later to encompass most of the remainder of the country, except for Bucharest.[2] By the time of the revolution, the official monthly ration for many Romanians had been reduced to a kilo of flour, sugar, and meat, half a kilo of margarine, and five eggs, with there being no guarantee that

1. For a description of Romania in the 1980s see Almond (1991), 279–329.
2. Shafir (1985), 117.

Map of Romania.

even these meager supplies would be forthcoming.[3] Everywhere there were lines for even basic staples of life, such as bread, which was also rationed, and no Romanian would dream of leaving home without a plastic bag in case of chancing upon an unexpected delivery—the better-connected flaunting their status through a bag sporting a western design. Gas, when it was available, was rationed to thirty liters or less per month and other energy supplies were equally curtailed. A drive to save electricity left the streets dimly lit at night and the country vulnerable to unpredictable power cuts. The enormous centralized heating systems, which each supplied thousands of city apartments, might only produce hot water once a week, and in many flats the temperature never rose above eight degrees centigrade, even in the coldest weather. In Bucharest, during the bitter winter of 1985, the family of the economist Alin Teodorescu slept wrapped in their overcoats, while elsewhere in the city fear of hypothermia drove others to sleep in their kitchens.[4] Here, kept warm by the naked flames of their stoves, they ran the risk of asphyxiation if the gas supply was cut while they slumbered and then turned on again unexpectedly.[5] In 1985 it was reported that energy consumption per household was a meager 20 percent of the 1979 level, and the extent of the economic downturn was fully revealed in official CMEA statistics, which recorded that between 1980 and 1985 annual state expenditure on housing declined by 37 percent, on healthcare by 17 percent, and on education, culture, and science by a crippling 53 percent.[6]

From this land of scarcity there also emerged persistent reports of serious human rights abuses.[7] Anyone who dared openly doubt the "triumphal age" in which they resided ran the risk of losing their job, harassment from the security forces, and detention, sometimes in psychiatric hospitals.[8] The chief agents of control were the forces of the Ministry of the Interior: the militia and the Department of State Security, popularly known as the *securitate*. Like Ceaușescu, the latter since 1989 has become almost a byword for tyranny of the worst kind, although in reality they ruled as much by the fear they inspired as actual terror.[9] Under Ceaușescu the loss of life and suffering cannot be equated with the horrors of the Soviet Union in the 1930s, China during the Cultural Revolution, or even Romania under Gheorghe Gheorghiu-Dej. Still, it was far from being an open society. By an order of April 1983 all typewriters had to be regis-

3. Deletant (1998), 178; Ionescu (March 4, 1988), 10–11; Brezinski and Petersen (1990), 79–80; Gallagher (1995), 65; Oprea and Olaru (2002), 16 n. 9.
4. Teodorescu (1991), 69–82.
5. Anon [Câmpeanu] (October 23, 1986), 10–18.
6. Georgescu (1988), 78–79; Linden (1989), 301.
7. *Romania: human rights abuses* (1987); Gabanyi (2000), 369–78.
8. Adler, Mueller, and Ayat (1993), 3–17.
9. Jowitt (1991), 75.

tered with the authorities, special permission had to be gained to make a photocopy, and, from December 1985, failure to report conversations with foreigners became a criminal offense.[10] This did not stop Romanians from talking to travelers, but no encounter could take place without constant furtive glances over the shoulder to see who might be listening.[11] Rumors at the time of the revolution held that as many as 25 percent of the population were informers, and, not surprisingly in such an atmosphere, fear and suspicion came to predominate. In the absence of formal channels of communication—the news on the television each night dwelled almost exclusively on the activities of the presidential couple, also featured prominently in the print media—gossip and rumor tended to reach fantastical proportions.[12] Among the myriad of stories, it was claimed that human flesh was on sale in restaurants unable to secure normal food supplies, that Ceaușescu was negotiating with Indira Gandhi to secure the repatriation of Romania's Gypsies to India, and that Ceaușescu's son, Nicu, regularly knocked down and killed pedestrians in drunken driving sprees.[13]

Control permeated all levels of society and even entered the bedroom through the infamous pronatalist campaign that since 1966 had restricted abortions and made contraception virtually unavailable. Initially this had led to a growth in the birth rate, and ironically some of the young people who took to the streets in 1989 to depose Ceaușescu were probably the fruits of this campaign. However, by the time of the revolution, the number of births had long fallen away, prompting the imposition of ever stricter limits on abortions, intrusive gynecological examinations, and penalties against healthcare workers if one of their patients ended a pregnancy through an illegal termination.[14] Countless women died from illegal abortions in Romania, which had the highest rate of maternal mortality in Europe, with 159 deaths per 100,000 live births in 1989.[15] After the revolution, the full tragedy of the campaign was revealed. Haunting pictures emerged of dilapidated institutions crammed with an estimated 100,000 children under eighteen years old placed in care by their parents because of poverty or marital breakdown.[16] Over one thousand children—half from such institutions—were later found to be suffering from AIDS, the vast majority being less than four years old. In most cases the

---

10. Georgescu (1988), 84; Deletant (1998), 204; Gabanyi (2000), 397–400.

11. My own experiences seem to have been shared by other visitors to Romania at this time; see, for instance, Hall (1988), 3–88; Harding (1990), Chamberlain (1990), 76–96, 123–47.

12. Stefanescu (October 1, 1985), 15–17; Gross (1996).

13. Sampson (1984), 142–64.

14. Fischer (1985), 121–37; Cole and Nydon (1990), 469–76; Kligman (1992), 364–418; Johnson, Horga, and Andronache (1993), 875–78; Kligman (1998).

15. Hord et al. (1991), 231–40.

16. Reich (1990), 9–14; Johnson, Edwards, and Puwak (1993), 489–506.

disease had been contracted through unscreened blood transfusions or from the use of contaminated needles and syringes during therapeutic injections.[17]

Yet amid this deprivation and suffering, the Romanian people were constantly told by the state propaganda apparatus that they were living through a "golden epoch" of unparalleled achievements, as Ceauşescu embarked on a series of grandiose and costly construction projects of doubtful utility. A Trans-Făgăraşan highway, which purposelessly twisted and turned over the highest mountain chain in the country, was littered with rock falls within years of its completion. The newly finished Danube-Black Sea Canal, advertised as the largest construction project ever undertaken in Romania, with a claimed scale of work greater than that involved in digging the Suez or Panama Canals, languished to only a fraction of its capacity.[18] Dwarfing all was the Orwellian scheme of systematization through which at least 5,000 of the country's villages were slated to be bulldozed to the ground and their inhabitants transferred to blocks of flats in a network of new agro-towns.[19] Ostensibly the scheme was driven by a desire to rationalize the use of agricultural space and raise the status of rural communities. Migration to the cities was to be halted and professional people, especially doctors, were to be given reason to work in the countryside. More invidiously, social control would also be tightened and individualism eroded. In fact, only a few villages were actually destroyed during the campaign, and it was within the urban landscape, especially in Bucharest, that Ceauşescu was to do more irreparable damage. Here a large swath of the city center, including many historic houses and churches, was leveled to the ground to allow for the construction of a wide triumphal boulevard and an enormous administrative complex, known as the Casa Republicii.[20]

So poignant were the tales of human suffering emanating from Romania that since December 1989 the name of Nicolae Ceauşescu has become synonymous with dictatorship of the worst kind. Yet the paradox remains, that in the face of such hardship, for much of the 1980s, there were relatively few signs of revolt or dissent in Romania. The high level of coercion exercised by the state was obviously one reason for this, but two other explanations were offered by western analysts at the time, one broadly cultural in orientation and the other structural. The cultural view was best expressed by Michael Shafir, who, searching for an explanation

17. Hersh et al. (1991), 645–49.
18. Sharman (1983), 317–21; Socor (October 5, 1984), 7–14; Turnock (1986b), 65–79; Socor (November 6, 1987), 21–24; Gabanyi (2000), 401–6.
19. Shafir (August 23, 1988a), 3–8; Ronnås (1989), 543–59; Turnock (1991), 77–107; Deletant (1993), 53–74.
20. Giurescu (1990), Almond (1992), 153–71; Danta (1993), 170–82. Originally christened Casa Poporului, it was later renamed Casa Republicii (Deletant, 1995), 308.

for passivity, stressed the lack of a tradition of autonomy in Romanian political culture and the deep roots of peasant conformity, with its tendency toward resignation and fatalism grounded in mysticism and the Orthodox religion. These traits were supposedly expressed through the folk ballad *Miorița*, in which a young shepherd warned by a female lamb of the murderous schemes of his companions still passively awaits his death.[21] The clearest exponent of the structural view was Steven Sampson. He also drew upon cultural factors in searching for an answer to the question of passivity, but took them to markedly different conclusions, when he stressed the individuality of the Romanians and their apparent lack of faith in social organizations. Instead of passively conforming, he saw the Romanians as actively scheming to bypass the most unpleasant aspects of the system and to secure goods and services through the informal economy.[22] Family and friends supplied the food that ensured that despite the shortages there was no famine in Romania. And, although there was an oppressive level of formal censorship and uncontrolled public life was at a minimum, with restaurants and other places of entertainment closing by the early evening, a high per capita ownership rate of video cassette recorders meant that inside their homes many Romanians were watching the latest western films.[23]

Both these cultural and structural explanations for passivity are useful for understanding the lack of revolt in Romania during the 1980s, but they are less helpful for explaining why the country erupted in revolution in 1989. This is partially because they both start from a belief that conditions in Romania during the 1980s should have produced social unrest. But this is not necessarily true, because poverty and suffering in themselves do not produce revolt. If they did, then many parts of the world would be convulsed in permanent turmoil. To explain this apparent anomaly some theorists have suggested that instead of utter poverty or, as they style it, absolute deprivation, it is actually relative deprivation caused by a sharp downturn in fortunes after a period of prosperity that sparks revolution.[24] Could this be the case in Romania? The 1980s had seen a sharp economic downturn after a period of sustained economic growth and social development and this had, presumably, produced a sharp dislocation between expectations and achievements, but this was nothing new in 1989. The greatest decline in living standards had actually occurred in the years between 1980 and 1983 when, according to the calculations of Marvin Jackson, overall domestic consumption fell by 17 percent. Conditions had actually improved slightly in the mid-1980s, and

---

21. Shafir (1985), 132–35. For a translation of *Miorița* see Barsan (1975), 35–37.
22. Sampson (1981–83), 166; Kideckel (1992), 70.
23. Gross (1996), 51; note also the small ads for video recorders in any pre-revolution newspaper.
24. Davies (1962), 5–19; Gurr (1970), 23, 52–56.

then stayed more or less the same for the rest of the decade, although living standards remained only around 88 percent of the 1979 figure.[25] It seems that neither relative deprivation nor absolute deprivation can explain the outbreak of the revolution in Romania; and the failure of the decline in the country's economic situation after 1989, when for many the gap between hopes and reality became a gaping abyss, to produce further outbreaks of sustained revolutionary violence only serves to underline the absence of a causal link.

Revolutionary situations need more than deprivation, whether it be absolute or relative, and a sense of widespread popular grievance. They require the appearance of individuals or more probably a group or amalgamation of groups—a revolutionary coalition—willing to challenge the ruling regime. For a "true" revolution to occur, most would hold that this group should draw its strength from "below" and the crowd on the streets rather than from "above," although elements of the elite are usually present. Indeed, since in a revolution old faces often appear in new guises, some sort of division within the ranks of the old elite or at least a renunciation of the old regime by leading members of society, such as intellectuals, is normally expected prior to the event. Then, in order for these revolutionary contenders to succeed, the authorities' grasp on power has to have been sufficiently weakened for the regime to be relatively easily overthrown. The institutions of the state, and particularly the security forces, have to effectively cease to function, there has to be a degree of state breakdown. Finally, the outside world has to be prepared to "allow" the revolution to occur and not to intervene. Any survey of the causes of the Romanian revolution has to be built around all these factors, because, although successful mobilization is not possible without state breakdown, the latter will only result in paralytic stasis if no political contenders emerge; and neither mobilization nor state breakdown will lead to a revolutionary outcome if a neighboring power is determined to prevent such an event, as occurred in Romania in 1848 and Hungary in 1956.

The Romanian Neo-Stalinist and Neo-Patrimonial State

Turning first to state breakdown, to understand the mechanics of this in Romania it is necessary to consider the nature of the state. Still bound in the rigid communist monolithism, which had already begun to slip elsewhere in Eastern Europe, in 1989 Romania displayed all the signs of an arrested political development. If comparisons are to be made, it is better to equate the Romanian revolution, not with elsewhere in Eastern Europe in 1989, but with the violence unleashed during de-Stalinization, es-

25. Jackson (1989), 313.

pecially in Hungary in 1956.[26] However, rather than a pure Stalinist state, Romania in the 1980s can be more accurately called "neo-Stalinist," because, while Ceauşescu in terms of his personality cult and form of rule emulated Stalin (and even more so Mao Zedong and Kim Il-Sung), the changed historical context meant that he was unable to fully replicate the Soviet leader's system, even if he had so desired.[27] If for heuristic purposes, within the communist system, Romania in the 1980s can best be characterized as a neo-Stalinist state, then within the world political system it has been suggested that it shared many of the features that normally distinguish neo-patrimonial states—the most extreme of which are sometimes dubbed "Sultanistic."[28] These are highly personalized regimes in partly modernized societies that are "characterized by the chief executive's maintenance of state authority through an extensive network of personal patronage, rather than through ideology or impersonal law."[29] The overthrow in 1979 of both Mohammad Reza Shah Pahlavi in Iran and Anastasio Somoza Debayle in Nicaragua prompted a certain amount of literature regarding the susceptibility of neo-patrimonial regimes to revolution, and some attempts have also been made to fit Romania within the same model, notwithstanding differences in levels of development and geopolitical location.[30] However, even if the premise that Romania should be considered a neo-patrimonial state is accepted, this by itself would not necessarily explain why it succumbed to revolution, since relatively few of the world's many neo-patrimonial regimes have met such a fate. In fact, it may even be argued that neo-patrimonialism fosters stability, if the elite is effectively co-opted, or sufficient members of society are politically neutralized through either formal or, if the regime turn a blind eye, informal patronage networks—a situation which existed in Romania for much of the 1980s.[31] It is possible, though, to suggest that in certain circumstances neo-patrimonialism and neo-Stalinism might create the conditions that make certain states prone to revolution. Jeff Goodwin, who has taken into account the revolutions in Eastern Europe when formulating his model,

26. Sampson has also made comparisons between Romania in the 1980s and both the Soviet Union in the 1930s and the rest of Eastern Europe in the 1950s: Sampson (1984–86), 42; Sampson (1989), 221.

27. During an interview with an American journalist Ceauşescu is reported to have admitted to being a great admirer of Stalin; see Kligman (1992), 370 n. 15. For the revival of Stalinist imagery see Shafir (August 23, 1988c), 33–34, and for Stalinism see Tucker (1977).

28. For neo-patrimonial regimes in general see Goldstone (1986), 38–48; Goodwin and Skocpol (1989), 489–509. For sultanism see Chehabi and Linz (1997).

29. Snyder (1992), 379.

30. Goodwin (1994), 577–78, 594–96, 600 n. 29; Skocpol (1994), 312. For earlier attempts to place Ceauşescu within the neo-patrimonial model see Jowitt (1971), 147–49, 191–93; Linden (1986), 347–80; and the comments in Fischer (1992), 46. Chehabi and Linz (1998) consider the Ceauşescu regime to have been sultanistic and his name is even emblazoned on the cover of the book alongside Trujillo, Batista, Somoza, Duvalier, Pahlavi, Marcos, Mobutu, and Bokassa.

31. Eisenstadt (1978), 282–85, but see Shafir (1985), 62.

suggests this is because they display certain attributes: (a) the exclusion of mobilized groups from state power or resources, (b) the use of indiscriminate, but not overwhelming, state violence against mobilized groups and opposition political figures, (c) weak policing capacities and infrastructure of power, (d) a corrupt and arbitrary personalistic rule that alienates, weakens, or divides counterrevolutionary elites, and (e) state sponsorship or protection of unpopular economic and social arrangements.[32] It is true that all these attributes were present in Romania in 1989, but again it may be argued that most of them had been present throughout much of the communist period. What changed during the 1980s is that several became more pronounced—in particular the first, as power became concentrated in fewer and fewer hands.[33]

At the apex of the pyramid of power in Romania was Nicolae Ceauşescu. By all accounts, he was a tough-minded and resolute man. The third of ten surviving children, he was born on January 26, 1918, into a family of poor peasants in the village of Scorniceşti in the county of Olt in southwest Romania.[34] At the age of eleven, after only an elementary school education, he was apprenticed as a shoemaker in Bucharest. In the capital he met his future wife, Elena Petrescu, the daughter of a peasant and small trader from the village of Petreşti, in the county of Argeş. Soon after arriving in Bucharest, the young Ceauşescu drifted into left-wing politics, eventually joining the tiny RCP, which in 1933 boasted only 1,665 members.[35] The Party was officially proscribed and Ceauşescu spent a number of spells in prison, but nonetheless he rose to become a secretary of the central committee of the youth organization. After the Second World War, when the communists took power, he occupied a number of posts in both the ministries of agriculture and armed forces before being promoted by the Party leader, Gheorghiu-Dej, to full membership in the

32. Goodwin (1994), 578; Goodwin (1997), 17–21. On the basis of a limited analysis Goodwin suggests that the events in Romania amounted to an aborted social revolution comparable with the situation in Haiti after the ousting of Jean-Claude "Baby Doc" Duvalier. Aside from any superficial similarities there may be between the Tontons Macoutes and the *securitate*, Goodwin's interpretation largely rests on his assertion that the NSF regime was neocommunist. However, his argument is considerably weakened when he openly states that he terms the regime as such, not because it was attempting to maintain the institutions of communism but "because of the background (and certain mentalities) of its principal leaders." Such a judgment would seem to make the leopards of communist politics unique in not being able to change their spots. For a well-reasoned rebuttal to the idea that the Iliescu regime was neo-communist see Verdery and Kligman (1992), 122–30. Snyder (1998), 77–78, also suggests that the closest parallel for Ceauşescu is Duvalier in his discussion of the sultanistic qualities of the regime.

33. Fischer (1989), 232–33. For the growing concentration of power see Gafton (July 3, 1987), 3–5.

34. Considerable problems remain in disassociating fact from fiction in Ceauşescu's life story. For his life see Fischer (1989), and the biographies produced after the revolution: Sweeny (1991), Behr (1991), Almond (1992).

35. Graham (1982), 30.

Politburo in 1955. When Dej died in 1965, Ceauşescu used his position as central committee secretary for organization and cadres to skillfully elevate himself to the leadership. The bare outline of this career is enough to suggest that Ceauşescu was shrewd and sharp-witted. He was also highly competitive, to the point of being vindictive against those who he thought had got the better of him.[36] Many observers, including former USSR leader Mikhail Gorbachev, have remarked on Ceauşescu's inflated concept of his own self-worth, which was paralleled by an equal lack of respect and even contempt for those he considered inferior.[37] These traits seem to have become more pronounced as time passed, and by 1989 Ceauşescu was over seventy years old. His age must have had some effect on his ability to deal with the unfolding revolution, and John Sweeny, after talking to Iulian Mincu, one of Ceauşescu's physicians, has suggested that poorly treated diabetes may also have made his behavior more erratic and possibly even impaired his mental capacities.[38]

Below Ceauşescu, the concentration of power was generally perceived by the wider population in terms of nepotism and favoritism, particularly after the promotion of Elena Ceauşescu and other family members to prominent positions in the regime.[39] Elena was elevated to membership of the PEC and to the position of first Deputy Prime Minister, and presented to the world as a chemist of international standing, the focus upon her was a distinct feature of the cult of personality in Romania that underlined the state's neo-patrimonial characteristics. The joke was of "socialism in one family" and much was made in the West of the process of "party familiarization," with lengthy lists appearing of the high offices occupied by supposed family members, although in many cases the links were far from proven.[40] In fact, it may be questioned how much power other family members actually wielded, especially given their performance during the revolution, when aside from Elena, only Nicu, Ilie, and Nicolae Andruţa Ceauşescu played limited roles. Even the posting of Nicu, always said to be the heir apparent, as Party Secretary in Sibiu can be seen as either a

36. This character sketch draws upon the observations of two jaundiced observers who had both once been close to Ceauşescu, Pavel Câmpeanu, a sociologist who had shared a prison cell, and Sergiu Celac, diplomat and later ambassador to the United Kingdom, who was Ceauşescu's interpreter. Sweeny (1991), 50–51, 100–101; Deletant (1998), 166.

37. Gorbachev (1996), 475, writes "it is hard to imagine a major politician without his share of vanity and self-confidence. In this sense, though, Ceauşescu was in a class of his own. An absolute ruler for decades, he always wore an arrogant smirk, treating others with apparent contempt, everyone from retainers to equal partners."

38. Sweeny (1991), 173–74.

39. Fischer (1985), 121–37; Tismaneanu (1989b), 371–74. For Elena's position in the regime see Ionescu (January 28, 1988), 11–13.

40. Shafir (1986b), 124–27. Typifying the accepted image is the illustration to be found in Brucan (1993), 105, where Nicolae and Elena Ceauşescu are graphically depicted as being at the center of nine grasping octopus tentacles each bearing the name of a family member. This view is also supported by the title *Romania: a case of dynastic communism* (1989). For a balanced appraisal of the various claims see de Fleurs (1984), 165–74.

springboard for future promotion or a way to partially sideline a man of limited talents.[41] When, in the 1970s, Ion Iliescu was sent to Timişoara and Iaşi in the same position, it was seen as a demotion, and in various interviews after the revolution Nicu hinted that his transfer should also be seen in the same light, because of his difficult relationship with his parents.[42] Rather than creating a strong ruling dynasty, Ceauşescu, by distributing rewards to relatives, was merely acting as countless Romanians had done before him.[43] By behaving in such a manner, however, he not only reinforced the "federation of families" culture and legitimized the nepotism of others, but also undermined his own regime, by sapping its moral authority and giving grounds for popular discontent.[44]

Besides the ruling couple, the leadership also incorporated a number of longstanding cronies of advanced age, who (according to their detractors) were "anti-intellectual, xenophobic, isolationist, anti-technocratic, and hostile to change."[45] Alongside Ceauşescu and his wife, the powerful permanent bureau of the PEC had only six other members: Emil Bobu, Constantin Dăscălescu, Ion Dincă, Manea Mănescu, Gheorghe Oprea, and Gheorghe Rădulescu. This small group ruled over a country that was in total crisis, yet none of them showed any overt signs of opposing Ceauşescu's policies or seem to have contemplated leading a "true" palace coup against him. In many ways this is perhaps not surprising, since promotion to such an elevated status could only be achieved through a blind loyalty to Ceauşescu, which, judging by the PEC transcripts released after the revolution, often seems to have bordered on servile submission. Probably they all shared his weltanschauung but, if not, Ceauşescu was also careful to emphasize how "indispensable" he was to the running of the system.[46] Any PEC member tempted to participate in a coup would have had to carefully weigh up the possible consequences. In particular, there was the risk that the overthrow of Ceauşescu might lead to the disintegration of the whole system, as, in fact, did happen.[47] Instead, the geriatric ruling clique cut themselves off from society. With minimal feedback in an atmosphere of intellectual stagnation they developed an enclosed mentality, which at times seemed almost totally divorced from reality. This is nowhere better shown than in Ceauşescu's in-

41. Gabanyi (November 6, 1987), 9–12.

42. Sweeny (1991), 160.

43. For the "traditional" and defensive nature of Ceauşescu's behavior see Jowitt (1978), 6–21, especially 7–8; Shafir (1985), 79–80; Eyal (1990), 150.

44. Sampson (1981–83), 170.

45. Georgescu (1988), 81. Georgescu (1983b), 184, draws on Mihai Botez, who also blamed Romania's decline on the mediocre intellectual qualities of the ruling group.

46. Tismaneanu (1989b), 336, argues that Romanian communism had a worldview inherently suspicious of diversity, never having "given much credence to critical Marxism, heterodoxy, and the values of dialogue and tolerance."

47. For the concept of indispensability see Goldstone (1986), 42.

terpretation of the revolution as being nothing more than the work of a few domestic malcontents aided by foreign agents provocateurs and in his abiding belief, even after his ouster, that the workers would still come to his rescue.

Ceauşescu had been able to concentrate power in his hands so success-fully partly because of the strategies he employed to prevent any rivals es-tablishing a power base. Chief among these were the closely related poli-cies of "divide and rule" and "circulation of the elite," but certain key groups, such as journalists, had also been subject to a policy of co-option. This raised their professional status, without giving them any concomitant increase in autonomy.[48] "Divide and rule" multiplied the number of indi-vidual posts, directorates, and institutes and then played them off one against another, while "circulation of the elite" saw officeholders arbitrar-ily moved from one post to another.[49] The pace of this circulation, which was between both Party and state bureaucracies and local and central ad-ministrations, intensified during the 1980s. However, rather than offering opportunities for advancement, this circulation mostly resulted in offi-cials being shunted sideways, because there was little risk of demotion so long as strict fidelity to Ceauşescu was maintained.[50] With political loyalty the sole criterion determining movement, there was also no incentive to improve governmental performance. The ruling elite became solidified, and with the effective closing of channels of advancement those excluded from high office, the "able and energetic lions" of Vilfredo Pareto's cele-brated formula, were prompted to search for alternative mechanisms by which to take power from the ruling "weak and cunning foxes," one of which was to be forcible and violent change.[51]

The concentration of power may have temporarily allowed Ceauşescu to maintain control of the system but ultimately it was to be totally self-defeating. By making him responsible for all major day-to-day decisions it imposed a rigid hierarchy on policy making, leaving it inelastic when con-fronted with a fast-evolving revolutionary situation. The narrow base of the regime also dictated the shape of the opposition when it arose, since it gave the political space for the formation of the widest possible anti-Ceauşescu coalition.[52] Through Ceauşescu the fortunes of the state were so tightly bound to that of the ruling regime that a situation was eventu-ally produced in Romania somewhat similar to Russia in 1917. Then the

48. Fischer (1989), 182–89.
49. Skocpol (1994), 255 n. 8, suggests that such tactics are used by all patrimonial lead-ers. For an example from Iran see Tien-lung (1988), 157.
50. Shafir (1985), 72–73.
51. Krejčí (1983), 37. Arjomand (1995), 147, also considers what he terms the "Aris-totelian-Paretian" ideal type and suggests it was particularly applicable to the Eastern Euro-pean revolutions.
52. This appears also to have been the case in the Cuban, Nicaraguan, and Iranian revo-lutions, where narrow regimes faced broadly based mass movements.

collapse of the tsarist regime also brought down the state, allowing the Bolsheviks to seize power with only limited popular support. In Romania, the ruling RCP was formally bound to the state, with the "marriage" being symbolically tied with Ceaușescu's accession to the post of state President as well as Party head in 1974.[53] The merging of Party-state positions also augmented Ceaușescu's power, since it enabled him to exert personal control through a succession of local "clones" who replicated his own position. From top to bottom corruption thrived as minions, emulating their leader, carved out their own petty tyrannies.[54] This fusion was ostensibly done in the name of efficiency, but at all levels Party officials were in the ascendant as central control increased. The fate of the Party and the state were thus irrevocably bound together, and any weakness on the part of the former would necessarily reverberate through the latter.

At first sight in 1989 the RCP appeared in a powerful position. With 3.7 million members it was the largest communist party in Eastern Europe outside the Soviet Union, including within its ranks approximately a quarter of the total adult and a third of the working population.[55] Yet the size of the Party was a mask for weakness rather than a sign of strength. Within the precepts of "multilaterally developed socialism," as propounded by Ceaușescu, society was supposed to wither away to be taken over from "within" by the Party. In the promised Utopia every "expert" was to be "red." Yet, as the Party grew and turned from being a vanguard grouping into an agent of mass inclusion, so the high degree of revolutionary belief required to effect such a takeover from within was necessarily diluted. To try and offset this a special emphasis was placed on recruiting certain key groups seen as being particularly loyal. During the 1980s, 68 percent of all new members were stated to be workers (what constituted a worker seems to have been variable), with only 16 percent of the intake being intellectuals and 15 percent peasants.[56] This move to reproletarianize the Party, rather than producing a more ideologically committed body, merely created one that was disproportionately poorly educated; 47 percent of members in 1980 had only a primary education and a relatively small segment, 11 percent, higher education, the remainder having finished some form of secondary schooling.[57] During the 1970s and early 1980s, the huge size of the RCP may have worked in favor of the stability of the regime, as it permitted the application of a semblance of Party discipline to

53. Shafir (1985), 58–59. A famous picture shows Ceaușescu holding a scepter in a Napoleonic pose as he assumes the office of president; see the example in Govender (1982) and also Ionescu (January 22, 1985), 13–19.

54. Chirot (1991), 10–11.

55. Gafton (April 29, 1988), 9–11; the figure is for 1987.

56. All figures derive from Fischer (1989), 191–200.

57. Fischer (1989), 197. Georgescu (1988), 81, suggests that, by the late 1980s, 80 percent of Party members and 78.5 percent of the Party *apparat* had a peasant or working-class background.

a large proportion of the adult population. Many, however, had only joined for career and material advancement and as the crisis deepened and the expected rewards of access to scarce goods, preferential treatment, and upward mobility failed to materialize, discontent among Party members rose and their loyalty to the regime waned. During the revolution, fifty-three of those arrested in Timişoara prior to Ceauşescu's overthrow were RCP members.[58] The mediocre qualities of what was frequently a poorly educated cadre, rigid and highly formalized Party structures that stifled all traces of initiative, half-hearted commitment by an often disaffected middle-ranking leadership, and a lack of ideological cement all combined to produce a hollow facade that had little durable content. During the revolution the RCP imploded and, as noted above, this produced a concomitant breakdown of state institutions.

Legitimacy and the Cult

The fact that after more than forty years in power, upon the flight of its leader, this huge communist party simply dissolved, as if conjured away in a puff of smoke, suggests not only that it had become so totally identified with Ceauşescu that it no longer retained any separate autonomy but also a collective loss of self-belief on a colossal scale. Yet only twenty years earlier, in 1968, the picture had been completely different. Then Ceauşescu, addressing a vast crowd in the center of Bucharest, had won genuine popular acclaim for himself and the Party by calling the Warsaw Pact's invasion of Czechoslovakia "a great mistake and a grave danger to peace."[59] The late 1960s and early 1970s had been the high point of Ceauşescu's popularity, as the coercion of the Dej years was relaxed and a greater diversity of views permitted. Efforts were also made to step up production of consumer goods, as, like elsewhere in Eastern Europe at the time, the Party attempted to substitute a legitimacy based on symbolism and ideology with one founded on material reward. By the mid-1970s, however, this brief "Romanian Spring" had begun to wither, as ideological uniformity was reimposed by Ceauşescu alongside a growing cult of personality and extensive use of national symbols. The two were coupled in a propaganda that regularly placed Ceauşescu in a lineage of Romanian heroes stretching from the Dacian king, Burebista, to the medieval monarchs, Stephen the Great and Michael the Brave.[60] The regime embraced nationalism with a fervor tying it to Marxism-Leninism in a formula that held that it was only through the ending of class conflict and the building of a Stalin-

58. Pitulescu et al. (1995), 112.
59. Cited in Almond (1992), 2.
60. For examples see the journal *Romania: Pages of History* throughout the 1980s.

ist heavy industry base that the true national destiny of Romania could be realized.[61]

The cult of personality of Ceauşecu and his wife has been compared to that of Stalin and Mao Zedong.[62] The whole country was bedecked with banners lauding the achievements of the regime. From the smallest village to the largest city roadside placards chronicled the surpassing of production targets and Ceauşescu's role in promoting world peace. Huge signs praising the Party and its leader sprawled across the roofs of factories and everywhere there were pictures of the Ceauşescus. Elaborate rituals were staged in their honor, the most celebrated being the national festival "Song to Romania." In 1985, 3,593,316 people organized into 153,040 groups participated in its displays. Holding placards aloft, they formed "living pictures," offering synchronized praise to the ruling couple, who ultimately were the only real spectators.[63] In this sycophantic world, no publication could appear without it being embellished with some words of wisdom from Ceauşescu, and when the printing presses were not churning out multiple volumes of the "genius of the Carpathian's" speeches they were producing such "Stalinist kitsch," as the 1988 collection of children's poems: *Our Ardent Love for the President of the Country.*[64] The collection includes the cloying poem "The Epoch of Gold":

> We live in a land of legends
> In the epoch of great deeds
> The epoch that bears
> The lofty name
> of the most brave *conducător.*
>
> Comrade Nicolae Ceauşescu is
> the loving father of all children,
> he shows us the road
> towards communism,
> built with heroism under the tricolor.[65]

In its symbolism the cult bore many of the characteristics of a secularized religion. Early Soviet thought in the idea of "God Building" had held that socialist man would turn from the worship of a transcendental divinity to

61. Tismaneanu and Pavel (1994), 402, consider Ceauşescu's ideology to have been a "syncretic mixture of decayed Marxist tenets, self-aggrandizing ethnocentric myths, and the unabashed celebration of Ceauşescu himself. Xenophobia, autarchy, isolationism, anti-Occidentalism, and anti-intellectualism were the main motifs underlying this ideological construct."

62. Fischer (1981), 117–41; Georgescu (1983a), 129–42; Tismaneanu (1986), 65–90; Fischer (1989), 160.

63. Giurchescu (1987), 163–71.

64. Rupnick (1989), 151.

65. *Dragostea noastră* (1988), 18. *Conducător* means leader, while tricolor refers to the Romanian flag.

find religious expression through the socialist earthly Utopia, and, miraculously in the case of Romania, the apotheosis of Ceaușescu does seem to have occurred within his own earthly paradise, with one of his court poets, Corneliu Vadim Tudor, describing him as a "secular-God."[66] Among Party members of little education, in a wider popular culture infused with traditions of religious iconography, the omnipresent portraits of Ceaușescu and his wife were to prove simple but potent legitimizing devices cementing the authority of the leadership. The cult image may have been a lie, but, as Leszek Kolakowski has noted, "Obvious lies uttered aloud with impunity are excellent proofs of the health of the system."[67] Ceaușescu was short in stature and a poor speaker, and aside from his eyes he was unprepossessing.[68] His cult generated some of the charisma he naturally lacked, and, while it lasted, the grossness of the lie merely served to illustrate his power, since it brought the image partially to life. Later, after the revolution, Pavel Câmpeanu was to remark how despite their coarseness and transparency, the subterfuges of the cult had the strange, somewhat contradictory effect of both "reinforcing an obscure fear that Ceaușescu was immortal" while at the same time breeding a passivity as "little by little the population's obsession with his ubiquitous presence turned into an obsession with his death."[69] However, the cult was a double-edged sword, for in extolling the virtues of Ceaușescu as the supreme decision maker it also laid the ground for him to be branded as the universal scapegoat and focus of grievance. Through the cult Ceaușescu had become not an authentic leader or an example to be emulated but an idol to be obeyed. He developed no meaningful relationship with a society that remained mere onlookers or dragooned participants in his spectacles.[70] The resulting structure was a hollow shell, a false image open to ridicule, which needed just one crack in the facade—or, as it was in this case, one glance of consternation during the mass rally in Bucharest on December 21, 1989—for the whole edifice to crumble to the ground.

The cult became the mirror in which the regime saw itself, and so rosy was the image produced, that, like Narcissus, Ceaușescu fell in love

66. For the deification of Ceaușescu see Ionescu (January 28, 1988a), 7–10; Gabanyi (2000), 35–43. Ceaușescu also often presented himself in semi-regal guise. One of the more bizarre manifestations of his seventieth birthday celebrations was the appearance in the Romanian press of a number of bogus messages of congratulation apparently cobbled together from old texts, including one from the Queen of England, Elizabeth II.

67. Kolakowski quoted in Schöpflin (1993), 162. For the cult as a lie glossing over the contradictions in society see also Giurchescu (1987), 164.

68. Fischer (1993), 5.

69. Câmpeanu (February 1, 1990), 30; see also the joke reproduced in Almond (1992), 1, where one man asks another why he reads the front page of the newspaper first. The reply is that he is looking for an obituary and when told these are to be found on the back page he sharply replies: "Not the obituary I am looking for!"

70. Fischer (1989), 162–63.

with his own reflection and came to believe that the hymns of praise he received were as real as the improbably youthful portraits held aloft by his beloved workers.[71] Yet this picture also had its reverse, and for the remainder of the Party elite the other image they caught sight of was less reassuring, eroding their faith in Ceauşescu and his policies and fatally weakening their own sense of self-legitimation. This other image was generated by an angry and impoverished society which by the 1980s had lost all faith in the ruling elite. Their sense of outrage emerged in the form of exaggerated rumor and gossip that cast the leadership as nothing less than grasping and debauched tyrants surrounded by sycophantic and parasitical minions.[72] In this world, the Ceauşescus were not the subject of adulation but the butt of bitter jokes and crude stories.[73] Yet, to a certain extent, Nicolae Ceauşescu, perhaps by virtue of his secondary cult image as a hard-working and somewhat puritanical revolutionary, was protected from the worst of these stories prior to 1989. No such reticence, however, was shown toward Elena Ceauşescu. She was regularly presented as the real evil genius behind the throne, who in her love of opulence and finery was something of a cross between Imelda Marcos and Madame Lupescu, the mistress of King Carol II of Romania.[74] The Ceauşescu children were also not spared. Nicu Ceauşescu in particular was regularly portrayed as a debauched playboy presiding over bacchanalian orgies.[75] In fact, the reality appears to have been rather more prosaic and shabby. After the revolution, Nicu drank himself into an early grave and much of Elena's fabled haute couture, following years in store, was eventually donated to Europe's last remaining leper colony.[76] Nevertheless, the stories of excess in a land of poverty undercut the last vestiges of popular support enjoyed by the regime.

This perception of moral degeneracy, when combined with poverty and economic hardship, fuelled a widespread sense of injustice. By what right did this small ruling clique inflict such suffering on the nation? Instead of the failed vision of Ceauşescu, many Romanians sought an alternative future that would bring both political and economic gains—most commonly expressed in terms of basic human rights and consumer goods. The support for such an alternative vision naturally varied, partly because perceptions of injustice were greater within some groups than others. It was, for example, particularly high within the ethnic Hungarian

71. Schöpflin (1993), 228.
72. Sampson (1984), 142–64.
73. Banc and Dundes (1990).
74. For a cutting description of Lupescu see Quinlan (1994), 95–104.
75. For a series of scandalous stories about the debauched lifestyle of the Ceauşescu elite see Pacepa (1989). For a corrective to stories about their fabulous wealth, see the description of the Ceauşescus' living quarters in Simpson (1992), 274–76.
76. *Guardian*, November 5, 1998, 17.

minority, which considered itself the subject of illegitimate assimilatory pressures and even spoke of cultural genocide.[77] Partly in reaction to the excesses of the ruling regime, this popular vision of a more just future was invested by Ceaușescu's opponents with a moral rigor which was often expressed in terms of a collective need to cleanse the nation's soul. Through this they were able to both define the gap between themselves and the regime, which they presented as being the incarnation of tyranny in its barbarous oppression of the "people," and give themselves an aura of moral rectitude.[78] This alternative vision was then projected toward the outside world, where it fed the images of tyranny encountered at the beginning of this chapter, and back onto society in Romania, where it produced a stark black and white picture of a battle between good and evil. This was to raise the stakes in the coming revolutionary struggle, because, by placing Ceaușescu and his *securitate* henchmen outside the moral pale of normal society, it marked them as targets for extralegal retribution.

By the eve of the revolution, the Ceaușescu regime was widely seen as illegitimate for reasons ranging from the economic catastrophe besetting the country to the wider collapse of communism. However, whether the regime was any more illegitimate in 1989 than it had been in 1985, or even earlier, remains open to question. The loss of legitimacy is more useful in explaining the vulnerability of the Party-state and the rise of popular discontent than the actual outbreak of revolution. It did, however, have a significant impact on the events after the overthrow of Ceaușescu, since the NSF was to a certain extent legitimized by the lack of legitimacy of the RCP regime it replaced. The bounds of post-revolution legitimacy, however, were far from clear. In particular, nobody knew how much of the past was no longer acceptable. Obviously the inner regime would have to leave office, but what about members of the *nomenklatura*, and the *securitate*? And which ideological modes of legitimation were beyond the pale? Certainly Ceaușescu's debased amalgam of neo-Stalinism and nationalism, but what about Marxism-Leninism? In December 1989 it did not seem altogether inconceivable that the cult of Ceaușescu and his stress on nationalism might have left the political space for some form of reform socialism, as propagated by the likes of Silviu Brucan and Iliescu, to still retain some legitimacy.

Ceaușescu and the Romanian Elite

At the center of many theories of revolution lie the intellectuals. If they withdraw their support, a process Crane Brinton termed the "desertion of the intellectuals" and Lyford Edwards "the transfer of the allegiance of

77. *Witnesses to cultural genocide* (1979).
78. This line of argument stems from Arjomand quoted in Goldstone (1991), 43.

the intellectuals," then many theorists argue the regime is destined to fall.[79] Certainly this phenomenon can be seen in Romania, but rather than the "transfer of allegiance of the intellectuals" it may be better to talk of the "alienation of the elite." Intellectuals, when strictly defined, constitute a somewhat narrow band, while elite (people whose skills and positions are such that they are able to influence large numbers of others) implies a broader category, embracing all the higher echelons of society, including intellectuals, higher members of the intelligentsia, and other social leaders.[80] Also, since relatively few of the elite in Romania went into open opposition, alienation may be preferred to "transfer of allegiance," as it implies a withdrawal of consent, allowing for an intermediate posture of passivity, perhaps with an internalization of sentiment giving an outward appearance of loyalty.

The decline in the moral authority of the regime echoed throughout the whole of society, but it was particularly felt by members of this alienated elite who chafed at being ruled by those they perceived as their inferiors.[81] Ceauşescu had received no formal education beyond the age of eleven and his peasant origins were always betrayed by his thick Olteanian accent. In contrast, many of the members of the incoming NSF regime, including Brucan, Alexandru Bârlădeanu, Iliescu, and Petre Roman, had been highly educated, often abroad. Yet in spite of their disillusion, few Party members openly expressed their hostility to the regime. Prior to 1989, the chief dissenting voices were Károly Király, a former alternate member of the PEC, who, since 1977, had sent a series of letters of protest to prominent Party members, with one of the last being published in the West in January 1988, and Constantin Pârvulescu.[82] The latter was one of the founding fathers of the RCP, who, at the 12th Party Congress in 1979, after being given the floor by Ceauşescu himself, launched a bitter attack on the leader and pledged he would not vote for his reelection. For his impertinence Pârvulescu was stripped of his Party posts and disappeared from public view until 1989, when he reappeared once again as one of the signatories of a bitter indictment of Ceauşescu's years of misrule, dubbed the "Letter of the Six." Broadcast on the BBC World Service on March 10, 1989, this was the most significant piece of Party dissent to appear during Ceauşescu's long years of rule. The origins of the letter are contested, but alongside Pârvulescu it was also written in the name of Brucan, who at one time had been Romanian Ambassador to the United States and the

---

79. Brinton and Lyford Edwards are both quoted in Krejčí (1983), 35–36; see also Goldstone (1991), 38–40; Gurr and Goldstone (1991), 332–34; Lachmann (1997), 73–101. For examples from Hungary and Iran see Schöpflin (1993), 119–22, 228, and Skocpol (1982), 265–83.
80. Gurr and Goldstone (1991), 332–33.
81. Krejčí (1983), 32.
82. Socor (January 13, 1988a), 29–31; Shafir (1985), 82.

United Nations; Gheorghe Apostol, a previous first secretary of the Party (1954–55) and rival of Ceaușescu, who was long-rumored to have been Dej's chosen successor; Bârlădeanu, a leading economist and former member of the PEC; Corneliu Mănescu, a former foreign minister (1961–72); and Grigore Răceanu, a veteran member of the Party.[83] Beginning "at a time when the very idea of socialism, for which we have fought, is discredited by your policy," the "Letter of the Six" took Ceaușescu to task on a number of counts: for failing to observe the stipulations of the Romanian constitution safeguarding civic freedoms, for proposing to raze thousands of villages and destroying part of the center of Bucharest, for economic mismanagement which through food exports—they charged—threatened the very "biological existence of our nation," and, finally, for damaging Romania's international standing.[84] By cracking the facade of unanimity that had previously signified the Romanian leader's near absolute control of the public sphere, the letter helped sow the seeds of doubt as to his ability to hold on to power.[85] Yet it is still more relevant to collapse than overthrow, since at the time the letter was written the six co-signatories were far from the center of power and posed no immediate threat to Ceaușescu, while, in contrast, the upper echelons of the Party gave every appearance of monolithic support.

Outside the Party in the early 1980s dissent was almost the sole preserve of a few courageous individuals, such as Doina Cornea, a professor of French from Cluj, whom Dennis Deletant considers "the conscience of Romania" during this period.[86] Cornea penned a number of open letters to Ceaușescu, but for most of the 1980s hers was a lone voice in the wilderness, apart from occasional stirrings from shadowy groups, such as the anonymous "Romanian Democratic Action," and a former giant of Romania's precommunist political past, the National Peasant Party.[87] More active were Romania's ethnic Hungarian and German communities. Again protests were mostly centered on individuals, such as Király, but wider groupings were also occasionally involved, such as Aktionsgruppe

83. Brucan (1993), 136, had earlier made a statement on the Brașov disturbances. For Apostol see Fischer (1993), 18 n. 34.

84. For the text of the letter see Brucan (1993), 153–55; and for additional details Tismaneanu (1989a), 23–24; *Adevărul*, March 14, 1991, 2; Betea (1998), 216–25; Ivan (1998), 174–77; Răceanu (2000), Mănescu (2001), 236–54. According to some reports Iliescu was asked to sign the letter but declined.

85. For the importance of cracks in the "surface unanimity" see Schöpflin (1993), 229–30, although note that he does not consider this to have occurred in Romania until the outbreak of the revolution in Timișoara.

86. Deletant (1989), 26–27; Deletant (1998), 199.

87. Cornea (1991), Gallagher (1995), 65. For Romanian dissent during the 1980s see Tismaneanu (1989b), 334–35, the list in Deletant (1998), 195, and various reports in *Index on Censorship* and *Radio Free Europe Research*, such as Socor (August 7, 1987), 1–6; Stefanescu (October 14, 1988), 13–16. For Romanian Democratic Action see Socor (March 2, 1988), 1–3, and for the National Peasant Party see Socor (November 6, 1986), 33–34; Socor (February 6, 1987), 23–26.

Banat, a group of German writers in the Banat, most of whom were dismissed from their jobs and forced into exile during the 1980s. Samizdat journals also appeared, one of which, *Ellenpontok* (Counterpoints), featured a young pastor, László Tőkés, among its contributors.[88] The dissent of Hungarian intellectuals offered a new focus of identity for a disorientated Hungarian population, but in a state that stressed total conformity and countenanced no opposition, it also intensified regime distrust and offered Ceaușescu an opportunity to mobilize public opinion against the Hungarian "enemy within."

It was only in the late 1980s that dissent became more widespread among ethnic Romanians. In August 1988 the poet Mircea Dinescu gave an interview to Radio Moscow's Romanian Service, in which he praised Gorbachev and called for reform, and afterwards, in March 1989, to the Paris daily *Libération*, in which he denounced the absence of human rights in Romania.[89] Dinescu's stand created something of a crisis of conscience among Romanian intellectuals, who were faced with making a choice between dissent and compliance. A few took up the challenge, including the critic Octavian Paler and the essayists Andrei Pleșu and Mihai Șora, who with four others signed a letter of support for Dinescu.[90] Other open letters to Ceaușescu appeared, including one, in March 1989, from the veteran poet Dan Deșliu and another, a month later, from Aurel Dragoș Munteanu, protesting his dismissal from the staff of a literary weekly and calling for freedom of speech.[91] The state responded harshly. The signatories were unable to publish their work, lost their jobs, and, in some cases, such as Dinescu, were placed under house arrest.

Obviously the coercive practices of the regime were an important factor in ensuring that Romanian dissent was so muted for much of the 1980s, but other factors also played a role. First, the putative dissidents were operating within a society that did not necessarily place value on the expression of opposing views. Within what was still largely a peasant or first generation worker society, conformity and social solidarity were at least equally prized—attitudes reflected in the popular proverb "the sword will not sever the bowed head." Among intellectuals such ideas may also have been reinforced by the teachings of the influential Romanian philosopher Constantin Noica. He argued that life could be more fulfilling under difficult conditions and put a premium on resistance through cultural develop-

---

88. For Hungarian dissent see Schwerthoeffer (1985), 79–92; Koppany (March 21, 1989), 1–3. For Károly Király's last letter see *Independent*, January 7, 1988, 10; Socor (January 13, 1988a), 29–31. For earlier letters written in 1977 see *Witnesses to cultural genocide* (1979). For German dissent see Pompei-Cojocaru (October 29, 1985), 27–30; Ionescu (April 18, 1986), 7–10; and for examples of German writings see Wagner (1990) and Müller (1989).

89. Deletant (1995), 279–84.

90. The letter is reproduced in *Index on Censorship*, 18:8, 1989, 33.

91. For Deșliu's letter see *Index on Censorship*, 18:8, 1989, 28; for Munteanu see Stefanescu (November 9, 1988), 29–30.

ment rather than outright dissent.[92] Second, the outside world also failed to adequately recognize Romanian dissent. This may have been because of a lack of interest in a distant and closed land but, according to some Romanian dissidents, it sprang also from the West's infatuation with Ceauşescu and his semiautonomous foreign policy.[93] Only through desperate acts, such as that of Liviu Babeş, who died after setting himself on fire in front of a group of western tourists at Poiana Braşov in March 1988, did it seem that Romania could be brought to the attention of the outside world.[94] Finally, to a certain extent the need to engage in open dissent was blunted by the fact that the system was sufficiently malleable and arbitrary to allow intellectuals to make their protest within its bounds, even if, in the process, they became experts in the use of metaphors and symbolic disguises in what Adam Sorkin has called "ventriloquisms of irony."[95] Books as critical of communism as Marin Preda's *Cel mai iubit dintre pământeni* (The most beloved of the earth dwellers) and Augustin Buzura's *Refugii* (Refuges) were published in the 1980s, when poems as outspoken as Dinescu's *Indulgenţă de iarnă* (Cold comfort) also appeared:[96]

> God preserve me from those who want what's best for me
> from the nice guys
> always cheerfully ready to inform on me
> from the priest with a tape recorder under his vestment
> from the blanket you can't get under without saying good evening
> from the dictators caught in the chords of the harp
> from those angry with their own people
> now when winter's coming
> we have neither tall walls
> nor geese on the Capitoline
> only great provisions of tolerance and fear.[97]

Intellectuals were alienated from the regime in Romania, but, for a variety of reasons they rarely came to openly state their opposition. Their voice was limited and reached few beyond their own circle. They denied the regime their support but did not actively foster its collapse. During the revolution, this lack of open dissent was to have important ramifications, since it made it difficult for them to gain the moral credibility they

92. Pleşu (1995), 61–71.
93. See the pungent remarks of Mihai Botez in *Romania: a case of dynastic communism* (1989), 53.
94. *România Liberă*, March 3, 1998, 3.
95. Sorkin (1991), 26–38; Cornis-Pop (1989), 3–19; Deletant (1989), 121–61.
96. Buzura (1994).
97. Dinescu (1985), 46. Originally published in *Democraţia naturii* (1981). The translation is by Andrea Deletant and Brenda Walker. I would like to thank Brenda Walker for permission to reproduce this poem.

craved and forestalled the appearance of any well-known figure who might rival Iliescu.

The Economic Catastrophe

At the heart of the causes of state breakdown, but also of the sense of grievance which was to fuel popular mobilization, was the economic catastrophe sweeping the country. Romania was not alone in facing problems—all the command economies of Eastern Europe were entering terminal decay by the 1980s—but in Romania the crisis was particularly acute due to the policies pursued by Ceaușescu. The factors behind the economic crisis are complex, but at its heart lay the stifling rigidities of a command economy in which all transactions were politically determined by plan, with little attention paid to questions of supply and demand or to international and domestic market forces. Within this system it was impossible to measure efficiency, since there were no real prices and money played a purely passive role as a unit of account, following politically determined allocations rather than acting as a constraint.[98] The overriding rationale was not the provision of goods and services for profit but the procuring and, then, controlling of resources. Central bodies accumulated resources to generate further resources, factory managers hoarded and padded their budgets so as to be able to fulfill the dictates of the plan, while shop assistants keeping goods aside for relations or favored customers left other consumers short of scarce items.[99] The result was an economy of shortage in which the lines were endless and goods were invested with a high degree of political significance.

After the sharp growth of previous decades, by the 1980s the Romanian economy was in desperate need of reform, but for a number of reasons this was effectively off the agenda. Ceaușescu's counter to perestroika, "perfecting" (*perfecționarea*)—a variant of the Stalinist "ideology of perfection"—although it allowed for the possibility of room for improvement, was firmly rooted in the assumption that the Romanian leader was the sole guide to the construction of a "multilaterally developed socialist society." Ceaușescu permitted no real challenge to his vision, and whatever discussion was allowed usually focused on how to implement policies rather than matters of real substance. Since major policy mistakes could not be countenanced, let alone be publicly admitted, error from the ideological standpoint was out of the question and a change of direction from that prescribed by Ceaușescu was effectively impossible. Moreover, since policy could not be at fault, then mistakes and poor performance could

98. Bruz (1991), 179.
99. Verdery (1995), 222–23, 227.

only be explained in terms of incompetence or lack of loyalty by subordinates.[100] The crippling power shortage of the late 1980s was not blamed on Ceaușescu's nonsustainable drive for development, which was based on obsolete and energy inefficient equipment, but on the human failings of Gheorghe Petrescu, deputy prime minister in charge of the energy sector, and Ioan Avram, minister of electric power, both of whom were dismissed in 1987.[101] The inflexibility of the command economy made change difficult in all communist states, but in Romania the concentration of power in Ceaușescu's hands multiplied the problem. Instead of any meaningful reform, the Romanian economy under Ceaușescu only experienced repeated "simulated change" in which a superficial attention to form was matched by an almost total lack of content.[102]

The spark for the crisis of the early 1980s largely came from adverse developments in the global economy. Building on Romania's traditional interests in the oil industry, a great deal of investment had been poured into facilities for the processing of secondary petroleum products as well as other energy intensive sectors, such as steel manufacturing and aluminum refining. Oil refining capacity, for instance, rose from eighteen million tonnes in 1973 to thirty-three million tonnes in 1980.[103] The Romanians intended to cover the cost of these new investments by exporting the goods produced to the West, but not only was this fateful decision made at a time when reliance on oil imports was increasing because of a decline in domestic production—this fell by 20 percent between 1982 and 1988—but also the new plant began to come on stream just as the price of oil tripled during the second OPEC crisis. This was largely caused by the revolution in Iran, a country that had traditionally been an oil supplier to the Romanians. As a result, Romania's oil supplies were seriously disrupted at the same time as export markets were hit by a worldwide recession. When the price of secondary oil products failed to rise proportionately in relation to the cost of imported crude oil, it was estimated that the Romanians were losing $25 on every ton of refined products sold to the West.[104] By 1980 the country was posting a $1.5 billion trade deficit at a time when the financial backing previously supplied by the West began to evaporate, as bankers fearing a Polish default of outstanding loans proved unwilling to refinance Romania's debts. An unexpected slump in agricultural production, partly caused by adverse weather conditions but fundamentally resulting from years of neglect, merely added to the woes, as it

100. Sampson (1989), 222.
101. Gafton (October 15, 1987), 7–9.
102. Shafir (1985), 107–26. An example is the New Economic and Financial Mechanism. See Shafir (1985), 121–26; Gafton (June 23, 1988), 21–22; Gabanyi (2000), 428–32.
103. Linden (1989), 295.
104. Turnock (1986a), 272; Georgescu (1988), 73 n. 8.

brought shortfalls for both domestic and export markets.[105] The result was that in 1980 the spectacular growth of the 1970s was brought to a shuddering halt. Ceaușescu's reaction to the crisis was belated but, when it came, it displayed the same single-mindedness which had earlier driven his quest for industrialization. A massive campaign of export promotion and import substitution was launched in which the most marketable products, especially foodstuffs, were shipped abroad, leaving only "patriots" such as pig's feet at home.[106]

The 1980s were years of crisis as the domestic economy was squeezed dry to pay off the foreign debt. At its peak, in 1982, the debt had stood at around $11 billion, but by 1986 it had already been cut to $5.5 billion, and by 1989, the year in which the Grand National Assembly passed a law prohibiting the taking of any new credits, it was virtually paid off.[107] Yet even with the debt crisis largely overcome, Ceaușescu still remained unwilling to lessen demands for the mobilization of ever greater resources in favor of intensive growth based on technological innovation and efficient use of resources. Why Ceaușescu continued with the policy of consumer austerity long beyond the point when it was, even by his criteria, necessary, remains difficult to fathom, but it seems quite possible that it was the realization that it would continue, even after the debt had been repaid, that finally tipped the Romanians into taking to the streets.

The initial response of the population to the deterioration in economic conditions was to seek ways to bypass the system as, in time-honored fashion, they turned to the informal secondary sector, which was largely parasitical on formal institutions. Through the trading of mutual favors, bribery, and even petty theft from the workplace, many scarce goods were secured by those who knew the "right people"—a situation well caught in the popular paronomasia that the initials PCR stood not for Romanian Communist Party (Partidul Comunist Român) but for "connections, acquaintances and relations" (*pile, cunoștințe și relații*).[108] So important were both the legal secondary economy of peasant markets and artisans' workshops and the illegal secondary economy of shady deals that, by the mid-1980s, it was estimated that together they accounted for between 35 and 40 percent of the income of the Romanian people.[109] The long-term consequences of this excessive use of the informal sphere were socially disastrous, as it led to anomie, falling public standards, and increased social atomization (at least to the family level). In the short term, however, during

105. Jackson (1986), 489–542.
106. Ionescu (December 2, 1988), 12.
107. Georgescu (1988), 77 n. 22; Gafton (December 29, 1988b), 7–9; Jackson (1989), 308; Linden (1989), 301.
108. For corruption in the Party see [Shafir] (July 2, 1986), 33–37.
109. Ionescu (November 14, 1985), 13–16; Brezinski and Petersen (1990), 75.

the first half of the 1980s, it seems that, in spite of the continued failure of formal institutions to provide the required goods, sufficient products remained available in the informal sector to satisfy enough of the population to ensure public quiescence. Sampson has even suggested that inability to obtain scarce resources at this time was interpreted not in terms of a failure of the system but rather as a personal failure to cultivate the correct contacts. The system may have been malfunctioning, but it continued to "muddle through" or stagnate for much of the 1980s.[110] It was only at the end of the decade, when the shortages became more acute and fewer and fewer people, even with the requisite connections, were able to acquire the goods they required that the system began to topple over into crisis, as the vast majority began to question their own ability to find solutions even within the informal sector.[111]

Popular Mobilization

Romania on the eve of the revolution was displaying all the attributes Goodwin has stated are necessary for revolution. Power was concentrated in relatively few hands, and the fusion of the Party—which despite its huge size was in reality little more than the ruling clique—with the state meant that the collapse of the one would invariably bring the other tumbling to the ground. All predictable norms had been eroded, leaving the system to rest on a highly personalized and arbitrary decision-making process, in which Ceaușescu himself increasingly "began to ignore some of the formal structures and procedures he himself had created to demonstrate the legality and institutionalization of the political process."[112] The system became highly malleable as laws and decrees, often totally unrealistic in their aims, were flouted or only half-enacted, ultimately producing a state of chronic paralysis. In the process the vast majority of the elite had become alienated from the regime, but for a variety of reasons dissent was relatively limited, although when it did occur it was quickly repressed. At the same time, a highly politicized economy, incapable of reform, was in a state of catastrophic breakdown. All contributed toward state breakdown and the growth of widespread popular discontent but, as noted before, this was not something new in 1989. Romania had been in a state of crisis for much of the 1980s, and so what is perhaps most remarkable is the resilience of the system during this period.

110. Sampson (1981–83), 170, actually distinguishes between "muddling through" and "stagnation" but in his later work he treats the two as being synonymous; see also Brezinski and Petersen (1990), 77.

111. Sampson (1981–83), 175–76; Sampson (1985–86), 44–66; Sampson (1984–86), 41–51.

112. Fischer (1989), 191.

There had been serious challenges to the regime prior to 1989, but these had all been successfully overcome. In 1977 miners peacefully occupied their pits in the Jiu Valley to protest moves by the regime to curtail social benefits and increase working hours and the age of retirement. A delegation headed by PEC member Ilie Verdeţ was dispatched to the coal field to open negotiations, but after the group was effectively taken captive by the strikers, Ceauşescu arrived in person. Amid chaotic scenes he conceded the bulk of the workers' demands and the strike collapsed.[113] The response of the authorities to the 1977 strike established a model for dealing with future unrest. Initially, the regime gave the appearance of acquiescing to the workers' demands and meeting local grievances. Then, once the strikers had returned to work, they moved to isolate the ringleaders by imprisoning them or sending them into internal exile, while at the same time clawing back the initial concessions. The Jiu Valley strikes were followed by other disturbances, but due to the rigid news blackout imposed by the authorities the true extent of these remains unclear, although reports reached the West of factory disturbances in a number of cities, including Cluj, Turda, and Iaşi, where students and workers in two separate protests were said to have marched through the streets of the city to the Party headquarters.[114] All these protests appear to have passed peacefully and, as the demands in most cases seem to have focused on local problems within the factory or, in the case of the students, with living conditions in their dormitories, they were relatively easily defused by timely concessions from the regime. There were, however, some exceptions to this general rule of peaceful protest, with two incidents involving miners from the early 1980s reportedly leading to violence.[115] An attempt to create a "Free Trade Union of the Working People of Romania" (SLOMR) in 1979, centered on workers and intellectuals in Drobeta-Turnu Severin and Bucharest but also drawing support from elsewhere in the country, was forcibly quashed by the authorities too.[116]

The most violent and significant protest prior to the revolution was to occur in Braşov on November 15, 1987. On that day workers from the Red Flag factory, proceeding to vote in local elections, began to shout anti-regime slogans. In scenes that prefigured the revolution in Timişoara, the workers were joined by other townspeople as they ransacked the local Party headquarters and tore down and burnt in a huge bonfire much of the panoply of communist symbolism that festooned the city.[117]

---

113. Socor (August 13, 1986), 1–5; Csalog (1989), 5–11.

114. Socor (November 25, 1987), 5–9; Gabanyi (2000), 428–32.

115. *Financial Times*, November 17, 1981, 2.

116. Karatnycky et al. (1980), 78–86; Freund (1983), 61–62; Georgescu (1983b), 187–88, 193 n. 24. For reports of unions being formed in the 1980s see Tismaneanu (1988), 57–58.

117. *Independent*, November 28, 1987, 6; Socor (December 4, 1987), 1–7; *East European Reporter*, 3:2, 1988, 61–63; Brucan (1993), 134–35; Deletant (1995), 249–53; Oprea and Olaru (2002).

Major-General Emil Macri, head of the II Directorate of the *securitate*, and Major-Generals Constantin Nuţă and Mihalea Velicu of the militia were sent from Bucharest to mount an inquiry. Scores were arrested, some as young as thirteen years old. Aside from general grievances over food shortages and rationing, the disturbances seem to have been triggered by an effective cut in wages at the factory due to a failure to fulfill plan requirements.[118] After the Braşov disturbances, there were reports from all over Romania of other sporadic protests against the regime, but these seem to have amounted only to the shouting of some anti-Ceauşescu slogans, the scattering of opposition leaflets, and occasional abortive attempts to organize demonstrations, as occurred in Iaşi on the very day before the revolution broke out in Timişoara.[119] Thus, although it remains true that for most of the 1980s Romania remained generally quiet, there were periodic outbreaks of unrest and it is conceivable that the protests in Braşov might have triggered a revolution. To try to understand why this did not happen and why the revolution only broke out in December 1989, it is necessary to first look at the reaction of the security forces, then at the mechanisms of revolt, before concluding with a survey of the changed international environment.

Ceauşescu and the Security Forces

The crucial determinant in deciding the fate of any popular uprising is the actions of the security forces of the state. For a revolution to occur the apparatus of coercion has to fail and, if this is not due to military defeat, it has to be because the security forces feel that the regime is so lacking in legitimacy that it no longer warrants their support. This is what eventually happened in Romania, but the crucial difference with elsewhere in Eastern Europe in 1989 is that, prior to December 22, not only did Ceauşescu possess the political will to use force but also the security forces were initially willing to respond to his orders.

To deal with an outbreak of civil unrest, the principal forces Ceauşescu had to draw upon were the army, its civilian paramilitary associate body, the patriotic guard, the forces of the Ministry of the Interior, the *securitate*, and the militia, as well as the 15,000-strong border guards. The largest of the available forces was the army, which in 1989 had 140,000 personnel. This, however, was far from being a professional fighting force, since 95,000 (68 percent) of its complement were conscripts, undergoing at sixteen months

118. Ionescu (March 4, 1988), 9–12.
119. Socor (January 13, 1988b), 21; BBC, EE/0698, B/12, February 26, 1990; *Adevărul,* February 23, 1990, 1, 3; *Adevărul,* February 24, 1990, 1, 3; Suciu (1990), 6–9; Spiridon (1994).

the briefest period of military service of any of the Warsaw Pact states.[120] The patriotic guard was theoretically even larger. With participation mandatory for all men until the age of sixty-two and for women until fifty-seven, it had a potential strength of six million. In fact, its actual core was far smaller, with perhaps 12,000 fulltime staff.[121] Of the Ministry of the Interior forces, the militia numbered 32,595, with 7,132 officers, 23,475 other ranks, and 1,988 civilian staff spread in stations across Romania.[122] The *securitate* was slightly larger, directly employing 38,682 personnel.[123] Of these, 23,370 belonged to the *securitate* troops, which had four main brigade headquarters in Bucharest, Constanța, Timișoara, and Cluj, each with four to five battalions. The remainder of *securitate* personnel were divided between national directorates, special units, the technical and transmission command, training centers, and county offices. There were six main directorates: I (domestic intelligence), II (economic counterespionage), III (counterespionage), IV (military counterespionage), V (protection of the party leadership), and VI (penal investigation). There was also a Center for External Information, which served as a foreign intelligence service.[124] Aside from the *securitate* troops, the most likely combatants from the Ministry of Interior forces in any conflict were the 484-strong V Directorate and the 795 members of the USLA special antiterrorist unit. The bulk of the *securitate* troops were also conscripts. They received better rations than their army counterparts, but this did not mean they were necessarily more loyal. Indeed, it is noticeable, particularly in the light of myth of the *securitate* as a specially favored service, how Ceaușescu employed units from all the main branches of the security forces during the revolution.

An army can be effectively used as an instrument of repression within an insurrectionary context only by virtue of the military values and discipline that give it a sense of institutional separateness from society as a whole. Only if this sense exists will it be able to act against domestic civilian populations, and then probably just for a limited amount of time, because even the most professional of forces operate under important constraints. These arise from both the weight of international opinion and the strains that are placed on internal discipline through excessive use against unarmed co-citizens. In Romania this sense of institutional separateness was weak. The largely conscript army perceived itself not as a "separate caste" but as part of society. Under the taunts of the crowd it was to prove unwilling to execute any more than a limited amount of repres-

120. For the army see Alexiev (1982), 149–66; Jones (1984), 348–411; Nelson (1989), 737–41.

121. Crowther (1989), 213; International Institute for Strategic Studies (1989).

122. Pitulescu et al. (1995), 15.

123. Deletant (1995), 380.

124. Ibid., 377–80.

sion, effectively collapsing as a disciplined force after a single operation in both Bucharest and Timișoara. However, before this had occurred, the unarmed crowd had, time and again across Romania, in acts of great heroism, stood their ground before the security forces, even after they had opened fire on the protesters. Similar behavior has been noted in other revolutions, which has led some theorists to suggest that such indomitable courage must be driven by ideological commitment.[125] It is difficult to argue this was the case in Romania, but nevertheless, aside from drawing on a sense of grievance and a concomitant belief that their actions were legitimate, the members of the crowd, well before there was any discernible evidence that it really was the case, do seem to have been driven by the idea that the army was about to defect to the side of "the people."[126] Fired by this belief, demonstrators unhesitatingly moved forward to fraternize with the troops and as a result so sapped military morale that eventually the security forces were unable to continue the repression. However, rather than being acts of reckless folly, closer study suggests that such actions by the crowd did have a certain rationale.

At a purely emotional level, few seem to have felt that the soldiers were capable of firing in cold blood at a crowd of innocent civilians. Many of the demonstrators had once been conscripts themselves and often still had friends and family who were serving within the army. Indeed, stories abound of conscripts coming face to face with relatives within the ranks of the demonstrators during the revolution.[127] The sense of solidarity between the conscripts and workers in the crowd was also increased by Ceaușescu's habit of using military labor on construction sites and in industrial and agricultural work, an onerous burden that seems to have been disliked by all ranks.[128] This not only allowed the conscripts to still feel part of the civilian body but also minimized their military training, leaving them unexposed to military values and unfamiliar with firing live ammunition—every bullet had to be accounted for after the rare training exercises. Indeed, having served in the army and knowing about such restrictions, many of the protesters thought it highly unlikely that live ammunition would be issued, leading them to think that warning shots fired at the crowd were nothing more than blank cartridges. Ceaușescu's use of nationalist ideology compounded his problems. Nationalism stressed the same patriotic values that traditionally lie at the heart of the military value system, thereby reestablishing the organic relationship between the army and the nation that had been diluted by internationalist tendencies in the immediate years after the communist takeover, when the Red Army was

125. Skocpol (1994), 249; Krejčí (1994), 37–38.
126. Milin (1990), 35, 42–46; Suciu (1990), 46–47, 209.
127. See, for instance, Ursu, Dolghin, and Lăcustă (1990), 4.
128. Gafton (November 14, 1985), 7–11; Gafton (December 17, 1985), 27–32; Suciu (1990), 213; *RUSI Soviet-Warsaw Pact Yearbook 1989* (1989–90), 270; Crowther (1989), 217.

stationed in Romania. Following the embracing of nationalism, the Romanian army, as the chief forum for patriotic socialization, had taken on a renewed importance as the "schoolroom" of the nation. This led to a widespread tendency both within the ranks of the military and society as a whole to identify the army with the nation—that is, "the people"—at their widest extent and to correspondingly downplay loyalty to the Party.[129] During the revolution it was this identification that was to bear fruit on the streets of Timișoara, Bucharest, and elsewhere when the protesters chanted at the troops: "We are the people, whom do you defend?"

The professional officer corps also seems to have been deeply disgruntled, but there is little evidence of middle and junior officers refusing to obey orders prior to the flight of Ceaușescu. In Târgu Mureș on December 21, 1989, a lieutenant colonel was relieved of his duties for having a "weak political, patriotic and revolutionary conscience and commenting negatively on the actual measures taken," and in Timișoara at least one officer refused to give his unit orders to suppress the demonstrations, but few examples appear to exist beyond these.[130] The roots of officer discontent were many and varied but they included the relatively low rates of pay, with the monthly wage of an army captain at the time of the revolution being approximately 15 percent lower than his equivalent in the *securitate* troops. Unlike elsewhere in Eastern Europe, army officers in Romania also suffered the indignity of having to line up alongside civilians for even basic foodstuffs. Under the doctrine that the army should produce as well as consume, large numbers of troops were also employed on building projects, often under civilian command.[131] Deployment on construction or agricultural duties was a particularly irksome burden for lower- and middle-ranking officers and contributed to a general decline in professional self-esteem. This was compounded by the introduction of the "Entire Peoples War" military doctrine. With its stress on the preservation of national independence through mass mobilization to harry an invading force, this put a premium on sheer numbers and the patriotic guard rather than traditional military values.[132] Indeed, for much of the 1980s, defense spending had actually been frozen, with the policy being legitimized by a national referendum in 1986, and by 1989 the perception, at least among army officers, was that Romania had one of the lowest rates of defense spending in the world.[133] Together with shortages of fuel and lack of spare parts, this all meant that by December 1989 few units were at

129. Bacon (1978), 173.
130. Milin (1990), 162; Suciu (1990), 213; *Expres*, April 6–12, 1990, 3; Lungu (1997), 249.
131. Urdăreanu (1996), 32.
132. Chaplin (1983), 267–82.
133. Nelson (1988), 185–86; Gafton (December 29, 1988a), 3–5; Eyal and Anthony (1988), 99, 111; *RUSI Soviet-Warsaw Pact Yearbook 1989* (1989–90), 272–73; Eyal (1989), 80–85; Crowther (1989), 218; Nelson (1990), 30.

proper fighting capacity. Higher ranks had been incensed by Ceaușescu's failure to promote 2,152 senior officers as expected on August 23, 1989, and the severing of professional contacts with other members of the Warsaw Pact, leading to Romania's absence from military exercises, also continued to alienate a number of older generals who had received their training in the Soviet Union.[134] Indeed, Ceaușescu's policy towards the Warsaw Pact left him with a tricky contradiction to resolve in general. The differences with his powerful eastern neighbor created the need for strong domestic security forces, but the more powerful these became the more vulnerable he was to a military coup. And, indeed, before 1989, rumors of coup attempts had surfaced periodically over the years, suggesting there were serious levels of dissatisfaction within the military.[135]

The forces of the Ministry of the Interior included the militia and the *securitate*. As in all Stalinist states, in Romania the intelligence services were effectively under the control of the leader and not the Party; indeed, they were expected to monitor the activities of party members. This has led some to argue that they really were a state within a state and the chief repository of political power, with the political elite being strictly subordinate.[136] As might be expected, the former officers of the *securitate* deny this and, in general, during the revolution, they do not seem to have displayed any greater loyalty to Ceaușescu than other sections of the security forces, perhaps partly because their control of the channels of information made them well aware of the weakness of the regime.[137] Indeed, one source has even suggested that Ceaușescu was frightened of the *securitate*, seeing them as most likely to launch a coup.[138] From their dominant position within Romania's import-export companies, *securitate* officers may also have looked at their Polish and Hungarian counterparts who had embraced "political capitalism" and established "private" profit-orientated companies within the bureaucracy.[139] If so, this may in part explain their apparent lack of commitment to the Ceaușescu regime, as they came to realize that their best interests might be served by a freer economic environment. Certainly, after the revolution, former members of the *securitate* acquired the resources to build sizeable business empires.[140] As noted previously, the *securitate* were also the main source of information for the

134. Codrescu et al. (1998), 39; Alexiev (1982), 162.
135. Crowther (1989), 208.
136. Tismaneanu (1993), 316.
137. For an unsubstantiated but credible report see Săndulescu (c1996), 246–82.
138. Domenico (1999), 75.
139. Staniszkis (1990), 77–78; Verdery (1995), 235.
140. *România Liberă*, September 13, 1994, 1, claims that in 1994 over 1,000 of the 1,549 businesses with assets of more than one billion lei were owned by former members of the *nomenklatura*. John Simpson in the *Independent*, December 16, 1994, 21, reported that the *securitate* major who arrested him before the revolution was driving a Mercedes and ran an import company. For the commercial interests of the *securitate* see Deletant (1994), 39–41.

Party leadership. Indeed, many claim that they were the only source, although again the former leaders of the *securitate* disagree. Whatever the case, the leadership and the *securitate*, as was the case with the *Stasi* in East Germany, do seem to have become locked in a fatal symbiosis, with each conditioning the other's worldview.[141] This was partly because of the structures in which they found themselves. Members of the counterespionage directorate, for example, were expected to spend their lives looking for spies. Perhaps because of this, many members of the *securitate* do seem to have embraced Ceauşescu's national-communist rhetoric, and willingly confirmed his suspicions that Romania was infested with foreign agents and their domestic accomplices.[142] Like the *Stasi*, the *securitate* also seem to have considered themselves as an elite, leading and shaping society. This produced a rather condescending stance toward a society that was largely perceived as consisting of passive peasants. Following the old adage of "familiarity breeds contempt," it may be that the successes of the 1980s lulled the *securitate* into a false sense of security about their ability to keep the lid on popular dissatisfaction. There had been one serious outbreak of unrest in Braşov, but this had been confined within the city and quickly defused. Could they not deal with any future disturbances in a similar fashion?

The Mechanisms of Revolt

In any discussion of why the Romanians rose in revolution it is necessary to explain two apparent paradoxes. First, Ceauşescu was toppled by a series of mass protests, but, until the end, he seems to have believed that his regime enjoyed genuine popular support. This may be attributed to simple delusions on his part, but it also implies that there had been a significant shift in his relationship with the people, which, for reasons best known to himself, he failed to concede. Second, it has been widely recognized that Stalinism produced considerable social atomization and, in the case of Romania, the continuing high levels of coercion, which eroded all sense of trust, made this so acute that it has often been cited as a prime explanation for the passivity of the population during the 1980s. Yet huge crowds took to the streets in December 1989, and such mass mobilization requires a certain degree of social cohesion, implying that, even within the confines of a state that had undergone such severe dislocations, alternative forms of societal organization had emerged.

Both a consequence and an aim of Stalinist forced modernization, with its attendant urbanization, industrialization, and collectivization, was the destruction of the "traditional" fabric of society through the dissolving of

141. Popplewell (1992), 37–63.
142. Teodorescu (1992).

social bonds and the overturning of age-old norms. The goal was a new homogenized society cleansed of class antagonism, but the result was a collapse in social cohesion.[143] Alcoholism and delinquency increased, as an increasingly disorientated and atomized population either lapsed into passive anomie or actively schemed to bypass the system.[144] In Romania this process of homogenization (*omogenizare*) produced both positive and negative levers of social control. Firstly, it allowed Ceauşescu to construct a "contract" with society in which new flats and urban facilities in a vigorously independent state were traded for political impotence. During the 1960s and 1970s, the "contract" had largely been kept. The economy had performed strongly enough to allow for surplus resources to be diverted to improve living standards among most sections of the population. Many villages for the first time had been connected to the electricity grid and received paved roads, while levels of personal consumption rose in the towns, where new apartment blocks were seen as a definite step up the social ladder from poorer village housing. Although conditions had worsened in the 1980s, for many Romanians, particularly in the countryside and smaller towns, the Ceauşescu era was one of considerable progress, partly explaining some of the ambiguity subsequently felt about the revolution and the nostalgia for the communist era that resurfaced remarkably quickly after 1989.

More invidiously, the denial of identity inherent in homogenization facilitated social control. Years of turning up at poorly maintained institutions for nonexistent work led many people, including skilled scientists and technicians, to feel a sense of powerlessness bordering on the very edge of nonbeing.[145] In a society divorced from a framework of normal values, with minimal room for personal initiative, their disorientated lives seemed without any discernible direction and, as George Schöpflin has stressed, this purposelessness ultimately eats away at the legitimacy of the system.[146] Yet while helping "explain" the apparent passivity of the population during the 1980s, the same characteristics by a neat reversal can also be used to account for much of the dynamic of the revolution. The homogenized structure of the state, which was characterized by an absence of differentials and an ideological stress on egalitarianism and centralized decision making, produced a commonality of experience, which during the 1980s increasingly became a commonality of grievance. This ensured that any explosion would include broad swaths of society.

143. Kligman (1992), 364–418.
144. Stefanescu (March 2, 1984), 21–24; Gafton (May 17, 1984), 13–16; Kideckel (1984–85), 431–46; Beck (1984–85), 395–413. For atomization see Schöpflin (1993), 169–71; Sampson (1984–86), 42–44.
145. *Guardian*, January 12, 1990, 23, quotes the expressive words of a Romanian author: "In Romania the clock seemed dumb, the hours and minutes passed without any meaning. We were drifting in the belief that we were forgotten in a play for nobody, for nothing"; see also Kligman (1992), 367.
146. Schöpflin (1993), 78–80, 191–92.

Sampson has plausibly suggested that the cold winter of 1984–85 was the defining moment in this process. Then, to save fuel, the huge central heating systems supplying thousands of apartments were turned off and no amount of personal connections could provide the necessary leverage for the boilers to be refired. The barriers between "us" and "them" were eroded, building a sense of collective suffering that underwrote the deep feeling of betrayal permeating all levels of society.[147] This shared experience of suffering and domination—reinforced, as years passed, in the solidarity of waiting in lines—brought society as an entity increasingly into opposition to the regime, so that, for instance, the workers in response to the "official 'cult of work' " that was propagated to motivate fulfillment of the plan developed an "oppositional cult of *non*-work."[148] The sense of shared suffering, which was powerful enough to bury deep-seated ethnic and social differences, laid the ground for a popular uprising en masse against Ceaușescu—although, once he departed from the scene, the underlying anomie and lack of social discipline also partly explains the violent excesses of the revolution. However, this commonality of grievance could not in itself lead to mobilization because, as Theda Skocpol has noted, to turn mass lower-class discontent into revolution, (semi-)autonomous collective organizations have to be present.[149] These will probably be well embedded within society and possess a degree of cultural significance. In a case study of the Iranian revolution, Skocpol identified the traditional networks centered on the bazaar merchants as forming such a nucleus, and in the Bolivian revolution of 1952 the miners seem to have formed a similar organizational group with a "special cultural resonance."[150]

Turning to the Romanian case, three such organizational forms can be identified, each dominant at a certain stage of the revolution. Firstly, the origins of the demonstrations in Timişoara were rooted in the Hungarian Reform Church, which provided the key organizational base for protests in support of the dissident pastor László Tőkés. The first demonstrators were almost entirely drawn from the ranks of his congregation. Secondly, a number of observers have drawn parallels between the behavior of the protesters on the streets of Timişoara and elsewhere, and that of a soccer crowd, noting that, barring the slogans shouted, their conduct was virtually identical.[151] Indeed, prior to 1989, Sampson had already suggested that the local soccer club was one of the few intermediary organizations in Romania that possessed the mobilizing potential of primary organiza-

147. Sampson (1984–86), 44; Pompei-Cojocaru (March 25, 1985), 3–6.
148. Verdery (1995), 224 (emphasis in original).
149. Skocpol (1994), 241.
150. Ibid., 245–50 for bazaar merchants, and 314–15 for Bolivia.
151. Even some of the slogans resembled soccer chants, especially those beginning with "óle óle"; Granqvist (1999), 63 n. 78.

tions. Soccer matches in the country had also been marked by protests and violence. In June 1988 a local Derby between the two great Bucharest rivals, Steaua and Dinamo, was brought to a halt when opposing fans battled on the field after a controversial goal had been disallowed; and in Timişoara, on November 15, 1989, in a virtual dress rehearsal for the revolution, Romania's victory over Denmark in the World Cup qualifying competition brought jubilant supporters flooding onto the streets of the city chanting slogans such as "Down with Ceauşescu."[152] During the revolution, the camaraderie of the terraces appears to have provided some type of model for the collective behavior of the young men who predominated in the demonstrations during the first days of the protests. The last and most important organizational forum was the factory. It was not to be the soccer fan–style demonstrations that brought down Ceauşescu, because the authorities were able to suppress the protests in Timişoara on December 17 and in Bucharest on December 21 and regain control of the streets. Instead, it was the mass demonstrations in public places on December 20 in Timişoara and December 22 in Bucharest that were to prove decisive. The only place the protesters could gather beforehand was their place of work. In the forecourts of the factories they adopted some basic organizational form before they issued onto the streets, completely overwhelming any remaining vestiges of military opposition they encountered. Thus, with some irony, it can be said that Ceauşescu was toppled by mass protests that stemmed from an organizational form, the factory, that communism had elevated to be both the actual and also the mythical heart of the state.

Marx and Engels argued that workers, following their concentration in the new urban factories and reduction through capitalism to universal poverty (which Marx termed "immiseration"), would subsume their individual interests within a wider class consciousness and form trade unions to defend their common position.[153] However, as noted previously, immiseration, even in poverty-stricken Romania, does not seem to have sufficed to prompt a revolution, and under communism trade unions had evolved into little more than ciphers charged with mobilizing the workforce on behalf of the regime. Bereft of effective bodies to air their grievances, the workers had no means of bargaining for change, leaving violent protest one of the few alternatives. The factories were, therefore, not so much the source of formal revolutionary structures, although it seems that in some enterprises the workers took over the trade unions and workers' councils during the revolution, but rather they served as centers

---

152. Sampson (1981–83), 169; for the analogy with football supporters see Suciu (1990), 90; for the November 1989 events see Ibid., 7, 56–57; for the June 1988 violence see Leicand (July 20, 1988), 41–43.

153. Calhoun (1988), 135.

of mobilization.[154] Craig Calhoun has argued that in the absence of formal organizations well-integrated "traditional" communities are normally required for mobilization, but in atomized Romania these were not present, and instead the workplace came to act as a substitute community.[155] The lack of formal organizations, however, was to produce a fundamentally weak revolutionary movement, characterized by many small clusters rather than one coherent whole. Largely defined through negative reference to Ceaușescu, the revolutionary coalition was little more than an agglomeration of individuals, which made it potentially highly vulnerable to oligarchic takeover. The factories were the organizational base that lay at the heart of the mass mobilization that overthrew Ceaușescu, but the same was also true of the disturbances in Brașov. The essential difference between 1987 and 1989 was the international context.

The International Context

The events of December 1989 cannot be divorced from the other Eastern European revolutions of that year and the breakup of the Soviet bloc, which provided the permissive international context required. Prior to 1989, previous attempts at revolution in communist Eastern Europe, such as Hungary in 1956, had been crushed by the Soviet Union. But, now, in 1989, once their monopoly of power was challenged, the various communist parties of Eastern Europe were allowed to collapse one after another in quick succession like a house of cards. Beginning in February, with the Polish round table talks and the decision by the Hungarian Communist Party to abandon its leading role, the pace of events escalated throughout the year until they culminated in the months of November and December with the fall of the Berlin Wall, the velvet revolution in Prague, and the Romanian revolution.

This permissive environment arose because of changes in the Soviet Union's perception of the world, and of Eastern Europe in particular, which came to be seen in strategic and economic terms as more of an encumbrance than an asset. Gorbachev's "new thinking" in foreign affairs,

154. Photographs taken on December 22 in Bucharest show large numbers of workers marching into Piața Palatului just before the flight of Ceaușescu, carrying makeshift banners calling for his resignation. However, they are noticeably being shepherded by some of their own number wearing armbands, which raises important questions as to how much formal organization was deployed at this time. Did the workers spontaneously create new structures or adapt old ones, such as the trade unions? Evidence from Bucharest and elsewhere shows worker councils being established after the flight of Ceaușescu, but were some created beforehand?

155. Calhoun (1988), 149–50.

with its stress on mutual security in an interdependent world, left little room for the old Cold War divisions—exemplified par excellence by the Berlin Wall. With this realization, the road was opened for the revocation of the so-called Brezhnev Doctrine and, ultimately, the Soviet Union's withdrawal from Eastern Europe.[156] The changes in the Soviet Union were crucial in providing a permissive environment for revolution in Eastern Europe but they did not provide a detailed strategy for managing any transformation. Consequently, for much of the period, rather than setting the agenda the Soviet Union seems to have been merely reacting to the powerful dynamic of revolution that gripped the region. This seems to have been as true for Romania as elsewhere. Gorbachev's reforms undermined the position of Ceaușescu both at home and abroad. In the international arena, Romania, outpaced by the Soviet Union, lost its carefully cultivated image of an eastern bloc maverick and was consigned by the West to diplomatic isolation. At home, they raised hopes for similar reforms, effectively cutting the ground from under the feet of Ceaușescu, who continued to combat ideas of radical change. But there was to be no direct transfer of revolution to Romania. Not even an indirect trigger, as happened with East Germany, when the Hungarians opened their borders on September 11, 1989, sparking the "crisis of emigration." Romania was isolated with few contacts with its neighbors and, paradoxically, the absence of Soviet troops may have contributed to the violence of Ceaușescu's overthrow, because, unlike elsewhere in Eastern Europe, Gorbachev possessed no effective leverage to persuade the Romanian leader to leave power peacefully.

Prior to 1989, the Romanians had long been accustomed to making unflattering comparisons between their country and the West, which was often seen in unrealistically utopian terms.[157] What changed in 1989 was that, as the boundaries of the East-West divide started to dissolve, the Romanians suddenly found themselves in an invidious position vis-à-vis not only the West but also other Eastern European states. On November 10, 1989, even the elderly Todor Zhivkov, the leader of Bulgaria (whose television channels could be received in Bucharest) was removed from power. In the case of Timișoara the contrast was even more striking, since Hungary—the state which had progressed furthest along the road of reform in Eastern Europe and one with which the ethnic Hungarian population of the area could obviously identify—lay just across the border. Great changes were taking place across Eastern Europe: was Romania to remain the only country (save Albania) shackled under an enfeebled neo-Stalinist dictator? The prospect was too hard to bear, and it was this real-

156. Holloway (1988–89), Dawisha (1990), Pravda (1992), Lévesque (1997).
157. Câmpeanu and Steriade (1993), 917.

ization voiced by many of the revolutionaries that it was "now or never" that drove the dynamic of revolution.[158]

Romania and Its Neighbors

As Romania was part of the Warsaw Pact, the revolution can be placed within the ambit of the wider collapse of communism in Eastern Europe. Yet Romania also occupied a distinctive position within the Soviet bloc, as for years it had sought to persuade the outside world that it followed its own autonomous, nonaligned foreign policy, distinct from that of the USSR. The reality might well have been that under a veneer of autonomy Romania was careful to cultivate its intra-bloc links and refrain from any true independence of action, but the rhetoric of the leadership often suggested otherwise.[159] Throughout much of the 1980s, Romania was engaged in a protracted and vitriolic war of words with Hungary and, to a lesser extent, with the Soviet Union. Judging from transcripts of the PEC meetings, Ceaușescu was obsessed with the fear that he was to be toppled by a Soviet-backed coup, and post-1989 many analyses of the events of December have stuck to this line. These allegations are discussed in some detail later in this book and to put these into context this section concludes with a short review of relations between Romania and both the Soviet Union and Hungary immediately prior to the revolution.

By 1989 Romania had ceased to be of any great importance to the Soviet Union. It presented no ideological challenge, held no great geopolitical significance, and, aside from the continuing tensions with Hungary over minority rights in Transylvania, it was not politically destabilizing, unlike Poland. In his memoirs Gorbachev stresses that he was not intrinsically hostile to Ceaușescu and that the latter also seems to have desired better relations, if only, according to the Soviet leader, because it pandered to Ceaușescu's aspirations to be a global leader. To this end, Ceaușescu used to enter into elaborate charades, such as when he stumbled in a park, so that he could be caught on camera arm-in-arm with the Soviet leader.[160] Marking the improvement in relations, on May 25, 1987, Gorbachev became the first CPSU general secretary to visit Bucharest since Leonid Brezhnev in 1976. In his main speech, which was carried live on Romanian radio and television, the Soviet leader fully embraced the idea of separate national roads to socialism.[161] However, any sense of security Ceaușescu may have gained from this endorsement of a policy he

---

158. Gurr and Goldstone (1991), 331–32, emphasize the tendency for such "copycat" revolutions.

159. Shafir (1986a), 366.

160. Gorbachev (1996), 475–76.

161. For the 1987 visit see Gabanyi (2000), 343–54.

had long championed must have been curtailed by Gorbachev's call for the removal of all those who "cannot keep up with the times; . . . who have tarnished themselves with dishonesty, lack of principle, and nepotism, and who, in the pursuit of profit have sacrificed the moral image proper to a party member."[162] Nonetheless in the years immediately prior to 1989, there was, if anything, a slight thaw in Soviet-Romanian relations. Polemics were still occasionally traded in newspapers, but they gave the appearance of being ritual exchanges, devoid of any real meaning and largely intended for domestic consumption. Most of the time the Soviet press played down its criticism of the Romanian regime, although this in itself was not unusual, because the same was also true of its coverage of other hard-line states, such as Czechoslovakia and East Germany.[163] On the occasion of his seventieth birthday in January 1988, Ceaușescu was awarded the Order of Lenin, although according to Soviet sources it was a normal gesture made at the request of the Romanians, and later that year in October, at a summit in Moscow, Elena Ceaușescu was finally accepted by the Soviet Union as an official representative of Romania.[164]

The reasons for the improvement in relations between the two countries are not entirely clear, but there seems to have been a growing realization of mutual dependence. Trade had increased sharply since Gorbachev's accession to power, so that the Soviet Union accounted for 33 percent of Romania's total trade in 1988.[165] Soviet exports to Romania were mostly in the energy sector, including oil, which had to be paid for in hard currency (one of the costs of Romania's semiautonomous foreign policy), while in return the Romanians supplied the Soviet Union with agricultural products, particularly meat.[166] The Soviet leader's visit to Romania in 1987 and no doubt his return in July 1989 for a Warsaw Treaty Organization meeting also seemed to have confirmed Soviet fears that economic collapse in Romania could bring political turmoil, which might conceivably spread into Soviet-controlled Moldova.[167] So, as Jonathan Eyal has suggested, it seems quite possible that the preferred option at this stage was to shore up Ceaușescu rather than encourage his removal from office, which could cause further problems and might even lead to a costly intervention.[168] From the Romanian point of view as well, better ties were desirable, as diplomatic isolation had forced the virtual abandon-

---

162. BBC, EE/8579, C1/9, May 28, 1987. For Ceaușescu's reply see BBC, EE/8579, C1/2, May 28, 1987. Gorbachev's speech was not fully reported in the Romanian press and, according to the Soviet leader, he later had a very frank exchange of views with Ceaușescu over a private dinner; Eyal (1992), 196; Gorbachev (1996), 476.

163. Lévesque (1997), 194.

164. Ibid.; Socor (November 9, 1988), 3–8.

165. Eyal (1992), 191.

166. Lévesque (1997), 193.

167. Falin (1990), 24.

168. Eyal (1992), 198.

ment of the semiautonomous foreign policy. The failure of Károly Grósz in Hungary and Wojciech Jaruzelski in Poland to stem the flow of power to the opposition confirmed to Ceaușescu that his view, that only closer collaboration between the socialist states could avert catastrophe, was correct. This was a consistent theme in his speeches throughout 1989 and appears again in his last meeting with Gorbachev, which took place in Moscow on December 4, 1989.[169] Touching upon the recent events in East Germany and Czechoslovakia, Ceaușescu urged Gorbachev to take a more active stance. By this the Romanian leaders seems to have been seeking the convening of a congress of communist parties, rather than military intervention, although it has long been rumored that earlier he had called for Warsaw Pact action after the success of Solidarity in the June 1989 Polish elections.[170] Much of the meeting was devoted to discussions about bilateral economic ties and, generally, the picture that emerges is of Ceaușescu striving unsuccessfully for closer ties between the countries while the Soviet leader remains wary.

One of the chief concerns of the Soviet Union was Romania's acrimonious high-profile confrontation with Hungary, which also cast the country in an unfavorable light on the world stage.[171] During the late 1980s, the rhetoric between the two countries increased in intensity, as, with the crumbling of the communist system, the old debate couched in terms of Leninist nationalities policy was abandoned in favor of outright chauvinism.[172] The result was a raising of the minorities issue to the top of the Hungarian political agenda and an increase in levels of distrust between the two countries. The Romanians were intent on raising the specter of Hungarian revanchism to foster regime legitimation, but in Hungary the same issue was employed for the opposite purpose of undermining the ruling party.[173] The treatment of the minority in Romania and particularly the systematization campaign, which was seen as targeting ethnic Hungarian communities, became a rallying cry used by the opposition to berate the Hungarian authorities, with the Hungarian Democratic Forum mustering an estimated 40,000 protesters in Budapest in June 1988.[174] In response the new Hungarian leader, Grósz, met Ceaușescu in August 1988 in Arad, but, naïvely accepting Ceaușescu's assurances that conditions in Transylvania would improve, he was humiliated by his host's subsequent

169. A transcript can be found in Sava and Monac (2001), 80–97. For a suggestion that the meeting was stormy see Codrescu et al. (1998), 27, 41–42 n. 6. Shevardnadze (1991), 117, also suggests confrontation but does not say when.

170. Dobrynin (1995), 632.

171. Among the extensive literature on the Romanian-Hungarian dispute see for instance: Gabanyi (April 20, 1987), 11–15; Shafir (January 28, 1988), 15–19; Schöpflin and Poulton (1990).

172. Schwerthoeffer (1985), 86.

173. Joó (1994).

174. Hunya (1989), 327–41; Rady (1992), 73.

denunciation of "intolerable interference in Romanian affairs."[175] A mutual expulsion of diplomats followed in November 1989.[176] The war of words also spread to international forums. On February 27, 1989, the Hungarian Deputy Foreign Minister, Gyula Horn, condemned Romanian policies on minorities and human rights in a speech at the UN Commission on Human Rights in Geneva. And, the following month, the Hungarians cosponsored a resolution calling for an inquiry into human rights abuses in Romania, with other Eastern bloc countries, including the USSR, Bulgaria, and East Germany, abstaining.[177]

Notwithstanding the polemics, Hungary was seen as a welcome sanctuary by many Romanians. By late 1989, it was reported that over 24,000 refugees had fled from Romania to Hungary, and this figure was probably an underestimate, as many more were unregistered. By the end of 1989, the flow was more than 300 per week, of which 25 percent was said to be ethnic Romanians, the most famous being the Olympic gold medal-winning gymnast Nadia Comăneci, who fled in November 1989. Some commentators saw the exodus as a deliberate ploy to rid Romania of potential troublemakers and silence Hungarian complaints about the fate of their conationals, but it did little for the public image of the regime and, at a time when the rest of the Eastern bloc were dismantling their defenses, in 1989 Ceaușescu started to extend the border fence between Hungary and Romania to universal condemnation.[178]

By 1989 Romania faced international isolation. Uncertain about its allies and openly opposed by its neighbor Hungary, the much vaunted semiautonomous foreign policy lay in tatters, as the West turned its back. Systematization and the destruction of Bucharest had brought universal condemnation not only from inside Romania but also from outside the country, including a rare intervention into international politics by the Prince of Wales in the United Kingdom.[179] The response of the Romanian regime was to turn its back on the outside world, including the unilateral renouncing of the prized Most Favored Nation trading status with the United States in February 1988. The collapse of the Romanian economy in the 1980s meant that few American businessmen were willing to lobby for a continuation of the agreement and, with the arrival of a conservative American ambassador in Bucharest, the Romanians decided it

175. Almond (1992), 206–7, makes the interesting observation that Hungarian policy on an open border with Austria was directly concerned with securing similar rights of travel for their co-nationals in Romania.

176. Deletant (1995), 137.

177. Deletant (1998), 199–200.

178. Eyal (1988), 130–32; Eyal (1992), 198. A further 5,000 refugees were in Yugoslavia.

179. For examples of protests both inside and outside the country see Shafir (August 23, 1988d), 17–22; Socor (September 16, 1988), 19–20; Ionescu (October 20, 1988), 1–12; Doina Cornea's appeal to the Krakow Independent Human Rights Conference reproduced in *East European Reporter*, 3:4, 1989, 21–22.

Nicolae Ceauşescu is applauded by his wife, Elena, and the other delegates during the 14th Congress of the Romanian Communist Party, November 1989. Courtesy Associated Press.

was better to abandon the agreement to forestall Congress from scrutinizing its human rights record.[180] Romania also pointedly refused to be bound by the provisions relating to human rights and freedom of worship in the final document of the Conference on Security and Cooperation in Europe (CSCE), and in April 1989 the European Commission suspended negotiations on trade agreements because of human rights abuses.[181]

With Romania increasingly isolated and beset on all sides, amidst the turbulent scenes of hope shining brightly elsewhere in Eastern Europe, on November 20, 1989, the 14th Congress of the Romanian Communist Party opened in Bucharest. It seems that all Romania waited with bated breath for the opening speech from their leader, hoping against hope for either news of a last-minute conversion to Gorbachev-style reforms or, perhaps, a challenge from the audience, like that at the 12th Congress of the RCP when Pârvulescu had risen to denounce Ceauşescu's abuse of power. Instead, in a familiar declamatory drone punctuated by frequent bursts of carefully orchestrated applause, they heard Ceauşescu launch into a monologue in which he promised only to maintain the leading role of the Party. No respite was offered on the painful road of socialist con-

180. For MFN trading status see Harrington and Karns (1988), 71–97; Harrington and Courtney (1991), Kirk and Raceanu (1994).
181. Gafton (March 4, 1988), 3–5; Linden (1989), 302.

struction, and many remember turning off the radio or television with heavy hearts.[182] When Ceaușescu was "unanimously" reelected Party leader, the loss of hope seems to have been palpable and, as the last prospects for peaceful change evaporated, the only option left was to be a violent overthrow.

182. A feeling apparently shared by the Soviet delegates; see Gorbachev (1996), 484.

Chapter Two

The Overthrow of Nicolae Ceauşescu

The Contexts of Revolution

The Romanian revolution broke out in December 1989 in the city of Timişoara, which lies in the far west of the country, in an area known as Banat. The time of year in which it occurred, the geographical position of Timişoara, and the distinct historical development of the Banat all played a role in shaping the nature of the revolution. December normally sees the onset of the harsh Romanian winter, but in 1989 most of the month was blessed with unseasonably mild weather. This encouraged the crowds to stay on the streets and, to a certain extent, rendered the tactics of the authorities ineffectual, since the blasts of cold water discharged by water cannons did not have the same impact as if they had been delivered in more wintry conditions. A prominent revolutionary from Timişoara, Claudiu Iordache, was later to say that the weather had been worth five divisions in their victory.[1] Strangely, on either side of the revolution, the country experienced a cold snap. In the early days of December the first arrival of wintry weather, with its attendant power and food shortages, must have fueled the desperation of the demonstrators, while after the events, the return of the chill weather at the beginning of January helped quench the zeal of those who wanted to continue the struggle on the streets against the new regime. Midwinter also brought early nights, which in the low wattage twilight of communism were frequently pitch black. Much of the revolution was played out against a backdrop of dark-

---

1. Galloway and Wylie (1991), 175.

ness, and this had a profound influence on the events. The night aided the first demonstrators, giving them a cloak of anonymity in which to hurl stones and petrol bombs at the security forces, but it also made it easier for officers to order scared and ill-trained conscripts to fire on their fellow citizens, who were glimpsed only as nocturnal half-images rather than in the full glare of day. Darkness also helped conceal the face of repression compounding the problem of identifying both those who were guilty of shooting at the crowd before December 22 and, more lastingly and bafflingly, the identity of the terrorists who fired in the nights following that date.

Timișoara is closer to Belgrade and Budapest than it is to Bucharest. The proximity of the Yugoslav and Hungarian borders allowed for the relatively easy passage of news about the early demonstrations to waiting Western journalists, despite the news blackout declared by the regime. Details of the events were then speedily broadcast via Western radio stations, such as the BBC, Radio Free Europe, and Deutsche Welle, to other parts of Romania.[2] Inside the country information about the disturbances also continued to flow informally, not only via the gossip of the stairwell and the rumors whispered in the long food lines but also through the telephone system. Throughout most of the period this continued to function within Timișoara, with calls also sometimes possible to other localities in Romania, if not through the normal telephone system, then via the network operated by Romanian railways.[3] Only foreign calls were almost impossible to make, although even here there were exceptions, with, among others, Radio Free Europe, the BBC, and Hungarian radio and television all broadcasting telephone interviews with residents of Timișoara.[4] Telex services also seem to have remained uninterrupted, as were the trains, so travelers were freely able to relay news of the events in Timișoara to the remainder of the country.

Attempts to identify why Timișoara was the cradle of the revolution usually stress the distinct historical development of the Banat, which was long part of the Habsburg Empire.[5] The Habsburgs had encouraged large-scale immigration into the area from the mid-eighteenth century onward, making it one of great ethnic diversity. By 1989, however, the traditional multiethnic structure of the Banat was fast waning. Like so many other cities in Romania, during the Ceaușescu era, Timișoara had experienced a massive increase in population, virtually doubling in size from

2. Suciu (1990), 222; Ratesh (1991), 35–36. In 1989 between 1:00 a.m. and 1:00 p.m., CNN was also relayed every day from Belgrade and the signal could be received in Timișoara; *Washington Post*, December 31, 1989, A30.

3. Suciu (1990), 58, 138, 170–71, 183–86, 225, 238; Milin (1990), 155–56; Haidău (1997), 159.

4. For the broadcasts see the examples in Sârcă (1998), 34–57; *Independent*, December 21, 1989, 1.

5. Birăescu (1990), 11–15; Ratesh (1991), 17–19.

174,243 in 1966 to 334,278 in 1992 (the closest available figure to 1989). Most of these newcomers had been drawn from elsewhere—43 percent of the urban inhabitants of the county of Timiş in 1977 were born outside the county—and when taken in conjunction with the exodus of the Germans and the deportation of the Serbs in the 1950s, this meant that by 1989 the vast majority of the population was Romanian in ethnic origin. In 1977, the last available census figure prior to 1989, 71 percent of the urban population were recorded as being Romanian, 13 percent Hungarian, 12 percent German, and only 2 percent Serbo-Croat.[6] During the revolution, Ceauşescu may have railed against agents of foreign irredentism but, in reality, aside from the undeniable facts that László Tőkés was a Hungarian and that the bulk of the initial protesters were drawn from the congregation of his Hungarian Reformed Church, it is difficult to argue that the history of ethnic diversity had much bearing on the outbreak of events. Among those arrested during the revolution in Timişoara, each ethnic group was represented more or less in proportion to its number in the city as a whole.[7] Only in the way it pandered to the Romanian leader's anti-Hungarian prejudices did it perhaps influence developments, leading him to misjudge the causes of the demonstrations and order inappropriate actions.

The immigrants, especially the Germans, had acted as something of a catalyst for the development of the Banat as a whole, introducing advanced agricultural and manufacturing techniques.[8] This, coupled with a tradition of good schooling for the members of all ethnic groups, meant that the region and especially Timiş and Timişoara came to enjoy a level of economic and social development above that of much of the rest of Romania. This situation seems to have even continued during the Ceauşescu era, since it was only in October 1989 that food rationing was reported as being introduced on a large scale in the region.[9] It seems quite possible that the lateness of this further decline in the quality of life may have played a significant role in the triggering of the revolution, especially as the Banat was a noted food-producing region. The greater level of development, ethnic diversity, and geographic position of the Banat all helped give the region a distinct identity, and Traian Birăescu has stressed the higher civic culture of the area, writing that *Homo Timisiensis* is characterized by tolerance, understanding, and a predisposition to civic harmony.[10] Traditionally, Timişoarans have taken pride in their orientation westward, and other Romanians have tended to view the region with respect for its

6. All figures are drawn from *Recensămîntul* (1980), and *Anuarul statistic al României 1992* (n.d.).
7. Pitulescu et al. (1995), 111–13.
8. Lampe and Jackson (1982), 78.
9. *Washington Post*, December 31, 1989, A.30.
10. Birăescu (1990), 12.

identification with Western values. The isolationism and corruption of the Ceauşescu regime were the diametric opposites to these traditions, and the strains imparted by this local political culture coming to terms with the Romanian leader's vision of the world appear to have played a role in sparking the revolution. Miodrag Milin has noted that the Romanian revolution did not break out where the misery was greatest but where the shame was strongest.[11] However, this still does not fully explain why Timişoara was the seat of the unrest rather than Bucharest, Braşov, Cluj, or any of the other major cities that were to see violence in the coming weeks. Unlike Timişoara, though, none of these had the trigger for the events: László Tőkés.

László Tőkés and the Outbreak of Revolution

László Tőkés, a fresh-faced but determined looking thirty-seven-year-old priest of the Hungarian Reformed Church, had a long history as a troublemaker who was often at loggerheads with his church authorities.[12] After attending Cluj Theological Institute he was posted first to Braşov and then to the town of Dej. Here he came into conflict with the authorities over his advocacy of the Hungarian cause and, following a lengthy court action, was eventually evicted from the church premises and forced to return to live with his parents in Cluj. Convinced his dismissal was illegal, in a pattern of behavior remarkably similar to the one he adopted in Timişoara, Tőkés stubbornly protested his case for two years until he secured a hearing before a review committee. As a result, in 1986 he was awarded the post of assistant pastor in Timişoara. The authorities probably thought this would be a relatively safe posting, because the city was away from Tőkés's home territory of Transylvania. Timişoara's Hungarian population was also relatively small and had not been particular active in its dissent. During the 1980s there had been several reports of unrest in the county of Timiş, but none of these seem to have reached any great proportions, perhaps for lack of focus, and, according to Filip Teodorescu, deputy-head of the III Directorate of the *securitate*, an internal DSS "audit" in October 1989 judged the county to be "quiet."[13]

Tőkés was not long in Timişoara when, in January 1987, following the death of the incumbent, Leo Peuker, he was appointed probationary pastor. This indeterminate status was held by 70 percent of the other pastors in the diocese, leaving them all directly under the jurisdiction of the

11. Milin (1990), 31.

12. For full details of László Tőkés's career see Tőkés (1990); Corley and Eibner (1990).

13. For details of incidents after a Romanian victory in a football match against Denmark in November 1989 and an abortive protest at a Timişoara factory over the reelection of Ceauşescu at the November Party Congress, when the 300–400 workers who gathered were dispersed by the management, see Suciu (1990), 6–7; Teodorescu (1992), 45.

Bishop of Oradea, László Papp. According to Tőkés, Peuker had been a notorious "red priest" who collaborated with the authorities, and under his care the congregation of the church had dwindled to a mere shadow of its former self. With his customary zeal Tőkés set about reversing this decline in fortunes and in the process he seems to have won the admiration and loyalty of many of his parishioners. Over the coming months they were to work tirelessly on his behalf, addressing petitions to the local bishop and even smuggling food and fuel into his apartment when he was placed under virtual house arrest. They also formed a secret communication group which ensured that a constant flow of news about Tőkés's case reached Hungary and, thence, Western Europe.[14] According to Tőkés, the authorities moved from a passive acceptance of his activities to active intimidation following two events that occurred in the autumn of 1988. The parish of Timişoara was part of the Arad Deanery, and in September of that year this body delivered an open letter to the Bishop of Oradea criticizing Ceauşescu's policy of systematization. The letter had been written by Janos Molnar, but the authorities strongly suspected Tőkés was responsible and brought him in for questioning. The incident brought an official reprimand and raised the authorities' suspicions that Tőkés was again causing trouble. Shortly afterward, in October of the same year, apparent confirmation of these suspicions came when a joint Catholic–Reformed Church ecumenical service was held in Timişoara. Attracting young people and intellectuals from both religious faiths, this raised the specter of organized dissent in the eyes of the authorities, and they responded by beginning proceedings to evict Tőkés from his living in Timişoara. A formal notice of suspension was filed on March 31, 1989, but, as he had before in Dej, Tőkés vigorously contested this in the courts, with the main points at dispute being who had the right to determine who was to reside in the church premises and whether the correct procedures had been followed in securing the eviction notice.[15] Eventually, after nearly a year of intense legal wrangling, the final eviction decree was issued on December 7, but, while the wheels of justice had slowly ground forward, the extralegal pressure had increased on Tőkés. He was subjected to a campaign of intimidation that at one point saw him attacked in his own home by masked men, and by December was effectively under house arrest.

In his last Sunday service prior to the planned eviction, Tőkés appealed to his parishioners to gather outside his church on the morning of Friday, December 15, to witness the event. The prospect of a demonstration seems to have alarmed the authorities, who urged Tőkés to retract his re-

---

14. For the importance of publicity as a shield see Deletant (1995), 144.

15. Tőkés (1990), 4, 137–38; BBC EE/0649, B/7, December 29, 1989. Tőkés's lawyer gives his version of events in *Adevărul*, December 26, 1989, 2, and Kincses (1992); for László Papp's justification for the eviction see BBC EE/0647, B/6–7, December 23, 1989.

quest, suggesting his removal would not occur before the next week at the earliest. Their pleas fell on deaf ears, and on the morning in question some thirty to forty mostly elderly retired members of the congregation gathered outside the nondescript turn-of-the-century block that houses the Hungarian Reformed Church and the residence of its pastor to observe events and offer Tőkés their moral support. The building lies just off a small square over the canal from the center of Timişoara, where a cluster of worn houses momentarily widens to allow for the concrete platform of a tram stop. In December 1989, the crowded passing trams were to act as a grapevine, spreading news of the events outside the church throughout the city. Waiting passengers mingled with the members of Tőkés' congregation, swelling the size of the crowd so that, in the restricted space, it appeared more numerous, giving heart to the parishioners and drawing in the curious.

The continuous bustle on the boulevard meant that any events had to be played out against a public backdrop, and this may help explain why the authorities allowed the small, peaceful assembly to continue, even though it blatantly contravened the draconian laws governing public gatherings. Since the revolution, it has been suggested that the inactivity of the *securitate* at this point was part of a deliberate strategy aimed at fostering violence so as to destabilize a regime it wished to see changed, with accusations even appearing that Tőkés himself was a *securitate* informer.[16] In fact, it seems to have been Ceauşescu who refused *securitate* requests to speed up the process against Tőkés, probably because he wanted to avoid the adverse publicity that might arise from the use of open coercion against the pastor, who during 1989 had become something of an international cause célèbre.[17] Tőkés's plight had been regularly featured on Hungarian radio and in July he had attracted wider attention when, in an interview broadcast on Hungarian television, he attacked the Hungarian Reformed Church authorities in Romania. News of his activities had also spread beyond Hungary to Western Europe and all the main Western shortwave radio stations broadcast to Romania, so that by the beginning of the demonstrations there was some consciousness of Tőkés and his protest, not only in Timişoara and Romania but also within the wider world. One consequence of this was that both the British and American embassies in Bucharest dispatched officials to Timişoara to report on the situation.[18] Although they were subsequently forced to leave the scene,

16. For a review of the literature suggesting such a scenario see Hall (1997), 154–57. The accusations regarding Tőkés have appeared periodically since 1990. See, for instance, BBC, EE/2189, B/4:12, December 30, 1994; BBC, EE/2193, B/3:8, January 5, 1995; FBIS-EEU-98–175, June 24, 1998.

17. This is the view of Teodorescu (1992), 45–46.

18. The French embassy may also have sent an observer; Nicolaescu (1999), 34.

the appearance of these officials around mid-morning on December 15 may have persuaded the authorities to keep the security forces in the background in the hope that the affair might blow itself out.[19] This cautious approach, however, misfired, since, by giving Tőkés's parishioners free access to the pastor in his house for the first time in several weeks, it only produced a strengthening of his and their resolve. As one of the parishioners was later to note, the longer the demonstration lasted the more the perception grew "that we had power. We were able to control what was happening. We had driven the Securitate away. It was like living a wild dream, a forbidden fantasy."[20] By the next day, rumors were sweeping Timișoara that the *securitate* and the city's authorities had been powerless in the face of open defiance and this, in turn, brought many more people to the church to see if the story was true.

As December 15 progressed, Romanian Pentecostalists and Baptists, who had been told of the planned eviction earlier in the week, began to mingle with Hungarian Calvinists. When Tőkés addressed the crowd in mid-afternoon he spoke in Romanian and, by the early evening, the numbers had grown sufficient to bring traffic to a virtual standstill on the nearby boulevard. The mood of the gathering now began to alter. Adopting a more radical and markedly anti-government tone, the protesters began to show a brazen contempt for those in positions of authority. When the mayor of Timișoara, Petru Moț, arrived and tried to disperse the gathering by promising to issue a temporary permit to allow the pastor to stay in Timișoara and to repair windows and doors broken in earlier incidents, he was met by so much hostility that Tőkés had a real fear that the mayor would be lynched by the crowd. The pastor had to negotiate with the demonstrators not only in order to protect Moț but even to be allowed to talk to him and, afterward, despite countless pleas, few of the throng outside the church were willing to depart quickly. As Tőkés heard chants of "Freedom" rising from outside his window, he sensed that control of the protest was slipping away from his hands and, as the crowd began to gain a sense of its own power, so it can be said that the Romanian revolution of December 1989 had begun. However, at this stage there was still no violence. Scuffles had broken out on the fringes of the crowd that evening, as the authorities apparently tried to make some arrests, but there were few overt signs of coercion, and the day seems to have drawn peacefully to a close with fifteen to twenty people still maintaining a vigil outside the church into the early hours of the next morning and beyond.

19. This view is supported by the British official involved; see also Tőkés (1990), 7; Corley and Eibner (1990), 21; and Teodorescu (1992), 54–55, who in an inventive passage presents the two as spies.

20. Lajos Varga quoted in Tőkés (1990), 10. Much of what follows is based on the full description of the events in this book.

The Protesters Take to the Streets

In the middle of the next morning of December 16, Mayor Moţ appeared again outside the church, this time accompanied by some workmen, to fulfill his promise to repair Tőkés's flat. He also brought three doctors to examine Tőkés's pregnant wife, Edit. At this stage the authorities still seem to have hoped that they could defuse the situation through minor concessions and dialogue, so talks took place between the mayor and an ad hoc negotiating committee of six Romanians and four Hungarians. The presence of Romanians within this committee marks an implicit acceptance that the issue had now broadened beyond the confines of the Tőkés dispute, but, despite this, the mayor was still only able to give assurances relating to the pastor. When even these were not kept, with Moţ failing to produce a written guarantee that Tőkés would not be evicted, despite promising that it would be faxed from Bucharest, the suspicions of the already mistrustful crowd were only heightened—perhaps correctly, because at the same time Ceauşescu was apparently ordering the RCP county secretary, Radu Bălan, to arrange Tőkés's removal.[21]

Throughout December 16, at the request of both the mayor and deputy mayor, Tőkés had made repeated attempts to disperse the crowd but had been unable to do so, and later he was to write: "the crowd looked to me as a figurehead, in truth I was a prisoner of their anger."[22] Indeed, there had been a perceptible change in atmosphere as the protest broadened in scope and the slogans chanted by the crowd took on a politicized edge. Earlier calls for bread and meat were now replaced with "Down with Ceauşescu," "Down with tyranny," and the all-pervasive "Freedom."[23] By the early evening, the number of protesters had swollen sufficiently to block the passage of the trams passing through the square. Impromptu orators leaped onto the bumpers of the stranded vehicles to address the predominately Romanian and youthful crowd, and incited by their fiery words the protesters began to break the windows of nearby shops. Turning their backs on Tőkés and leaving a long trail of damage in their wake, groups of demonstrators then began to drift toward the center of town, with one of the largest heading for the county Party headquarters. Unable

21. Nicolaescu (1999), 54.
22. Tőkés (1990), 155.
23. Milin (1990), 24; Suciu (1990), 209. The following account of the events in Timişoara leans heavily on many eyewitness accounts of the revolution contained in these two valuable books. In using such sources two problems have emerged. The first relates to the fragmented nature of the revolution in Timişoara, particularly during the first days, which narrows the perspective of every account and frequently leads the evidence to be contradictory. The composite picture presented here is based on a correlation of these varied accounts. Second, it would appear, perhaps naturally, that the evidence supplied by some of the leading actors in the revolution has a tendency to become self-congratulatory and occasionally carries marks of hindsight. In these cases due caution has been shown.

to enter the deserted building, because the door was barred, the protesters turned their attention instead to nearby shops, setting fire to the tomes of Ceaușescu looted from a bookstore, before the appearance of riot troops prompted them to turn tail and run into the night. Meanwhile, uniformed troops of the security forces had appeared in the vicinity of Tőkés's church, but, insufficient to control the crowd, their presence instead only seems to have incited the demonstrators further. When reinforcements arrived, with the aid of fire engines, which moved up and down the boulevard drenching the protesters in cold water, the troops eventually secured control of the area, but not before a two-hour running battle had left the streets strewn with broken glass and at least one burned out vehicle. Clashes and arrests continued until the last demonstrators were dispersed sometime around 4 o'clock in the morning, but before then, in the early hours of December 17, Tőkés and his wife were seized from his church together with seven friends.[24] In his account of the events, Tőkés states that he was brutally beaten before being brought into the presence of Ion Cumpănașu, head of the Department of Religious Denominations, who forced him to sign a blank piece of paper effectively accepting his dismissal and eviction. Subsequently, he and his wife were taken in separate cars to Mineu, an isolated village in the county of Sălaj, which had been designated his new residence.

It seems that the authorities still considered Tőkés to have been the focus of the revolt and that by removing him the problem could be cut at its roots. However, the next day was a Sunday and in the absence of work even larger crowds were to gather on the streets, many curious to see the testimony of the rioting of the night before. For, aside from being a purely emotional response, the breaking of so many windows by the crowd had an important practical significance. Traces of previous anti-Ceaușescu outbursts, such as the incidents in the autumn of 1989, had been expunged from the historical record through lack of visible markers. Unreported by the authorities, they had been destined to remain mere unsubstantiated rumors. But the wreckage left by the violence of December 16 was of such proportions that even when the authorities tried to cover the evidence, as they apparently did at the Party county headquarters, enough remained for news of the scenes of devastation to quickly spread throughout the city, bringing yet more people on the streets to see if the stories were true.

All morning large numbers of people circulated through Piața Operei in the center of the city. The crowd was expectant and amidst sporadic outbreaks of booing and chanting occasional strains of the old patriotic anthem *Deșteaptă-te Române!* (Romanians Awake!) could be heard. Around midday a sizeable portion of this crowd, about two thousand strong,

24. Corley and Eibner (1990), 30–31.

started to drift toward the county council building. Here, in front of the local Party headquarters, they found a double cordon of troops together with fire engines. As they approached, one of these moved forward and began spraying water. However, instead of cooling their ardor, this only seems to have infuriated the crowd further, which rushed the vehicle, breaking its windscreen before setting it on fire. In the pitched battle that followed, hand-to-hand fighting predominated, in marked contrast to the long-range stone-throwing of the night before. Gradually, the crowd pushed the cordons far enough back to allow a small group of mostly young demonstrators to break into the building. Before the security forces regrouped to drive them out, the protesters had time to ransack the ground floor and part of the first, throwing all that easily came to hand out of the windows and attempting to set fire to the rest.[25] After a few minutes the security forces gained the upper hand and pushed the protesters away from the building, but not before several military vehicles and fire engines had been badly damaged and set on fire. Most of the crowd then streamed back toward the center of the city to join a mass of stone- and petrol bomb-throwing protesters outside the Hotel Continental. This crowd was held at bay by two newly arrived armored vehicles, and another tank seems to have moved even further forward into the narrower confines of the tree-lined Piața Libertății, where there were several buildings used by the military, including the local army garrison headquarters. Already this square was the scene of devastation, with smashed shop windows and a burning newspaper kiosk. Now, unable to maneuver in the confined space and under attack from demonstrators, who tried to disable it by thrusting iron bars into its tracks, the tank became trapped. It was in this atmosphere of chaos and unrest, with the windows of part of the garrison headquarters broken and the furniture inside dragged out into the street and set on fire, that in the late afternoon of Sunday, December 17, 1989, gunshots were heard and the first dead and wounded of the revolution fell.[26]

Concomitant to these events in the center of the city, a major incident was also unfolding in Calea Girocului, on the other side of the Bega Canal.[27] Earlier in the afternoon, the armored vehicles that had later appeared in the center of the city had traveled down this road, crushing a car as they passed and drawing curious onlookers onto the street. When a

25. In one of the rooms the demonstrators found a large flag, and it is at this point that the most famous symbol of the revolution may have made its first appearance: a Romanian flag with the communist emblem cut from its center. See the account of Petre Boroșoiu in Milin (1990), 57. In doing so, although they may not have been aware of it, the demonstrators were following in the tradition of the Hungarian revolution of 1956 when a similar symbol appeared; Eyal (1990), 156.

26. Pitulescu et al. (1995), 103, reproducing extracts from Dossier no. 331/P/1991 of the Local Military Prosecutors' Office of Timișoara.

27. Milin (1990), 79–95; Suciu (1990), 66–124.

second column of tanks appeared, the crowd moved quickly to trap them in an ingenious snare. At one point, because of some roadwork in the middle of Calea Girocului, the tanks were forced to make a brief diversion from the main road through some side streets. When this occurred, the crowd moved to swiftly block the main road in front of them with trolley buses. Caught in the restricted space between this barricade and the excavations behind them, the vehicles were forced to a standstill. One part of the crowd rushed to block off all the remaining exit points, while the others moved to immobilize the tanks. When a few hotheads tried to set the stranded tanks on fire, the crews abandoned their vehicles. The crowd did not vent its anger, however; instead the officer in charge, bleeding from a scalp wound, was allowed to lead his men away.[28] By late afternoon on December 17, the authorities faced a critical situation. They had virtually lost control of the center of Timişoara, where an angry crowd was vandalizing property at will, part of the Party county headquarters had also been ransacked, and five tanks armed with 275 shells had fallen into the hands of the demonstrators, presaging a potentially dangerous escalation in the conflict.[29]

The Response of the Authorities

During the first days of the revolution, the authorities oscillated between policies of dialogue and coercion. Neither were successful. The negotiations had been conducted at too low a level to carry any real authority with the crowd. And, when troops had been deployed to crush the demonstrations, they had been too few in number, allowing the protesters to achieve a series of minor "victories" that built their confidence for future confrontations. The failure to take decisive action meant that the security forces during these first days were mostly reacting to the agenda set by the demonstrators, and it was the inability of the authorities to prevent the conflict spreading from the restricted area around Tőkés's church to the center of Timişoara that led to the situation spiraling out of control.

From the beginning, Ceauşescu paid close attention to the unfolding events. During the night of December 16 he constantly telephoned Tudor Postelnicu, the minister of the interior, ordering a vigorous dispersion of the demonstrations and a "show of strength" to cow the protesters into submission.[30] However, a rather bizarre military parade that passed through the center of Timişoara on the morning of December 17 with flags flying and bugles blowing, instead of demoralizing the crowd,

---

28. The story of the officer can be found in *Adevărul*, December 21, 1992, 3.

29. Some reports also speak of demonstrators seizing guns from the security forces at this time; Nicolaescu (1999), 65.

30. Nicolaescu (1995), 277.

merely seems to have left most of the onlookers thoroughly bemused and, in fact, provided a pretext for the crowd to gather and solidify.[31] Likewise, the order for armored vehicles to be deployed in the center of the city not only meant that the army would be the chief instrument of repression in Timișoara on December 17, but also, as has been seen, it turned a local disturbance into a crisis that would convulse the very foundations of the regime.

After the ransacking of the Party's county headquarters in Timișoara, Bălan and Ilie Matei, the secretary of the central committee, who came from the city, rang Ceaușescu to tell him what had happened.[32] A full meeting of the PEC was then convened around 5:00 p.m., followed, one hour later, by a teleconference between Ceaușescu, county Party heads, and senior officials.[33] Ceaușescu, occasionally abetted by his wife, dominated the PEC meeting. In many ways, what is most interesting about the proceedings is not the detail that is revealed about the revolution, but the insights that are given into the mind of the Romanian leader and the atmosphere in the central committee building at this time. In the carpeting of ministers and the ritualistic self-abasement of Postelnicu, it is difficult not to see the whole meeting as being a charade, a piece of political theater, perhaps designed to strengthen waverers, but with little meaningful content.[34] Ceaușescu started the proceedings by giving a short synopsis of the events as he perceived them. Beginning with Tőkés and the problem of securing his removal, Ceaușescu noted that the issue had been allowed to drag on too long but, voicing a full commitment to the norms of "socialist-legality," even within such an intimate gathering, he stressed that the eviction fell within the remit of the judicial process and was not directly the concern of the PEC. More pressing were other aspects of the case, because, according to Ceaușescu, the actual violence in Timișoara was the work of a few "déclassé" elements and Tőkés was a mere front for more sinister forces. The Romanian leader was adamant that "foreign circles are involved, foreign spy agencies, beginning with Budapest because

31. Milin (1990), 48–49; Suciu (1990), 80, 83, 86, 120; *Adevărul*, May 25, 1992, 2; Teodorescu (1992), 68.

32. Pitulescu et al. (1995), 85.

33. The transcript of the PEC meeting can be found in Nicolaescu (1995), 274–88, and the teleconference in ibid., 289–91. All extracts cited below come from these sources. The transcripts are said to have been discovered in a desk in the central committee building during the revolution and were later to form the chief evidence for the prosecution at the trial of former PEC members. They have been treated as authentic by scholars working on the revolution; see, for instance, Tănase (1999), 265. Quite large numbers would gather to hear a teleconference, although there was no guarantee that the machinery would function correctly. Few in Cluj, for instance, were able to hear Ceaușecu on December 17. Nicolaescu (1999), 280–81.

34. The impression of political theater would be heightened if the story from an unidentified source is true, that Ceaușescu, at the end of the PEC meeting, in a fury threatened to resign and only reconsidered his position at the imploring of his minions; see *Adevărul*, January 14, 1990, 1, 3.

he [Tőkés] also gave an interview. Actually the facts are well known. Moreover, it is known that both in the East as well as in the West everyone is saying that things ought to change in Romania. Both East and West have decided to change things and they are using any means possible."[35]

Taken with his address to the nation of December 20 and his speech in Bucharest the next day, these statements confirm that Ceaușescu's reading of the protests in Timișoara was conditioned by his understanding of events elsewhere in Eastern Europe.[36] He was convinced that the Soviet Union and other Warsaw Pact allies, joining forces with the West in planning his overthrow, had infiltrated agents into the country in order to foment unrest and pave the way for a high level coup d'état. Romania, according to Ceaușescu, was in a state of war, and the consequences of this interpretation of the events for decision making were to be considerable. Once the picture was formed and became received wisdom, it seems to have become immutable with all available evidence being manipulated to fill it. Ceaușescu's brother, Lieutenant-General Ilie Ceaușescu, even falsely reported to the Ministry of Defense from Timișoara on December 19 that 100 of those arrested came from Târgu Mureș, a distant city with a large Hungarian population; and the next day in Cluj, he apparently could only reiterate that the events in Timișoara were a terrorist diversion organized by Hungary, with the support of the United States, the Soviet Union, and Western Europe, aimed at sparking an armed conflict so that Hungary could annex Transylvania.[37] Indeed, soldiers leaving for Timișoara were told that they should be prepared to fight Hungarian insurgents.[38] By seeing the unrest as the work of foreign agents and domestic malcontents, Ceaușescu seems to have been able to convince himself that the vast majority of the population would rally to his cause once the situation was clearly explained to them. His position seems to have been based on a rose-tinted view of 1968 when, in a rousing rally in the center of Bucharest, he had condemned the Warsaw Pact invasion of Czechoslovakia and made a stirring declaration of Romania's independence of action.[39] At the time, this had won him great popular acclaim and, now, although he was aware that the situation was more serious than in 1968, he seems to have believed that the threat to Romania's territorial sovereignty was acute enough to allow him to successfully play the same national card one more time. This time, however, it was not the Soviet Union but Romania that was the reactionary bulwark against liberalization, and all efforts to rally the population to Ceaușescu's side were only to reveal the

35. Nicolaescu (1995), 275.
36. For a translation of the December 20 speech see BBC EE/0646, B/1–2, December 22, 1989, and for the December 21 address BBC EE/0647, B/5–6, December 23, 1989.
37. Nicolaescu (1999), 109, 295.
38. Watts (1992), 106–7.
39. For the 1968 speech see Costello (September 6, 1968), 1–11.

weakness of his position, most conspicuously during the calamitous public meeting in Bucharest on December 21.

Ceauşescu's deep-seated fears of a coup d'état seem to have fueled his continuing suspicions as to the loyalty of the security forces, and at the PEC meeting he was to accuse them of defeatism and capitulation. According to his analysis of the disturbances, their inability to control events in Timişoara was rooted in the failure of the senior commanders in Bucharest to enact his commands. During the PEC meeting, he repeatedly asserted that the orders he had given for all units to be armed with live ammunition and to move in firmly to crush the demonstrations had been ignored by Postelnicu, Minister of Defense Colonel-General Vasile Milea, and Colonel-General Iulian Vlad, head of the *securitate*. Both Milea and Vlad admitted to not ordering their forces to carry live ammunition on December 16, but whether this amounted to a calculated act of insubordination on their part must be questioned. Ceauşescu himself seems to have had an unfounded confidence that in the face of a little more resolute action from the security forces, the protesters would rapidly turn tail, and from their elevated position above society the leaders of the Romanian army and the *securitate* may well have come to share a similar belief. The orders given by Ceauşescu also seem to have been somewhat vague and, perhaps as might be expected, Milea, Postelnicu, and Vlad all allude to this in their responses to his hostile questioning at the PEC meeting. Given the fluidity of the disturbances in Timişoara, which appear to have left even the officers on the ground uncertain as to what was actually going on in the city, the clarity of the picture of the events transmitted to the center might also be questioned, and at the PEC meeting Milea was to state that he did not think things would reach such proportions.[40] With few trained riot troops at their disposal, the military commanders may have been reluctant to sanction the deployment of the armed forces in the knowledge that, if the demonstrators did not heed warnings to disperse, they risked embroilment in a massacre.

Instead of the armed forces, Ceauşescu continued to place greater reliance on the institutions of the Party and, particularly, the working class. When giving his final orders before embarking on his trip to Iran, he left full responsibility for their enactment in the hands of the RCP county leadership, with a stipulation that all military operations should be controlled from the local Party headquarters. This additional stress on the political leadership of the operation may have further undermined the willingness of senior army commanders to persevere with the struggle. Indeed, Ceauşescu continued to contrast the wavering loyalty of the army and the forces of the Ministry of the Interior with what he saw as the reliability of the patriotic guard. At the PEC meeting he fondly reminisced of

40. Nicolaescu (1995), 282.

the time when the workers had been mobilized to secure the communist takeover in 1945, and he attributed his success in 1968 to the same root. But, now, after he had first berated Postelnicu, Vlad, and Milea and threatened them with dismissal, Ceauşescu granted each an apparent reprieve, as he gave clear orders for the demonstrations to be vigorously suppressed.

To quell the disturbances in Timişoara the authorities had a variety of forces at their disposal. Aside from the army, a confusing mélange of units from the *securitate* troops, USLA, militia, border guards, and patriotic guards as well as some Party activists all seem to have been deployed on the streets of the city.[41] A steady stream of senior generals also arrived to deal with the crisis, first by train and then by air. A team led by Major-General Emil Macri, head of the economic counterespionage directorate of the *securitate,* and the two highest commanders of the militia, Lieutenant-General Constantin Nuţă and Major-General Mihalea Velicu, had arrived separately in the city on the morning of December 17. Now, in the afternoon of the same day, they were joined by Colonel-General Ion Coman, secretary of the central committee responsible for military and security affairs, and a number of senior army generals including Major-General Ştefan Guşă, first deputy defense minister and chief of the general staff; Lieutenant-General Victor Stănculescu, deputy defense minister; and Lieutenant-General Mihai Chiţac, head of the chemical forces and commander of the Bucharest garrison. The arrival of these senior generals and army reinforcements transformed the situation. On the morning of December 17 troop deployments had been largely defensive with concentrations around the Town Hall, RCP county headquarters, and Tőkés's church but, as live ammunition was distributed to the soldiers, in the late afternoon the security forces began an offensive operation designed to ruthlessly crush the demonstrations.[42]

As the light began to fade, the crowd still remained in control of the city center, occasionally smashing windows and looting stores, including in Piaţa Operei, a fur shop and a perfumery. Only a small number of people were involved, and some of the demonstrators even seem to have made an effort to stop the vandalism, but this incident has attracted some infamy, as it has been suggested that the shops were deliberately ransacked and set ablaze in order to form a pretext for subsequent events.[43] The looting in Piaţa Operei, however, was only a small part of what had become a general rampage throughout the center of Timişoara. According to official assessments, over three hundred shops were damaged at a

41. Pitulescu et al. (1995), 77.
42. Nicolaescu (1999), 66.
43. Milin (1990), 65; Suciu (1990), 71; for descriptions of dubious characters present at this time see Ratesh (1991), 29, and for a general discussion of the subject Hall (1997), 172–75.

cost of five billion lei at this time, and well into the next year people were still being sent for trial for theft of clothing and electrical goods.[44] Given the seriousness of the situation and the fact that shots had already been fired elsewhere, the security forces hardly needed to produce a further "excuse" for the massacre which was to follow. There may have been shouted commands for the demonstrators to disperse, followed by some warning shots, but increasingly the guns came to be trained directly on the unarmed crowd, perhaps initially shooting at their legs but then, it seems, to kill. In the grisly carnage that followed the greatest number of victims fell in the center of the city around the Cathedral and Piaţa Operei, where twenty-one died and nearly one hundred were wounded, but incidents also occurred in more outlying districts, such as Calea Lipovei, where shooting in the vicinity of an army unit left six dead, and Piaţa Traian, where another six fell.[45] That night detachments of troops continued to roam the streets firing at the demonstrators and arresting virtually anybody upon whom they could lay their hands. The army also set about recapturing the tanks left stranded in Calea Girocului. A detachment of troops had arrived in the area early in the evening, but the size of the crowd had been sufficient to force a stand-off. It was not until later, when reinforcements arrived from the center, that the tanks were finally recovered, but again only after shooting had left further casualties among the civilian population. By the time a heavy rainstorm broke in the early hours of the morning, the security forces had regained control of Timişoara from the demonstrators but at a fearsome price. Over sixty civilians were dead and more than two hundred lay wounded in local hospitals, with many others probably refusing to seek medical assistance for fear of the *securitate*. Around seven hundred had been arrested.

Ceauşescu Flies to Iran

Faced with the greatest threat his regime had ever encountered, at 8:30 on the morning of December 18, Ceauşescu flew to Iran for a three-day state visit. The two countries had a recent history of reciprocal high-level diplomatic visits. The Iranian president had visited Bucharest in February 1989 and the arrangements for Ceauşescu's trip had originally been made in the summer. However, given the seriousness of the situation he left at home, Ceauşescu's reasons for continuing with the engagement have long been subject to speculation. At the time of the revolution rumors arose that he had taken with him to Iran a large shipment of gold either for his personal use in the event of being forced into exile or for the pay-

44. *Adevărul*, May 25, 1992, 1; Pitulescu et al. (1995), 96–97.
45. Nicolaescu (1999), 101.

ment of armed intervention by Arab or Iranian terrorists.[46] As might be expected, the Iranians have persistently denied these stories and the evidence that has emerged to support such accusations is hardly conclusive. A small group of seven Iranians did arrive in Romania, supposedly to visit factories, on December 20, but their whereabouts remain totally unknown until they left the country on December 31 via Giurgiu.[47]

For the Iranians the presidential visit was initially much welcomed, because, like the Romanians, they had become something of a pariah nation and Ceauşescu's arrival was seen as breaking their diplomatic isolation. However, when the first news of the events in Timişoara began to filter through, it is possible that they made a last-minute attempt to cancel the visit. Certainly, when Ceauşescu did arrive, there was a degree of embarrassment, and after the revolution, the Iranian ambassador in Bucharest, Mohammad Jamshid Gowhari, was recalled and fired for failing to give Tehran an accurate picture of the situation in Romania. Under attack from radicals in the Iranian parliament, the Majlis, Foreign Minister Ali Akbar Velayati felt constrained to defend the visit in a speech, which in its reference to vital defense agreements also gives some indication of why the Romanian leader remained so adamant that the visit should still go ahead.[48]

It seems that Romania and Iran were close to clinching an enormous arms deal that reportedly involved the sale of 155 T55 tanks and possibly the IAR-93 fighter at a reputed unit cost of around $10 million. The Romanians were also rumored to be close to sealing an agreement to overhaul and modernize all the Warsaw Pact military equipment secured by Iran during the long Iran-Iraq war of 1980–88 and to be involved in the building of an Iranian naval base as well as the conversion of a tractor plant to produce military vehicles. In exchange, Romania was to receive 130,000 tons of crude oil and one billion cubic meters of natural gas per year, and altogether Ceauşescu is reported to have signed contracts worth more than $2 billion during his stay in the country.[49] The considerable arms exporting business built up by the Romanians during the 1980s was in sharp decline by 1989 and the possibility of securing such important contracts was probably sufficient to persuade Ceauşescu of the merits of

46. *Adevărul*, December 26, 1989, 1. For an Iranian denial of such claims see the *Washington Post*, December 25, 1989, A40, and for a markedly anti-Iranian Western newspaper report upholding much of the speculation concerning Ceauşescu secreting millions in gold in Iran and the presence of Iranian revolutionary guards during the revolution see ibid., January 17, 1990, E17; see also *România Liberă*, September 28, 1990, 1, 3.

47. Nicolaescu (1999), 106.

48. *Financial Times*, December 27, 1989, 4; *Independent*, January 3, 1990, 10.

49. For details of the arms sales see Socor (December 23, 1986), 17–21; Brzoska and Ohlson (1987), 105, 124; Eyal (1989), 85; *Guardian*, April 29, 1989, 8; *Independent*, May 20, 1989, 14; Stockholm International Peace Research Institute (1990), 246–47, 280.

keeping to his original schedule. The need to preserve a display of normality and a desire not to lose international prestige may also have played a role. Ceauşescu departed from Bucharest with the customary presidential honors, and his behavior does not seem so bizarre when placed against the fact that a week after the November 1987 disturbances in Braşov he had also left Romania on a state visit, that time to Egypt. At this stage, the situation in December 1989 must have looked somewhat similar. At 5:30 in the morning of December 18 Coman had reported the situation in Timişoara under control, so Ceauşescu could have thought that the worst of the crisis was over. He may have foreseen the state of emergency continuing until the new year, but this in itself indicates that he expected the storm to be weathered, just like previous disturbances.

When he flew to Iran, Ceauşescu, in a departure from his usual practice, left Elena behind in Romania to coordinate Party and government work with Manea Mănescu and Emil Bobu. However, in reality the political process was frozen. The policy of repression was not checked and no attempt was made to establish a dialogue with the demonstrators in Timişoara until the situation had effectively passed out of the control of the authorities. The absence of Ceauşescu during such a crucial period can only have weakened the position of the regime and, in particular, appears to have undermined the willingness of the security forces to continue to suppress the demonstrations. His departure also led to rumors that he had fled the country, and this perhaps created an additional sense of disappointment when he returned, strengthening the feeling of desperation.

The Growth of Unrest in the Factories

From December 18, with the security forces patrolling the streets, a state of emergency applied in Timişoara in all but name. People were instructed to pass only two at a time and any larger gathering was quickly dispersed. In consequence, the protests were largely driven from the public spaces into the only alternative place of mass socialization that was available, the factory workplace.[50] The communist penchant for constructing factories in large industrial complexes allowed for a concentration of sentiment and facilitated the free flow of information between the many workers. At cigarette breaks and informal gatherings news circulated of casualties among the families of workers, and the innocence of the victims was graphically contrasted with tales of barbaric behavior by the security forces, who were widely rumored to have bayoneted pregnant women. Ironically, the passage of news about the disturbances was now

50. A state of emergency in Timiş county was only officially instituted by presidential decree on December 21; BBC EE/0646, B/2–3, December 22, 1989.

also further aided by the authorities who ordered the convening of a series of workplace meetings. Ostensibly held to "explain" the events and denounce the perpetrators as hooligans, these for most workers merely offered confirmation of the rumors about the extent of the damage and unrest. Indeed, among the commuters from outside Timişoara, who until that point had probably little idea of what had passed in the city over the weekend, the meetings served to inform them of the violence. Speeches delivered by representatives of the county Party leadership or higher management appear to have normally been heard in silence. However, in some of the larger factories, such as Electrobanat (ELBA), these gatherings were to provide a forum for debate. After preliminary meetings with senior management and local Party leaders, section heads in this factory returned to address their workmates, but, not holding the same stamp of authority as higher officials, their accounts sometimes led to cross-questioning and heated debate, thereby providing a platform for criticism of the regime.

While it was trying to mobilize the workforce in its support, the regime was also making an attempt to disguise the extent of the massacre. During the night of December 18–19 the bodies of forty victims were taken from the mortuary in Timişoara and loaded into a refrigerated truck. Taken first to the local militia headquarters, they were then transferred to Bucharest, where they were cremated and their ashes scattered at the mouth of a canal in Popeşti-Leordeni, on the outskirts of the capital.[51] This act of subterfuge, however, was to badly backfire on the authorities, because by closing the mortuary area for the duration of the operation they only prompted the spread of rumors. During the days that followed, one of the most emotive and sustained rallying cries among the demonstrators was for the return of the bodies of the dead for decent Christian burial. The snatching of the bodies is another incident that has entered the mythology of the revolution, and it lies at the root of the uncertainty that long existed over the exact death toll of December 17 and 18, especially since most of the hospital records relating to this period also seem to have been destroyed.

Indeed, as the unrest progressed, rumors became increasingly significant in mobilizing the crowd, with two incidents, one at the Cathedral and the other outside the ELBA works, coming to be seen as symbolizing the conflict. On December 18, in the late afternoon, troops opened fire on a group of young protesters gathered on the steps of the Cathedral, leaving a twenty-two-year-old man dead.[52] In the minds of many of the

51. Suciu (1990), 151–54, 160–63; Teodorescu (1992), 294–99; Pitulescu et al. (1995), 114–120; Nicolaescu (1999), 97–100. Details of the identity of the corpses removed from the mortuary appear in *Adevărul,* March 13, 1991, 5.

52. Suciu (1990), 154–58. Two others died nearby and four were wounded. In total seven died this day; Pitulescu et al. (1995), 100.

protesters the precincts of the Cathedral seem to have represented an ideal of sanctuary—a place at which the forces of repression would not dare shoot. Thus, when it occurred, this incident, underpinned by ideas of sacrilege, seems to have embodied the image of a Manichean battle between good and evil. It vividly struck the popular imagination and, as stories circulated exaggerating the youth and number of people killed, it contributed to a perceptible rise in tension. The incident at the ELBA works happened the next day, when the discontent simmering within the factories throughout Monday broke to the surface in a series of wildcat strikes. An armored personnel carrier had been stationed in the vicinity of the ELBA factory since Monday, and on Tuesday, at the outbreak of a strike, troops seem to have entered the actual premises or at least come to the gate. Thus, when the workers laid down tools and marched on the offices of the management, among demands for improved conditions there also appeared more politicized calls for the withdrawal of the army from the area. When the management proved unable to persuade the strikers to return to work, Bălan, Moţ, and another local Party official, Constantin Posa, arrived followed later by Guşă to negotiate with the workers. Eyewitness reports say they were initially greeted enthusiastically, but the workforce still refused to disperse, despite repeated promises that more formal negotiations would be opened to address their grievances.[53] The visit to ELBA brought the chief of the general staff face to face with the grassroots protest in Timişoara. Even if he had previously harbored some misconceptions about the nature of the disturbances, these were now dispelled as, in his own words, he saw that the protesters "were not hooligans but serious people."[54] The seeds of future doubt were perhaps being sown, presumably helped by the reports of an army intelligence team working in the city since December 18, but at this time the policy of repression was still in force.[55] As the talks continued within the factory, a crowd attracted by rumors of unrest gathered outside, near the bridge over the Bega Canal. More armored vehicles and soldiers arrived and, shortly afterward, the security forces opened fire. One of the victims, a woman, seems to have been brought for emergency treatment in the factory's dispensary. In the streets around the factory the situation then ignited into the by now familiar pattern of protest. Windows were broken, vehicles and a newspaper kiosk set ablaze, and stones and petrol bombs thrown at armored vehicles and troops, with the latter retaliating by opening fire.[56] During this day, two more demonstrators were to die.

53. Milin (1990), 111.
54. *Adevărul,* February 1, 1991, 2, gives Guşă's version of the events.
55. Nicolaescu (1999), 76, 82–83.
56. For full accounts of this incident see Milin (1990), 112–14; Suciu (1990), 164–65, 174–76; Tatomirescu (1990), 152–64.

The strike at ELBA and the shooting and rioting in the area wove a further strand in the mythology of the revolution, with the rumors following the incident being particularly graphic. The most striking story was that a young boy had been shot on the bridge and his body thrown into the Bega Canal.[57] Gradually, as these rumors spread, the events seem to have become conflated and the distinction between factory and street blurred. The news was not only of a strike but also of shootings at ELBA, so that instead of a single person, Tőkés, the symbol of the revolution now became a whole factory.[58] Soon sympathy strikes were being reported and the next day, as the strikers marched from their factories toward the center of the town, slogans were chanted in support of the ELBA workers, with the main column even marching across Timișoara to the factory before turning toward the center. The violence of December 19 marked the failure of the policy of repression. Even with large numbers of troops and armored vehicles in the city, the authorities seemed powerless to halt further outbreaks of unrest and, during the coming day, their resolve was to be tested until it broke.

The dénouement of the revolution in Timișoara came on Wednesday, December 20, 1989. As the morning shift appeared for work, protests seem to have swept through most of the larger factories, with crowds gathering in the open spaces shouting slogans. The authorities reacted by resorting to the same tactics as the day before. Representatives of the local Party leadership toured the larger factories, trying to negotiate a return to work. Moț and Posa again went to ELBA, Bălan and Deputy Prime Minister Cornel Pacoste to UMT, and Vasile Bolog to Electrotimiș.[59] They were to meet with no greater success than the day before, although again it seems the anger of the workers was focused more on the security forces and the central authorities than local officials and management. At ELBA Moț and Posa seem to have been met with indifference rather than hostility and at the Electromotor factory the workers even seem to have tried to persuade the management to join them in marching to the center. At first, in many of the factories, there seems to have been some discussion as to the relative merits of remaining united within the protective walls of the workplace or risking dispersal on the streets of the city. But then, often encouraged by news via those telephones still functioning that others were on strike or by seeing fellow demonstrators on the road before them, the workers poured forth in steadily increasing numbers. The exact circumstances that surrounded the exodus from the factories remain unclear, and especially the degree of organization and leadership involved.

57. Milin (1990), 111; Suciu (1990), 170–71, 211; Tatomirescu (1990), 163.
58. Milin (1990), 116.
59. Pacoste had arrived in Timișoara at 11:00 p.m. on December 17, 1989.

Workers on the margins of the columns of demonstrators wearing white arm bands seem to have acted as marshals, and some reports even suggest that workers' councils first appeared at this stage of the revolution, giving shape to what had previously been a spontaneous and unorganized protest.[60] Nor is it clear what proportion of workers actually joined the demonstrations, because it seems the turnout varied from factory to factory, with the management in some cases blocking exit by locking the gates. As the marchers set out for the center, the security forces were still in position to halt their advance, but, when confronted with such vast crowds, they seem to have shown little resistance. There is no agreement on whether they were still under orders to fire that morning. Eyewitness accounts speak of shooting and one person seems to have died that day, but the circumstances in which this occurred are unclear.[61] There were several columns of protesters; the largest, which reportedly took a quarter of an hour to pass any single point, chose a long, meandering route to the center in order to gather support on the way. It traveled from the industrial complex on Calea Buziaşului to the ELBA factory before turning to reach Piaţa Operei shortly after midday. Here it was confronted by a cordon of troops and armored vehicles in the area around the Town Hall, but after a few moments of hesitation, the crowd surged forward and, while shouting "The army is with us" and "Without violence," overwhelmed the soldiers. Clambering over the armored personnel carriers they placed flags in the barrels of the machine guns and handed cigarettes, meat, and bread to the young conscripts. From this moment onward the security forces were effectively neutralized in Timişoara.

The dense crowd flooded up the open space toward the Opera House, with the remaining members of the security forces retreating before them. The main door of the building was barred but, as the troops withdrew up a side street, access was allowed through a back entrance. Details as to how some members of the crowd were able to force their way into the building differ slightly, with different positions and times of arrival presumably leading to varying perspectives, but Claudiu Iordache is credited with making a passionate appeal for the troops to withdraw at this time.[62] Around 2 o'clock in the afternoon the first person arrived on the balcony of the Opera House and, announcing that he was Lorin Fortuna, a professor at the Technical University of Timişoara, he urged the crowd not to leave the square but to stay united and strong.[63] Quickly Fortuna

60. Socor (February 2, 1990), 21; Nicolaescu (1999), 84.
61. Milin (1990), 117; Pitulescu et al. (1995), 100.
62. Milin (1990), 124–25; Galloway and Wylie (1991), 126.
63. Fortuna's memories of the day can be found in Fortuna (1997), 162–66. A loudspeaker system was already in place on the balcony in anticipation that the prime minister, Constantin Dăscălescu, who was due to arrive in the city that day, would use it to address the crowd; see Teodorescu (1992), 106; Pitulescu et al. (1995), 125.

was joined by other figures and throughout the afternoon a steady stream of speakers representing various factories and ethnic groups appeared to address the 40,000-strong crowd that thronged the open space. Shortly after the speeches began, some of the armored personnel carriers overrun earlier in the day arrived in the square still covered with protesters. They were followed a little later by a group of senior officers who walked unhindered through the crowd to reclaim the vehicles and lead them back to barracks. This marked a general withdrawal of the army from the center, apparently ordered by Guşă, with the bulk of units leaving the county council building in the late afternoon.

Another section of the crowd had gathered outside the county Party headquarters. Earlier in the day, the prime minister, Constantin Dăscălescu, and Emil Bobu, a senior PEC member and one of Ceauşescu's closest aides, had arrived from Bucharest, and now there were repeated calls for these two to come onto the balcony to address the crowd. About 4:00 p.m., Dăscălescu, and possibly Bobu, appeared only to withdraw when shouted down. A request then seems to have been made for a deputation of demonstrators to enter the building to conduct negotiations with the representatives of the regime, and subsequently a small group of between thirteen and eighteen protesters coalesced. The numbers are imprecise, because they entered in several batches, with the last group including Fortuna not arriving until late in the evening.[64] The delegation that entered the county Party headquarters was drawn from a wide range of professions and places of employment and included at least two women.[65] None seem to have been publicly known before the revolution, although several, notably Sorin Opera and Petre Boroşoiu, had achieved some prominence during the violence of the preceding days. The talks began around mid-afternoon with the chief negotiator on behalf of the regime being Dăscălescu, supported by Bălan and the deputy prime minister, Cornel Pacoste.[66] Many of the senior generals were also present. According to Ioan Savu, one of the members of the deputation, it was a genuine ad hoc body, with no preparation of a common negotiating position beforehand. This, together with the fact that the delegates were somewhat overawed by the senior officials facing them, led the talks initially to

64. Galloway and Wylie (1991), 129.

65. The following negotiators are named in two or more sources: Sorin Opera, 27, mechanic; Ion Marcu, electrician; Petru Petrişor, lawyer; Dumitru Cornel Pop, 49, economist; Ioan Savu, 39, store-man; Simona Tomuţa; Petre Boroşoiu, 28, actor; Lorin Fortuna, 41, university professor, and Valentin Vârtan. A further member of the delegation may have been Adela Săbăilă. The various accounts of the negotiations all differ and are mostly from the side of the protesters, with each narrator apparently striving to place his own personal contribution in an optimum light. The following draws on short accounts by Opera, Boroşoiu, and Bălan and a longer detailed account by Savu, including some poor photographs of the lists of demands drawn up in his diary at the time; see Suciu (1990).

66. Pacoste had previously been first secretary of Timiş and chairman of the county peoples' council between 1982 and 1985.

follow the regime's agenda, focusing on relatively minor issues, such as passports, housing, and the supply of services. However, against a background of continuous chanting from outside, the representatives of the protesters seem to have gradually become more assertive. At first they shaped a series of demands that were almost entirely concerned with the situation in Timișoara, being little more than a coherent articulation of the slogans of the demonstrators, but then they became broader with calls for the resignation of Ceaușescu, and the government, as well as free elections.[67] By late afternoon, the talks had ground to a stalemate, with Dăscălescu playing for time by constantly referring to the need to confer with Bucharest. Feeling in a vulnerable position the negotiators asked that their names and demands be communicated to the Yugoslav consulate in Timișoara, presumably in the hope that they would relay the news to the wider world. One of the negotiators, Valentin Vârtan, seems to have gone in person to the consulate and a short five point manifesto was duly faxed to the Yugoslav Embassy in Bucharest and then to Belgrade.[68] And, on December 22, whether from this source or another, some of the international press did carry a fairly accurate report of the negotiations—although in *The Times* they were erroneously dated as taking place on December 21.[69] Eventually, it became clear that the authorities were only willing to concede three of the lesser demands, guaranteeing the immunity of the delegates, the release of detainees, and the return of the bodies of the dead. After Ceaușescu's uncompromising speech to the nation at 7 o'clock that evening, in which he blamed the disturbances on hooligans and foreign agents provocateurs and offered no respite from the road of socialist construction, the negotiations gradually fizzled out, although Dăscălescu and Bobu remained in Timișoara until the early hours of the following morning.[70]

With the end of the negotiations and the withdrawal of the security forces from the center, an uneasy stalemate settled on Timișoara. Power rested fully neither with the demonstrators, ensconced in the Opera House, nor with the representatives of the regime, left in the county council building. In Piața Operei the demonstrators set about consolidating their position, but in contrast to the euphoria of earlier in the day, as the numbers in the square dwindled to a few hundred, the prevailing atmosphere became one of suspicion and apprehension, with rumors spreading that troop trains were approaching the city. These fears were not without foundation, because that night plans were being drawn up for an assault on Piața Operei, as between ten and twenty thousand workers

67. Suciu (1990), 274.
68. Atanaskovici (1997), 184.
69. *The Times*, December 22, 1989, 7.
70. The text of Ceaușescu's speech is reproduced in BBC EE/ 0646, B/1–2, December 22, 1989. For the freeing of detainees see Suciu (1990), 177.

from Oltenia headed toward the city on a series of special trains.[71] Most of the workers had been dragged straight from their shifts, roughly armed with makeshift clubs and truncheons, clothed in the uniform of the patriotic guard and told they were going to fight "hooligans" and "drunks" who were playing the game of foreign security services on the streets of Timişoara. The operation had been personally ordered by Ceauşescu and was organized by his close aide and PEC member Ion Dincă, together with the leaders of the patriotic guard and the Party secretaries in the counties of Dolj, Olt, and Vâlcea.[72] If they had arrived earlier and received adequate local leadership, the workers might have been able to wreak havoc in the city but, when the first train arrived in Timişoara the next morning, December 21, the Oltenian workers found nobody to meet them except for a few hundred protesters. Nine other trains followed at regular intervals until 11:15, but tired, hungry, and confused, most of the workers remained on board, waiting to return home, with only a few journeying to Piaţa Operei to see the unfolding events for themselves. Five more trains were stopped at various stations in the Banat in the early evening, when, with the approval of Ceauşescu, they were all allowed to head home.

During the night of December 20, many of those who had been most prominent in the day seem to have departed from the scene exhausted. Stamina was at a premium, as physical presence at the Opera House now seems to have become the main criterion for holding power. Earlier in the day, Fortuna had established the Romanian Democratic Front with himself at the head of a leadership of five. During the evening, the membership had been expanded with the introduction of some of those involved in the negotiations at the county council building, but the next morning, as the numbers on the balcony once again swelled, pressure was exerted for the bounds of the new Front to be widened even further. It soon became clear to all that there was little cohesion among the leaders of the uprising. Eventually, a program drawn up by Fortuna the night before was redrafted. In what appears to be a compromise text, a call for the resignation of Ceauşescu was placed alongside a statement that the Romanian Democratic Front had been formed as a political organization in order to negotiate with the government with the express goal of securing the democratization of the country. Following this, there was a list of demands relating to political freedoms, including free and democratic elections, freedom of the media, and respect for human rights, as well as calls for economic reform and for improvements in both medical care and the supply of food. According to Savu, troops intervened to stop the program being printed on December 21, and it was only on December 22, shortly

---

71. Nicolaescu (1995), 39; Durac (1997), 117–18.
72. *Adevărul,* January 31, 1990, 3; Milin (1990), 170–71.

after Ceaușescu had fled from Bucharest, that it finally appeared as a leaflet headed "The Tyranny has Fallen!" and was broadcast on Romanian radio.[73]

In truth, the new leaders were very tired, having slept and eaten little for several days. Tempers were frayed and the continuing uncertainty and possible dangers of the situation only added to the stress. The crowd bombarded them with demands and, from December 22, the pressures were to intensify following the arrival of the international mass media. Savu is open when he states that they just did not know what to do for the best, as over many years they had been painfully schooled in dissatisfaction but not in the skills needed to construct a revolution. Wild rumors that more trains full of patriotic guards were en route to the city and that the water supply had been poisoned only destabilized the situation further. It was in this atmosphere of confusion and doubt that Bălan appears to have been asked by some of the protesters to join the leadership. In general, the Party first secretary seems not to have been unpopular in the city and he was applauded when he first spoke from the Opera House balcony. His return may have been requested because of the growing chaos in Timișoara and the pressing need to normalize the situation and ensure a regular supply of foodstuffs. The overtures toward the local Party head could also have been a deliberate ploy by some of the rivals of Fortuna to undercut his power base. At least this seems to have been the intention of Savu, who says it was he who fetched Bălan to the Opera House.[74] By the morning of December 22 events in Timișoara had followed a course that Bucharest was soon to emulate, as inexperienced new leaders drawn from the crowd tried to come to terms with "untainted" representatives of the old regime.

The Revolution outside Timișoara

By December 21 the authorities were facing a sharply escalating crisis, as the disturbances spread from Timișoara, first to other towns in the Banat and Crișana and then into Transylvania. On December 20 the protests had spread to a number of towns and villages near Timișoara, including Jimbolia, Sânnicolau Mare, Deta, and Lugoj, with the evening demonstrations in the latter leaving two dead.[75] The next day they reached Buziaș, also in Timiș county, as well as the chief towns of neighboring counties, including Reșița and Caransebeș in Caraș Severin,

---

73. The leaflet is reproduced in Milin (1990), 173, and the translated text of the radio broadcast can be found in BBC EE/0648, B/7–8, December 28, 1989.
74. Suciu (1990), 246–48; Mioc (2000a).
75. Codrescu et al. (1998), 81–82; Pitulescu et al. (1995), 130.

Oradea in Bihor, and Arad, where, following the lead of Timișoara, a fifteen-member Romanian Democratic Front was formed.[76] Further afield the most serious incidents on December 21 were to occur in the big cities of Cluj, Sibiu, Târgu Mureș, and Brașov, and the capital, Bucharest, although disturbances were also reported from a number of smaller Transylvanian towns, including Cugir and Cisnădie. By the morning of the next day, December 22, the protests had spread to encompass other urban centers, including Alba Iulia, Bistrița, Miercurea-Ciuc, Sfântu Gheorghe, and Turda, leaving only the southern and eastern extremities of the country generally quiet.[77]

The patterns of protest within these urban centers broadly seem to have corresponded to the forms already encountered in Timișoara, but a division can be made between those cities that experienced conflict and those that did not, with the fine line between the two being largely drawn not by the protesters but by the actions of the security forces. Among the cities that experienced violence during this period, some of the most telling images emanated from Cluj. Here, around midday on December 21, there had been the first signs of trouble during the change of shifts in the city's factories. That afternoon, watched by crowds of onlookers, a small number of protesters seems to have gathered in part of the central square of the city and started to chant anti-Ceaușescu slogans. When armed troops appeared, the protesters began to jeer and a young actor, Călin Nemeș, stepped forward taunting the soldiers to fire if they dared. In the confused melee that followed at least one of the protesters, Lucian Matiș, was left dead, and Nemeș, as well as the officer in charge of the unit, wounded.[78] There have been claims that the shot which wounded Nemeș came not from the square but from a neighboring building, but a senatorial commission of inquiry found this unlikely and suggested instead that in a scuffle with Nemeș the revolver of the officer discharged, wounding him in the shoulder. As he fell, the officer had panicked and shouted "fire" and the young and scared conscripts had responded by shooting in all directions.[79] As news of this incident spread, columns of demonstrators marched into the center of the city. Cordons of troops tried to block their approach and throughout the night there were further violent clashes, as the demonstrators repeatedly challenged the security

76. For Buziaș see Suciu (1990), 196–97; for Arad see Șimăndan (1999); Codrescu et al. (1998), 79–81; Nicolaescu (1999), 346; for Oradea see Bradu and Moisa (2000); for Reșița see *Raportul SRI*; for Caransebeș see Codrescu et al. (1998), 82–83.

77. Some indication of the events in the various counties of Romania can be found in Popa and Ștefan (n.d.), 22–28 and Codrescu et al. (1998), 108–9.

78. *Sunday Times*, January 21, 1990, A13–A16. Altogether eleven seem to have died in and around the square that day.

79. Codrescu et al. (1998), 88, 144–45; Nicolaescu (1999), 260–65.

forces. By morning twenty-six people lay dead in Cluj and many more were wounded.[80]

Elsewhere in Transylvania there was also violence. In Târgu Mureș the protests were initially peaceful, and it was only after nightfall that serious violence erupted, accompanied by the breaking of windows. As demonstrators and troops clashed, a soldier, whose gun had jammed, reached for the machine gun fixed to an armored car. In twenty seconds enough rounds were fired to leave four dead.[81] In Sibiu the confrontation was particularly significant, because it was partly responsible for setting the dynamic of the events after the fall of Ceaușescu. The revolution in the city was also given a special resonance through the presence of the Romanian leader's son, Nicu, who was first secretary of the county. Although news of the demonstrations in Timișoara circulated freely, Sibiu remained quiet until December 21. On that morning protesters clashed with the security forces and set a jeep ablaze, before the troops called in to quell the demonstration opened fire.[82] This occurred while they were regrouping, and the shots may at first only have been in warning, but nevertheless it seems two protesters were left dead and many more injured. For most of the afternoon there was a tense stand-off in the city, with knots of protesters shouting slogans outside key buildings, such as the Party headquarters and the militia station. Widespread fraternization broke out between the crowd and the troops, most of whom were young conscripts from the local Military Academy but, as night fell, stones were thrown, more cars were set on fire, and the shooting began again, leaving a number of protesters dead.

The next morning Sibiu saw further demonstrations. By noon, a crowd of approximately 1,000 had gathered outside the joint militia and *securitate* headquarters demanding the release of all those arrested the day before. A dialogue seems to have opened between those in the building and the protesters outside in a tense but still peaceful atmosphere. Vasile Avram paints a vivid and plausible picture of confusion and doubt, as the occupants inside the building, having apparently been instructed to defend it at all costs, found themselves effectively leaderless. With Nicu Ceaușescu already having left the city, and all the senior officers in a nearby army base, the breakdown in communications seems to have been total, with all attempts to gain clarification of orders eliciting only evasive and inconclusive replies. While those inside prevaricated, the crowd out-

80. For the revolution in Cluj see Cornea (1997), 239–44; Lungu (1997), 245–58; Cocan (1999).

81. *Raportul SRI*. Two others were also to die that night. Pitulescu et al. (1995), 161–63.

82. This description of events in Sibiu is largely taken from Avram (1992). See also Codrescu et al. (1998), 98–106, 266–76; Nicolaescu (1999), 317–42; *Adevărul*, December 21, 1992, 2; also the probably rather exaggerated claims in *Washington Post*, January 9, 1990, A1, A15.

side grew ever more eager to see this bastion of the Ceauşescu regime in Sibiu fall and those who they believed were held inside following the demonstrations of the day before released. Amid much pushing and shoving the protesters eventually forced the gate of the building and, brushing aside a cordon of soldiers, streamed into the internal courtyard. Here, they were met by clouds of tear gas and gunfire, which created pandemonium. The occupants of the building must have feared for their lives and shortly afterward a group of between twenty-five and thirty seem to have made a break for the nearby army base. Surprised, the soldiers inside the base seem to have mistaken them for a hostile attacking force and opened fire, killing and injuring twenty-three.[83] After peaking in the early afternoon, sporadic firing continued until around 4:30, when the army and members of the crowd entered the Ministry of Interior building and took control.[84] In the turmoil a number of protesters and inhabitants of nearby buildings were also killed and it was reports of this shooting—apparently the first in Romania after the flight of Ceauşescu—that, when it reached Bucharest during the afternoon of December 22, sparked some of the fears of a "terrorist" onslaught by the *securitate* on the capital itself.

In contrast to Timişoara, Cluj, and Sibiu, the demonstrations in Braşov, the center of the 1987 disturbances, were largely peaceful with no fatalities recorded prior to the flight of Ceauşescu from Bucharest. After demonstrations in the central square of the city on December 21, the local Party leaders had opened rather desultory negotiations with a committee of twenty-three protesters. They had presented a seven-point program of demands headed by calls for the removal of Ceauşescu and elections in which those without Party affiliation would also be able to run. Little, however, was gained other than a promise that the demands would be forwarded to Bucharest. The following day, demonstrators again gathered in the center of the city, outside the county council building. Chanting and burning pictures of Ceauşescu, they remained peacefully outside until, hearing the news of his flight from Bucharest, they surged inside.[85] In smaller centers the demonstrations also seem to have been usually peaceful. In Făgăraş after an initial demonstration on December 21, large crowds gathered the next day and marched on the factories asking the workers to join them in their protest. Some supervisors seem to have allowed their staff to join the crowd, but elsewhere factory security guards tried to prevent the workers' exit by posting notices warning them of the consequences. They were ignored and a vast crowd marched on the Party

---

83. Nicolaescu (1999), 328.
84. Codrescu et al. (1998), 267.
85. For the revolution in Braşov see *The Times*, December 29, 1989, 10; *Le Monde*, December 31, 1989/January 1, 1990, 3; *New York Times*, January 5, 1990, 14; ibid., January 9, 1990, 12; David (1990), 3–5; *Adevărul*, December 21, 1992, 3; Codrescu et al. (1998), 95–98, 276–83; Nicolaescu (1999), 372–77.

headquarters in the town where, after an hour, they broke in and, as elsewhere, ransacked the premises, throwing portraits of Ceaușescu out the windows.[86]

However, there were exceptions to this general rule of peaceful protest in the small centers. In Cisnădie, near Sibiu, on December 21 a crowd gathered outside the local militia station apparently in the belief that some of those arrested in nearby Sibiu were being held inside. Some members of the crowd seem to have tried to force a passage through the blocked entrance of the building with a bulldozer, and in response the members of the militia trapped inside opened fire, killing two civilians. In Caransebeș the demonstrations on December 21 also turned violent as night fell. When a group of protesters tried to break down the door of the militia station with a mobile crane, those inside opened fire, killing one and wounding thirteen. Other buildings were then attacked, including the Party headquarters, town hall, courts, and even the post office.[87] In Cugir, workers reacted to a rumor that there had been arrests after a demonstration in which books by Ceaușescu were burned in the streets by besieging the local militia headquarters. In scenes of turmoil, as some of the protesters vented their anger on vehicles parked outside the building, while others used a bench to break down the door, the occupants opened fire. Nearly forty of the protesters were wounded in the shooting that followed, mostly in the arms and legs, yet far from subduing the crowd, it only enraged it further. Protesters burst into the building, trashing the ground floor and setting fire to the furniture. As the flames climbed higher, members of the militia began to jump from the windows only to fall into the hands of the demonstrators outside who beat some of them so severely that two were killed—the only members of the security forces, it seems, to die in the revolution prior to the overthrow of Ceaușescu.[88]

The Revolution in Bucharest

Simultaneously, as the revolution was spreading like a brushfire through towns and cities across the Banat and Transylvania, demonstrations also broke out in the capital, and from this point onward this was to be the main seat of the disturbances. On December 20, Ceaușescu had arrived back from Iran at 3:00 p.m., apparently three hours earlier than scheduled. In the early evening he held a teleconference with senior Party leaders before making the defiant broadcast to the nation that effectively scuppered the negotiations then taking place in Timișoara.[89] After the

86. Kideckel (1993), 213–14.
87. Pitulescu et al. (1995), 152–53; Nicolaescu (1999), 90; 418–19.
88. *Raportul SRI*; Pitulescu et al. (1995), 153–56; Nicolaescu (1999), 343–44.
89. Sava and Monac (2001), 176–84; BBC EE/0646, B/1, December 22, 1989.

broadcast, workplace meetings were convened across Romania at factories and other places of work, including military barracks, to mobilize support for the regime and to denounce the events in Timișoara. These were probably arranged at short notice, and noticeably those in Bucharest seem to have been addressed only by union and works' Party officials, not by any major political figures.[90] At the same time, at a session of the permanent bureau of the PEC the decision was being taken to mount a similar spectacle on a far greater scale the next morning in Piața Palatului, in the heart of Bucharest. This huge mass meeting, to be covered live on national television and radio, was intended to display to the Romanian public the widespread popular support the regime continued to enjoy, and thereby legitimize the repression of the demonstrations in Timișoara. Given the rising tensions, it was a high risk strategy, which in hindsight Postelnicu was to say "made little sense," but Ceaușescu, who held an abiding belief that he still enjoyed the support of the working population, seems not to have seen it in that light.[91]

The organization for the meeting seems to have been entrusted mostly to Barbu Petrescu and the Party apparatus in Bucharest, principally, the municipal committees and first secretaries of the sectors of the capital. News that the meeting would take place seems to have been circulating around Bucharest from late on the evening of December 20, becoming more widely known the next morning, when the Party organization within the factories sprung into life to mobilize the workers. Various accounts speak of the meeting being postponed and then reinstated. None of these tally as to precise times, but, if true, they do suggest that there was some doubt within the regime about the wisdom of holding such a gathering.[92] Selected by work unit, the participants were bused to the center, where they were issued with placards and banners and formed in a column for the march to Piața Palatului. On their arrival, they were screened to weed out any potentially disruptive elements. Eyewitnesses describe the mood as being subdued and, when the meeting began, around midday, the apathy was evident in the muted response given to the warm-up speeches by Party representatives from some of Bucharest's biggest industrial plants. The large but loosely packed crowd stretched to the furthest confines of the square, holding aloft banners proclaiming the successes of communism and portraits of an improbably youthful ruling couple. Before them, on the balcony of the central committee building, Ceaușescu stood with Elena at his side, surrounded by many of the Party leadership. Then, following an introduction by Petrescu, Ceaușescu approached the

90. For accounts of such meetings together with photographs showing unenthusiastic workers see *România Liberă*, December 21, 1989, 2.
91. Postelnicu interviewed by Andon and Roveli (n.d.), 19.
92. Ratesh (1991), 38; Ioniță (n.d.), 16.

microphone and began to speak at 12:31. Barely had he begun passing through a few brief introductory sentences when he was interrupted by a commotion in the crowd and high-pitched screams. Quickly the live radio and television transmission was cut short, but not before a look of startled bemusement on Ceaușescu's face had been captured by the cameras and fixed in the minds of viewers throughout the country. As they watched him waving feebly to the crowd, many Romanians trace this moment as the turning point in which they realized the frailty of Ceaușescu's grasp on power and the possibility that he could be overthrown; and it seems not improbable that similar thoughts also began to pass through the minds of his Party colleagues and the commanders of the security forces.[93]

The source of the disturbance has never been properly determined. It has been suggested that it was caused by a loud noise, but it remains unknown whether or not this was the result of a deliberate act. Some have claimed it was caused by the letting off of a firework in the square and, according to Postelnicu, this was the view of those on the balcony, but equally it may have come from an entirely accidental source, such as a collapsing lamp stand or from the snapping pole of a dropped banner.[94] Inevitably allegations have surfaced that the disturbances were deliberately triggered by the *securitate*, with claims that they arranged for the loudspeakers to broadcast the sound of approaching tanks and strange subliminal messages.[95] More credible are suggestions that loudspeakers short-circuited or that the noise was caused by the firing of tear gas grenades at protesters, who were already gathering on the edge of the square. Bulgarian and Yugoslav correspondents covering the rally reported that this was the case and transcripts of conversations between different units of the forces of the Ministry of the Interior made available after the revolution also point to the same conclusion.[96] It seems probable that the exact cause of the disturbance will never be known, but whatever its source the noise led the crowd, which was already tense and rife with rumors, to panic, and in the pushing and shoving that followed fifteen were injured.[97] Simultaneously, or possibly shortly afterward, some muffled protests were also shouted, although these were only loud enough to be indistinctly picked up by the recording microphones.[98] Over the years various people have claimed responsibility. Leon Nica is often mentioned,

93. *New York Times*, January 5, 1990, 14. It seems that in some units of the security forces the troops were ordered to watch the speech allowing them to witness Ceaușescu's moment of consternation; see *România Liberă*, January 7, 1994, 7.
94. Nicolaescu (1995), 41; Postelnicu interviewed by Andon and Roveli (n.d.), 19.
95. Ratesh (1991), 107.
96. Hall (1997), 206–19.
97. *Adevărul*, May 25, 1992, 2.
98. Galloway and Wylie (1991), 134; Postelnicu interviewed by Andon and Roveli (n.d.), 19.

but also a group of young workers from the Turbomecanica factory, who have said they started chanting "Timișoara."[99]

After a few minutes, enough of a semblance of order was restored for Ceaușescu to resume his speech. The Romanian leader first announced a series of measures to improve living standards, raising the minimum wage from 2,000 to 2,200 lei and also increasing children's allowances, pensions, and social security benefits. These increases had been approved at a meeting of the PEC held earlier that morning, but they cannot be seen as a serious attempt to buy popular support, as the figures involved were relatively small and the hikes had all been announced earlier during the 14th Congress of the RCP.[100] Then, turning to the events in Timișoara, Ceaușescu sought to win the support of the crowd by calling for national unity to meet the many dangers faced by Romania in a hostile world. To Ceaușescu it was obvious that in Timișoara the country was facing "action orchestrated by circles who want to destroy Romania's integrity and sovereignty, halt socialist construction and again put our people under foreign domination. . . . We have to work in complete unity and with determination against all those who are trying to weaken the strength and unity of our nation and who are in the service of various espionage services and imperialist circles to divide Romania again and to subjugate our people." In the face of these threats he exhorted his compatriots that it was "better to die fighting in full glory than again to be slaves in the ancient land."[101] His tired words elicited little enthusiasm and, by the end of the speech, he was again being interrupted by indistinct chanting, and so, after Ceaușescu had spoken for only twenty minutes, the rally seems to have been brought to a peremptory end. Confused and alarmed, the crowd streamed rapidly away so that within a few minutes the square was virtually deserted. Placards were left heaped on the pavement or strewn on the ground and, as the television crew began to pack up their cameras, squads of cleaners entered to tidy up the square. The first deployments of troops also began to appear.

The authorities seem to have taken some precautions to forestall unrest in the capital. A watch had been placed on student dormitories to prevent demonstrations, and later that night several known dissidents, including Dumitru Mazilu and Gabriel Andreescu, were rounded up by the *securitate*

99. Confusingly he is often called Nica Leon. Only the day before Nica had had an open letter denouncing the Ceaușescu regime published in a Canadian paper. For a good discussion of Nica and how his relationship with the press soured as they reevaluated his role in the revolution see Hall (1997), 209–13. For the Turbomecanica workers see *România Liberă*, March 17–April 25, 1990.

100. BBC EE/0647, B/7, December 23, 1989. However, there is some evidence the crowd may have perceived it as an attempt to buy them off; see *Washington Post*, December 23, 1989, A1, A15.

101. BBC EE/0647, B/5–6, December 23, 1989.

and moved out of Bucharest.[102] Units of the patriotic guard had been partly activated, and since December 17, like the remainder of the military, the Bucharest army garrison had been placed on a state of alert under the code name "Radu cel Frumos." In preparation for the December 21 mass meeting, eight platoons of *securitate* troops had been placed in buses at strategic points throughout the center of the capital, while others joined a detachment of soldiers in Piața Palatului. However, news of the meeting had traveled far and wide within Bucharest, attracting people toward the center and now, as these new arrivals mingled with the workers leaving the square, there were isolated disturbances.[103] Scattered groups of youths moved through larger crowds of onlookers and passing shoppers, shouting slogans and urging their fellow citizens to join them in protest. Some shop windows were broken on Calea Victoriei and, once reinforcements arrived, the security forces moved in to break up the protests with tear gas and baton charges. The demonstrators fled down side streets and there were many arrests.

While it was relatively easy to disperse demonstrations in the narrow confines of Calea Victoriei, it was to prove more difficult in the broader expanses of Bucharest's main squares, especially Piața Universității. As much a road junction as a square, this area under the windows of the towering Intercontinental Hotel, a traditional refuge for many of the foreign visitors to communist Romania, was now to be the focal point of the revolution in Bucharest. The crowd seems to have gathered here at around the same time as the meeting began to unfold in nearby Piața Palatului, with reports speaking of demonstrators climbing onto the low wall at the entrance to an underground parking garage to address the gathering throng. Shortly after the official meeting had dispersed, a section of this restless crowd appears to have tried to push up a side street back toward Piața Palatului, but their progress was blocked by a line of shield-bearing troops. As the two sides came into open confrontation, an officer of the militia stepped forward and, firing directly into the unarmed gathering, wounded two of the protesters. The injured were taken to a local hospital, where they were admitted at 1:30 p.m., the first of the many casualties of the revolution in Bucharest.[104] Soon, military reinforcements arrived in the square, but there was at first no further shooting and the demonstration remained peaceful, as the crowd began to fraternize with the troops. Facing the protesters in Piața Universității were shield-bearing riot troops behind which were ranged several fire engines and armed soldiers together with their armored personnel carriers. In the late afternoon, some

---

102. The same tactic as regards the student dormitories had been employed at the recent Party Congress; see *Adevărul*, January 25, 1990, 5. For the arrest of dissidents see *România Liberă*, October 20, 1994, 16.

103. Codrescu (1991), 35.

104. *Adevărul*, December 21, 1994, 1, includes a photograph.

fresh military reinforcements seem to have arrived and, according to submissions to the senatorial commission of inquiry, at that time, an army
truck became partially blocked by the crowd, which called for its withdrawal.[105] When this was not forthcoming, someone threw a brick that
shattered the windscreen of the truck and struck the driver a blow on the
head.[106] Hurtling out of control, the vehicle sped forward, knocking down
and injuring twenty-three civilians and three or four riot troops, before
coming to a halt just inches short of an armored personnel carrier. The
incident inflamed the crowd and, surging forward toward the wounded
demonstrators, they knocked the riot troops aside. In the ensuing chaos
shots were fired and seven demonstrators fell dead. This outbreak of
shooting was to herald a night of mayhem out of which it is difficult to
make any discernible pattern, as security forces and demonstrators continued to battle in and around Piața Universității. At times both Milea and
Postelnicu came to the scene in person to direct operations.[107] In the
early evening, fire engines seem to have been used to try and disperse the
crowd but, as midnight approached, protesters were still ranging freely
and blocking most of the side streets in the area. In one widely reported
incident, a barricade built across Bulevardul Bălcescu was set ablaze.
When armored personnel carriers under the cover of clouds of tear gas
and gunfire moved forward to try and dismantle the barrier, one caught
fire before they succeeded in the task. By 3 o'clock in the morning, when
the streets finally quieted and cleaning crews moved in to paint over the
slogans daubed on the walls and remove the debris of battle, 49 demonstrators were dead, 463 wounded, and 698 arrested.[108]

The revolution in Bucharest was to follow a pattern remarkably similar
to that in Timișoara. During the afternoon and night of December 21, the
disorganized street protests, mostly by youths, were ruthlessly crushed by
the authorities. The sound of the shooting reverberated across the city
and news of the violence also rapidly spread via the telephone. As fleeing
demonstrators mingled with changing nightshift workers, a deep-seated
public anger began to arise that harbored, alongside emotions of utter re-
vulsion at the actions of the regime, a growing sense of expectation. In
the early hours of the next morning the situation was described as calm,
with municipal transport operating and food shops open, but gradually
knots of demonstrators began to assemble.[109] In some cases factory direc-

---

105. Ibid., May 25, 1992, 2. For a view from the side of the protesters see Dolghin, Lăcustă, Matei, Ștefan, and Ursu (1990), 6.

106. For the testimony of the soldier see Codrescu et al. (1998), 151.

107. Troops from both the Bucharest army garrison and the Ministry of the Interior were
deployed. For a detailed discussion of the part USLA may have played see Hall (1997),
219–24.

108. Nicolaescu (1999), 122.

109. For the situation that morning see the Tass report reproduced in BBC EE/0647, i,
December 23, 1989.

tors ordered gates to be welded shut in a vain hope of keeping their workers inside, while overhead a helicopter hovered, dropping leaflets warning the demonstrators that they had embarked on a dangerous road and calling on them to abandon their protest.[110] At various strategic points army units also tried to stem the flow of the crowd: outside the Turbomecanica factory, on Drumul Taberei, in Piața Gorjului, on Bulevardul Republicii, among others.[111] Volleys of warning shots may have been fired in places, but these had little effect, as the crowds continued to stream toward the center, often swamping the military units facing them. The soldiers broke ranks and began to fraternize with the crowd and, as it became clear that the existing forces could not bring order to the streets, instructions were issued for heavy military reinforcements to proceed to the capital, although none were to arrive before the flight of Ceaușescu. Then, as the situation continued to deteriorate for the regime, at 10:58 a declaration of a national state of emergency was broadcast on the radio that put all units of the armed forces, the Ministry of the Interior, and patriotic guard on full alert and banned public gatherings of more than five people.[112] This was immediately followed by a terse announcement that Milea had committed suicide. The statement made constant references to treacherous behavior by Milea, accusing him of orchestrating rumors and lies in "close cooperation with the traitors within the country and with the imperialist circles" and of giving "false information in connection with the situation in our country."[113]

The circumstances surrounding Milea's death have long been the source of debate. Some argue that he committed suicide, as was announced at the time, while others suggest he was murdered on the orders of Ceaușescu.[114] The oration of Colonel-General Ion Hortopan at Milea's funeral was ambiguous when it spoke of "one who was and will remain in the conscience of the Romanian army . . . , killed by Ceaușescu's dictatorial clique."[115] However, submissions to the senatorial commission of inquiry follow the official line of suicide, as pronounced by Ceaușescu to his colleagues at a PEC meeting immediately after the death. They state that, after he came out from a meeting with Ceaușescu, Milea went to the office he occupied as head of the patriotic guard on the sixth floor of the

110. *România Liberă*, January 7, 1994, 7.
111. For an account of the incident in Piața Gorjului see ibid., December 23, 1993, 10; for Bulevardul Republicii see Ursu, Dolghin and Lăcustă (1990), 4.
112. BBC EE/0648, B/9, December 28, 1989.
113. Ibid.
114. Among English language commentators, Sweeny (1991), 211, and Rady (1992), 103, both suggest Milea was murdered, while Behr (1991), 3, and Ratesh (1991), 42, refrain from any absolute judgment but appear to lean toward a verdict of murder. Almond (1992), 12, adopts a neutral view, while Galloway and Wylie (1991), 143–44, cleverly incorporate both possibilities by suggesting Milea committed suicide after Ceaușescu ordered him shot for treason.
115. BBC EE/0652, 13:23, January 3, 1990.

Crowds moving into the center of Bucharest on the morning of December 22, 1989, pass isolated military vehicles on Bulevardul Magheru. Courtesy Rompres.

central committee building and asked for a pistol on the pretext that he was preparing to go out onto the streets. Then he retired into his office alone and around 9:30 a.m. shot himself. He apparently did not perish immediately but died either on the way to or in hospital.[116] According to Stănculescu, both the postmortem and coroner's report gave verdicts of suicide, and the last person who appears to have seen Milea alive, Colonel

116. Bunea (2000), 10.

Corneliu Pârcălăbescu, also later testified at the trial of Bobu, Dincă, Mănescu, and Postelnicu that it was suicide.[117] Earlier, during the same trial, however, Bobu had told the court that Ceauşescu had ordered Milea to be shot, and this version of the events, which was being broadcast on the radio as early as December 23, was judged credible by many in Romania.[118]

Immediately after the fall of Ceauşescu an elaborate myth of the martyrdom of Milea began to be propagated. On December 28 he was posthumously promoted from the rank of Colonel-General to full Army General, and Mark Almond has remarked how his death metamorphosed him "from villainous minion of the tyrants into their innocent victim."[119] As the body of Milea lay in state, the image of the noble officer who defied the orders of the dictator and refused to order his troops to fire on defenseless civilians was assiduously cultivated by members of the new regime to proclaim the innocence of the army from the charge that they had opened fire during the revolution. Submissions to the senatorial commission of inquiry make constant references to Milea issuing an order for the army not to open fire on the morning of December 22 just before he committed suicide, and it is widely presumed that it was his defiance of Ceauşescu that led to his death. Already reports were reaching the central committee building that soldiers had been disarmed by the crowd, and it seems not inconceivable that, as the soldiers fraternized with civilians, Milea may have been faced with the possibility of not only having to order his troops to fire on the demonstrators but also on their own brothers-in-arms. Perhaps this possibility drove him to commit suicide, and such a scenario was evoked by Dumitru Mazilu in his oration at the funeral. While affirming that the death of Milea was "the symbol of the Romanian revolution, marking a turning point which changed the course of events and helped us emerge victor" he also added that "when he received the loathsome order to fire at the army, he said 'I am also the army. Hence I shot the army.' "[120]

Despite claims to the contrary, there are few signs that Milea was universally loved within the lower ranks.[121] Rather than leading to an out-

117. Codrescu et al. (1998), 126–30.

118. For a fuller account of Pârcălăbescu's evidence see *Washington Post*, January 31, 1990, A10; *România Liberă*, January 31, 1990, 5. For doubts about the official version of Milea's death see also Captain Alexandru Borbu interviewed in *Tineretul Liber*, June 2, 1990, 1–2, and also the observations by Săndulescu in Bunea (2000), 9–12.

119. Almond (1992), 12.

120. BBC EE/0652, 13:23, January 3, 1990.

121. Milea had been appointed minister of national defense in place of Constantin Olteanu in December 1985. He had been associated with the patriotic guard as much as the army and was reported to be a staunch supporter of Ceauşescu's policy of using the military within the domestic economy, a form of forced labor detested by many soldiers; Eyal (1989), 104–6; Maier (January 10, 1986), 7–10. For a typically scurrilous pen portrait of Milea see Pacepa (1989), 157.

pouring of grief, news of his death provoked a sense of confusion and even panic, not only within the armed forces but also, if the transcript of the PEC meeting held that morning is any guide, within the regime itself.[122] On the streets of Bucharest it gave a common topic of conversation between the crowd and the army units and, when it was coupled with rumors circulating that some militia vehicles had been burned during the previous night and their occupants killed, it further undermined the soldiers' will to resist.[123] After the visit to Iran and the meeting of December 21, the public announcement of the suicide of Milea was a third major error by Ceaușecu.[124] Following the death of the Minister of Defense, Stănculescu was ordered to take command but he had only returned to Bucharest himself earlier that morning and, on his own admission, had gone to some length to render himself incapable of playing any further role in the events, not least by feigning a broken leg and having his limb encased in plaster.[125] He eventually arrived at the central committee building sometime after 10 o'clock. Present at the same time in the building were Lieutenant-General Nicolae Eftimescu, First Deputy Chief of General Staff, and Major-General Gheorghe Voinea, commander of the First Army based in Bucharest and, with Gușă still in Timișoara, in the next few chaotic hours some sort of collective leadership seems to have prevailed.[126]

After the dispersal of the demonstrations of the night before, on the morning of December 22 troop dispositions were changed, so as to move the heaviest concentrations into the immediate vicinity of the central committee building. By 7:00 a.m. there were fourteen tanks, forty-five armored personnel carriers, and over a thousand troops of both the army and the *securitate* in the area. However, by mid-morning these tanks and the troops had all been withdrawn from in front of the central committee building. According to representations made to the senatorial commission of inquiry, the order for units to withdraw was given by Stănculescu at 10:45, with the process beginning at 11:00.[127] Other submissions state that slightly earlier, at around 10:00, Colonel Dumitru Pavelescu of the *securitate* troops also ordered his men to withdraw, although the last of these did not leave until 1:30 to 2:00, long after the flight of Ceaușescu. It

122. Nicolaescu (1995), 289–91.
123. *România Liberă,* January 7, 1994, 7. Nicolaescu (1999), 516, suggests that six members of the security forces died in Bucharest that morning but gives no details.
124. Nicolaescu (1995), 46.
125. Galloway and Wylie (1991), 131–44; Almond (1992), 11; *Adevărul,* November 3, 1993, 1.
126. Codrescu et al. (1998), 152, n. 72; Nicolaescu (1999), 134.
127. Some accounts suggest that other generals were still trying to regroup their forces in the square at this time with Voinea giving an order to this effect at 11:24 and General Constantinescu at 11:38; see Deletant (1995), 357. See also Codrescu et al. (1998), 113, 120, 153 n. 76.

is stated that Pavelescu gave this order on his own volition, with the decision being relayed to Vlad, who concurred.[128] At 11:20 a further order was passed from Stănculescu and the army high command in the central committee building to Major-General Iosif Rus, head of military aviation, for four or five helicopters to fly to Bucharest.[129] These took off from the nearby Otopeni airbase at 11:33, with the first landing on the roof of the building shortly after 11:40. An order for so many helicopters would seem to suggest that it was initially planned to land in Piața Palatului and evacuate most of the political leadership, although this was to prove impossible, once the demonstrators had seized control of the central committee building.

The decision to pull back the troops from the area in front of the Party headquarters was crucial for the revolution. It moved the security forces out of direct confrontation with the demonstrators, effectively allowing them to abrogate their responsibilities to Ceaușescu, and it gave the demonstrators unhampered access to the central committee building, thereby ultimately paving the way for the downfall of the regime. Whether the order to pull back was given independently of Ceaușescu or with his sanction remains one of the chief mysteries of the revolution. By 10:00 the army was already breaking ranks and military discipline crumbling fast. The Tass correspondent in the city reported that a wave of demonstrators chanting "The army is with us!" had mingled with bewildered soldiers and that "hundreds of people" had climbed onto tanks and armored personnel carriers.[130] There were also persistent rumors that guns were falling into the hands of the protesters. With the effective ending of the fighting capabilities of the security forces, did the high command—some reliving again the scenes from Timișoara—give the order to return to barracks in an effort to protect their troops and equipment and retain at least a semblance of order and military discipline? This is the standard response to fraternization and is usually the prelude to a regrouping of the armed forces, perhaps involving the drafting of reinforcements from elsewhere, hitherto uncontaminated by contact with civilian populations, before embarking on a further attempt to crush the demonstrations. Such a

128. For these details see *Adevărul*, May 25, 1992, 2–4. Note also the contention by an officer of the army unit U.M.01210 that they received the order to withdraw at 10:25 and were nearly all back in barracks by 11:00; *România Liberă*, September 8, 1993, 8. The commander of the Ministry of the Interior troops at the television station, Lieutenant Mihai Dițiu, reported receiving an order not to fire from the commander of UM0596 Bucharest, Major Ilie Gorjan, around 11:00; Televiziunea Română (1990), 336. Members of the III Directorate of the *securitate* also claim to have been ordered to hand in their arms between 11:30 and 12:00; *România Liberă*, October 20, 1994, 16. USLA units deployed on the streets also say that they returned to barracks around 11:00; *Tineretul Liber*, March 7, 1990, 1, 3. At the radio station the picture is confused but it seems the order to return weapons to the guardroom was not given until after 12:30. *România Liberă*, January 7, 1994, 7.

129. The order was also passed by General Neagoe; Domenico (1999), 54.

130. Report from *Izvestia* translated in *The Current Digest of the Soviet Press*, 41:51, 1989, 14.

pattern seems to have been followed in China in 1989, when, following fraternization between civilian protesters and members of the Beijing garrison, the authorities appear to have called upon forces from outside the capital to suppress the Tiananmen Square demonstrations. Likewise, in the final days of the Iranian revolution, as over one million demonstrators marched through Tehran, the high command also took the decision to withdraw their troops from the streets so as to forestall any possible mutiny.[131] Once the Romanian army in Bucharest engaged in widespread fraternization and had effectively merged with the crowd, the senior officers had little option but to withdraw their forces, whether or not this was under the direct orders of Ceaușescu. Indeed, there is some evidence to suggest that in places this was a spontaneous decision by the troops on the ground.[132] It is not necessary, therefore, to invoke the need for a conspiracy on the part of the high command of the Romanian army to explain the actions taken. However, this is not to rule out the possibility that one or more of the senior officers were privy to the intentions of those who had been conspiring against Ceaușescu or, indeed, may have been participants in these plans. Certainly, given the tide of events, considerable doubts must have surfaced within their minds about the wisdom of maintaining the security forces' association with the embattled Ceaușescu. It is not unlikely that by mid-morning on December 22 they were looking for alternatives, and again it is interesting to compare the events in Romania with the Iranian revolution where, before the final overthrow of the government on February 11, 1979, a number of senior Iranian generals, including the chief of staff, had already come over to the side of the opposition.[133]

Although Ceaușescu had long had his doubts about the security forces, he still seems to have believed that the workers and the patriotic guard remained loyal. During the previous evening, attempts had been made to mobilize 5,000 members of the patriotic guard to crush the demonstrations in the center of Bucharest, but only about 300 had arrived late at night. One unit had fraternized with the protesters, while the others remained idle, until they were sent back to their factories in the early hours of the morning.[134] Now, in the morning of December 22, senior party officials were again dispatched to the major factories to try and rally the workers to Ceaușecu's cause.[135] Their task was impossible, and as the envoys returned with news of columns of workers chanting anti-regime slogans marching on the center, along with the rest of the PEC, Ceaușescu was forced to decide whether to fight or not. For once, his was not the only

131. For China see Calvert (1990), 43; for Iran see Moshiri (1991), 128–29.
132. Deletant (1995), 356.
133. Moshiri (1991), 129.
134. *România Liberă,* January 20, 1990, 1.
135. *Adevărul,* January 28, 1990, 3.

voice to be heard, as the members of the PEC debated the options. They could agree that a countrywide state of emergency should be imposed, but what should they do when the protesters, some of whom, they were told, had taken guns from soldiers, reached the central committee building? If they started to shoot, they could legitimately call upon the army to defend them, but if the demonstrators came peacefully, could they as "representatives of the workers" sanction a massacre? As Ceaușescu continued to ramble about betrayal, the discussion was agonized and inconclusive.[136] The Romanian leader's options were fast diminishing. The staff of the television center still expected him to address the nation from the television studio in the central committee building at 1 o'clock, perhaps to announce the formation of a new government. But, before then, as an enormous crowd surged into the square below, he stepped onto the balcony for the last time.[137] It was quite in keeping for Ceaușescu to make one final attempt to address the crowd, but in the square below the excited talk was already of an alternative government and, when he began to speak at approximately 11:30, he was soon interrupted by boos and catcalls and ushered inside.[138]

As the embattled leader left the public stage for the last time, the crowd below rushed the doors of the central committee building and, meeting little opposition, streamed inside. Most of the stories relating the flight of Ceaușescu tell of an undignified scramble to the roof of the building after an elevator became blocked between floors.[139] Then at a few minutes past noon, just before the first members of the crowd reached the fleeing leadership, an overloaded helicopter staggered into the air carrying Nicolae and Elena Ceaușescu, Bobu, Mănescu, and two members of the presidential bodyguard, Major Florian Raţ and Captain Marian Constantin Rusu. Ten minutes later it touched down at the presidential residence at Snagov, just north of Bucharest. Here the fugitives seem to have quickly gathered some possessions, while Ceaușescu made a series of telephone calls to try to discover the situation in the country as a whole. Around 1:15 the helicopter departed again, but this time with only the two Ceaușescus and their bodyguards on board. Bobu and Mănescu left separately by road and were eventually captured near Găeşti, halfway between

136. The transcript is reproduced in Nicolaescu (1995), 289–91.
137. Televiziunea Română (1990), 177.
138. *Financial Times*, December 23, 1989, 2; *Independent*, December 23, 1989, 1. Perva and Roman (n.d), 26–27.
139. There are many accounts of the flight of the Ceaușescus and, although most are rather full of hyperbole and implausibly contrast the pitiful and dejected state of the fleeing couple with the heroism of those who were forced to drive them, the basic facts seem to be fairly uniformly acknowledged, even if the motives of many of the participants still remain unclear; see Sweeny (1991), 213–14, 218–21; Behr (1991), 4–17; Ratesh (1991), 70–73; Almond (1992), 13–18; Galloway and Wylie (1991), 168–72; *Adevărul*, April 4, 1991, 3; ibid., January 19, 1990, 3; Pitulescu et al. (1998), 17–26; Nicolaescu (1999), 472–73.

Bucharest and Pitești, in the evening of December 22. According to the pilot, when he took off from Snagov, he initially tried to return to base at Otopeni, but was forced by his passengers to, first, make for the military airbase at Boteni and, later, when Ceaușescu changed his mind, for Pitești. Brucan, however, has alleged that from the beginning Ceaușescu planned to head for Târgoviște to establish a base of resistance. Some support for Brucan's position comes from documents published after the revolution. These purport to show that Ceaușescu had long possessed detailed plans for an evacuation from Bucharest at times of foreign invasion or internal coup. It should be noted, however, that the veracity of these documents has not been fully established and that the originals seem to have been handwritten, implying, if nothing else, an extremely limited circulation.[140] First drawn up in 1970 under the code name Rovine-IS-70 the escape plan later came to be known as *Luceafărul* and, after its publication by the Romanian media, as "Plan-Z."[141] However, the existence of a plan does not mean that it was ever put into action and, certainly, the text nowhere envisages the series of events that were to follow.

According to the pilot of the helicopter, Lieutenant-Colonel Vasile Maluțan, after he had warned Ceaușescu of the danger that they were being tracked by radar and might be shot down, he was ordered to land, which he did in a field near the village of Serdanu, just outside Titu.[142] Here the first car on a nearby road was flagged down for a lift. The vehicle was driven by a local doctor, Nicolae Decă, and he took the Ceaușescus to the village of Văcărești, just outside Târgoviște.[143] At Văcărești, either in fact or invention, the doctor seems to have run out of gas and the couple transferred to another car driven by Nicolae Petrișor. He took them to Târgoviște, where one of the bodyguards left the couple, possibly because he was dispatched to find the local Party first-secretary—the other bodyguard had already been lost somewhere en route. Petrișor was left alone with the presidential couple and at around 2 o'clock they arrived at the local Center for Plant Protection. The couple stayed at the Center for a short time until two vehicles arrived to collect them, one from the local militia and one from the presidential fleet, which one source says had been on alert since the day before.[144] The militiamen seem to have tried to take the Ceaușescus straight back to their station, which they shared

140. For revelations that plans existed see *Evenimentul Zilei*, July 8, 1993, 3; ibid., July 10, 1993, 3.

141. Deletant (1995), 84–88. In its original form the security of the fleeing leadership was to be the responsibility of Colonel Dumitru Penciuc, a figure later associated with the plots against Ceaușescu, which would suggest that the existence of a plan was known to those conspiring against Ceaușescu, even if its contents were not, since it had undergone many revisions over the years.

142. For Maluțan's story see *The Times*, January 2, 1990, 6.

143. Nicolae Decă interviewed in *România Liberă*, December 23, 1993, 15.

144. Domenico (1999), 113.

with the *securitate*, but the sight of a hostile crowd besieging the building forced them to abandon this plan. As they turned away, the two vehicles became separated and to protect their charges from hostile crowds the two militiamen, who had the Ceașescus in their car, headed for the nearby village of Rățoaia, where they hid among reeds on the edge of a lake. Here they seem to have waited, maintaining radio contact with the militia station in Târgoviște, until they were told that the bulk of the demonstrators had left and the army had restored order. Around 6 o'clock in the afternoon they returned to the station with the Ceaușescus eventually being transferred to a nearby army garrison around 6:30. News of this was relayed to Stănculescu in Bucharest about an hour later.

CHAPTER THREE

"The Bloody Bacchanalia"

And we are here as on a darkling plain
Swept with confused alarms of struggle and flight,
Where ignorant armies clash by night.

MATTHEW ARNOLD, *Dover Beach*

If the events leading to the flight of Ceaușescu can now be seen with relative clarity, those that directly followed still languish under deep layers of
obfuscation. Yet the salient fact remains that it was the period following
the flight of the deposed leader that witnessed by far the greatest bloodshed of the revolution. The official death toll for the whole of the revolution is 1,104, with 3,352 wounded.[1] Of these, 162 died and 1,101 were
wounded in the period between December 17 and noon on December 22.
Following the flight of Ceaușescu, the numbers escalated sharply, so that
by January 10 a further 942 people had lost their lives and 2,251 had been
wounded. Only in Timișoara and Cluj did the greatest number of casualties occur before noon on December 22. Of the casualties afterwards, 493
died in Bucharest and 1,275 were wounded.[2] Of the those who died elsewhere, the various sources give different figures, but it seems that approximately 99 died in Sibiu, 66 in Brașov, 42 in Brăila, 29 in Buzău, 29 in Constanța, 24 in Craiova, 20 in Timișoara, 19 in Arad, 13 in Turda, and 11 in
Reșița.[3] The vast majority of those who died were civilians, but, according

The title of this chapter is taken from a remark in Falin (1990), 24.
1. *Adevărul*, December 22, 1994, 1. Ionițoiu (1998), 145, records 1,247 dead. Of these,
120 died before the flight of Ceaușescu and the rest afterward. Nicolaescu (1995), 342–43,
gives a total figure of 1,207 dead based on hospital records.
2. Ionițoiu (1998), 145, gives a total death toll of 617 for Bucharest, while Nicolaescu
(1995), 342–43, suggests 563.
3. This is only a list of towns where more than ten people died. Deaths were also
recorded elsewhere, including Târgoviște, Alba Iulia, Blaj, Hunedoara, and Sfântu Gheorghe. Nicolaescu (1995); Codrescu et al. (1998); Ionițoiu (1998); Pitulescu et al. (1998);
Nicolaescu (1999); *Adevărul*, December 21, 1991, 2–3.

Table 3.1.   Revolutionary events in local areas

Have these revolutionary events occurred in your local area?	Yes	No	Don't know
Violence	31%	57%	10%
Arrests	15	57	24
Demonstrations	50	38	10
Attacks upon institutions	26	53	17
Public gatherings	60	23	14
Personal participation in events	23	76	0
Participation of members of the family in events	21	74	4

Source: Câmpeanu (1993), 179–80.

to the army, 221 soldiers also perished and 633 were wounded.[4] It is more difficult to assess casualties among the Ministry of Interior forces, since the *securitate* was amalgamated with the army at this time, but 97 members of the militia and the *securitate* troops died, mostly in Bucharest, Sibiu, and at Otopeni airport.[5] Of those who died after the flight of Ceaușecu in Bucharest, most fell within a space of little more than forty-eight hours, stretching from the evening of December 22 until the evening of December 24, with the majority dying on December 23.

After the revolution eyewitness accounts offered vivid pictures of the fighting. They spoke of "a massive attack with an extremely large force" being launched on the Ministry of Defense by "successive waves of terrorists," while in Timișoara the fighting of the night of December 22–23 was described in almost apocalyptic terms: "After the massacre we felt that on Saturday morning we would all be picked up from our homes and lined up against the wall. We felt that it was not just the end of the revolution, but of the entire world."[6] The number of casualties leaves little doubt as to the intensity of the shooting, and in a December 1992 opinion poll 31 percent of the respondents were to say that they knew of violent events occurring within their locality during the revolution (Table 3.1).[7] The quantity and range of ammunition expended, including antiaircraft missiles and tank rounds, also suggests a conflict of considerable proportions. According to a past chairman of the senatorial commission of inquiry into the events of December 1989, during the period of the revolution the

4. Codrescu et al. (1998), 462–74. A figure of 224 army dead is given in Sava and Monac (2001), 460.

5. Pitulescu et al. (1998), 433–43.

6. General Traian Dafinescu in a March 1990 interview quoted in Perva and Roman (n.d.), 73; *East European Reporter*, 4:2, 1990, 33.

7. Câmpeanu (1993), 179–80. The poll covered Bucharest and urban and rural areas in all counties.

army fired in total over five million rounds of ammunition, with one unit alone in Bucharest, which mobilized alongside its infantry fourteen tanks and sixty-one armored personnel carriers, using 176,351 cartridges and 1,216 grenades.[8] Yet despite the use of this vast amount of ammunition, the level of physical damage recorded to key installations, even in the center of Bucharest, was surprisingly small. Buildings at the center of the fighting, such as the television station and the central committee building, emerged virtually unscathed, although surrounding structures fared badly. The university library next to the central committee building was left a burned out shell, and in the vicinity of the television station seven buildings were destroyed totally and five more partially out of the fifty-four reportedly hit by gunfire.[9] In the heat of the battle this discrepancy was barely noticed, but afterward it was to feed suspicions about the artificial nature of the violence and suggestions that the pattern of destruction had not been accidental but somehow contrived.[10]

However, this violence was to be only one facet of the revolution, because after the flight of Ceaușescu, the range of activity that might be considered revolutionary broadened to encompass the storming of state and party institutions, and public gatherings in support of the incoming NSF. It would be difficult and not particularly illuminating to chart the path of the revolution in every city in Romania but, if the figures in Table 3.1 are taken in conjunction with available military reports, then, based on patterns of revolutionary action (or inaction), the country's population centers can be divided into three distinct categories: (a) those that experienced fighting involving the security forces accompanied by mass demonstrations and the destruction of property, (b) those that saw peaceful mass demonstrations often accompanied by the sacking of public institutions, and (c) those that experienced only limited demonstrations or no activity at all.

Those population centers that fall into the first category were the focus of media attention at the time of the revolution and obviously take pride of place in any account of the events. Yet according to the army, only thirty-seven of Romania's cities and towns actually saw shooting during the revolution.[11] Often these were the larger cities, because a clear pattern is apparent of the chance of conflict rising in direct relation to the size of settlement. Of the fifteen biggest cities, shooting broke out after December 22 in Bucharest, Timișoara, Brașov, Sibiu, Constanța, Craiova, Cluj, Brăila, Galați, Bacău, and Arad, while among the smaller towns some of the most serious acts of violence seem to have been recorded in Alba

8. *Daily Telegraph,* December 12, 1994, 10; *România Liberă,* September 8, 1993, 8.
9. Televiziunea Română (1990), 173.
10. Ratesh (1991), 59.
11. Out of a total 260. Codrescu et al. (1998), 392.

Iulia, Buzău, Caracal, Caransebeș, Giurgiu, Hațeg, Hunedoara, Mihai Bravu, Reșița, Râmnicu Sărat, Râmnicu Vâlcea, Sfântu Gheorghe, Slobozia, Târgoviște, and Turda.[12]

Even when it did break out the fighting in most of these cities was not constant. Instead, it was a scrappy warfare, with long periods of quiescence being punctuated by intervals of heavy localized firing, which often took place during the hours of darkness. In Bucharest the shooting was chiefly confined to zones around the television station, the radio station, the Ministry of Defense, the central committee building and, outside the city center, at Otopeni airport. Outbreaks also occurred in the vicinity of barracks near the Ghencea cemetery and Șoseaua Olteniței as well as elsewhere.[13] It is probably true that in each city the causes of the conflict were distinctive. In Sibiu in particular, it seems to have been related to fears and expectations arising from the residence of Nicu Ceaușescu in the town. However, it is noticeable that the shooting did tend to be located in urban centers that had military garrisons within their bounds or nearby.

In some rural areas, deep-rooted tensions also boiled over into petty vandalism or worse. When, shortly after the revolution, the German-Romanian author Richard Wagner returned to his parental home in the mixed Romanian and German village of "P," which lies close by the River Maroș midway between Arad and Timișoara, he discovered what had transpired:

> They chucked out the mayoress and her deputy; the second deputy took over the official duties, till a week later they chucked him out too. They sacked the mayoress's husband who ran the cooperative society, the manager of the corn-mill, the director of the hat factory. The people dragged out the chief of the local police—or militia, as the Communists called it, consisting of three men whose main occupation was harassing or beating people and getting bribed by would-be emigrants—and gave him a thrashing. Since then he has slipped away to his home town, four villages away. The second militiaman is in prison for brutal assaults. The third is still in office under the new public order authority, now called "police" again like before the War.[14]

Worse was to occur in the counties of Harghita and Covasna in Transylvania. Here not only were militia stations attacked—thirty-five in Harghita allegedly suffering some damage—but six members of the militia were apparently killed in revenge attacks, with a further twenty-three injured

---

12. Codrescu et al. (1998); for Giurgiu see *Daily Telegraph,* December 27, 1990, 3.
13. *Nouvel observateur,* February 15–21, 1990, 4–10; Codrescu et al. (1998).
14. Wagner (1990), ix.

and hospitalized.[15] In Dealu a local militia officer died after his home was attacked by a crowd of up to 300 villagers, aggrieved over what they saw as years of mistreatment. Eight Hungarians were convicted and jailed for this and other incidents in the region before eventually being pardoned in March 1994 after a lengthy campaign.[16]

The second category of the typology encompasses some of the cities, such as Pitești, and many other urban centers, including nineteen of the county towns of Romania.[17] Here revolutionary activity was usually limited to mass demonstrations and the storming of local RCP and Ministry of the Interior offices, including militia stations. Revolutionary committees, usually bearing the name "National Salvation Front," were established, barricades thrown across streets, and worker militias mobilized, but serious shooting did not ensue.[18] In these centers the revolution was largely peaceful, as it was in the last category, which was by far the most common of the three and encompassed nearly all the smaller towns and the vast majority of the many villages of Romania. In these, apart from the occasional roadblock established by eager youths and the sporadic ousting of a particularly compromised local official, little more seems to have followed, except for possibly some form of mass meeting. This was the most frequent type of revolutionary activity in both larger and smaller centers, but even many of these must have been only sparsely attended, because, according to the opinion poll mentioned above, less than a quarter of the population aged seventeen or over actually took part in some action in support of the revolution, defined at its widest extent. Although this still means around four million people did participate, the inescapable conclusion is that for most Romanians the revolution was essentially a passive event. Many seem to have followed the example of the workers who normally commuted into the industrial centers from their villages in the Brașov-Făgăraș area. At the first sign of the revolution they left their factories and returned home, remaining there for the duration of the events.[19] For these workers and the other inhabitants of the many small villages of Romania, the revolution remained nothing more than a slightly unreal drama played out on the television, which made it seem, as a Romanian teacher noted at the time, as "if it was happening in another country."[20]

15. Parlamentul României (1991). Dragoș (c1995) offers an interpretation of events that stresses ethnic antagonisms, but note that three of the dead militia officers bore Hungarian names.

16. BBC EE/0920, B/9, November 13, 1990; BBC EE/1992, B/4:12, May 9, 1994; BBC EE/1957, B/3:9, March 28, 1994.

17. Codrescu et al. (1998), 392.

18. For the Revolution in Pitești see *The Times*, December 30, 1989, 10.

19. Kideckel (1992), 71.

20. Quoted in *Sunday Times*, January 7, 1990, A.14.

The Collapse of the Old Regime and the Search
for a New Order

As noon passed on December 22, 1989, and the Ceauşescus fled from Bucharest, the people milling in the broad expanse of Piaţa Palatului before the central committee building were joined by thousands of others who poured out of their apartments onto the wide boulevards of the city. Swelling ever larger, the exuberant, chanting crowd was euphoric as the naturally expressive Romanians drank in the feeling of freedom and release after long years of repression.[21] The barriers of society were cast aside. Generals and the future political elite rubbed shoulders in apparent equality with workers and students, and the future seemed to hold unlimited vistas for a people reveling in new found possibilities. Yet while they were carried along in this mass celebration, members of the crowd were also conscious of their own individuality, with many remembering the revolution as being, above all, an intensely felt moment of personal self-deliverance.

Already, as Ceauşescu's helicopter took to the skies from the roof of the central committee building, members of the crowd were surging through the doors below. Meeting no opposition—the guards on duty seem to have melted away—the tide of mostly young demonstrators swept through the huge building, commandeering offices and scattering papers as they mingled freely with bewildered Party apparatchiks and troops of the army and Ministry of the Interior. Protesters clambered onto the balcony recently vacated by Ceauşescu and began to address the mass of people below. The identities of many of those who spoke that day have long since been forgotten, as also have their often inarticulate utterances, but on December 22, 1989, their words fired the throng, which responded in unison like a Greek chorus, elongating the syllables of their chanted replies: *"Li-ber-ta-te," "Ro-mâ-ni-a," "Nu ple-căm"* (We are not leaving). Some of the speakers seem to have been merely content to revel in their newly found freedom of public expression, with one man reported as intoning over and over again the words "Ceauşescu has gone," but others had a more serious messages to relay.[22] Throughout the afternoon a succession of aspiring leaders came to address the enormous crowd in the hope of gaining legitimization through public approbation. Some were familiar faces, among those who tried to address the crowd that afternoon was Dăscălescu, while others were young hopefuls.[23] Most were to quickly slip back into obscurity but one early speaker in particular, a young university professor called Petre Roman, who made a declaration on behalf of a

---

21. See the observations in Granqvist (1999), 50–54.
22. Galloway and Wylie (1991), 153.
23. Scurtu et al. (1990), 48.

grouping he called the People's Unity Front, was to have a more lasting impact.[24] The balcony of the central committee building was not to be the focal point of the revolution. The real leaders of post-Ceaușescu Romania were to be introduced to the nation elsewhere, but the crowd in Piața Palatului was to remain an important source of legitimization and later that day even Iliescu was to find it politic to come and speak from the balcony. Inside the central committee building the situation was no different from outside. The atmosphere has been likened to a madhouse with people rushing hither and thither and governments being formed one after another.[25] One report says fourteen were formed "one for each floor and one for every corner."[26] Most of these "governments" seem to have disappeared without trace almost immediately, but some lingered longer, becoming a radical alternative focus of the revolution and the seat of the first anti-Front demonstrations.[27] The young people in the central committee building retained legitimacy as the voice of the revolution, and at one point there even seems to have been discussions about institutionalizing them as a revolutionary guard, but at the beginning of January they disbanded peacefully, with some being given jobs in the new administrative structures.[28]

The speed of the revolution seems to have caught many of the senior leaders of the RCP off their guard. Some were still outside Bucharest, where they had been sent by Ceaușescu to try and restore calm in provincial centers, but others were inside the central committee building. As the crowd filled the RCP headquarters, there seems to have been some last-ditch attempts at achieving an orderly transfer of power. When he appeared on the balcony, Dăscălescu is said to have announced he was forming a new government. After he was shouted down, he retreated inside only to appear a little later to publicly tender his resignation.[29] Meanwhile, inside the building, old leaders, new leaders, and unknown revolutionaries were forming fleeting alliances, with the most discussed configuration involving the former prime minister, Ilie Verdeț, another Party official, Vasile Vâlcu, and Colonel-General Vlad.[30] Several sources have

24. *Le Monde*, January 5, 1990, 1, 4; Televiziunea Română (1990), 34–36, 234–35; Ratesh (1991), 45–46; Galloway and Wylie (1991), 148–50; Roman (1994), 112–14.

25. Liviu Viorel Craciun, an early "Minister of the Interior," quoted in Ratesh (1991), 46.

26. Nicolaescu (1999), 174.

27. The BBC journalist John Simpson stumbled across a "cabinet" of a taxi driver, soldier, cinema stunt man, sociologist, paranoiac sculptor, and "hostess" from the Intercontinental Hotel, in the former central committee building several days after the overthrow of Ceaușescu; Simpson (1992), 271–74; see also *Independent*, December 27, 1989, 8.

28. Mazilu (1991).

29. Ştefănescu (1995), 23; Ratesh (1991), 46.

30. After apparently falling out with Ceaușescu, Verdeț had been demoted to the post of a section head within the Central Committee; Maier (September 11, 1986), 13–18. The semantic difference between a "committee" and a "government" has allowed Verdeț to truthfully declare that he made no attempt to be prime minister at this time. Brucan, without

suggested that they tried to form an action committee as a first step to choosing a provisional government.[31] The proposed committee would have included some of the young revolutionaries, but even this was not enough to grant it the legitimacy to succeed. The revolution was in full flow and it soon became clear that any new leader would have to be drawn from outside the ranks of those intimately connected with the old regime.

Ion Iliescu and the Foundation of the National Salvation Front

From mid-morning on December 22, people had been congregating around the tower and studio complex of the television station, which stand in a quiet suburb north of the city center. Initially the protesters had remained outside, but eventually a delegation was allowed into the building to negotiate a resumption of broadcasting so as to spread news of the events in Bucharest to the rest of the country. The accounts of these meetings are extremely uneven, but a general feeling emerges that the management of the television station was evasive and prevaricated for as long as possible, using the excuse of technical problems, perhaps because the director, Constantin Petre, had been away at the central committee building, apparently preparing for Ceaușescu to make another broadcast to the nation. The mood changed with the arrival of the first armored vehicles laden with demonstrators around midday together with the actor Ion Caramitru, dissident poet Mircea Dinescu, and, shortly afterward, the film director Sergiu Nicolaescu.[32] All morning the television had been carrying Ceaușescu's pronouncement of a state of emergency, and now the presence of these three well-known figures, perhaps together with the return of Petre with firsthand knowledge of what was happening in Piața Palatului, seems to have been enough to secure the beginning of live transmission around 1:00 p.m.

The first person to appear on Romanian television following the flight of Ceaușescu was Caramitru, who opened with the words: "Brothers, thanks to God we are in the television studios, we managed to reach here on the back of tanks, with the army and with students and with the people whom you see and with thousands and thousands of Romanians."[33] For

---

ever clarifying the circumstances in which the offer was made, has alleged that Iliescu was prepared to accept Verdeț in this post; see *Expres,* February 9–15, 1993, 6.

31. *România Liberă,* January 5, 1990, 1; *Linia Întîi,* September 1991, 8–9; Mazilu (1991), 55.

32. Dinescu was first approached and informed of developments by the Dutch ambassador Coen Stork; Stork (1993), 70–71. Dinescu's account of his arrival at the television station can be found in *Independent,* January 6, 1990, 15.

33. Televiziunea Română (1990), 21. This book on pages 19–130 contains a transcript of the television broadcast on December 22, 1989. When checked with transcriptions of some of the more important pronouncements made by the BBC, it appears to be accurate. How-

many Romanians these words heralded news of the revolution. After the stultifying tedium of broadcasts during the Ceauşescu years, the appearance of the rather disheveled Caramitru and Dinescu together with the open appeal to God were the clearest possible indications of a transcendent break with the past, and this was immediately reinforced when Dinescu approached the microphone and announced that "the dictator has fled." After the long years of sycophantic adulation, with these four words the cult was overturned and the all powerful *conducător* reduced to a mere fugitive. The sight of this poet and actor, which was paralleled by the early appearance of the poet Ana Blandiana on the radio, instantly gave a sense of real revolution and a color and romance to the proceedings that equaled the projection center stage of Václav Havel in the Czechoslovak "velvet revolution."[34] They gave the Romanian revolution a human face, providing an acceptability both at home and abroad, which perhaps would not have been so forthcoming if the first images presented to the world had been of the old soldiers and former Party officials Militaru, Tudor, Iliescu, and Brucan. In one sense, it might be alleged that Caramitru and Dinescu probably unwittingly, served as a mask to legitimize the incoming Iliescu group, but their melodramatic appearance also undoubtedly raised expectations of real change.

The imagery conjured by Caramitru of a journey to the building on the back of a tank instantly set a mood of excitement and tension, and during the first hour, several short breaks of transmission, which were covered by music or an eerie silence, served to sharpen the sense of drama. This feeling can only have been heightened when the live relay switched to the seething courtyard below, where figures scrambled to utter a few incoherent words into the microphone. Hardly less calm were the crowded broadcasting studios above, where jostling figures and competing voices struggled to announce tidings of the great victory, as Caramitru and Dinescu strove manfully, but not entirely successfully, to bring some order to the proceedings. The prevailing image conveyed to the viewers was one of confusion interlaced with uncertainty and unease. The early appearance of Captain Mihai Lupoi and Generals Voinea and Chiţac meant that the army appeared to be on the side of the revolution, but victory was by no means assured, with strong suspicions remaining over the intentions of the *securitate* and the whereabouts of the Ceauşescus unknown.[35] Faced

---

ever, it is not complete and in places has been reconstructed from a variety of apparently overlapping video recordings—note, particularly, the identical language on pages 69 and 89. There are also differences from the excerpts reproduced in a later book published by Romanian radio, Sârcă (1998). A weakness of both books is that neither give any indication of the exact time at which statements were broadcast (all timings derive from BBC transcripts).

34. Sârcă (1998), 78–79.
35. Televiziunea Română (1990), 25.

with the need to end the sense of uncertainty and to fill the political vacuum, some tentative efforts were made to try and install some order. Dinescu, rather impracticably, asked for the air force to be ready to ferry representatives of every county to the television station to form a provisional government later that day. The pressures that lay behind this and other moves were later revealed by Dinescu, who commented that the army—without being specific as to whom he actually meant by this term—at an early stage in the proceedings had demanded the appearance of "serious politicians" instead of "a few crazy poets and intellectuals."[36] The only figures with such experience were serving or former high officials within the RCP and one of these, in particular, was to prove ready to step forward and fill this role: Ion Iliescu.

The next phase of the revolution, as portrayed by the television, began after one of the breaks in transmission. In place of Dinescu and Caramitru there appeared the broadcasters Teodor Brateş and Petre Popescu, and these two were to hold the floor during the rest of the day's transmission.[37] A stream of speakers then began to appear who, in a confusing mix of the old and new, can broadly be divided into five groups. First, there were representatives of the current military leadership: Generals Voinea, Chiţac, Guşă, and Colonel Marius Oprean as a proxy for Stănculescu; also General Câmpeanu and Colonel Ruşi of the militia. Second, former members of the security forces who had fallen foul of Ceauşescu: Generals Nicolae Militaru, Nicolae Tudor, Nicolae Doicaru, Stelian Ţârca, and First-Rank Captain Emil Dumitrescu. Third, former senior Party members who had also come into conflict with Ceauşescu: Ion Iliescu, Silviu Brucan, and Alexandru Bârlădeanu. Fourth, prominent intellectuals, some of whom had been dissidents: Mircea Dinescu, Ion Caramitru, and Sergiu Nicolaescu. Finally, there was a large number of then unknown civilians, some of whom had been members of the RCP and a few of whom came to prominence later, including Petre Roman, Cazimir Ionescu, Ion Mânzatu, and Gelu Voican Voiculescu.

They were each to use television for their own purposes because, as much as relaying the spectacle to a watching world, television was to play an active role in shaping events. In particular, it was to be another forum through which aspiring leaders of the revolution tried to win popular support. During the afternoon of December 22, several groups used the television to present their political programs to the country. Boris Zingher spoke in the name of the Romanian Democratic Movement, Florin Filipoiu for a group calling itself Social Action, and, most important, Iliescu appeared representing the group which was to take power,

36. Ratesh (1991), 52; Rady (1992), 107, quoting from an interview in *Frankfurter Allgemeine Zeitung*.

37. Brateş's memories of the day can be found in Brateş (1992).

the NSF.[38] In a popular culture long exposed to the politics of personality, television familiarized previously unfamiliar faces, cementing their authority and turning them into icons of the revolution transmitted into every Romanian home. It was no coincidence that opinion polls taken after the revolution recorded the highest levels of public confidence in figures who had appeared on television at this time. Through television the incoming leaders legitimized themselves in the eyes of the people as the new authority in the land, and during the first days of the revolution it was the primary conduit by which the NSF reached its constituency once the RCP had imploded.

Several of the earliest people arriving at the television station had moved quickly to bring Iliescu to the building. Militaru states that he called Iliescu by telephone and Nicolaescu seems to have sent Mihai Bujor Sion to fetch the future president, but it was Dumitrescu who made the call for his former colleague to come to the television center on the air.[39] Iliescu says that he was in his office at work when he saw the momentous events unfolding on television. The *securitate* shadow that had tailed him for a number of years had disappeared, and so with a group of colleagues he set off for his home where he met Bujor Sion, who took him in his own car to the television station. Iliescu seems to have made some efforts to prepare the ground before he arrived. He admits to telephoning ahead both the director, Petre, whom he seems to have known personally, and Stănculescu at the Ministry of Defense to ascertain the situation. Iliescu also telephoned cabinet room "number one" in the central committee building, presumably in an attempt to contact senior members of the Party. It would be interesting to know what message he intended to relay, but at the time it was all passed off as something of a joke, with Iliescu saying that instead of the "number one" person in the room he only found a Comrade Luca, who had never heard of him, to which Bujor Sion presciently added, "He will know you."

Most observers of Iliescu's arrival at the television studio speak of him entering with an immediate sense of authority. Rumors had long been circulating in the West that he was Gorbachev's preferred choice to succeed Ceaușescu, and with some irony, given later polemics, these stories had been disseminated inside Romania by Radio Free Europe and other short-wave radio stations.[40] Iliescu was also known for a daring, if rather opaque, call for reform published in *România Literară* in 1987. This had been widely interpreted as an open claim to be Ceaușescu's heir pre-

38. For Zingher see Televiziunea Română (1990), 36–37; for Filipoiu see ibid., 53–54, and BBC EE/o648, B/7, December 28, 1989.

39. Televiziunea Română (1990), 40.

40. It was first mentioned in a story in *Der Spiegel* in November 1986. Almond (1990a), 489; see also the entry for Iliescu in the pre-revolution, Stroynowski (1989), 2: 466 and Gilberg (1990), 122–23.

Ion Iliescu speaks in front of the cameras at the television station in Bucharest during the afternoon of December 22, 1989. Courtesy Rompres.

sumptive, and according to the historian Dinu Giurescu, after it was published, Iliescu's name was "the only one on people's lips."[41] The result was that when Iliescu strode into the television studios on December 22 there already existed, at least among intellectual circles in Bucharest, something of an expectation that he would be the next leader à la Gorbachev.

Undoubtedly, any expectation that Iliescu would assume power was more than matched by his own hopes, and the lengthy speech he now delivered in stark contrast to the babble that had proceeded him shows obvious signs of a degree of preparation. In a powerful, if at times muddled, piece of rhetoric, peppered with the wooden words of socialism, the incoming leader launched into a searing indictment of Ceaușescu. Unequivocally pinning the blame for the disasters heaped upon Romania on his despotic rule, through constant references to "the people" and "the country" Iliescu presented a message of collective suffering that sharply contrasted the callous disregard of Ceaușescu with his own heartfelt understanding. "The principal culprit is Ceaușescu. . . . This man without heart, without conscience, without brain . . . without reason . . . who did not want to give way, a fanatic who ruled this country with medieval methods and went as far as this dramatic point of opening fire, . . . of ordering

41. Galloway and Wylie (1991), 288.

[troops to] fire against the people of this country. And he had the effrontery to speak in the name of the people! To speak in the name of the defense of sovereignty and national independence! Who! He? He who placed the fate of this country in peril and pushed its people into misery. And as you see, he fled, he shamelessly ran away, when possible he must be brought to reckoning before the people."[42] A few minutes later Iliescu continued in the same vein when he attacked Ceauşescu over the legitimacy of his self-appointment while offering a pointed defense of both the RCP and communism. In bitter tones he denounced those "who appointed themselves leaders, who made themselves chosen by the people, they appointed themselves communist, they had nothing to do neither with socialism nor with ideology . . . [of] scientific communism. . . . They just defiled the name of the Romanian Communist Party, they just defiled the memory of those who gave their lives for the cause of socialism in this country."[43]

The immediate task facing Iliescu and his supporters was the organization of a forum to take control of the situation with a key first objective being the securing of a return of public order. To this end Iliescu called upon all "responsible" people—and here he particularly referred to those who had signed the "Letter of the Six"—to come to the central committee building at 5:00 p.m. to form a Committee of National Salvation. As the appointed hour approached, the square outside the building remained thronged by a noisy crowd. Several vans from Romanian television, each carrying a powerful loudspeaker system, were already present, and now they were joined by some large floodlights whose beams cut the darkening sky. It is possible that by the time Iliescu appeared on the balcony around 5:30, flanked by Guşă, Militaru, Lupoi, Voiculescu, and Roman, among others, shooting may already have broken out in the vicinity, but while he spoke it appears no further gunfire was heard. Iliescu first addressed the security situation by telling the people that the process of change was irreversible and that effectively the *securitate* no longer existed, since it had been incorporated into the ranks of the army. He then announced he was withdrawing to establish the National Salvation Front Council, which he hoped would give the lead for the formation of similar local institutions, because, as he underlined, "The old structures—the Party, the government, and so forth—have actually been eliminated."[44] Appealing for public support for the new provisional authority to be established before elections he closed with the popular news that there were unconfirmed reports that the Ceauşescus had been arrested near Târgovişte.

42. Televiziunea Română (1990), 42.
43. Ibid., 46.
44. Ibid., 84–85.

When he had finished speaking, the microphone was soon handed to Dumitru Mazilu, who now launched into a passionate speech that was noticeably more populist and visionary than the cautious words of Iliescu. Mazilu was a former head of the foreign ministry's legal department who had been stripped of his official post, apparently after drawing up an unexpectedly critical report on Romania for the UN Human Rights Subcommittee toward the end of 1987. In the early hours of December 22 he and his family had been forcibly removed from Bucharest by the *securitate* and taken to the nearby town of Alexandria. Following the flight of Ceauşescu, his guards had brought him back to his home, and after retrieving a political program he had been working on from behind the refrigerator, where it had been thrust by his wife when the *securitate* officers entered the house, he arrived at the central committee building between 5:30 and 6:00.[45] In his speech Mazilu made a concerted appeal to the emotions of the crowd by attacking the odious dictatorship of Ceauşescu and praising the heroism of the martyrs of Timişoara and Bucharest. Directly saluting the serried ranks below him, he then began to enunciate the outline of his political program. Later he claimed to have penned this alone in the days after the demonstrations began in Timişoara, loosely basing it not only on the Magna Carta, Thomas Jefferson's Declaration of Independence, and the French Revolution's Declaration of the Rights of Man and of the Citizen but also what had been written about the changes elsewhere in Eastern Europe.[46] Indeed, the speech does bear many of the hallmarks of the reformist ideas then current in Bucharest and elsewhere in the region, with prominent references to such key concepts as "restructuring," "efficiency," and "competence." Noticeably, though, Mazilu openly rejected the doctrine of Marxism-Leninism when in rousing words, amid constant interruptions from a cheering crowd, he proposed:

> Let us organize free elections at the latest in May, next year. Let us separate legislative, executive, and judicial power in the state. Let all political leaders be chosen for one or at the most two terms. Nobody should be able to claim power for life. Unlimited power clothed in abnormal garb. Two, the restructuring of the whole national economy on the criteria of efficiency. Let us restructure agriculture and let us halt the plan of murdering the villages of our country. Let us respect the peasant! Let us reorganize education, and beginning from today . . . cast aside, Marxism-Leninism, this dogma. . . . Let us eliminate lies . . . falsehoods. . . . Let us establish criteria of competence, responsibility and of devotion to Romania! . . . Press, radio, and television to pass into the hands of the people, and never again to belong to one family or

45. *România Liberă*, January 24, 1990, 3; Mazilu (1991), 46–47; Mazilu (1999), 50–51, 281–82; for Mazilu's early career see Shafir (August 23, 1988b), 23–26.
46. Mazilu (1991), 13; Mazilu (1999), 281.

one clan. . . . Let us respect the rights of all citizens, without distinction of nationality. We are not indifferent to nationality, as the tyrant used to say, we love the minorities, and we want to live quietly and peacefully with all the country's minorities. Don't forget that among them there are martyrs. . . . All foreign policy and external commerce to serve the interests of the people. Beginning from today to put an end to the export of any food so the country will starve no more. . . . Our principal objective to be: THE INDIVIDUAL. THE INDIVIDUAL to be respected. We should be the ones to rejoice at the honor of living in this land. Let us be proud, let us be proud that we are Romanians! . . . Fellow-countrymen, our country has outstanding men, men who in these days knew how to regain their . . . freedom and dignity, with the price of blood.[47]

The speech closed with a call for the formation of citizens' committees throughout the country, including a national citizen's forum in Bucharest, and, at this time, Mazilu does seem to have become involved with the formation of such a group. Discussion with a large crowd in the great hall of the central committee building produced a list of about thirty names, including a number of well-known dissidents. It is unclear whether Mazilu ever saw this as a potential springboard to mount a bid for the leadership, because by the end of the day he had surfaced within the ranks of the Iliescu-led NSF, in which he was eventually appointed to the post of deputy leader. Nevertheless, during the first days of the revolution, Mazilu seems to have maintained a sense of separateness from the main body of the Front, as he positioned himself between the young revolutionaries in the central committee building and the remainder of the new leadership.[48]

While Mazilu was delivering his speech, the meeting to formally inaugurate the NSF had already begun in a small office elsewhere in the central committee building, with the proceedings being recorded for posterity by a videotape.[49] The meeting was attended by a select group, hardly numbering more than a dozen. Among those present were Iliescu, Roman, Guşă, Militaru, Lupoi, Pârcălăbescu, Colonel Ardeleanu, the head of the elite antiterrorist troops USLA, and two secretaries of Ceauşescu, Dumitru Apostoiu and Vasile Nicolcioiu. Later, they were joined by Brucan and Bârlădeanu, but others who tried to attend, includ-

47. Televiziunea Română (1990), 69, 89.
48. Mazilu (1991).
49. Subsequently this videotape reached France and was broadcast on New Year's Day by the French television channel FR3, with a transcript appearing in the newspaper *Libération* on January 2, 1990. Various transcripts appeared in the Romanian press; see, for instance, *România Liberă*, May 10–12, 1990, and a copy can also be found in Pitulescu et al. (1998), 241–48.

ing Gheorghe Apostol, were apparently refused entry, probably because Brucan thought he had collaborated with the *securitate* after the publication of the "Letter of the Six."[50] Although the main item on the agenda was the formation of the NSF and the drawing up of a communiqué to announce its formation, this was surprisingly little discussed. Instead, the meeting soon degenerated into a series of scrappy exchanges, during which Iliescu spent much of the time on the telephone, and the others took the opportunity to catch up on the news of the day, with Roman at one point recounting to Guşă and Militaru how Ceauşescu had escaped to their obvious surprise.

Like his earlier address on the television, the main statement made by Iliescu at this meeting was muddled and showed no clear vision. Indeed, he even seems to have had some doubts as to whether they were gathering to resurrect the old regime or to create a new one—at one point in contradictory fashion, he referred to the restructuring of a new mechanism of power. In contrast to the crowd on the street, Iliescu spoke not of "revolution" but of "change" and "transformation."[51] Beyond the restoring of order and a commitment to ensure the supply of the necessities of life, his vision seems to have held surprisingly few concrete plans. This was significant not only in terms of ideology but also as regards his apparent failure to grasp the need of presenting an uplifting and inspiring program for the future that would win both the support of the crowd outside and galvanize the waiting nation. Some of the others present seem to have realized the shortcomings of such an approach, with Bârlădeanu arguing that any communiqué must mention fulfilling the needs of the people and moving toward democracy. Brucan had also voiced similar sentiments earlier on television, when he had stated that the principal problem facing Romania was the transition from dictatorship to democracy. At the time he had called for committees of "honest men," untainted by the Ceauşescu years, to be organized in every town and for the formation of a provisional government until free elections could be held.[52] Now, however, he added little and Iliescu seems to have been seeking inspiration from elsewhere when he insistently asked of the whereabouts of Mazilu.

To all appearances, the new leaders had been overwhelmed by the sheer pace of events and were floundering in the face of the need to adapt to the dynamics of a mass popular uprising. Only Militaru, in the blunt manner of a soldier, seems to have retained something close to a clarity of purpose. When the question of what relationship any new organization might have with the state was raised, he firmly stated that like the RCP be-

50. Ratesh (1991), 53–55, 163 n. 11. Silviu Brucan interviewed in *Adevărul*, January 16, 1990, 1, 5; Brucan (1993), 162–63. Brucan (1993), 172, has also stated that Vlad was present at the meeting, although this has not been confirmed in other sources.

51. *România Liberă*, May 10–12, 1990.

52. Televiziunea Română (1990), 43–44.

fore it, "The Council of National Salvation is an organ of Party and of state."[53] In this he was supported by Iliescu, who silenced Roman when he spoke in favor of the separation of powers. The first signs were already appearing of the dissension which over the coming months was to solidify into the fault lines of more serious conflict; and this surfaced once again, when Roman's declaration that the new grouping should have a single head, Iliescu, was challenged by Brucan, who spoke in favor of a collective leadership. The most significant part of the discussion, however, was the rather heated debate that followed over the name of the new organization. Iliescu had used the name Committee of National Salvation at the television station, but now an anonymous voice objected that "salvation is not good [because] . . . it belongs to a coup d'état." Iliescu smoothly replied that "democracy is with everybody," but again he was questioned, "What does 'salvation' mean?" and later someone baldly stated, "It creates a state of panic when you say salvation."[54] Roman mentioned that he had spoken under the name of People's Unity Front, but this name was rejected by Brucan. Then other voices entered the fray, arguing that the word "democracy" should appear, before Roman correctly pointed out that Democratic Front was impossible because it had been used in the past. The debate was momentarily silenced by Militaru's statement that it had to be called the National Salvation Front, because that organization "has existed for six months." Then Iliescu, after asking what name was in use in Timișoara and being told by Roman that it was Democratic Socialist Unity Front, began to muse on the words "democratic socialist." However, Roman argued that the word "socialist" was untenable, and the debate closed with Iliescu agreeing that more time was needed to ponder the matter. The meeting ended abruptly about 6:15, when Nicolaescu rushed into the room with the alarming news that they must flee, because the building was mined, prompting the new leadership to disperse, with most returning to the television station, where they established their headquarters on the eleventh floor of the building.

At first sight in its decision to eschew the title "party," the National Salvation Front was following the example of its counterparts elsewhere in Eastern Europe, such as the Civic Forum in Czechoslovakia, the New Forum in East Germany, and the Union of Democratic Forces in Bulgaria. Indeed, not only in Bucharest but elsewhere in Romania during the revolution there appeared a number of organizations that included the word "Front" in their name. As already seen, in Timișoara Fortuna had christened his organization the Romanian Democratic Front and the same name was also used in Arad. In Iași the abortive demonstration of December 14 was called in the name of the Romanian Popular Front, while in

53. Pitulescu et al. (1998), 245.
54. Ratesh (1991), 54–55.

Braşov there briefly appeared a National Renaissance Front and in Alba Iulia a Front of Patriotic Freedom.[55] The reminder of Eastern Europe in 1989 may have abandoned the label "Front," considering it tainted after years of communist contamination, but in Romania, and several of the new states carved out of the former Soviet Union, including Moldova, it was still seen as retaining legitimacy. Perhaps the NSF was influenced in its choice of appellation by its desire to map a consensual political future that minimized confrontational politics. However, with its quasi-messianic overtones the name carried, rather than the promise of a resurgent civic future inherent in the titles of the new citizen bodies of the other East European countries, hints of an exclusivity of purpose, which left little room for bargaining or compromise.[56] Indeed, in terms of name, the closest relative to the NSF in Romanian history was the National Democratic Front, a bogus coalition of parties formed in 1944 through which the communists seized power; after 1989, the appellation was to gain greater infamy, when it was used by a group of Russian military officers, former communists, and extreme nationalists, which was initially banned by President Boris Yeltsin in October 1992.[57]

The program of the NSF was finally presented to the nation at 11:35 in the evening of December 22, when Iliescu once more appeared on the television. In outline it was strikingly similar to the earlier declaration made by Mazilu from the central committee balcony and it must, therefore, be presumed to be largely his work, although a few changes were made by Brucan and later, during a longer session at the television station, by Iliescu.[58] The most significant emendations were the introduction of a passage on the need to observe Romania's commitments to the Warsaw Pact and the replacement of the name National Civic Forum by the National Salvation Front.[59] While still eschewing the word "revolution," the scope of the changes envisaged in the program was far wider than the vague pronouncements made earlier by Iliescu and, it is noticeable, the cause of the past misfortunes was no longer confined to the excesses of Ceauşescu but to the years of "totalitarian tyranny." After paying tribute to the spirit of sacrifice of the young, "who restored to us the sentiment of national dignity with their blood," Iliescu presented to the nation a vision that seemed to imply a steady evolution at best, as he spoke of all functions of the state passing in their entirety to the CNSF and all ministries and central bodies continuing to function for the time being in their current form. In a formulation that notably stressed abstract goals rather than process, Iliescu announced that the aims of the Front were to esta-

55. Pitulescu et al. (1998), 50; Neacşu (c1999).
56. Fischer (1992), 53.
57. Slater (September 24, 1993), 1–6; *Independent*, October 28, 1992, 10.
58. Mazilu (1999), 282–83.
59. Brucan (1993), 173–74.

blish democracy, freedom, and the Romanian people's dignity and, to this end, the new body would encompass "all" the country's "healthy forces" as well as those who "bravely rose to defend freedom and dignity in the years of totalitarian tyranny." Strikingly, the address made virtually no mention of the security situation apart from stating that the Higher Military Council, which was charged with coordinating the activities of the army and Ministry of the Interior forces, would be subordinated to the Council of the National Salvation Front.

There were eleven main features of the program. (1) The leading role of a single party was to be abandoned and a democratic and pluralist system of government established. (2) Free elections were to be organized in April. (3) The legislative, executive, and judicial powers of the state were to be separated, with the election of all political leaders being limited to one or two mandates, at the most. (4) The economy was to be restructured in accordance with the criteria of profitability and efficiency. Administrative-bureaucratic methods of centralized economic management were to be eliminated and free initiative and competence promoted in the management of all economic sectors. (5) Agriculture was to be restructured, with greater assistance given to small-scale peasant production. The destruction of villages was to be halted. (6) Education was to be reorganized in accordance with current requirements, eliminating ideological dogmas. The development of national culture was to be based on a new foundation. The press, radio, and television were to be removed from the hands of a despotic family and placed in the hands of the people. (7) The rights and freedoms of national minorities were to be assured and full equality granted with ethnic Romanians. (8) The country's trade was to be reorganized with the prime aim of satisfying the need of the domestic population. To this end, the export of agricultural foodstuffs was to be halted and that of oil products reduced so as to allow the diversion of resources to meet the energy requirements of the population. (9) Foreign policy was to be based on the principles of good-neighborliness, friendship, and peace, with the integration of Romania into the process of building a united Europe and a common home for all the people of the continent. All Romania's international commitments were to be met, especially those to the Warsaw Treaty. (10) All domestic and foreign policy was to be subordinated to the needs and interests of developing the "individual," ensuring the complete observance of human rights and freedoms, including the right to free movement. (11) By organizing themselves into the Front, the new leaders underlined their commitment to do their utmost to reestablish a civil society in Romania and to guarantee the triumph of democracy, freedom, and dignity for all citizens of the country.[60]

60. BBC EE/0648, B/8, December 28, 1989.

After the proclamation of the manifesto Iliescu read out the composition of the new Council of the National Salvation Front.[61] The first names heard were those of a number of prominent dissidents, including Doina Cornea, Ana Blandiana, Dan Deşliu, Mircea Dinescu, and László Tőkés. Several of these had not been contacted by the Front at this stage and, although Iliescu declared that these well-known figures were included because they had demonstrated a spirit of sacrifice during the years of tyranny, later accusations were to be leveled that they were only added as window dressing to cover the real leadership of the regime which lurked below.[62] Here, alongside a group of serving military officers who had openly sided with the revolution, at the core of the new regime there was a group of former RCP members who had fallen foul of Ceauşescu, including Iliescu, Brucan, Bârlădeanu, and Marţian. By the evening of December 22 the boundaries of the new leadership had been largely set. Over the next months, names were to be added and subtracted, but many of the men who were to rule Romania for the coming years were already installed in office. Within the space of less than twelve hours the political succession had been decided but the new leaders still had to bring under control the forces unleashed by the revolution, and this was to prove a more difficult and protracted task than they had expected.

The Descent into Anarchy

After the collapse of the old regime in the morning of December 22, with the notable exception of Sibiu, the post-Ceauşescu era in Romania began in relative peace. The exertions of the military leadership were largely successful and in most cities their units started to withdraw to barracks. However, the departure of the military from the scene left a critical power vacuum, because, as the afternoon of December 22 wore on, it became clear that the revolution had unleashed passions and forces beyond the expectations of the new leaders. Charged with adrenaline and freed from traditional constraints, after years of numbing tedium, ordinary Romanians began to play an active role in the unfolding events. Each was

61. The composition of the first CNSF in order of announcement: Doina Cornea, Ana Blandiana, Mircea Dinescu, László Tőkés, Dumitru Mazilu, Dan Deşliu, Gen. Ştefan Guşă, Gen. Victor Stănculescu, Aurel Dragoş Munteanu, Corneliu Mănescu, Alexandru Bârlădeanu, Silviu Brucan, Petre Roman, Ion Caramitru, Sergiu Nicolaescu, Mihai Montanu, Mihai Ispas, Gelu Voican Voiculescu, Dan Marţian, Capt. Mihai Lupoi, Gen. Gheorghe Voinea, Capt. Emil Dumitrescu, Vasile Neacşa, Cristina Ciontu, Marian Baciu, Bogdan Teodoriu, Eugenia Iorga, Paul Negroţiu, Gheorghe Manole, Cazimir Ionescu, Adrian Sârbu, Constantin Cârgan, Géza Domokős, Magdalena Ionescu, Marian Mierlă, Constantin Ivanovici, Ovidiu Vlad, Valeriu Bucurescu, and Ion Iliescu. *Monitorul Oficial al României,* 1:1, December 22, 1989, 2.

62. It has been suggested that, like the main program of the Front, this list of names was also the product of a fusion of one drawn up earlier that afternoon; for Mazilu's Citizen's Forum with those of the Iliescu centered NSF, see Neacşu (c. 1999).

driven by different needs. For many, motivation probably lay no deeper than pure curiosity or a desire to participate in such historic events. There was also a sense in which the nation, both collectively and as individuals, sought to expunge past humiliations through revolutionary glory—as Iliescu termed it, "the restoration of national dignity." For a significant minority, however, less edifying motives were paramount. Some looked to cover past misdeeds by establishing themselves as part of the new political process, while many others simply took advantage of the chaos to extract material recompense for years of humiliation and poverty. The most obvious way of showing commitment to the revolution was joining the huge mass on the streets. Many participated spontaneously, but others were encouraged by the voices on the radio and television that broadcast constant appeals throughout December 22 for the inhabitants of the capital to form a "living wall" safeguarding the nerve centers of the revolution.[63] The defenders of the revolution came not just from Bucharest itself but from throughout the country, with the radio interviewing youngsters who had arrived from as far afield as Bihor, Galați, and Râmnicu Vâlcea.[64] Arriving at the main railway station, the Gara de Nord, they chose their own leaders and were grouped according to their counties of origin, before being bused to the fighting.

From the outset some among the crowd on the street felt the need to take more direct action in support of the revolution. Within hours of Ceaușescu's departure and, it seems, before the renewal of shooting, a barricade had been thrown across Calea Dorobanților, north of the city center. Following appeals on the radio and television that called on truck drivers to block roads with their vehicles, including concrete mixers, by early evening there were reported to be between six and eight such obstacles spanning the road between the city center and the television station.[65] As the revolution progressed and the terrorist threat heightened, the number of these barricades grew rapidly, spreading from Bucharest to encompass towns across the country. Checking and checking again, they only served to magnify the climate of suspicion on which they were founded. Cars could be searched three or four times in the space of two hundred meters and the whole exercise often held an air of total unreality, as a journalist from *The Times* found in a town outside Bucharest: "In Slatina, as in many other towns, a faintly surreal situation is emerging out of the initial chaos. Young, self-appointed guardians of the revolution, handwritten 'badges' pinned to the lapel, tear around checking the papers of people they have known all their life and diligently search the shopping bag of a former teacher. They work alongside but not exactly

63. Sârcă (1998), 228–29.
64. Ibid., 107.
65. Ibid., 81–82, 91; Televiziunea Română (1990), 134, 153, 173.

under the orders of a handful of conscripts—perhaps a year older than them—who sometimes find them a source of irritation."[66] The roadblocks gave those who had been powerless for so long a sense of power. More inimically, they also set the stage for numerous tragedies, as cases of mistaken identity, failures to obey orders to halt, and countless breakdowns of communication between the different defenders of the revolution led to scores of cars being riddled with bullets and many dead throughout the country.[67]

The breakdown of order also posed more base temptations, because, like all revolutions, alongside its undoubted heroism and bravery, the Romanian revolution also had its darker side, with vandalism and looting never far from the surface. Frequently blamed on Gypsies, most of these incidents went unreported, although the scale of the lawbreaking is evident from the constant appeals to desist broadcast on the radio and television.[68] In the afternoon of December 22 Ceauşescu's residence in the north of Bucharest was entered and plundered, and during his first appearance on the television Iliescu made a direct reference to the destruction of shops.[69] The next day, when Guşă spoke on television, he also specifically called on the population to "act against those who are trying to destabilize us and who break into shops."[70] Most alarming for the new leadership was the news that crowds were also breaking into government offices, seizing files, and burning documents and, as late as December 27, a Western correspondent could still write: "Such is the state of anarchy in the capital that looters are still able to break into the now abandoned government buildings despite the presence of the army only yards away."[71]

Alongside attacks on state property, the revolution also saw a number of vicious assaults on personnel connected with the old regime, with an appeal broadcast by the new regime on December 24 asking "individuals or groups of individuals, who have made use of weapons for absurd revenge" to stop, because "these excesses have assumed alarming proportions."[72] Many of these pleas, including those broadcast on the radio on December 28 and January 8, 1990, were specifically prompted by vigilante actions against *securitate* and militia officers, and, as the revolution pro-

---

66. *The Times*, December 30, 1989, 10. For similar reports see *Daily Telegraph*, December 27, 1989, 3; *The Times*, December 26, 1989, 6; *Independent*, December 27, 1989, 1.

67. See the countless examples in Codrescu et al. (1998); also *Washington Post*, December 27, 1989.

68. See, for instance, Sârcă (1998), 92–93, 180, 184, 189, 222.

69. Televiziunea Română (1990), 46; *România Liberă*, May 10–12, 1990; Scurtu et al. (1990), 47.

70. BBC EE/0648, B/10, December 28, 1989. Sârcă (1998), 197–98.

71. *Independent*, December 27, 1989, 1.

72. BBC EE/0649, B/3, December 29, 1989; see also the communiqué of the CNSF read by Măgureanu on the same day, BBC EE/0648, B/13, December 28, 1989.

gressed, an increasing number of Western journalists, one of whom narrowly escaped being lynched himself, began to file stories in which they reported such attacks.[73] One saw a man shot through the head with his own revolver, while others report seeing suspects dragged from their cars and beaten to death. In another incident, a journalist describes how he saw a member of the *securitate* denounced by an angry crowd. Ignoring his pleas of innocence, they chanted for his death and he was summarily executed by two shots to the head.[74] Even after the end of the fighting reports continued of local *securitate* chiefs being beaten and killed outside Bucharest and, as late as January 6, Mazilu still felt compelled to make a front-page appeal in *România Liberă* for an end to vendettas and anonymous denunciations.[75] The notion that some suspected terrorists and former members of the *securitate* may have fallen victim to mob violence during the revolution remains highly controversial and the details of such instances, perhaps understandably, are difficult to corroborate. Aside from the stories mentioned above, hints that a suspected terrorist may have been lynched in Brăila by an angry crowd appeared in a trial in 1993, although again it is difficult to disentangle the facts surrounding the case.[76]

In considering the progress of the revolution after the fall of Ceaușescu, the chaos and disorder that is reflected time and again in eyewitness accounts cannot be stressed too strongly. The violence that shook Romania during these days can only be understood if it is firmly placed within the context of the prevailing heady atmosphere of elation, tinged with fear, suspicion, and rumor, and a total breakdown of political and social control, which saw the effective erosion of all constraints on behavior. In this atmosphere of anarchy, the first task of the new leadership was the reestablishment of public order. Following the flight of Ceaușescu, the general order issued by Ilie Ceaușescu earlier in the morning from the Ministry of Defense calling on units to take all steps necessary to apply

73. For such stories see *Independent*, December 27, 1989, 21; *The Times*, December 26, 1989, 1; *Guardian*, January 12, 1990, 23. The radio broadcast calls to eschew revenge attacks on December 28, 1989 and another appeal was made as late as January 8, 1990; see BBC EE/0650, B/11, December 30, 1989; and BBC EE/0658, B/11, January 10, 1990. For continuing reports of revenge attacks see *The Times*, January 10, 1989, 6.

74. *Sunday Telegraph*, December 24, 1989, 1; *Independent*, December 29, 1989, 8; reported that a dozen *securitate* officers "worse than monsters" had been lynched in Sibiu. Simpson (1992), 260–61; also gives an eyewitness account of the unlawful killing of a suspected terrorist when it was discovered that he held *securitate* documents. *The Times*, December 26, 1989, 6, carries a report from a local Romanian journalist of a village idiot casually shot in cold blood. The most high profile victim of a revenge attack was Nicu Ceaușescu, who was stabbed when he was brought to the television station on December 22; see Nicolaescu (1999), 210.

75. *New York Times*, January 2, 1990, A12; *România Liberă*, January 6, 1990, 1.

76. *Adevărul*, November 19, 1993, 2.

the state of emergency and to only obey orders issued by the supreme commander, his brother Nicolae, had been canceled and replaced by a new one instructing all units to return to barracks as quickly as possible and to arrange for the protection of military premises. This was then, in turn, superseded a little later by a new general order from Stănculescu, which called upon commanders to arrange for the protection of key strategic objectives after liaising with local authorities, but not to open fire unless they were fired upon—an instruction that, by its very nature, presupposes that this could happen.[77] In response, as the afternoon of December 22 progressed, army units once more left their barracks. By the time darkness began to fall, between 5 and 6 o'clock, they were in position at the radio and television stations and other key locations in Bucharest, including the central committee building, the national bank, and the airports of Otopeni and Băneasa.

In their quest to restore order the new leadership was to be severely hampered by the deficiencies of the military forces under their command. The army possessed neither the equipment nor the training for such a task, and was anyhow unwilling to undertake any action that would jeopardize its newly won position as the guardian of the people, effectively precluding any possibility of it acting on behalf of the authorities against the people. The forces of the *securitate* were rapidly placed under army control, while the militia, long held in popular contempt and the butt of countless jokes about their stupidity, were put in the impossible situation of being commanded to keep order in a situation in which, if they took any decisive action, they ran the risk of being branded counterrevolutionaries. More than a few militia officers seem to have felt the vengeance of the crowd, as following the flight of Ceaușescu, militia stations were occupied in scores of towns and villages. Sometimes the buildings were seized out of revolutionary enthusiasm, sometimes in a search for vengeance, as in the cases from the Banat and Transylvania already mentioned, and sometimes it seems purely out of a desire to free from the cells those held on criminal charges, as allegedly happened in Târgoviște.[78] Tainted by their association with the previous regime, all the branches of the security forces for a variety of differing reasons were unable to act effectively to restore order, but now, as night fell on December 22, they found a new purpose, because out of the chaos there appeared an enemy for them to fight.

---

77. Codrescu et al. (1998), 156–57. There was also room for confusion in the fact that the complexities of the command system meant that orders were received in different units at different times. Ilie Ceaușescu's order was received in Brăila at 12:15 p.m. but not in Brașov until 2:30, while Stănculescu's arrived in Brăila at 2:00 but in Buzău only at 5:45. See Nicolaescu (1999) for all times.

78. Nicolaescu (1999), 440.

An Enemy Emerges

On the streets of Bucharest, following the flight of Ceauşescu, the feeling of triumph was buoyed by the very density of the crowd, but, within its ebbs and flows, there lurked abiding fears, for the huge mass was also fickle in mood, as it was swept by rumors. The extent of the victory was not yet clear. Ceauşescu had fled, but to where? Could he be overthrown so easily? How could such a mighty regime, which had kept the whole nation shackled in misery for so long, not possess a powerful backlash? What had happened to the feared *securitate?* In the wild mélange that was Bucharest, suspicions were easily stirred not only among the crowd, but also in the minds of some of the military leaders who had come to the side of the revolution. General Chiţac, in one of the earliest broadcasts on television, warned the retreating military units to be vigilant and to be prepared to give a decisive riposte in case any should challenge the new democratic socialist political orientation of the country.[79] This and other announcements broadcast on radio and television merely exacerbated the growing nervousness. A ham-fisted attempt to forestall the spread of rumors only ended with the totally counterproductive warning that tall stories would be manipulated by the *securitate,* and soon the tale, already familiar from Timişoara, arose that it was really *securitate* officers dressed in civilian clothes who were staging the looting of shops as agents provocateurs. As the afternoon of December 22 progressed, the news became wilder and wilder. The *securitate* was said to have blown up a blood bank in Bucharest to hinder the treatment of those wounded in the fighting the night before and to have poisoned the water in Timişoara and Sibiu and possibly even Bucharest itself.[80] More immediately threatening, a hostile armored column was said to be heading toward a nuclear plant and oil refineries in Piteşti as well as a nearby dam, while Bucharest was told to be on full alert to repulse a countercoup about to be launched by the head of the militia, General Nuţă.[81] The culmination of these stories came at 4:10, when Brateş made the dramatic announcement that a column of terror-

---

79. Televiziunea Română (1990), 35.

80. Ibid., 51. Assurances that the water of Bucharest was safe were issued within twenty-four hours but such was the fear that these had to be constantly repeated for the next few days.

81. Ibid., 58, 61. In fact, Nuţă and his deputy Velicu had not flown back from Timişoara with Guşă but had boarded a later TAROM flight. Among their fellow passengers were Lorin Fortuna and other revolutionaries from Timişoara. In Arad the plane was grounded because of bad weather and the passengers placed for the night in local hotels. The next morning, when it became clear that the plane would still not be able to fly, Nuţă and Velicu took a train for Bucharest. Stopped in Simeria, they were taken by a minibus to Deva. Here they were collected by a helicopter, which was to take them to Sibiu, but this crashed outside Alba Iulia during the evening of December 23, 1989, killing all those onboard. Some shots seem to have been fired at this time by a guard at a local reservoir and possibly also by members of

ists, which confusingly were in fact antiterrorist troops, by which he meant USLA, were heading toward the television station. A few minutes later the news was hysterically repeated by a revolutionary, identified in the pages of *Revoluția Română în direct* as Costin Țugui, who desperately cried for the population to come to their rescue: "Help us, help us, defend us army, defend us someone!"[82] The danger was imaginary, the USLA troops never arrived, and it may be that jittery nerves mistook the army detachments, coming to guard the television station, as hostile forces.[83] Whatever the case, taut nerves had been tightened further, and when immediately after this statement the screen went blank for the better part of an hour, apparently due to the overheating of some equipment, the tension reached an almost unbearable level. The television and radio stations had both fed on and in turn fed popular prejudices, and, caught center stage in the excitement and drama of the events, they came to reflect the fears and suspicions of the country as a whole. With the radio freely giving out telephone numbers throughout the day, all manner of rumors and stories had been broadcast just as they were received, without the slightest attempt at verification. But the medium transformed the message, because the television and radio, like the army, had now become the television and radio of the people, as they were magically transformed from gray mouthpieces of the Ceaușescu era to bearers of the news of his downfall. In the process they were freed from their legacy of lies and became a repository of the revolutionary truth, given the power to transform fiction into fact.[84] The popular expectation was that there would be an enemy and now, as darkness fell, that foe was to emerge.

When the television station returned to the air, it soon passed to a live transmission from Piața Palatului, presumably so as to be able to catch the moment when Iliescu made his address from the balcony. The crowd, already restless from news of the fighting in Sibiu and the impending attacks on the television and radio stations, were further alarmed by warnings to be watchful as among them there were "enemies . . . who smuggle arms . . . who fire."[85] The exact time of the first shots is unknown, but reports of isolated gunfire appeared during the broadcast from the central committee building beginning around 5:00 p.m. Gradually the shooting became heavier and more pronounced with television beginning to show images of bullet holes in windows. The source of these shots remains un-

---

a military unit in the vicinity but the actual cause of the crash remains unclear; see Nicolaescu (1999), 231–57; Codrescu et al. (1998), 371–73.

82. Televiziunea Română (1990), 64–65; BBC EE/0647, i, December 23, 1989. A similar announcement was made on the radio Sârcă (1998), 187.

83. There is some indication of this in Televiziunea Română (1990), 144, 146.

84. An early opinion poll recorded an 89 percent approval rating for the television service, higher than for the NSF.

85. Televiziunea Română (1990), 82.

known. Perhaps with guns already falling into the hands of the demonstrators they were merely the product of revolutionary enthusiasm, or possibly they were fired in an attempt to control the crowd and dissuade looters. Those on the balcony of the central committee building, while making constant calls for the crowd to keep calm, tried to explain them away as blanks designed to scare or as attempts by soldiers loyal to the revolution to blow open the locks on steel doors for which they lacked the keys. In one instance it was even stated that a sudden shot was the result of a captured rifle still loaded falling to the ground by accident. However, as night fell and the firing began to commence in earnest, an announcement that "bandits" had been captured in the basement of the central committee building suggested that the opponents of the new regime were beginning to take on a more tangible form.

Most of the shooting seems initially to have focused on the former royal palace, which lay on the other side of Piaţa Palatului from the central committee building. The northern wing of the palace housed the national art gallery and, sometime during the afternoon, members of the crowd seem to have entered the complex, because after announcing "irresponsible groups had forced the doors" at about 5 o'clock, the radio broadcast an appeal calling upon citizens to defend the works of art and "not to let terrorist groups enter the building."[86] The fear may have been of looters but, as darkness fell, sections of the crowd outside seem to have become convinced that forces hostile to the revolution had occupied the building and, despite desperate appeals from the balcony for those with guns to stop firing, the shooting continued and even grew in intensity. The live television broadcast relayed both the drama but also the absurdity of the situation, as the revolution was publicly fought out before watching crowds to the exhortations of the loudspeakers. At one point, a crazy duet broke out with one loudspeaker appealing for a cease-fire, while another hysterically pointed out the locations from which the terrorists were firing.[87] As midnight approached, Ion Caramitru reappeared and tried vainly to reestablish order by making constant appeals to those in the square to stop firing and for all civilians with arms to come and deposit them safely at the central committee building. But his pleas only seem to have fallen on deaf ears and, as the firing continued and waves of panic passed through the crowd, speakers on the balcony above—feeling as exposed as their compatriots had in Timişoara earlier—implored them not to leave the scene. Many seem to have responded and stayed, as foreign journalists paint a vivid picture of knots of people standing and refusing to run for cover, as they watched tracer bullets criss-cross the night sky. Cheering and applauding, they encouraged the soldiers as they directed

86. Sârcă (1998), 82.
87. Televiziunea Română (1990), 126.

heavy machine-gún fire onto the windows where the enemy was perceived to lie.[88] As the fighting intensified, tanks once more rolled into the center of Bucharest and Piaţa Univérsităţii again echoed to the roar of gunfire, with the shooting not abating until the dawn of the next day.[89]

As the evening progressed, the news relayed via television became more and more alarming and the situation at the radio station was reported as being particularly critical, with frantic appeals being broadcast for crowds to gather for its defense.[90] A host of other targets were also announced as being under attack, including the Ministry of Defense and the Dorobanţi and Rahova telephone exchanges. However, almost as soon as the news was broadcast retractions and corrections started to appear. The nest of terrorists in the basement of Casa Scânteia was actually a civil defense command post, and the Dorobanţi telephone exchange was not under threat.[91] The false alarms only sowed deeper the seeds of confusion, increasing the sense of confrontation as the rumors became wilder and wilder. Soon it seemed all Bucharest was criss-crossed by a multi-layered network of secret bunkers and tunnels through which the terrorists passed with ease, as they moved from target to target. This underground labyrinth was held to have enormous dimensions, with tunnels reportedly everywhere. They linked the central committee with other important buildings in the center, the Cotroceni Palace with the Sala Palatului and the Casa Republicii, which was also connected to the Izvor metro station. They were at the IMGB works. The list was endless.[92] Appeals were made for anybody who knew the exact layout of the underground labyrinth to come forward, while vigilant citizens were called upon to block entrances and exits.[93] Yet the tunnels proved to be almost as elusive as the gunmen who were said to use them. There was a series of bunkers under the central committee building, and Ceauşescu does seem to have drawn up elaborate plans for escape that were partly based on tunnels, and rumors of these had even reached the West before the revolution.[94] However, the juncture at which a tunnel becomes a sewer, or vice versa, remains a moot point, and all the stories of underground tunnels really only served to hide the hidden terrorists even further. The Romanian American poet and journalist Andrei Codrescu was to perceptively ob-

88. *Washington Post,* December 23, 1989, A1, A15.

89. For some of the first foreign news reports see *Independent,* December 23, 1989, 1; ibid., December 27, 1989, 21; *Washington Post,* December 23, 1989, A1, A15; *The Times,* December 23, 1989, 1.

90. BBC EE/0648, B/8, December 28, 1989. For the situation at the radio station see *România Liberă,* January 7, 1994, 7; Sârcă (1998), 81, 85, 92, 95–98, 101, 194–95.

91. Sârcă (1998), 234.

92. Ibid., 206.

93. For examples of newspaper coverage emphasizing the extent of the tunnel network, see *Washington Post,* December 25, 1989, 38; *The Times,* December 26, 1989, 7.

94. *Sunday Times,* November 19, 1989, A19; for Ceauşescu's plans see *Evenimentul Zilei,* July 10, 1993, 3.

serve: "The underground labyrinth below our feet was a fit image for the nightmare the dictator had built for his people on earth. We stood on top of it, but inside our heads we were still looking for ways out."[95] Still, the truest appreciation of the tunnel stories, perhaps, came from a poet interviewed by Codrescu. In reply to his assertion that he could think of nothing comparable to these tunnels in the modern world, the poet merely added: "I can . . . the Romanian mind after forty-five years of dictatorship."[96]

Then, the television center itself came under attack. The first isolated bullets seem to have been fired around 9:00 that evening, but the size of the complex together with the constant coming and going means that the various accounts tend to give differing times. The battle that followed was long and bloody, claiming at least sixty-two lives, the vast majority of whom were civilians. For the best part of three days the area resounded with gunfire, but during this time the fighting was never continuous, being essentially sporadic in nature, reaching several crescendos, and then subsiding into a fitful warfare of occasional isolated shots. The television station lies in one of the most exclusive areas of Bucharest; richly verdant, it was a favored location for the houses of the *nomenklatura*. Since they were the homes of the Ceauşescu elite, many of these villas were easily invested with a malign aura, often, it seems, transformed into terrorist havens purely by virtue of the identity of their owners. The residence of Valentin Ceauşescu, for instance, was reported to be the source of much shooting. Consequently, these houses drew heavy fire from the tanks and other weapons defending the television center, leaving many of them destroyed or heavily damaged, while the television center itself emerged relatively unscathed.

The Defenders of the Revolution

Deployed against this enemy were a varied collection of forces that at their heart had the army. From the demonstrations in Timişoara the slogan "The army is with us" had been on the lips of the protesters and now, following the overthrow of Ceauşescu, it at last took on a ring of reality. General Voinea from the balcony of the central committee building had declared the army was on the side of the revolution and then together with Captain Lupoi and a host of other senior army figures he had repeated this message on the television. The theme was relentlessly hammered home throughout the day, so that by the time Guşă spoke alongside Iliescu on the central committee building balcony and declared to the crowd that "the army will always be with *us* and with you," it was clear

95. Codrescu (1991), 20–21.
96. Ibid.

that the army had become the bastion of the revolution and its commanders an important force in the new leadership.[97]

As they arrived to take up their new defensive positions, the soldiers were totally unprepared for the situation that confronted them. Many of the defenders of the television station had only received two months of training or, in the case of the paratroopers, had never jumped from an aircraft.[98] Together with their heavy armor, which was better suited to the open battlefield than guerrilla street warfare, these young conscripts, many of whom had never trained under fire, were deployed in a densely populated urban environment to meet a vague and intangible threat. Around them thronged crowds of enthusiastic civilian revolutionaries, happily regaling them with all the gossip and rumor from the streets. Many barracks had been placed under a virtual news blackout since the beginning of the demonstrations in Timişoara, but now the young conscripts were exposed to frightening stories of imminent attack by elite units of the *securitate* armed with sophisticated guerrilla warfare equipment or by unspecified foreign forces using helicopters or seaborne raiding craft.[99]

In such an atmosphere, distinguishing between friend and foe became increasingly difficult, and pictures that were later captioned as showing surrendering terrorists in fact depict frightened volunteers raising their hands in the air so as to gain entry into the television center. Many people, including foreign journalists, still recall the dangers involved in having to run the gauntlet of trigger-happy troops in order to reach the building, and invariably accidents did occur.[100] One eyewitness recounts how one night a tank officer noticed suspected terrorists hiding in front of a tank positioned in the courtyard at the television station. He ordered them to surrender and they emerged with their hands raised, but hardly had they walked ten meters before they were cut down in a hail of machine-gun fire that also caught three or four civilians taking shelter by the perimeter wall. Although it is not stated, by inference one may conclude that the machine gun was fired by the defenders of the television station.[101]

Moreover, some units like U.M.01210, which only the day before had been involved in the thick of the fighting at Piaţa Universităţii, now found themselves defending the very people with whom they had previously been locked in bloody confrontation. This abrupt about-face required

97. BBC EE/0648, B/7, December 28, 1989; Televiziunea Română (1990), 84 (emphasis added).

98. Televiziunea Română (1990), 306.

99. Codrescu et al. (1998), 166–70, 192–99.

100. Simpson (1992), 264–65.

101. Televiziunea Română (1990), 157. It may also be another description of this incident that can be found in ibid., 142.

justification and may have fueled their enthusiasm to meet the terrorist threat. In Piaţa Palatului the BBC journalist, John Simpson, found himself remonstrating with a tank commander whose only motive for firing at the cupola of the university library seemed to be because he found it a "tempting target." Simpson concluded that:

> The soldiers were hot and nervous, with no clear orders about what they should be doing. The Army, weak and poorly trained, was anxious to demonstrate the extent of its new allegiance to the people. And so it used its overwhelming strength to hammer away at the grand buildings in the centre of the city, regardless of the damage it was doing. The noise and the damage were an end in themselves, the outward and visible sign of an inward and guilty desire to make up for its failure to side with the popular cause earlier. The Army was demonstrating its fitness to carry on serving the people. A few buildings destroyed were less important than the construction of a new public trust in its loyalty.[102]

As the soldiers of the army moved to defend strategic points in Bucharest and elsewhere, they were joined by contingents from other branches of the security forces, including members of the militia, *securitate*, USLA, patriotic guard, and even the navy. It was a true recipe for chaos and it was to breed bloody mayhem, as communication between the different branches of the security forces broke down, leaving various units firing at each other. The official army record of the revolution details many such incidents. In Brăila a platoon of soldiers, taking up positions in the vicinity of some garrison buildings, were mistaken as terrorists in disguise. According to one source this was because a number of the conscripts were speaking a foreign language—Hungarian. A military unit already deployed in the area opened fire, leaving five soldiers and a civilian waiting at a bus stop dead as well as five others wounded. In Arad a soldier, who was riding in an ambulance, was mistaken for a terrorist when he returned fire at some unspecified targets. Troops guarding the road upon which the ambulance was traveling opened fire, leaving it overturned in a ditch with one dead and two wounded. In Buzău an army officer, a fireman, and a revolutionary were taking suspects to the local army garrison when a detachment of militia, mistaking them for terrorists, opened fire on their car, killing the officer and fireman and wounding three more.[103]

Cases of mistaken identity did not only involve land forces. Fighter planes, including MiG-23s, and helicopters were also mobilized during the revolution. A squadron of twelve helicopters in Sibiu flew forty-seven sorties over December 22–23. Rumors of impending aerial attack were

---

102. Simpson (1992), 262.
103. Details in Codrescu et al. (1998), 317, 340, 306, respectively. For the incident in Brăila see also Alexandru (1988), 77–79.

commonplace, and in several cities the first shooting during the revolution was by antiaircraft guns firing at targets located by radar. Again, misunderstandings often occurred. A number of incidents were recorded of helicopters firing at troops on the ground and vice-versa, leaving yet more dead and injured. Most of these accidents were due to poor communications, but carelessness also at times seems to have played a role. In Caransebeş two officers literally wandered into a minefield, while in Haţeg a soldier was wounded by the splinters of his own grenade.[104] Elsewhere, sheer exhaustion took its toll after days and nights without sleep. In Buzău an officer of the patriotic guard opened fire with a machine pistol, killing four civilians and wounding one other. In the opinion of the army judicial service he miscalculated due to tiredness, fear, and uncertainty, and yet at the time his actions seem not to have been questioned, because eight hours later he wounded two more civilians.[105]

At the forefront of the confusion seems to have been the many patriotic guard units that were mobilized to protect strategic points throughout the country. Fourteen separate units, totaling over 300 men, arrived to defend the television station alone.[106] Few of these units, however, were acting under orders; the rest all came on their own initiative, spurred on by emotive appeals from the television and radio asking for their mobilization.[107] Many of the guardsmen arrived in civilian dress, without informing the central command at the television center or the local patriotic guard command that they were coming, and once in place each unit seems to have often acted as it saw fit, sometimes even carrying out searches without informing other defenders. Indeed, on the morning of December 23 a specific call was broadcast for better coordination between army and patriotic guard units.[108] Again many tragic accidents seem to have occurred. Three civilians, recorded by the army as "pretending to be from a patriotic guard unit," slipped into the compound of the television station behind a tank and opened fire, killing five paratroopers and seriously wounding three more.[109] Members of another patriotic guard unit, led, according to one witness, by a man who was drunk, started to shoot from the upper story of a first aid post, attracting fire from soldiers guarding the television station next door. It is not known if there were any casualties from this incident, but the members of the patriotic guard unit denied responsibility.[110] This is not to suggest that any

104. Codrescu et al., 354, 375.
105. Ibid., 305.
106. Nicolaescu (1999), 192–93.
107. An account of the actions of one patriotic guard unit at the television station can be found in Televiziunea Română (1990), 169–70. For examples of appeals for the patriotic guard to mobilize see Sârcă (1998), 82–83, 85, 92–93.
108. Neacşu (c1999).
109. Televiziunea Română (1990), 142, 305; Codrescu et al. (1998), 233.

of the many patriotic guard units, which were mobilized across Romania during these days, actively took up a position against the revolution, because there is no serious evidence to support such a view. However, it can be suggested that the enthusiasm of these units, as they rushed to support the revolution, was often tragically misplaced, since their presence in the firing line frequently seems only to have induced further confusion. In consequence, many of those arrested during the revolution as suspected terrorists do seem to have been members of the patriotic guard.[111]

However, most of those who descended onto the streets to defend the revolution were eager civilians responding to the desperate pleas heard on television and radio. Some were formed into ad hoc patriotic guard units, such as those established at the Gara de Nord and the radio station, where they were positioned on the roof and came under sustained fire, but most continued to operate independently.[112] Many of these civilians were "armed" with nothing more than stones or Molotov cocktails, but a surprisingly large number were given guns and effectively became armed irregulars. In Brașov over 600 weapons were distributed in this way.[113] Sometimes it seems only an identity card or service papers had to be shown to receive a gun. In Bucharest at the central committee building Gabriel Matei, who was there when the shooting began—he says around 4:30 p.m.—states that the young men present then demanded arms and were given them, and the same also seems to have occurred at the television station and the Gara de Nord.[114] For these armed civilians there were no formal structures of command, and frequently the only mark of distinction that proclaimed they were loyal to the revolution was a makeshift armband. Many were very young. In some places it has been estimated that 50 percent of the weapons were taken by adolescents, with one more mature revolutionary recording how he personally disarmed three youths whom he considered to be not much more than fourteen years old.[115] Often the guns came from patriotic guard armories located in party buildings or factories. In Brașov some came from a room under the main stairs leading to the prefect's office.[116] Others came from armories of the *securitate* and the militia seized by the crowd, while elsewhere civilians just grabbed old hunting rifles from home or took guns from dead or wounded soldiers.[117] There is a close correlation between the distribution of weapons and killing in the revolution. Where weapons were given to

---

110. Televiziunea Română (1990), 143.
111. Dolghin, Lăcustă, Matei, Ștefan, and Ursu (1990), 5.
112. Ursu, Dolghin, and Lăcustă (1990), 4.
113. Nicolaescu (1999), 380.
114. *România Liberă,* January 6, 1990, 3; Ursu, Dolghin, and Lăcustă (1990), 6.
115. Nicolaescu (1999), 377.
116. Ibid., 379.
117. *România Liberă,* July 25, 1990, 1, 3; *Independent,* December 27, 1989, 8.

Civilians join soldiers firing from behind an armored vehicle in Bucharest on December 23, 1989, after the flight of Ceaușescu from the city. © David Turnley/CORBIS

civilians the death toll was higher, and in hindsight it has been recognized that handing out guns so freely was a major mistake. Even at the time the new leaders were aware of the problem. There were constant pleas on the radio and television for guns to be handled carefully, and both during and after the fighting concerted efforts were made to recover firearms.[118] Finally, a deadline of December 25 was set by which they had to be handed in, otherwise those who continued to hold weapons faced the risk of being "punished most severely."[119]

The situation in Bucharest was a recipe for chaos, and a former chairman of the senatorial commission of inquiry, Valentin Gabrielescu, has graphically described the scene: "As well as the army and the police, thousands of civilians were armed, and under the stress of false rumours and false dangers from inside and outside. Everyone shot at everyone else. Everybody was a 'terrorist.' It was chaos. Everybody had a weapon in his hands. The army shot about five million rounds and the population as many as they could lay their hands upon—at first out of joy, then against the 'terrorists,' then because they were drunk."[120] The picture that emerges is of a plethora of military forces—army, units of the *securitate*, patriotic guard and militia—together with armed and unarmed individu-

118. See for instance Sârcă (1998), 78, 79.
119. BBC EE/0648, B/13, December 28, 1989.
120. *Daily Telegraph,* December 12, 1994, 10.

als congregating in a completely uncoordinated fashion. Some were under orders, but many were not, and in such circumstances it was almost impossible to identify who was with whom. In this atmosphere of chaos and uncertainty, and in the absence of adequate communications, rumor and innuendo seem to have all too easily triumphed. The inescapable conclusion is that many of the brave men and women who fell in defense of the revolution were the tragic victims of what has now come to be known as "friendly fire." This is among the most harrowing and unaccept-able of deaths in warfare, and the difficulties of admitting the truth about such incidents may lie at the heart of many of the revolution's dilemmas. The acceptance by the United States that they were responsible for the ac-cidental destruction of two British armored personnel carriers during the first Gulf War and the revelations about the bombing of Albanian refugees during NATO's Kosovo campaign were something of a first in the public admission of such mistakes. Previously, the tendency in all armed forces has been to cover up all details, sometimes to an extraordi-nary degree, long after the event. An interview with Gabrielescu revealed that the president of the senatorial commission of inquiry into the revolu-tion had come to the conclusion that most of those killed were "inno-cents, caught in the crossfire between panic-stricken soldiers and civilians firing at imaginary 'terrorists.' " An assessment of the fighting at the tele-vision center by the Romanian army also concludes with the following words that, in hindsight, must be judged to hold a kernel of the truth: "We are not able to omit that among the causes [of death] listed are acci-dents or mistakes of leadership generated by the specific conditions of ac-tion."[121] So far, the Military Procurator's Office has admitted that the army was responsible for the deaths of 333 and the wounding of 648 dur-ing the fighting, with the forces of the Ministry of the Interior killing a further sixty-three and wounding forty-six more.[122]

This interpretation—that many of the deaths of the second phase of the revolution were tragic mistakes—appears to be borne out by the cir-cumstances surrounding the greatest loss of life in a single incident at this time. This occurred at Otopeni airport during the morning of December 23, and as with most incidents in the revolution, it continues to be sur-rounded by controversy and conflicting claims. However, the broad de-tails seem to be as follow: after the flight of Ceauşescu by a helicopter sta-tioned at Otopeni, requests were made for the dispatch of reinforcements to the airport. In response to these pleas, in the early hours of the morn-ing of December 23, a detachment of troops from the training school for noncommissioned officers of the *securitate* troops, temporarily quartered at the *securitate* school in Băneasa, left for the airport. Three trucks full of

121. ibid.; Televiziunea Română (1990), 306.
122. *Adevărul*, December 22, 1994, 1.

young conscripts arrived at Otopeni shortly before dawn, having apparently passed through a series of checkpoints, which verified the legitimacy
of their mission, on the way. Indeed, at the last of these the army officer
on duty had climbed into the cab of the leading lorry in order to escort
the convoy to the airport buildings. The situation at the airport was already tense with antiaircraft guns firing at radar targets and stories circulating of approaching convoys of terrorists. Now, according to the army,
as the trucks advanced toward the airport, for some reason they left the
prescribed route and deviated to the right onto the main approach road.
Unable to make radio contact, as the vehicles were on the verge of reaching the main complex, the military positions lining the route opened
fire.[123] The shooting continued for some time and, when it ceased, forty
occupants of the trucks lay dead. At the same time, a bus carrying airport
workers, traveling on the same route, also came under fire, leaving nine
dead. The surviving officers and men of the *securitate* unit were immediately rounded up and placed under armed guard before being paraded as
captured terrorists on the television. A macabre photograph taken at the
time shows a forklift truck used to carry the bodies of the dead with the
word "terrorists" daubed on the side. The incident has been subject to a
detailed investigation by the Military Procurators Office, which has produced a report, and on December 17, 1993, legal action was initiated
against two officers held responsible for defenses at Otopeni in 1989,
Colonel Dumitru Drăghin and Lieutenant-Major Ionel Zorilă, as well as
the former head of the *securitate* troops, Major-General Grigorie Ghiţă.
They faced trial in the Military Section of the Supreme Court of Justice
for "murder and grave wounding" and the "dereliction of duty as concerns the organization and permanent coordination of the activity of the
groups under their command . . . [as well as] bad decision making and
bad transmission of orders."[124] Initially after the revolution, Ghiţă blamed
the incident on unidentified terrorists, but it now seems to be accepted
that the whole catastrophic episode was the result of poor communications, with one body authorizing the dispatch of the troops to the airport,
while others telephoned to warn that terrorists were approaching.[125]

Much of the blame for the confusion during the first twenty-four hours
after the flight of Ceauşescu can probably be laid on the general lack of
coordination between military forces. There was no unified command,
no plan of action, and the majority of military radios were either defective
or ineffective.[126] The breakdown of traditional hierarchies and methods
of command is exemplified by the use of television to give orders. At one

123. Codrescu et al. (1998), 251–57; *România Liberă,* January 5, 1990, 2.
124. BBC EE/1879, B/4, December 23, 1993.
125. *România Liberă,* January 5, 1990, 2.
126. Nicolaescu (1999), 173.

point a presenter was even to declare: "[There is] a military unit awaiting orders. . . . Who is it waiting for to give it orders? Now the orders are given by the people. To arms . . ."[127] Immediately after the flight of Ceaușescu, Militaru appeared on the television and, addressing many of the army high command personally by name (with the noticeable exception of Stănculescu), issued a dramatic appeal for both the army and Ministry of the Interior troops to "stop the slaughter!" and return to barracks.[128] Later that day, Dumitrescu on behalf of Gușă also used the same medium to order units in nearby cities to come to Bucharest to defend key installations. Yet by 12:20 the next morning on December 23, Gușă was telephoning Dumitrescu to ask him to stop giving orders in his name through this channel, as it was destabilizing the country.[129] In the hours immediately after the flight of Ceaușescu, three different communications centers came into being, each of which seems to have tried to determine the course of the revolution. Generals Gușă and Vlad, the nominal heads of the security forces, together with Colonel Pârcălăbescu of the patriotic guard, were based at the central committee building.[130] Gușă stayed at this command post until the morning of December 23 and Vlad until the same evening. Meanwhile, the political leadership of the NSF and some of the reserve generals were stationed at the television center until the morning of December 23. They then traveled to the Ministry of Defense, where a number of other generals, including Stănculescu and Chițac, seem to have been based throughout this period. In hindsight both Stănculescu and Gușă were to accept that the division of the command had been a serious mistake.[131] It was only when the three groups came together at the Ministry of Defense on December 23 and some coordination was established between the various strands of the leadership that the military situation was gradually brought under control. Indicative of the subsequent easing of tension was the decision of the political leadership to move from the Ministry of Defense to the old building of the Ministry of Foreign Affairs later on Christmas Day. Fragmentation of centers of command, however, was not just a problem in the capital. It also occurred elsewhere. In Brăila three separate centers functioned without cooperating, and in Sibiu it was only on December 25 that a unified command was established.[132]

---

127. Neacșu (c1999).
128. Televiziunea Română (1990), 38–39; BBC EE/0649, B/2, December 29, 1989.
129. Televiziunea Română (1990), 119; Sârcă (1998), 195 and, especially, 230.
130. This was already well endowed as a communication center but on the orders of Milea it had received extra equipment on December 21; A*devărul*, May 25, 1992, 2.
131. Codrescu et al. (1998), 206.
132. Pitulescu et al. (1998), 413; Codrescu et al. (1998), 271–72.

The Execution of the Ceaușescus

During the late 1980s from his vantage point outside the regime, Brucan, and presumably also some of the other leaders of the Front, had become convinced that the policies pursued by Ceaușescu were primarily designed to enhance his powers and that of the *securitate* at the expense of the Party.[133] On the basis of this analysis it is, therefore, perhaps not entirely coincidental that in the evening of December 24 as it set about establishing a new structure of power the new regime also proceeded to simultaneously remove what it saw as the twin pillars of the old regime: the Ceaușescus and the *securitate*.

These decisions were made at a time when the leaders of the Front still felt far from secure of their own positions. On the streets, rumors were circulating that they had been unseated from power, while they themselves continued to harbor doubts about the loyalty of a number of the military chiefs who had switched to support the revolution.[134] Among the latter, the finger of suspicion was especially pointed at Vlad and Gușă, largely it seems on the basis that, at various times during the night they spent at the command center in the central committee building, the two withdrew for secret consultations in an adjoining room. The continued presence in the building of Postelnicu and Dincă, who the generals consulted as they wrestled with the security situation, probably only exacerbated the suspicions.[135] Whether Vlad and Gușă were actually plotting to arrest the leaders of the revolution, as has been alleged, remains unknown, but at the time few would give them the benefit of the doubt.[136] The two generals were removed from office. Militaru was officially installed as the new Minister of Defense and a large number of more trusted reserve generals reactivated. Later, Iliescu was only to say that Gușă had been relieved from duty for making "mistakes impermissible for a military commander," but it is noticeable that he was the only one of the top brass of the army to be removed from his post at this time, although no serious charges were ever laid against him.[137]

Personal animosities may also have played a role in the decision to remove Vlad, as many of the incoming regime had suffered much at the hands of Ceaușescu. In particular Brucan, following his mistreatment at the hands of the *securitate* after the release of the "Letter of the Six," seems to have harbored deep antagonisms. Afterward Roman was to state that it

---

133. Silviu Brucan interviewed in *Financial Times*, December 29, 1989, 11.
134. BBC EE/0649, B/6, December 29, 1989.
135. Pitulescu et al. (1998), 259–60.
136. *Jurnalul Național*, December 23, 1997.
137. Quoted in Shafir (January 26, 1990), 40. For a trenchant rebuttal of the allegations against Gușă by a civilian in the central committee building that night, see *Adevărul*, July 6, 1991, 1.

was only Brucan who was fully aware of the power of the *securitate*, and certainly he seems to have taken the lead in denouncing its head.[138] The two came into open confrontation during the evening of December 24, when, according to Brucan, he asked Vlad why he had made no specific order for his troops to cease fire in his first radio broadcast to the nation on the morning of December 23. At that time Vlad had given broad assurances that his men were on the side of the revolution, stating that the *securitate* had "rid itself of elements loyal to the Ceaușescu clan" and that they were "fighting shoulder-to-shoulder with the Romanian army."[139] Any more explicit instruction from the head of the *securitate* for his forces to stop firing at this late stage in the proceedings would have been tantamount to an admission that they had been responsible for the night's conflict. Yet Brucan seems to have been convinced that the terrorists were members of the *securitate* and moreover that they were operating according to a master plan, which Vlad refused to divulge. According to Brucan, these accusations, which may have been aired at one or two meetings (his accounts vary), sowed such seeds of doubt regarding Vlad's loyalty in the minds of the rest of the leadership that he was later dismissed.[140]

Brucan's story offers a highly personalized account of events but, given the subsequent dismissal of most of the *securitate's* high command, it would seem to carry the flavor of what turned out to be a concerted strategy to remove the upper echelons of this powerful body.[141] On December 31 it was announced that Vlad, former deputy ministers of the interior Lieutenant-General Aristotel Stamatoiu and Major-General Gianu Bucurescu, and Lieutenant-General Gheorghe Vasile, head of the IV Directorate, had all been removed from active service and detained.[142] They were later officially placed in the reserve, alongside many other Ministry of the Interior generals, including Major-Generals Marin Neagoe, head of the V Directorate; Gheorghe Bucur; Emil Macri, head of the II Directorate; Ioan Moț, head of CIE counterintelligence; Alexandru Țencu, head of telephone surveillance and video monitoring; Vasile Moise; Ștefan Alexie, secretary of state for the DSS; Ioan Marcu, head of the Political Council of the DSS; Aurelian Mortoiu, head of the III Directorate; Victor Neculicioiu; Alecse Olteanu; Gheorghe Radu, head of the U.M.0525 cipher section; as well as Lieutenant-Generals Istifie Gearta and Epifanie Amohnoaie.[143] A few months later Stănculescu was to announce that the

---

138. *Le Monde*, January 5, 1990, 1, 4. According to Nicolaescu, Brucan was also prominent in the campaign against Gușă; Nicolaescu (1999), 177.

139. BBC EE/0648, B/10, December 28, 1989.

140. Compare Silviu Brucan interviewed in *Financial Times*, December 29, 1989, 11, with Brucan (1993), 178–81.

141. Hall (1997), 368–69.

142. BBC EE/0652, B/12:17, January 3, 1990.

143. *Monitorul Oficial al României*, January 8–10, 1990; ibid., January 19, 1990, 6.

IV and V Directorates had been dissolved and another 3,583 officers from Bucharest and other county units placed in what he termed "reserve functions." On the basis of the declared manning levels this amounted in total to some 33 percent of the personnel, if the *securitate* troops are excluded.[144]

The decision to place the Ceauşescus on trial was made on the evening of December 24. According to Brucan, it took place at a stormy three-hour meeting of the Executive Bureau of the NSF, where the main argument was between those who wanted an immediate military trial and those who wanted a civil trial several weeks later.[145] However, the presence of Roman at the discussions, who was not a member of the Executive Bureau, suggests that the decision was in fact made more informally, and Guşă has said that it was taken by a small group centered on Iliescu, Roman, Brucan, Stănculescu, Voiculescu, and Militaru.[146] A highly colored version of the events has been given by Galloway and Wylie, who place the onus for the decision on the personal intervention of Voiculescu and Stănculescu, who are said to have persuaded a reluctant and "idealistic" Iliescu to overcome his initial inhibitions.[147] Whether Iliescu was so unwilling to sanction such an action may be questioned, especially since he had already at the time of the arrest of the Ceauşescus declared: "The time for their just and harsh judgement by the people will come."[148] However, Brucan does suggest that Stănculescu had made some preliminary preparations for the trial beforehand, and all accounts agree that the final arrangements for the military tribunal were made by him and Voiculescu, who were both present as representatives of the regime, alongside Virgil Măgureanu.

The official explanation for the decision to execute the two Ceauşescus is that it was warranted by the military situation, since only through their deaths could the terrorists be persuaded to abandon their murderous campaign, allowing victory to be finally assured.[149] In hindsight this rationale may be questioned. Bucharest was peaceful enough on Christmas Day—the day of the executions—to encourage large numbers to venture outside to attend church services, and there were even reports that three

144. Sturdza (April 13, 1990), 33; *România Liberă,* January 10, 1991, 5. Later Iliescu was to suggest that 4,000 *securitate* officers from Bucharest alone had been transferred to other posts and in the neighboring county of Dolj it was claimed 181 had been removed; see *România Literară,* July 5, 1990, 14; for Dolj see BBC EE/0698, B/12, February 26, 1990.

145. Silviu Brucan interviewed in *Financial Times,* December 29, 1989, 11; Brucan (1993), 181.

146. Coruţ (1993), 145.

147. Galloway and Wylie (1991), 177–80.

148. BBC EE/0648, B/11–12, December 28, 1989.

149. BBC EE/0658, B/12:22, January 10, 1990. For similar views from Iliescu see Televiziunea Română (1990), 225; and Ion Iliescu interviewed in *România Literară,* July 5, 1990, 14; for Brucan see BBC EE/0654, B/11, January 5, 1990. For Mazilu's view on the legitimacy of the execution see *Independent,* December 28, 1989, 1.

weddings had taken place in Sector 5 of the city.[150] However, the evening before, when the new leaders met in the Ministry of Defense, the sound of firing still echoed from the streets outside, and when this is coupled with the doubts they held about the loyalty of their senior military commanders, the decision, perhaps, becomes more understandable. The deteriorating situation in Târgoviște probably also added to their concerns. The Ceaușescus had been in a military garrison in the city since the evening of December 22, but whether they were under arrest or merely there for their own protection seems to have been unclear even to themselves. Ceaușescu was respectfully addressed as "Comrade Commander-in-Chief" and "Comrade President" and, although the presidential couple were not allowed to leave the barracks, they were told this was because of the dangers posed by the revolution.[151] Throughout, the commander of the garrison, Colonel Andrei Kemenici, kept the Ceaușescus hidden, so few knew their exact location—at one point they were even dressed in military uniforms to be less obvious and put in a mobile command post—but nonetheless rumors quickly spread both within the garrison and outside. Members of the local NSF council became convinced that Kemenici had betrayed the revolution and was shielding the Ceaușescus. The long-standing rivalries between Kemenici and the military officers who headed the council no doubt deepened these suspicions, as did the continued presence of the deputy head of the local *securitate,* Lieutenant-Colonel Gheorghe Dinu, within the army garrison. The situation in Târgoviște was full of ambiguities and this exacerbated the psychological pressures placed on the troops defending the garrison. Day and night they lived in constant fears of attack from both ground and air, and when, late in the afternoon of December 24, it was reported that terrorists were firing from a nearby secondary school, they unleashed such a barrage of fire that the building was virtually leveled to the ground. With the situation fast slipping out of control, Kemenici seems to have decided that his only option was to evacuate the Ceaușescus to Bucharest. A convoy of vehicles was readied, and the presidential couple placed in an armored car, but when Kemenici called Stănculescu to inform him of his intentions, he was told it would be a disastrous move, because in Bucharest the situation was running out of control. The arrival of an emissary from Bucharest carrying insulin for Ceaușescu's diabetes, in the early hours of December 25 seems to have coincided with the abandonment of the evacuation, but news of these developments in Târgoviște must have influenced the decision to place the Romanian leader on trial.

At 7:00 a.m. on December 25 the garrison at Târgoviște was told that a flight of helicopters would be coming from Bucharest. The recognition

150. Neacșu (c1999).
151. This account rests heavily on Domenico (1999).

signal was to be a yellow lady's scarf carried by the lead helicopter. In preparation the Ceaușescus were dressed again in civilian clothes and once more placed in an armored car. According to Kemenici, they cheered up, believing, like him, that the helicopters were coming to take them to Bucharest.[152] Instead, they were carrying their executioners, although even as late as the pre-trial medical examination, the Ceaușescus still seem to have thought nothing particular was amiss, believing it was routine. The trial itself took place before a military tribunal in a lecture hall in the Târgoviște garrison.[153] On the tribunal sat the chairman, Colonel Gică Popa, together with five other assessors, three of whom were drawn from the Târgoviște unit. The chief prosecutor was Major Dan Voinea and the defense councils Nicolae Teodorescu and Constantin Lucescu.[154] The proceedings lasted no more than fifty-five minutes. No serious effort was made to investigate the charges laid against the Ceaușescus and nearly all independent observers have agreed it was little more than a kangaroo court.[155] The helicopters had brought a firing squad alongside the lawyers and, according to Kemenici, he was even asked to select a place for the execution before the trial began.[156] Even the very legality of the proceedings has been placed in doubt, with some arguing that under the state of emergency then in force there should have been a stay of execution of ten days after the death sentence had been passed, even if there was no appeal.[157] In the Ceaușescus' case such legal niceties were irrelevant. Indeed, one of the features of the trial was the ineffective defense councils, who in their summing up speeches embarked on a thinly veiled denunciation of their clients. For the most part the Ceaușescus answered for themselves, if only for Nicolae Ceaușescu to repeat endlessly that as president of the republic and supreme commander of the army he refused to accept the legality of the court and would only answer to the Grand National Assembly.

During the trial the prosecution brought four formal charges: genocide under Article 357 of the penal code; undermining the power of the state

152. Ibid., 100.
153. For the trial see Ratesh (1991), 73–77; Behr (1991), 13–23; Galloway and Wylie (1991), 181–203; Marcu (1991); Sweeny (1991), 221–24; Rady (1992), 114–21; Almond (1992), 231–36; Domenico (1992); Brucan (1993), 181–83; Ardeleanu, Savaliuc, and Baiu (1996); Domenico (1999). The transcript has not been fully translated into English. For a partial translation see BBC EE/0648, B/15–17, December 28, 1989; *Washington Post*, December 29, 1990, A26; and the transcript available at http://www.timisoara.com/timisoara/rev/trialscript.html.
154. Nicu Teodorescu interviewed in *The Times*, January 24, 1990, 12. Only three months later, on March 1, 1990, Popa was to commit suicide, further fueling speculation about the trial; see Hall (1997), 343–44.
155. See, for instance, Behr (1991), 18.
156. Domenico (1999), 105.
157. Galloway and Wylie (1991), 179; Behr (1991), 21.

by organizing armed actions under Article 162; destroying, degrading or bringing into disuse through explosion or other means industrial or other installations under Article 163; and undermining the national economy under Articles 165 and 145. The charges were little more than generalities and during the trial hardly any supporting evidence was produced, with strangely no reference made to the PEC transcript discussed in Chapter 2, which, according to at least one source, was available at this time.[158] When the charges were read on television the same evening, another, attempting to the flee the country with funds in excess of one billion dollars in foreign bank accounts, was added. At the same time, a figure of more than 60,000 was also given for the victims of the genocide. According to Voiculescu, this huge number was produced by adding those estimated to have died in recent years through cold and hunger to the 4,000 said by Yugoslav radio broadcasts to have died at Timişoara.[159] At one point in the trial, however, the presiding judge suggests that "There are *today*, due to the orders given by you, 64,000 victims in all cities" and, although this remark was made within a general attack on Ceauşescu's policies, a number of western newspapers subsequently carried an extract of the trial from the Yugoslav news agency Tanjug, which led to this being taken as the death toll in the revolution.[160] Just as only a fraction of this figure actually died at the time, so too the millions of dollars stashed in overseas banks also proved to be illusory. Immediately after the fall of Ceauşescu, the Swiss preempted any request from the NSF by putting a freeze on any assets that the Romanian leader may have held in their country, but an initial search did not reveal any money and neither it seems did the formal commission of inquiry, which was established in August 1990 under the chairmanship of Mugur Isărescu.[161]

The trial was a shouting match of mutual incomprehension—a dialogue between the deaf—but it is noticeable that Ceauşescu is not the totally bemused onlooker sometimes suggested and at times he even engages in his own defense, if only as "a citizen." He refuses to answer questions about the massacre in Timişoara and robustly denies that there had been any shootings in Piaţa Palatului, explicitly stating that he had given orders for troops not to open fire on the crowd in the square. Ceauşescu's position, consistent with his previous utterances, remained

158. Televiziunea Română (1990), 162, where it is suggested that there had been a debate within the NSF about whether the transcript should be read on the television.

159. Galloway and Wylie (1991), 184–85.

160. Ardelenau, Savaliuc, and Baiu (1996), 30 (emphasis added).

161. *Washington Post*, December 25, 1989, A40; *Financial Times*, January 16, 1990, 2. In March 1990, the Romanian government asked the international accountancy firm Peat Marwick to assist in the hunt for the supposed funds, but the leaks from their report suggesting that up to $1 billion was still held in foreign bank accounts remained unconfirmed; *Washington Post*, November 17, 1991, C1–2.

centered on an absolute belief in his own popularity with the working class. He proudly declared that conditions had never been better in Romania, displaying his own poverty of conception by pointing to the 200 kilos of wheat each person was supposedly receiving each year, as if peasant subsistence was sufficient to assuage the demands of the growing urban population. The deposed leader refused to recognize the legitimacy of the NSF and remained confident that the workers would rally to his side asserting that "the people will fight until they have eliminated this gang of traitors of the country who with foreign help organized a coup d'état." Underlying all this was the assumption that his overthrow had been brought about by foreign agency. When asked "What are these people fighting for throughout the country?," he replied, "For their existence, independence and sovereignty." It was the same closed mentality seen at the earlier PEC meetings.

The trial soon degenerated into a series of personal attacks, especially against Elena Ceaușescu, who was brought to task for her alleged taste in luxurious clothes, her false qualifications and the gold scales said to have been found in her daughter Zoe's apartment.[162] Elena reacted to the accusations with incredulity, countering them with the statement that she and her husband lived in an apartment just like any other Romanians. Other questions and the summary statements of the defense councils reflected the full gamut of rumors then sweeping Romania, with references being made to foreign mercenaries fighting on the streets, *securitate* officers donning the clothes of soldiers to avoid detection, killings in hospitals, and orphans being trained to be used against the Romanian people. The uncontested verdict was guilty, and the sentence immediate execution by firing squad. A group of soldiers surrounded the Ceaușescus and, roughly binding their hands behind their backs, dragged them struggling and protesting into the courtyard outside. The Romanian president and his wife probably died instantly, although even this has been the subject of debate, due to the fact that the actual execution appears not to have been filmed, the army cameraman apparently caught unawares as he switched to a portable power supply. The firing party consisted of an officer, a warrant officer, and six paratroopers, and the official version is that the Ceaușescus died when two members of this squad fired early without orders, but suggestions have also been made that the presidential couple were summarily executed with a single shot to the head. Such is the level of distrust in the revolution that it seems that no detail can be acknowledged by all sides, even though pictures of the bullet riddled corpses were

162. For the gold scales see *The Times*, December 28, 1989, 6. Also note the similarity with the tactics employed by the United States to justify their intervention in Panama against Noriega at the same time, *The Times*, December 28, 1989, 8.

later produced.[163] The bodies were almost immediately taken back to Bucharest, but due to a last ignominious mix-up of orders the corpses were left on the landing field at the Steaua soccer stadium for over twelve hours waiting for transfer to the Central Military Hospital, before being buried a few days later in military graves at the Ghencea cemetery in Bucharest.[164] Even in death the couple attracted a ghoulish fascination, with rumors continuing to circulate long afterward in Romania and elsewhere in the Balkans that Ceauşescu was not really dead and that his place during the execution and trial had been taken by a fanatical *securitate* doppelgänger.

Officially the death of Ceauşescu was one of the key moments of the revolution. Brucan asserted that "as of Monday evening, after people learned about the execution of the two, the situation changed radically. That was a turning point," noting, "Two of those who had been caught said that they would not consider themselves free of this oath [to defend the Ceauşescus to the end] until they had seen the film or picture in which it is clear that they are dead."[165] At the time most outside observers seem to have accepted such an explanation for the necessity of a rapid trial and execution, but in hindsight it punctured much of the romantic euphoria surrounding the revolution and marked the beginning of the end of the NSF's honeymoon with the outside world. Even at the time, as a harbinger of future differences, the United States expressed "regret" that the trial had not been a public and open affair.[166] The decision was also publicly regretted by prominent East Europeans, including Lech Walesa. Even the leaders of the Soviet Union seem to have had reservations, since Foreign Minister Eduard Shevardnadze subsequently admitted that the execution "left a really bad impression on me."[167] Within Romania such was the force of pent-up venom against the Ceauşescu regime that few voices initially spoke against the trial. An early opinion poll recorded 84 percent in favor of the executions, and afterward some commentators continued to argue that a proper trial could not have been organized in the chaos of the time.[168] However, a few voices of doubt were raised.

163. Ratesh (1991), 73–77; Calinescu and Tismaneanu (January–April 1991), 46 n. 14; Hall (1997), 340–46; for the "official" version of the execution see Galloway and Wylie (1991), 196–202. The charges and verdict were publicly announced in the evening of Christmas Day and a recording of the trial was shown on Romanian television at midnight the next day.

164. Even the date of burial is disputed with Codrescu et al. (1998), 302, and Nicolaescu (1999), 474, both suggesting it was December 28 while Marcu (1991), 80, and Ardelenau, Savaliuc, and Baiu (1996), 58 suggest December 30.

165. BBC EE/0654, B/12, January 5, 1990.

166. *Washington Post*, December 26, 1989, A26; Linden (February 2, 1990), 36–40.

167. *The Times*, December 29, 1989, 1. Eduard Shevardnadze interviewed by John Simpson on *Newsnight* (BBC2, December 16, 1994).

168. *The Times*, January 18, 1990, 6; Câmpeanu and Steriade (1993), 918.

Speaking on behalf of the new authorities in Timișoara, Valentin Vârtan expressed the feeling that the trial had been hurried and that it should have been broadcast live on television, and the writer Octavian Paler lamented the missed opportunity of staging a Romanian Nuremberg.[169] It was not an auspicious start for the new regime; instead of justice being seen to be done, the trial smacked of old communist practices, and even Iliescu was afterward to admit that it may have been a "mistake."[170]

The noted Romanian dissident Paul Goma has written that the rushed execution "stole Ceaușescu from those who suffered because of him" and it can be said that it did draw something of a veil across the communist era, a process encouraged by the new regime which tried, not entirely successfully, to equate the passing of Ceaușescu with the cleansing of the Romanian body politic from the evils of the past. Goma presciently also suggested that the trial "accomplished the extraordinary, the unheard and undeserved feat of turning the Ceaușescus into human beings," and it did indeed leave the door open for a later partial political rehabilitation of the Ceaușescus and their erstwhile supporters.[171] Moreover, by focusing only on unprovable genocide and not on the details of their misrule, the Ceaușescus' trial was to set an unhealthy precedent for the future court appearances of other RCP leaders, which resulted in a series of judgments of such dubious legality that the defendants were all released after serving only relatively short sentences.

By the time of the execution of the Ceaușescus life had more or less returned to normal in Romania. Already radio and television had became more relaxed—by the evening of December 24 the radio was even finding space to broadcast records by Tom Jones and Nana Mouskouri—and, reflecting the feeling that the revolution had triumphed, media coverage switched from the fighting to dwell on the evils of the Ceaușescu regime, with wide publicity being given to the arrest of Ceaușescu's daughter, Zoe, and the lavish opulence of her apartment, which was said to contain jewelry and $97,000 in dollar bills.[172] In Cluj, Craiova, and Mihai Bravu the shooting had virtually ceased by December 25 and during the next few days it was also to come to an end elsewhere, first in Brașov, Buzău, Sibiu, Timișoara, and Turda, and then in Arad, Constanța, Reșița, and Târgoviște. Yet as late as the evening of December 27, a soldier was shot dead while on patrol near Brăila and in Bucharest isolated acts of violence continued, with passersby in the streets still running for cover at the

169. *Washington Post*, December 27, 1989, A1, A14; *România Liberă*, January 14, 1990, 2; Ionescu (March 9, 1990), 45; note also the query in *România Liberă*, December 29, 1989, 1.
170. Shafir (January 26,1990), 38. Iliescu expands on this theme, suggesting the trial should have been public in *România Literară*, July 5, 1990, 14.
171. Goma quoted in Ratesh (1991), 77.
172. Neacșu (c1999).

sound of gunfire, as the army searched for terrorists.[173] On the same day the Front issued a final ultimatum for all remaining terrorists to surrender by 5:00 p.m. the next day, with the demand being repeated on the following morning in a lengthy communiqué that also established extraordinary military tribunals with emergency powers to try those accused of terrorism.

By this time, however, the radio was reporting that 85 percent of the working population of the capital were at work and, despite reports of a fierce gunfight lasting twenty minutes near the television station on December 28, official pronouncements were also beginning to record the end of the conflict.[174] On December 29, the Higher Military Command confidently declared that "the Army . . . fully controls the situation in all areas and localities in our country," with Chiṭac adding that no major "reconnaissance-diversion groups" remained at large in Bucharest and that the isolated groups that still existed elsewhere posed no real threat to the public.[175] Nevertheless, it was already clear that the legacy of the fighting would be lasting. There was still discussion on the radio about the extent of the tunnels amidst calls for *desecuritatization,* and, as late as January 4, 1990, the army was still registering casualties at the television station, although the circumstances in which this occurred remain unclear.

173. Codrescu et al. (1998), 317.
174. *Independent,* December 27, 1989, 1; *The Times,* December 29, 1989, 1; ibid., December 30, 1989, 1; BBC EE/0650, i, December 30, 1989.
175. BBC EE/0651, B/7:15, January 1, 1990; BBC EE/0652, B/12·18i, January 3, 1990. Note Chiṭac's avoidance of the word "terrorist."

CHAPTER FOUR

"The Most Obscure Problem"

The previous chapter, within a broad survey of the events after the overthrow of Ceaușescu, paid particular attention to the fighting that engulfed Bucharest and a number of other Romanian cities from the evening of December 22 and the means by which the incoming National Salvation Front established its hold on power. Mentioned, but left unexplored, were two of the most baffling questions of the revolution relating to the identity of the terrorists and the origins of the NSF. It is with these two key issues and the stories of conspiracy which surround them that this chapter is concerned.

The Army Is with Us!

The days of conflict after the fall of Ceaușescu had been long and bitter. Western news reports painted a vivid picture of hard-pressed defenders of the revolution locked in mortal combat with diehard loyalists of the old regime, who were said to "have orders to fight until the last moment and then commit suicide by biting on a cyanide pellet in their collars."[1] For a few days this reportedly highly trained and well-equipped foe—in a television interview Chițac claimed they possessed sophisticated weapons with night vision and even helicopters and light armored cars—seemed to threaten the very survival of the new regime. Then, as mysteriously as they

The title of this chapter is taken from a statement made by Iliescu concerning the terrorists in *România Literară*, July 5, 1990, 14.
1. *The Times*, December 26, 1989, 6; ibid., December 23, 1989, 1.

came, this enemy, usually called "terrorists" and identified with elements of the *securitate,* apparently disappeared without trace, leaving behind them the most perplexing enigma of the revolution: "Who were the terrorists?"

For most Romanians the *securitate* was virtually synonymous with the Ceaușescu regime, and few can have been surprised when television and radio started broadcasting appeals for them to side with the revolution. A melodramatic plea by army Captain Mihai Lupoi on the television was matched on the radio by Dan Cristescu, who called on the *securitate* to return to barracks and surrender their weapons. Speaking shortly afterward, another army officer, Major Pavel Lică, was also quick to emphasize that it was not the army but the *securitate* that had tried to stifle the peaceful demonstrations that morning.[2] Lupoi, Cristescu, and Lică were only stating what for most Romanians was to be expected: the army was on the side of the revolution and the *securitate* was against it. The new leadership did little to dispel this idea. Iliescu, when he first appeared on television, reported that Stănculesu had tried to make contact with the leadership of the Ministry of the Interior but had failed to find anybody in authority with whom he could talk. Iliescu quipped that this must be because the commanders of the *securitate* had fled with the political leadership.[3] The link between the previous regime and the *securitate* was confirmed, and Iliescu's subsequent call for the Ministry of the Interior forces to abandon the "vulgar clique of traitors," as he described the Ceaușescu regime, was to stand in sharp contrast to his effusive affirmations that the army stood shoulder to shoulder with the people.

The doubts about the *securitate* were also fueled by the apparent reluctance of senior officers of that body to appear on television and openly declare their adherence to the new order. Within hours of the revolutionaries seizing control of the television station, Voinea, Gușă, Chițac, and a number of other army commanders had appeared and pledged their loyalty to the new regime. Members of the militia, including the temporary commander, General Câmpeanu, also did the same on behalf of their forces.[4] In contrast, the first members of the *securitate* to appear on television were two relatively low-ranking officers: Lieutenant-Colonel Stan, a neighbor of Militaru and an officer in the II Directorate, and Colonel Apostolescu, who introduced himself as the head of the information service of the *securitate*.[5] Their semi-apologetic nature and half-hearted declarations, appealing to Vlad and fellow officers to put down their arms and work with the people, were the antithesis of the confident assertions of their colleagues in the army and militia. It was not until 6:03 a.m. on De-

2. Sârcă (1998), 222–24.
3. Televiziunea Română (1990), 42; Neacșu (c1999).
4. BBC EE/0649, B/2, December 29, 1989; Televiziunea Română (1990), 47–49.
5. Ibid., 52, 63, 209.

cember 23 that a message from the head of the *securitate* was finally read on the radio reassuring the nation that his forces were fully on the side of the revolution.[6] Stamatiou, head of the foreign intelligence service, made a similar statement shortly afterward, but by this time radio and television was already identifying the terrorists as members of the *securitate,* and, in response, an obviously puzzled Vlad could only weakly suggest that they must somehow be units connected with Nicu and Ilie Ceauşescu.

The Nature of the Enemy

On December 22 it was widely presumed that the *securitate* would stay loyal to the Ceauşescu clan, a conviction strengthened by the news from radio and television, especially after it was reported that fighting had broken out between the army and the *securitate* in Sibiu. That evening, as renewed shooting broke out in Bucharest and elsewhere, it became easy to believe that the *securitate* had taken up arms against the revolution. To most Romanians the *securitate* was a single monolithic entity but, in fact, it consisted of a plethora of directorates and units. During the revolution this multiplicity of forces was to lay the ground for considerable confusion, since few outside the ranks of the *cognoscenti* could distinguish between the various branches.[7] Initially, the whole *securitate* was viewed as potentially hostile but, as it became clear that elements of the Ministry of the Interior forces were on the side of the revolution, the enemy was subtly redefined to include only a few special units. The first real public effort to identify the enemy occurred in a short address made by Reserve Major-General Nicolae Tudor on television in the early evening of December 22, immediately after the transmission from the central committee building when Iliescu and Guşă had appeared on the balcony together. Speaking on behalf of the National Salvation Committee, Tudor authoritatively defined the enemy: "troops of the *securitate* led by General Ghiţă are at this actual hour, all, loyal to the people. They have orders and discharge orders on behalf of the National Salvation Committee. What is said, that troops of the *securitate* act against the people, is correct because of the actions of some special units. They are antiterrorist and other troops of the former dictator, few, small in number, but embittered, who act from different points. These points are in the course of liquidation by army forces."[8]

By the evening of December 22, alongside other terms such as "hooligans," "extremists," "fanatics," and "hostile elements of the old regime," the word "terrorist" was already in wide use to describe opponents of the

6. BBC EE/0648, B/10, December 28, 1989.
7. The best description is in Deletant (1994), 22–49.
8. Televiziunea Română (1990), 97. For the impact of Tudor's statement see Brateş (1992), 112–13.

new order, but confusingly Tudor did not speak of "terrorists" but "antiterrorist troops."[9] His statement thus naturally follows from the alarms involving USLA troops earlier that afternoon, but in labeling the enemy as a few special units of the *securitate* he was to set the pattern for many subsequent attempts to elucidate the identity of the terrorists. Tudor's definition was to be fine-tuned by Iliescu in the afternoon of the next day, December 23, when, mimicking the term used by Ceaușescu to describe the "hooligans" of Timișoara, he used the word "terrorist" to describe the enemy. Like Tudor before him Iliescu stressed the small number of terrorists but, while accepting they were Ministry of the Interior forces, he specified no particular units:

> [There are] certain bands of terrorists, specially trained to fight against the people's masses and defend the dictator, . . . certain fanatical individuals operating with unprecedented cruelty, firing on buildings and citizens, and claiming victims among the military [army]. . . . We want to say that all military units, and the great majority of militia and interior ministry units, are acting jointly against the terrorists. . . . Actually, I must tell you that we are not dealing with a large number of terrorist elements, but rather they are specially trained and equipped for this kind of actions, . . . the terrorists are not wearing uniforms. They are in civilian dress. Often, they try to create confusion and are even wearing arm bands, so as to be taken as people belonging to civic groups. They want to create confusion. They shoot from any position. Therefore, it is important for the armed citizens of our groups to refrain from acting, because they may be taken for terrorists and fall victim to clashes with military units.[10]

The terrorists wearing civilian clothes had begun to merge with the general population and this process was to be continued even further on December 28, when, following the establishment of extraordinary military tribunals, Oliviu Tocaciu, a member of the CNSF, provided a legal definition of terrorists in an official communiqué of the Front:

> Are considered terrorists and declared as such, persons who carry about themselves firearms and other offensive weapons, ammunition, explosives or any other types of weapons of destruction, or broadcasting apparatus, which . . . struggle against the National Salvation Front and the victors of Free Romania . . . also are considered terrorists and declared as such persons who spread or publish rumors as well as exaggerated and tendentious information about the exceptional situation with the goal of misleading the

9. Tudor spoke around 6:45 p.m., probably after the outbreak of shooting in Piața Palatului, but before firing was heard at the television station, and it remains unclear from where he received his information or if he had been in contact with those at the central committee building before speaking. For other terms in use to describe opponents of the regime at this time see Sârcă (1998), 82, 85, 92, 95, 101.

10. BBC EE/0648, B/11, December 28, 1989.

civil population and creating a state of panic. As terrorists will also be considered and declared as such people who hold relations with terrorists or favor terrorism.[11]

The terrorists still existed but now they were no longer members of the *securitate*. Instead, they were anybody who opposed the NSF, even a person who spread rumors. They had been transmogrified from fanatical units of the security forces to simple scaremongers. However, such an easy transformation was not accepted by all. The army, in particular, continued to play up the number of terrorists and their fighting capabilities, largely, it seems, to legitimate their own position and to "explain" the damage and destruction during the fighting. Even after the shooting had ended, Colonel-General Vasile Ionel, although admitting that the exact number of terrorists was still unknown, still suggested that there might have been several thousand.[12]

The view that the army had been fighting a more substantial foe was also supported by some prominent members of the new leadership, who argued that the terrorists had in fact been operating according to a carefully laid out plan. Iliescu on December 23 had spoken of "planned coordinated actions" by the terrorists,[13] and at the beginning of January Brucan was to emphatically state that the terrorists "were operating on the basis of a plan—that is, they had places to meet, they had places to train with ammunition and weapons, and they had well-functioning means of communication, they had well-functioning means of transport and they had underground passages in complete order. All these were, as a matter of fact, concentrated in a whole plan, which in military terminology is called a contingency plan, a plan for a certain eventuality, which they started implementing the moment they received the signal."[14] After the revolution, speculation continued over the existence of various plans, many of which bore abstruse code names such as Plan Z and Plan M, with stories about the latter apparently originating from Pacepa.[15] Most persistent was Brucan and Militaru's advocacy of the idea that the *securitate* were following Ministry of the Interior order 02600/1988 drawn up after the Brașov riots in 1987.[16] However, as might be expected, on closer inspection this turns out to be a means of securing order over a restless population by the authorities in power. It does not start from a premise of defeat and the need for isolated spoiling actions to hamper an incoming regime.

11. Neacșu (c1999).
12. BBC EE/0654, B/9:19, January 5, 1990.
13. BBC EE/0648, B/11, December 28, 1989; see also Chițac in BBC EE/0651, B/7:15, January 1, 1990.
14. BBC EE/0654, B/12:20, January 5, 1990.
15. *Independent*, January 7, 1990, 15.
16. *East European Reporter* 4:3, 1990, 74–77; *România Liberă*, December 17, 1992, 2; *Cotidianul*, May 25, 1995; the order is reproduced in Pitulescu et al. (1995), 28–38.

Just as Ceauşescu did not use any of the elaborate evacuation plans involving tunnels to escape from the central committee building, so it has not yet been adequately proven that any of these other plans, even if they existed, ever became operational. Their existence makes an interesting footnote to the history of the revolution and nothing more.

Who Were the Terrorists?

The terrorists were few in number and, according to Iliescu, they were practically indivisible from the general population. It is therefore hardly surprising that they have proved to be invisible. Nevertheless, many have sought to unearth their identity, with the most influential sleuths being Brucan and Militaru. Long after the revolution they continued to identify the terrorists as coming from a few special units of the *securitate,* although they rather weakened their case over the years by changing their minds over which units were involved. Following Iliescu, they seemingly borrowed freely from popular mythology in raising the terrorists to the status of a well-equipped elite: "All of them were snipers trained in the techniques of guerrilla-type urban warfare and equipped with the most modern machine guns (infra red etc.). . . . Some officers held two identity cards and passports, keys to two apartments stocked with food in freezers, civilian and military clothes, etc. They were called terrorists, because starting in the evening of December 22 they occupied positions in the buildings surrounding the TV and radio stations, the Ministry of Defence, the Central Committee of the Party and so on and began shooting soldiers and civilians indiscriminately."[17] Initially, Brucan and Militaru pointed the finger of suspicion at four special units of the *securitate:* the staff and students of the military academy for officers of the Ministry of the Interior at Băneasa, headed by General Nicolae Andruţa Ceauşescu, with a strength of about 2,000; USLA, headed by Colonel Gheorghe Ardeleanu, with a strength of 795; the V Directorate, headed by Major-General Marin Neagoe, comprising 484 men; and the Bucharest *securitate* forces, headed by Colonel Gheorghe Goran, with about 600 personnel.[18] However, in a later rendition, although like Militaru he maintained his insistence on the involvement of the staff and students of the Ministry of Interior military academy and USLA, Brucan dropped his allegations against the V Directorate and the Bucharest *securitate* apparatus, replacing them with the military finishing school for officers of the militia in Bucharest and the catchall phrase "other special units."[19]

It seems that many if not all of the above named units played some role in suppressing the demonstrations on the night of December 21 in

17. *East European Reporter,* 4:3, 1990, 74–77.
18. Ibid. This list was also reproduced in Brucan (1993), 185.
19. *Adevărul,* January 30, 1991, 2.

Bucharest, but little evidence has yet been produced to conclusively prove that they took up positions against the revolution after the flight of Ceauşescu. Indeed, if anything, the available evidence seems to point in the opposite direction. At the center of many of the allegations has been Ceauşescu's praetorian guard, the V Directorate of the *securitate*, with a number of stories also appearing in the Western media, suggesting that this unit harbored the terrorists.[20] These suspicions seem to have been partly grounded in the fact that the unit's headquarters, which lay next to the central committee building, was a source of shooting during the fighting and in consequence virtually razed to the ground.[21] However, an investigation by the respected editor of *România Liberă*, Petre Mihai Băcanu, found no evidence that the Directorate had been actively involved in the fighting after midday on December 22.[22] This was also confirmed by the head of the military procuracy, Major Mugurel Florescu, although he may not have been the most independent of judges.[23] After the flight of Ceauşescu, most of the Directorate seem to have fled. When soldiers came to occupy their headquarters in the late afternoon of December 22, they found it abandoned, except for a handful of armed civilians.[24] Technically, along with the rest of the *securitate*, after the fall of Ceauşescu, the unit passed immediately under the command of the Ministry of Defense. However, the exact whereabouts of its members is difficult to establish, although at least one senior officer, Colonel Octavian Nae, spent the night of December 22–23 with the revolutionaries in the central committee building, and another fell as a hero of the revolution defending the television station.[25] About one-third of the Directorate seem to have eventually ended up in the capital's militia stations, and from here, on January 7, Militaru ordered them transferred to a barracks on the outskirts of Bucharest for investigation.[26] However, few ever seem to have faced trial. Four members, including Raţ and Rusu, were charged in relation to the flight of the Ceauşescus, but were found not guilty on March 7, 1990, the first such acquittals recorded after the revolution. The head of the unit, Neagoe, and other senior officers were called to give evidence at this trial but noticeably faced no charges themselves.[27] Later, in May 1991, Neagoe was sentenced to seven years in prison, but this was for abuse of office ap-

20. *Financial Times,* January 2, 1990, 3; Rady (1992), 109, also points the finger of blame at the V Directorate, as does *Washington Post,* December 30, 1989, A1, A14; and, it seems, Mazilu as well, Hall (1997), 317–18. See also *The Times,* January 4, 1990, 8.

21. Pitulescu et al. (1998), 370.

22. *România Liberă,* July 25, 1990, 1, 3.

23. *Adevărul,* February 8, 1991, 2. For allegations by Militaru against Florescu see *România Liberă,* October 25, 1993, 3; Brucan (1993), 195.

24. Perva and Roman (n.d.), 61; Pitulescu et al. (1998), 369.

25. Hall (1997), 361; Pitulescu et al. (1998), 334. See also the report from Captain Ovidiu Soare of the V Directorate in Sava and Monac (2001), 456–57.

26. Băcescu (1994), 92; Hall (1997), 369.

27. *România Liberă,* February 17–March 8 1990.

parently involving the illegal sale of gasoline and not for any offenses specifically relating to December 1989.[28]

Another much suspected unit has been the elite antiterrorist force, USLA. It was at the center of the first alarms following the overthrow of Ceaușescu but, again, little conclusive evidence has appeared to suggest it actually took up arms against the new regime. The commander of this unit, Ardeleanu, appeared at the shoulder of Iliescu during the meeting held to formally constitute the NSF at the central committee building and, notwithstanding Gușă's evident shock at Ardeleanu's presence, this would seem to suggest that the USLA commander and his troops did rapidly align themselves with the new regime. Admittedly, Ardeleanu was later to be one of the few *securitate* commanders dismissed from his post during the revolution, but this seems to have been directly connected to a single confusing incident that occurred outside the Ministry of Defense during the night of December 23–24. The role of USLA in this episode, and in the revolution in general, was later investigated by Horia Alexandrescu in the newspaper *Tineretul Liber* and, although his articles undoubtedly painted a rosy image of the unit, they do seem to hold a kernel of truth.[29] During the night of December 23–24, it seems that three armored vehicles from USLA were summoned to the Ministry of Defense by Ardeleanu, who was inside the building. The order was probably initially given by Militaru, although the exact purpose of the mission remains veiled in some confusion.[30] One of the vehicles broke down en route, and, when the other two arrived, they came under heavy fire from units defending the building. Seven were killed, including the Chief of Staff of USLA, Lieutenant-Colonel Gheorghe Trosca, and two more wounded. Three other crew members escaped to a nearby block, where, the next morning, after telephoning their unit to announce their whereabouts, they were "captured" by the army and taken for interrogation. The USLA troops were immediately proclaimed terrorists, with this word daubed across their wrecked vehicles and the dead bodies left on public display in the street for some time. After the revolution, *securitate* apologists were to intimate that the USLA troops had been the victims of a cynical ambush, be-

28. BBC EE/1086, B/18, May 31, 1991.

29. *Tineretul Liber,* March 4–15, 1990; for a view of the same incident less favorable to USLA, see the article by members of the army in *Adevărul,* August 29, 1990, 1, 2, which, in turn, was a response to an open letter by the widows of the dead, *Adevărul,* August 26, 1990, 3. See also Galloway and Wylie (1991), 201; and for a photograph of one of the wrecked vehicles see *Adevărul,* December 26, 1989, 2. Ardeleanu was to die in 1993 after swallowing pesticides.

30. The situation around the Ministry of Defense was particularly confused but apart from this episode involving USLA there seems to have been at least two other incidents in which the soldiers defending the building fired on friendly approaching forces, causing loss of life. The first case, involving DIA officers from Buzău, killed four just before midnight on December 22, while the second, involving students from the Military Academy of Technical Studies, left five dead a few hours later in the early hours of December 23.

cause Trosca, as a military counterintelligence officer, had been involved in the unmasking of Militaru as a Soviet spy. There is about as much evidence to support this insinuation as there was to support the original view that they were terrorists. The soldiers were the victims of friendly fire and Iliescu did subsequently admit that the whole incident was an unfortunate accident.[31] Elsewhere USLA troops seem to have actively participated in a number of other actions on the side of the revolution, both in Bucharest and other cities, such as Arad.[32] In one incident, they were reported to have killed three terrorists dressed in patriotic guard uniforms. In another, a unit responding to a report that terrorists were firing on civilians raided an apartment on Șoseaua Mihai Bravu in Bucharest and shot dead two people dressed as civilians.[33] They were also involved in mounting searches of the basement of the television station on December 25 and other houses in the vicinity of that building, as well as the "tunnels" under Bucharest.[34]

As far as the other major *securitate* units are concerned, depositions made to the senatorial commission of inquiry state quite clearly that the troops from the officers school of the Ministry of the Interior at Băneasa remained in reserve on buses from 2 o'clock on the morning of December 22 until they returned to barracks around midday and that they were confined there from then onward. During the evening of December 22, on the instructions of Stănculescu, three officers of the Băneasa anti-aircraft command were dispatched to take control of the unit and seal their armories, which were intact but for six bullets.[35] The NSF was also noticeably slow in arresting the head of this unit, Nicolae Andruța Ceaușescu, which suggests that they did not think that either he or his men posed any great threat to the revolution.[36] From the available evidence concerning events at Otopeni, the soldiers of the school for non-commissioned officers of the *securitate* troops also seem to have been deployed on behalf of the revolution.[37] Earlier Brucan had also cast some aspersions about the loyalty of the *securitate* troops in general. However,

31. *România Literară,* July 5, 1990, 14; see also Iliescu (1994), 72–73. Hall (1997), 283–96, offers a full discussion of the literature in arguing that the USLA officers had "less-than-pure intentions." For a different point of view see Deletant (1995), 360–62. See also Nicolaescu (1999), 221–28; Codrescu et al. (1998), 244–45.

32. Codrescu et al. (1998), 225. For Arad, Nicolaescu (1999), 357. Controversy also continues to surround a commercial TAROM flight, which is alleged to have brought up to eighty USLA troops from Bucharest to Sibiu on December 20, 1989. It is not clear if the USLA forces were actually on the airplane or, even if they were, what they actually did in Sibiu. See Nicolaescu (1999), 340–42, and Săndulescu (c1996), 57–58, who suggests that they were not members of USLA but the DIA.

33. Filip (1999), 101.

34. *Nouvel Observateur,* February 15–21, 1990, 4–10; Televiziunea Română (1990), 337.

35. Codrescu et al. (1998), 217; Perva and Roman (n.d.), 84–85.

36. *Adevărul,* January 19, 1990, 1, 3.

37. See Chapter 2.

Tudor in his statement cited above had specifically praised the loyalty of this unit, and its commander, Major-General Ghiţă, had been present at gatherings of the new leaders from the afternoon of December 22, including a meeting at the Ministry of Defense.[38] Ghiţă and another commander of the *securitate* troops, Colonel Pavelescu, were also quick to rebut a statement by Postelnicu broadcast on the radio on December 23, calling on their troops to "cease all actions of a terrorist nature and establish effective means of surrendering."[39] Nevertheless, some suspicions seem to have lingered, because in January 1990 Ghiţă still felt it necessary to stress publicly in *Adevărul* that his men were on the side of the revolution from the beginning and that none were under investigation by the military procuracy.[40] The evidence that has become available about the smaller *securitate* units also seems to suggest that they aligned themselves with the revolution. For instance, during the night of December 22–23 Iliescu seems to have spoken with a number of individual commanders, including Major-General Ovidiu Diaconescu, head of the technical and transmission command, and Major-General Alexandru Ţencu, head of surveillance operations, both of whom were presumably acting on behalf of the new regime.[41]

Among army units, it is perhaps not surprising that doubts comparable to those raised about the various *securitate* units have only been voiced about the Intelligence Directorate of the General Staff, popularly known as the Army Intelligence Directorate or DIA, headed by Rear Admiral Ştefan Dinu, sometimes expanded to also include the special office of the Operations Directorate of the General Staff, headed by Colonel Dumitru Mircea.[42] *Securitate* apologists and others have repeatedly claimed that the DIA, which was said to possess gunfire simulators and other devices alleged to have been used in the revolution, mounted a sophisticated diversion.[43] As might be expected, Dinu and other members of his unit have robustly denied these charges.[44] They state that the primary task of the unit was to gather intelligence about overseas armies and that, although it saw service in both Timişoara and Bucharest, where it sustained casualties, its role in the revolution was little different from other military units. These allegations against the DIA are part of an alternative view of the revolution. This holds that the terrorists never existed and that the fighting

38. Codrescu et al. (1998), 157.
39. BBC EE/0648, B/12, December 28, 1989. Sârcă (1998), 245.
40. *Adevărul*, January 19, 1990, 2; see also ibid., May 25, 1992, 2–4.
41. Televiziunea Română (1990), 168.
42. Hall (1997), 256, 261; Hall (1999), 521–25; *România Mare*, June 29, 1992, 12–15; *România Liberă*, December 24, 1993, 16; FBIS-EEU-98–115, April 25, 1998; Săndulescu (c1996), 299–328. Mircea's superior was Lieutenant-General Eftimescu.
43. It has been admitted that the *securitate* possessed such simulators; Nicolaescu (1999), 215.
44. Codrescu et al. (1998), 414–18, 458–59; Săndulescu (c1996), 209–45, 299–328.

after December 22 was a sophisticated diversion designed to justify the NSF's takeover of power and a Warsaw Pact invasion of Romania, although the latter was foiled.[45] Finding the proof to sustain such an explanation of the events is as difficult as proving that special units of the *securitate* took up arms against the revolution. The NSF might have been guilty of playing to the gallery and making the most of the unrest so as to consolidate its hold on power, but there is little evidence that it deliberately started the shooting or prolonged it unnecessarily, and those who would argue otherwise have yet to present good reason for doubting more solidly grounded explanations of the events.

From the evidence so far available there is little to suggest that any of the larger *securitate* units per se came into open conflict with the forces of the revolution after the overthrow of Ceauşescu, although the absence of detailed information makes it impossible to discount the possibility that some members of these or other *securitate* units, acting as individuals or as small groups, did take up arms against the incoming regime. At first sight, some support for this view may be found in the ballistics evidence presented by Richard Hall, in which he stresses that during the revolution ammunition was fired which was not in the possession of the army.[46] Focusing particularly on 9mm machine guns of West German origin, which he says were only in the possession of USLA and the V Directorate, Hall points out that bullets of this caliber were found at various "hot spots" during the revolution, and in the corpse of a student of the military academy who died defending the Ministry of Defense building on the night of December 22–23. However, it may be questioned whether this evidence is quite so conclusive proof of the existence of *securitate* terrorists as Hall suggests. As of March 1990, thirty-one of these guns from the arsenal of the V Directorate still remained unaccounted for and, given the circulation of guns during the revolution, it is by no means certain that it was troops from these units that fired the weapons in question.[47] And, even if members of USLA and the V Directorate had been responsible for using these weapons, given the confusion at the time and the fact that some troops from these units were actively engaged in the fighting on the behalf of the new authorities, it does not follow that they were used against the revolution.

At first sight, some of the best evidence for the existence of individual terrorists comes from the indisputable fact that large numbers of suspects were arrested during the revolution. On the radio on December 28 two army officers, Major Pavel Lică and Colonel Gheorghe Suman, announced that seventy-five captured terrorists had passed through their

45. Hall (1997), 254–59.
46. Ibid., 319–23.
47. Codrescu et al. (1998), 208.

hands, and the new political leadership were soon reassuring an anxious population that thousands were under detention not just in Bucharest but also elsewhere in the country.[48] Yet the army now says that over December 22–31 military units only held 532 suspects, of which 516 were Romanian citizens and 16 foreigners.[49] Of these suspects, 299 were sent for investigation to the militia and 113 to civil procurators, with the remaining 120, mostly from military units, being interviewed by commanders of garrisons. However, a detailed Ministry of Defense breakdown of the time, which was subsequently produced by Brucan, seems to suggest that on January 4 the army held 608 suspects, with the vast majority being detained in four cities: Bucharest (179), Sibiu (171), Brăila (134), and Timișoara (89).[50] And, just over a month later, the number of arrests in Sibiu alone had reportedly risen to 522, of which 389 were former members of the Ministry of the Interior forces and 133 were civilians.[51]

Although there are some contradictions in the figures, it is clear that large numbers of people were detained during the revolution. Yet few terrorists were to appear in the dock. By the beginning of 1995, the military procurator's office had opened 4,495 files on incidents after December 22, 1989, but by December 1996 only 203 people had been sent to trial; 48 from the army, 93 from the forces of the Ministry of the Interior, and 62 civilians. In many of these cases, and virtually all of those relating to the forces of the Ministry of the Interior, the proceedings had begun prior to August 1990.[52] By that date, thirty had already been convicted for offenses relating to the revolution, according to one source, seventeen as "terrorists." Of these, ten were officers of the *securitate,* six members of the militia, and one a civilian.[53] Three of the earliest trials of suspected terrorists were partially televised in Romania and received much publicity in the Western media. All related to incidents that had occurred in Sibiu county, but in only one case was the defendant, Ioan Botarel, a member of the *securitate* and even he hardly matched the public image of a terrorist fanatic. Botarel was sentenced to nineteen years in prison and seven years deprivation of civic rights for firing on the crowd outside from the window of the militia-*securitate* building on the afternoon of December 22.[54] The other two cases both involved militia officers. On January 8, 1990,

---

48. Neacșu (c1999).
49. Codrescu et al. (1998), 188.
50. The table is reproduced in *Adevărul,* January 29, 1991, 2; see also ibid., January 30, 1991, 2, where it is shown that the majority of those held in Bucharest were arrested after December 27, probably because they were members of the V Directorate.
51. BBC EE/0690, B/6:20, February 16, 1990. Codrescu et al. (1998), 273–74, states that 494 were detained in Sibiu after December 22, 1989.
52. Stan (1997), 196; Ratesh (1991), 61; *România Liberă,* August 25, 1990; BBC EE/0856, B/10:30, August 30, 1990.
53. Perva and Roman (n.d.), 108–9.
54. *România Liberă,* January 13, 1990, 2.

Major Ioan Bunda was sentenced to nine years in prison together with four years deprivation of civic rights for attempted murder after he had been found guilty of shooting at five army officers and wounding another in Sibiu on December 22, 1989.[55] Then, the next day, Captain Liviu Vanga, the militia chief at Cisnădie near Sibiu, and Lieutenant-Major Aurel Marcu from Sibiu were each sentenced to twelve and a half years in prison, with nine years deprivation of civic rights for firing their submachine guns at demonstrators in Cisnăde on December 21, 1989, killing two and wounding eleven others.[56] Vanga and Marcu were pardoned in 1992, as were a number of other militia and *securitate* officers, often on the argument they had been acting in self-defense.[57]

After the initial flurry of trials, the pace of prosecutions from the second half of 1990 onward slowed, and even when convictions were secured, as in the case of Vlad, the prison sentences served were short.[58] This slowdown has often been blamed on a change in the political climate, which is said to have become more inimical to trials. However, it can also be seen as a sign of an increased determination to observe the rule of law, making it impossible to repeat the early show trials that had condemned the Ceauşescus and the members of the PEC. Under a positivist legal tradition that which was previously legal cannot easily be made illegal in retrospect, and many of those responsible for the worst bloodshed in 1989 had been acting under existing laws. Only when these laws had actually been breached could prosecution be considered, and this was not easy to establish. Following the elections of 1996, which saw the installation of Emil Constantinescu as president, the files on the revolution were reopened, partly it seems, at least in the case of Timişoara, due to pressure from revolutionary organizations.[59] New charges were laid, but, in contrast to the earlier trials, the focus this time was not on the terrorists and the *securitate* but on the army, as sixteen personnel, ranging in rank from generals to a private, were indicted for crimes committed during the revolution in Timişoara, Sibiu, Braşov, Buzău, Bacău, and Ploieşti, with more charges relating to Cluj following later.[60] The most prominent of these prosecutions relating to the revolution in Timişoara seem to have been mostly brought on the basis of the recommendations contained in a

55. For differing accounts of the trial see *The Times,* January 9, 1990, 8; *Financial Times,* January 9, 1990, 18; *Independent,* January 9, 1990, 8; *Washington Post,* January 9, 1990, A15. For a detailed investigation of the case see Pitulescu et al. (1998), 335–48.

56. *The Times,* January 10, 1990, 24; BBC EE/0690, B/6:20, February 16, 1990.

57. Pitulescu et al. (1995), 151. Other examples include Captain Adrian Tinca, a militia officer from Târgu Mureş, who was amnestied, and Majors Lupeş and Popovici of the *securitate,* who had their sentences quashed; ibid., 160, 163.

58. Vlad was found guilty of "favoring genocide" in July 1991 and sentenced to nine years in prison. On December 30, 1993 he was released on parole; Deletant (1995), 389.

59. FBIS-EEU-97–311, November 7, 1997; FBIS-EEU-97–314, November 10, 1997.

60. FBIS-EEU-98–105, April 15, 1998.

report drawn up by a governmental commission established in February 1990.[61] At the time the findings of this commission had been shelved, most probably because two of those recommended for prosecution, Stănculescu and Chițac, were senior ministers in the Roman government. Under the Constantinescu presidency these two men and a number of others were sent to trial, and, it seems, it was only his death on April 1, 1998, that prevented Gușă from joining them in the dock.[62]

None of those convicted for crimes committed during the revolution match the image of highly trained terrorists proffered at the time. Yet the fact that no terrorists have been convicted does not necessarily mean that they did not exist. It still remains the case that thousands of dubious characters were held as suspected terrorists during the revolution and, if they were not terrorists, why were they detained? From December 26, 1989, the military procurator's office began to investigate the cases of some 200 of those held in Bucharest.[63] They discovered that some of them were held for specific crimes related to stealing from the central committee building, RCP offices, or other state-owned premises, while others were armed civilians who had participated in the events and been detained for intemperate behavior. Some had been wrongly denounced to the authorities and a few had taken advantage of the situation to settle longstanding scores. However, most arrests seem to have been related to the general climate of all-pervading paranoia in which the level of fear and suspicion reached such a pitch that it sparked off an apparently never-ending cycle of arrest and release. This comes over particularly strongly in the accounts contained in *Revoluția Română în direct,* where it seems that, at one time or another, nearly every civilian in the television center was detained as a suspect terrorist, including even Dan Marțian, a leading light of the Front.[64] Often on the flimsiest of excuses arrests were made. Those lying wounded in hospitals were detained for wearing unusual clothes, while others were held for being in a different zone from where they lived, or perhaps because, without any valid reason, they were near a building

61. BBC, EE/3196, B/5, April 8, 1998; BBC, EE/3118, B/3, January 7, 1998; *Evenimentul Zilei,* March 9, 1999; BBC, EE/3198 B/3, April 10, 1998.

62. FBIS-EEU-98–007, January 7, 1998. The search for justice, however, has been painful and troubled. In June 1999 Stănculescu and Chițac were sentenced to fifteen years imprisonment but, following the victory of Iliescu in the 2000 presidential elections, their sentences were suspended. Their cases continue to be a political football. See FBIS-EEU-1999–0719, June 19, 1999; FBIS-EEU-1999–0716, July 16, 1999; FBIS-EEU-1999–0721, July 21, 1999; FBIS-EEU-2001–0212, February 12, 2001; *RFE/RL Newsline,* August 9, 2001, http://www.rferl.org/newsline/2001/08/090801.html; Siani-Davies (2001). In August 2002, Iliescu also pardoned—on "humanitarian grounds"—Major-General Constantin Rotariu, who, after a series of trials, had eventually been sentenced by the Supreme Court to ten years imprisonment for ordering his troops to shoot at the crowd in Calea Lipovei in Timișoara on December 17. *Evenimentul Zilei Online,* August 12, 2002, http://www.expres.ro/politica/?newsid=93461.

63. *Adevărul,* February 8, 1991, 2.

64. Televiziunea Română (1990), 225–29.

from which gunshots had been heard. One of the most striking images of the revolution, a photograph of a young terrorist under guard in a hospital bed, in fact showed an innocent young man, Cristian Lupu, who had gone to help defend the television station. When he was wounded on December 23 he was taken to the emergency hospital where, for some reason, he was declared a suspect terrorist before he died on December 25.[65] Lupu was later exonerated of all charges but his experience does not seem to have been unique. As early as January 6, 1990, *România Liberă* carried the details of a similar case involving a young revolutionary, Gabriel Matei. Taken from the central committee building to a hospital on December 25 with a bad infection in his leg, he was arrested as a suspected terrorist before being released.[66] The most emotionally charged picture of a man falsely charged as a terrorist, though, is the case of Dominic Paraschiv, which was later made the subject of the film *Requiem for Dominic* by his childhood friend, Robert Dornhelm. According to Dornhelm's research, Paraschiv, a deeply religious and essentially peaceful man, at the height of the revolution had joined a search party looking for terrorists at a factory in Timișoara. On December 24, 1989, exhausted after two consecutive nights on guard duty without any sleep, he seems to have suffered a nervous breakdown and at gunpoint forced his colleagues to kneel in prayer and repent their sins, saying that they had all collaborated in the forty-year lie of communism. Eventually Paraschiv was overwhelmed by soldiers, but in the process he was shot and had to be taken to the local hospital. Here the situation somehow got completely out of control, and a bleeding and naked Paraschiv secured in a net ended up being paraded before foreign journalists as a terrorist accused of eighty murders. Dornhelm suggests that the hospital staff, believing these wild rumors, withdrew treatment from their patient, apparently allowing him to bleed to death. Paraschiv was declared innocent of all charges in May 1990 and was, subsequently, listed as a victim of the revolution.[67] Yet his death while in the hands of the authorities was not unique, since there are reports of a number of other suspected terrorists being found dead in their cells or shot while trying to escape.[68]

It seems that even within the ranks of those held at the time there is still little evidence of the terrorists. Nearly all of those detained during the revolution were eventually freed. Most were clearly innocent but in some cases suspicions lingered. The military prosecutor stated that some of those released had been detained for fighting with supporters of the rev-

65. Ibid., 157–62, and the photograph in *Cronica însingerata* (1990).
66. His story can be found in *România Liberă,* January 6, 1990, 3.
67. *Requiem for Dominic,* directed by Robert Dornhelm (Austria, 1990). The film was first shown on British Television on December 26,1990; see Wilder (1995), 243–46, and the interview with Robert Dornhelm in *Independent,* December 20, 1990, 13.
68. Codrescu et al. (1998), 279, 281.

olution—he was not specific, but presumably these disputes were at the level of public arguments and fisticuffs rather than counterrevolutionary activity. More contentious were the cases of those held who were members of the *securitate*, even though they professed to support the revolution.[69] These arrests lie at the crux of the problem, because the accusation has often been made that many of those who were terrorists were surreptitiously released by their own comrades-in-arms once they were transferred to militia stations and other places of detention.[70] Brucan and Militaru have even charged that in this way many of those who took up arms against the NSF were allowed to flee to Hungary and Turkey.[71] No further information has been produced to substantiate these claims, although, prior to January 1, 1990, 10 of the 79 Romanians who fled to Yugoslavia during or immediately after the fighting were reportedly arrested as suspected *securitate* agents.[72]

The Image of the Terrorists

As might be expected, given the suggestion in Chapter 3 that many of the deaths in the revolution after the overthrow of Ceaușescu were caused by friendly fire, little tangible evidence can be found for the existence of the terrorists and even less to suggest that they posed any real threat to the new regime. Even the most suspect *securitate* units seem to have rapidly sided with the revolution, and from the available evidence few if any of those detained as terrorists fitted the popular image of the enemy. This raises an interesting puzzle, because if the terrorists did not really exist, why was the idea that they did so readily taken up by both the Romanians and the outside world?

Ceaușescu had called the demonstrators on December 21 "terrorists" and the use of the same word to describe those who opposed the new regime after his overthrow was just a neat reversal of terms. Yet there was also a sense of continuity, because those called terrorists after December 22 were the same people as those who had terrorized the population for so many years under communism; it was just that previously they had been known as the *securitate*. One of the first acts of the new leaders was to place the *securitate* under the jurisdiction of the army.[73] By doing this they may have hoped to conjure the *securitate* away, but through the medium of the terrorists it was resurrected as a foe. More than a physical entity the *securitate* for most Romanians, and later the outside world, was the very

69. *Adevărul,* February 8, 1991, 2.
70. *România Liberă,* December 17, 1992, 2.
71. *East European Reporter,* 4:3, 1990, 74–77.
72. *The Times,* January 1, 1990, 5.
73. BBC EE/0648, B/7, December 28, 1989; Televiziunea Română (1990), 84. This move was later legally enacted in a decree broadcast on December 26; see BBC EE/0649, B/5, December 29, 1989.

embodiment of the evils of the communist regime. An exaggerated myth had made them an omnipotent and omnipresent force of repression, and now, after Ceaușescu's downfall, that same myth was to make them capable of the most horrific atrocities. Western news reports drawing on local sources were graphic in their descriptions: "In Arad . . . [the *securitate*] stormed the maternity section of the main hospital. There, they riddled pregnant women and babies with bullets"; "In Bucharest, they attacked the main emergency hospital"; and "In Cluj . . . they descended from a lorry and fired into a small group of demonstrators. More than thirty people were shot dead."[74] In some places they were said to have poisoned the local water supply and in Brașov to have plans to blow up a nearby dam. The BBC journalist John Simpson had heard similar stories concerning poisoned water during the Iranian revolution of 1979, leading him to suggest that "certain ideas appeal forcibly to the self-dramatizing mind of the revolutionary."[75] Indeed, in Romania the wild storytelling to a certain extent was just another consequence of the tumult of the revolution. However, the imagery may also have served another purpose. According to Andrei Codrescu, when pushed far the Romanians instead of making physical recourse to action will use their imagination to make exemplary gestures. When Codrescu is told a story about *securitate* men being impaled on a wheel he notes that they "were neither more nor less dead for being impaled. But impaled, they were *unforgettable*. That was the point, whether any impalement had taken place or not."[76] A grotesque effigy of Ceaușescu left hanging by a rope from a tree in the center of Bucharest made a similar point and was indicative of how the ills of the past were heaped upon the deposed leader and his henchmen in a visceral hatred.[77]

The stories of atrocities fulfilled a real social need, because through them the Romanians as a people could indulge in a collective self-cleansing. All to a greater or lesser extent had been tainted by the Ceaușescu regime. Now, through the tales of horror, they were able to place the evil forces of that regime so far beyond the bounds of "normal" society that they were effectively able to distance themselves from the demons of the past.[78] There was also a sense in which it was *necessary* for the *securitate* to be so terrible: How else could the years of mute suffering under an enfeebled old tyrant such as Ceaușescu be explained and condoned?[79] The appearance of the terrorists allowed the Romanians to os-

74. *Financial Times,* January 2, 1990, 3. *Independent,* December 23, 1989, 1, carries reports of *securitate* officers killing thirty children in Timișoara.

75. Simpson (1992), 252.

76. Codrescu (1991), 93; emphasis in the original. Note the allusion to the Dracula myth in the reference to impalement.

77. *The Times,* January 10, 1989, 6.

78. Wagner (1990), vi.

79. *Guardian,* December 12, 1990, 23.

tracize the past but, as the atrocities spiraled uncontrollably, even the regular *securitate* officers became incapable of such deeds, since after all they were fellow Romanians. Instead, the terrorists were distanced from society, transformed into drug-crazed fanatics and mindless automata, until they stopped being Romanians altogether.

Stories about the terrorists being under the influence of narcotics began to emerge on December 28, when Bucharest radio's first "free transmission for the army" alleged that captured "enemy elements" were drugged. Soon Hungarian radio was broadcasting similar stories saying *securitate* agents had been captured in possession of heroin.[80] And, in an interview in the Western press two doctors responsible for the treatment of fifteen suspected terrorists, mostly in their early twenties in Bucharest, contended that their patients were: "really high on drugs and alcohol."[81] Later Gabrielescu was also to say that many of those who participated in the revolution acted under the influence of alcohol.[82] Much of this had presumably been stolen from vandalized shops, and it seems not inconceivable that many of those arrested as suspected terrorists at this time were drunk. A more fanciful attempt at distancing ordinary Romanians from the terrorists was through claims that they were zombie-like child orphans raised to obey without question the dictates of their beloved master. This "orphan myth," which circulated widely at the time and was even mentioned at the trial of the Ceauşescus, appeared in a number of Western news reports.[83] As an unfortunate consequence of Romania's widespread poverty and Ceauşescu's pronatalist policy, large numbers of children had been placed in institutional care, but there is no real evidence that they were specifically targeted for recruitment by the *securitate*. It seems more likely that, as with other stories about the seizure of children that have appeared with some regularity in Balkan history, this Romanian variant derives from the Ottoman practice of enslaving male Christian children into state service through the *devshirme*. Many of these children were later enlisted in the elite janissary corps of the Ottoman army—an institution that bore obvious parallels with the *securitate*.

This process of distancing was most evident in the widespread rumor that it was not really Romanians but foreigners who were responsible for much of the killing. Stories that foreign mercenaries were taking part in the fighting were broadcast by the Romanian media on December 23, with reports soon focusing specifically on Arab involvement.[84] In the early

80. BBC EE/0652, B/12:20, January 3, 1990.
81. *Washington Post,* December 30, 1989, A14; *Financial Times,* January 2, 1990, 3.
82. *Daily Telegraph,* December 12, 1994, 10.
83. *Washington Post,* December 24, 1989, A1, A24; *Independent,* December 30, 1989, 1; *Sunday Times,* January 14, 1990, A17.
84. Sârcă (1998), 263.

afternoon of that day, Romanian radio carried the dramatic news that "the radio building is being violently attacked by Arab troops. Our Caligula, the Caligula of Bucharest, has brought Arab troops to attack Romanians. . . . We are under attack."[85] And soon the foreign media were full of similar stories, with Hungarian Radio reporting that Colonel Muammar al-Qaddafi had sent 2,000 Libyan troops to support the *securitate*.[86] These stories prompted the Syrian chargé d'affaires in Budapest to request that the Hungarian people be informed that the Syrian army was not taking part in the fighting. Hungarian radio duly reported his statement, but in the process they noted that the chargé d'affaires had not specifically denied that any Syrian citizens were involved and, subsequently, on December 26, the Hungarians came under heavy criticism from the Federation of Arab News Agencies in Budapest for persisting with reports that people of Middle Eastern origin were involved in the conflict.[87] Vigorous denials from Syria and Libya that any of their citizens were involved also appeared in an edition of *Adevărul* dated December 25, 1989, and on Bucharest Radio on December 27 a Palestine Liberation Organization leader, Faruq Qaddumi, stated the same was true for his organization.[88] Finally, on December 30, after receiving a telephone call from Qaddafi, Roman made a public statement denying that any Arabs had participated in the conflict, adding that such "rumors" were being spread by those who wished to destabilize "the popular revolution."[89]

Roman's statement did not end the speculation about Arab involvement, because in their celebrated interview of August 23, 1990, Brucan and Militaru returned to the fray, claiming that the Ministry of Interior special units "were joined by about 30 Arab students, mostly Palestinians, who had been trained at Andruţa's [Ceauşescu] Military Academy. One of them was killed and many wounded but the corpse disappeared from the morgue, and the wounded, after undergoing surgery or being bandaged at the hospital, were taken away by their comrades and all left by air."[90] Once again these allegations were denied by the government, with Roman telling the Romanian language Israeli daily *Viaţa Noastra* that "no Arab terrorist had been captured" and that " 'the alleged training base for

85. Ibid., 264.
86. Ibid., 264–71; see also Shafir (October 12, 1990), 37; BBC EE/0649, B/3, December 29, 1989.
87. BBC EE/0649, B/8–9, December 29, 1989. For details of reports originating from Middle Eastern sources that Arabs and Iranians were involved in the fighting see *Independent*, January 3, 1990, 10.
88. BBC EE/0649, B/13, December 29, 1989; see also *Independent*, December 27, 1989, 8; *The Times*, December 28, 1989, 7.
89. Shafir (October 12, 1990), 37; see also the comments made by Corneliu Bogdan reported in the *Washington Post*, December 28, 1989, A26.
90. *East European Reporter*, 4:3, 1990, 76. An anonymous interview making similar claims also appeared that month in the magazine *Baricada*. Nestor Ratesh has argued this showed all the hallmarks of coming from Brucan and Militaru; Ratesh (1991), 65.

Palestinians terrorists' did not exist."[91] Yet rumors of such camps persisted, and in the light of the revelations of Romanian complicity in the activities of the international terrorist Ilich Ramires Sánchez, known as Carlos the Jackal, they were perhaps not so fanciful.[92] There were thirteen Libyans training in Romania in the schools of the Ministry of Defense in December 1989, but it still remains unproven that these, the seven Iranians mentioned in Chapter 2, Palestinians, Syrians, or indeed any Arabs actually participated in the conflict.[93]

Instead, it seems likely that the answer to the mystery of the Arab terrorists may again be found within the expectations of Romanian society. Prior to the revolution, Romania had a considerable population of Arab students, who in general seem to have been resented by most of the locals, because of their perceived arrogance and sometimes lavish display among domestic poverty.[94] Due to their skin coloring the Arabs were also associated in popular perception with the much-reviled Gypsies. Indeed, it seems possible that many of those identified as Arabs during the revolution were in fact Gypsies.[95] Latent tensions between the communities seem to have boiled over at the time, with PLO sources claiming Arabs were attacked and Cluj radio broadcasting an appeal for calm between the foreign students and local Romanians.[96] Indicative was a bizarre incident in Iași, where the head of the local branch of the NSF when telling the journalist David Binder how he ordered the army to attack upon hearing that a group of Arab students were at the local post office, drew a pistol, and declared "A revolutionary has to know how to . . . use arms."[97]

It is to be hoped that these Arab students escaped harm, but, willingly or not, it seems quite conceivable that others may well have become caught up in the fighting in some way. Whether any of these were military trainees will probably forever remain unknown. What seems more certain is that, even if a few Arabs did participate in some unknown way, they would have had little appreciable effect on the conflict. Indeed, all the reports of Arab terrorists are put into perspective by the experience of Philip Jacobson, a reporter from *The Times,* who entered Romania from Hungary with two South Korean journalists. When their car was stopped by the Romanian army, the two Koreans were roughly manhandled and nearly executed on the spot by excited soldiers before an officer appeared and explained that "Libyan and Syrian terrorists" had shot and

91. Quoted in Shafir (October 12, 1990), 37.
92. BBC EE/3121, B/6:13, January 10, 1998; *România Liberă,* January 22, 1998, 6; ibid., January 29, 1998, 6.
93. For the Libyans see Nicolaescu (1999), 111.
94. Angelescu (July 17, 1985), 19–21.
95. Nicolaescu (1999), 194. For anti-Gypsy sentiment see Dătculescu and Liepelt(1992), 139, where, in a poll, 68 percent of Romanians express antipathy toward Gypsies.
96. Sârcă (1998), 268; Neacșu (c1999).
97. *New York Times,* January 13, 1990, 17.

killed two of his men near Arad on Sunday night and that "his troops were naturally angry about this, and anyway, how could they be expected to distinguish between Libyans and Syrians and Koreans since they had never before laid eyes on any of them?"[98] Perhaps not surprisingly the Koreans, by now thoroughly unnerved, chose to return across the Hungarian border.

The passage of time has rendered the terrorists little more visible than they were during the darkest hours of the revolution. It was popularly charged that they were members of the *securitate* but, as has been seen, there is little evidence to suggest that any units of this organization per se took up arms against the incoming regime. However, this does not mean that some individual *securitate* officers, or even groups of officers, did not come to occupy a more ambiguous stance. The plain truth is that the whereabouts of many members of the *securitate* during the revolution remains a mystery. Typical of many were the eight officers and NCOs of USLA guarding Nicu Ceauşecu's residence in Sibiu. Following the departure of Nicu and the overthrow of Ceauşescu, apparently without waiting for any orders, they hid their guns and uniforms and headed home. Only during the evening of December 24 did they report to their unit, returning with representatives of the procurator the next day to recover their arms and equipment.[99] It was not just the lower ranks of the forces of the Ministry of the Interior who behaved in this way; senior members also went missing. Colonel Gheorghe Goran, the head of the *securitate* in Bucharest, left his post at 10 o'clock on the morning of December 22 and apparently did not reappear again until December 25.[100] In Târgoviste the local head of the *securitate*, Lieutenant-Colonel Ion Deaconu, left his office in the morning of December 22, he says to look after his handicapped son, and spent the night with his parents-in-law in Ploieşti.[101] Some *securitate* officers had even been ordered home before the collapse of the regime, as was the case with female officers in Sibiu during the evening and morning of December 21–22. In Brăila the local head ordered all his officers home, so that when the army came to take over the Ministry of the Interior headquarters in the city they found 75 percent of the staff absent. In Constanţa the figure was said to be 50 percent, while in Braşov forty officers were apparently unaccounted for.[102] This does not mean these officers took up arms against the new regime. Members of the *securitate* had much to fear, being so closely identified in the public mind with the sinking Ceauşescu regime. The crowds on the street were braying for retribution, sometime by name, and, as mentioned before, revenge at-

---

98. *The Times*, December 26, 1989, 6.
99. Nicolaescu (1999), 336.
100. Ibid., 124.
101. Domenico (1999), 173–75.
102. Respectively, Nicolaescu (1999), 179, 337, 363–66, 378, 415, 438.

tacks both on them and their property seem not to have been unknown. Like many of those in positions of authority, they were probably most concerned with saving their own skins while they waited to see which way the tide would turn. Amid all the stories of *securitate* terrorists, they floated in an ambiguous void, and it is the suspicions they engendered that may have led to some of the violence, as they were challenged by or perhaps even challenged the revolution. However, by the time Vlad and the other *securitate* leaders had made public protestations of loyalty to the new regime, both the populace and apparently many of the new leaders had embraced the idea of the *securitate* terrorists and, once set in motion, this idea proved impossible to halt, largely because the proffered image so closely matched popular expectations.

Internal Conspiracies

Aside from the identity of the terrorists, the other great enigma of the revolution relates to the origins of the National Salvation Front and the extent to which its seizure of power was due to a conspiracy. Initially, there was near unanimity within Romania that the events had been a spontaneous explosion of popular anger, with 90 percent agreeing with this description in an early poll.[103] Most observers abroad also held the same view, with an editorial in *The Times* the day after the overthrow of Ceaușescu headlined "An end to tyranny," unambiguously describing the events as a "classic popular uprising."[104] However, within days, nagging doubts had set in as to whether everything was really quite as it had first seemed. In particular, questions were asked about the NSF. Had it really grown out of the spontaneous revolution, as its leaders claimed, or had it been established earlier and taken power in an elaborate coup d'état? Doubts spread in Romania and abroad and, only a month after its first editorial, *The Times* under the headline "A revolution betrayed?" was making a rather hackneyed allusion to Shakespeare, in comparing Iliescu and Roman to Brutus and Cassius.[105]

The initial idea that the revolution was a planned conspiracy appears to have been a last gasp poisoned chalice from Ceaușescu, who at his trial raged against "this gang of traitors of the country, who with foreign help, organized a coup d'état."[106] Largely a recapitulation of his earlier allegations, that the revolution was the work of "reactionary, imperialist, irredentist, chauvinist circles, and foreign espionage services in various coun-

103. *The Times*, January 18, 1990, 6.
104. Ibid., December 23, 1989, 11.
105. Ibid., January 25, 1990, 13.
106. Ardeleanu, Savaliuc, and Baiu (1996), 31.

tries," the charge that the events were nothing more than a coup d'état was given added spice by the presence at his trial of Stănculescu.[107] Just as the terrorists grew out of the myth of the *securitate*, so Ceauşescu's assertion that he had been toppled by a conspiracy fell on particularly fertile ground. Romania has a longstanding domestic tradition of political intrigue, stretching back to the Phanariot period and beyond. Communism, with its all-pervasive climate of suspicion and a tendency to blame every problem on "plots" and "outside forces," merely reinforced this propensity.[108] Years of Marxist-Leninist instruction had imbued minds with the idea that revolution came about through the actions of a vanguard grouping, which was often a hidden and clandestine organization. Under communism too, there was no legitimate mechanism for promotion other than favor from on high, so conspiracy against one's rivals was the norm. Petru Dumitriu's informed novel *Incognito,* set among the higher echelons of the RCP, is redolent with intrigue, suspicion, and chicanery, and Vladimir Tismaneanu has described the tale of Romanian communism as "an endless succession of plots, vendettas, and assassinations."[109]

However, the longest shadow in 1989 seems to have been cast by the most famous Romanian plot of all, the coup d'état of August 23, 1944. This had removed Marshal Antonescu from power and led to Romania's abrupt change of sides from the axis to the allied cause in the Second World War. Some of the participants in 1989, such as Brucan, were old enough to have participated on the fringes of this earlier conspiracy, and it was surely no coincidence that Brucan and Militaru's celebrated interview about conspiracies against Ceauşescu was published in *Adevărul* on August 23, 1990. Following the downfall of the RCP regime, which had long usurped the coup of 1944 for its own political ends, a whole spate of books and articles appeared in Romania about the events of that year, and these seem to have helped, perhaps largely subconsciously, to consolidate the "culture of conspiracy." Indeed, some of the similarities between 1944 and 1989 at first sight do seem quite striking. Two eyewitness observers of the coup of 1944 noted: "There were so many plotters plotting, conspirators conspiring, traitors committing treason and cheaters cheating, including the very Sigurantza [Security Police] . . . that nobody knew who was who and what was what. We traced nine separate plots all striving for the same goal." However, before succumbing to a complete sense of déjà vu, it should be noted that the coup of 1944 proceeded so smoothly that "it really lacked the dramatic punch and the shooting and shouting with-

107. BBC EE/0648, B/1, December 22, 1989. For Stănculescu see Almond (1992), 233–34.

108. For the strength of the "culture of conspiracy" in Romania see Verdery and Kligman (1992), 119.

109. Dumitriu (1964); Tismaneanu (1989b), 330.

out which political upheavals in Bucharest were considered impossible."[110]

The Origins of the National Salvation Front

Past experience may have given the Romanians a predilection to believe in conspiracy stories but the doubts about the NSF would not have taken such a firm hold if there had not been real inconsistencies in the story that it told, especially about its own origins. After the public broadcast of the Ceauşescus' trial, speculation over this issue was fueled by the showing on French television of the video recording of the central committee building meeting of December 22 in which Militaru had declared that the NSF had already been in existence for six months before the revolution. In itself the statement is accurate, because an organization bearing this name had sent a series of letters to Radio Free Europe, two of which were broadcast: the first on August 27, 1989, the second on November 8. However, what is not initially clear from Militaru's comment is whether he was suggesting that those gathered in the room were actually part of an organization called the NSF or whether he was just stating that this existed, presumably because like many others he had heard it mentioned on Radio Free Europe. Interpretations of Militaru's words have tended to vary with political standpoint, with Iliescu somewhat contradictorily following the line that he was talking about another organization before noting his statement was "an exaggeration."[111] Only later did Militaru confirm that he was referring to an organization to which he already belonged, although by this time he can hardly be counted as the most reliable of witnesses, since he had long fallen out with many of his former colleagues.[112] However, even if Militaru did belong to an organization called the NSF it is still not certain whether this was the same as the group that had sent letters to Radio Free Europe, because according to Bucharest radio, which carried the story as early as December 30, 1989, at least one of the letters was written by Alexandru Melian, a Bucharest university professor, and this was later confirmed by Brucan.[113] Confusing the picture, Melian was subsequently to state that no real organization lay behind the letter and it is not entirely clear how his version of events fits with that of Radio Free Europe, which was told that the first letter had been smuggled out of Romania by a medical doctor, who was part of a

110. Bishop and Crayfield (1949), 34, 36.
111. Iliescu (1995b), 16.
112. General Militaru interviewed by John Simpson on *Newsnight* (BBC2), December 16, 1994.
113. Neacşu (c1999); Brucan (1993), 172; see also *Adevărul*, March 30, 1990, 1, 3.

larger organization, and that the same doctor had written the second letter while he was visiting relations in Germany.[114]

The link between the letter writing NSF and the NSF that took power during the revolution is not proven, but this does not mean that the latter organization did not exist prior to December 1989. Evidence that it may have been formed earlier comes not only from the various stories about conspiracies discussed later in this chapter but also from a closer consideration of the very name of the organization itself. In the argument over the origins of the National Salvation Front it has frequently been overlooked that, although Iliescu and the others took power formally in December 1989 under this appelation, it does not seem to have been the name that was first used for their organization. In the discussion at the central committee building when Militaru first spoke, he had actually called it the Council of National Salvation as well as Front, and in the hours immediately after Ceaușescu's overthrow both Iliescu and Tudor referred to it as the Committee of National Salvation. The semantic differences between the various forms might appear minor, but they become more interesting when it is recalled that the vehicle through which General Wojciech Jaruzelski declared martial law in Poland on December 13, 1981, was also called the Military Council of National Salvation. Was the imposition of martial law in Poland the model the Romanian conspirators had in mind?

There were obvious important differences between Romania and Poland, not least because in Romania there was no mass organization like Solidarity challenging single-party rule, and this left Western commentators doubtful that a Polish-style military coup could be mounted.[115] The coup in Poland, however, did set a precedent for the deposition of a party leader by the military and, as will be seen below, it does seem that some within Romania sought to replicate these events. The chief figure behind these plans for a coup, according to a fellow conspirator, Nicolae Radu, was General Ion Ioniță, a former minister of national defense and deputy prime minister, who seems to have acted out of a desire not to change the communist system but rather to place a greater emphasis on the state instead of the Party, as did occur in Poland.[116] Could the conspirators have chosen a name similar to that used by the Polish military in order to legit-

114. Shafir (January 19, 1990), 16, suggests that the language of the first letter, which includes references to God, indicates it was not written by a RCP activist. Ratesh (1991), 90.
115. Crowther (1989), 207–25, and the discussion in Sampson (1983), 139–44.
116. Săndulescu (c.1996), 104–5. Ion Ioniță during his career occupied many senior positions, including minister of national defense (1966–76). In 1976 he was promoted to deputy prime minister and became a full member of the PEC. However, in 1979 his career stated to go into sharp decline as he lost his place on the Defense Council and then the PEC before he was finally removed from the Central Committee in November 1984. According to Brucan, as early as 1976, Ioniță had become involved in the plotting of a military coup with the army chief of staff, General Ion Gheorghe. Both Brucan and Radu have suggested Ioniță died in highly suspicious circumstances; Brucan (1993), 132–34; Shafir (October 12, 1990). Nicolae Radu was formerly an officer in the Romanian navy and merchant marine. He has

imize their plans in the eyes of the USSR? Certainly the Soviet Union does seem to have been approached several times for help in mounting a coup. In 1984–85 discussions about this are said to have taken place between Vasile Patilineţ, the Romanian ambassador in Turkey, and his Soviet counterpart.[117] By his own admission, in 1987 Militaru asked the Soviet Consulate in Constanţa for material support, and in 1988 Brucan, also identified as a conspirator, may have done the same during his audience with Gorbachev. However, Militaru was rebuffed and according to Brucan, while Gorbachev expressed support for any well-organized plan that might secure Ceauşescu's removal, he specifically ruled out any Soviet intervention to aid such a scheme. Despite the nomenclatural similarities between the two bodies that came to power in Poland and Romania, preparations in the latter never reached a stage as advanced as in the former, where some sources suggest the detailed planning for the coup was settled in two meetings between General Jaruzelski and two officers from the USSR, General Kryuchkov and Marshal Viktor Kulikov.[118]

News of the contents of the video recording broadcast on French television rapidly filtered back to Romania, and under the sharp questioning of foreign journalists a number of senior CNSF members appeared to confirm Militaru's statement. A leading member of the Front, Cazimir Ionescu, told a foreign television journalist: "We have been planning this [the revolution] for the past two years. We never thought we would get it off the ground—but we kept on with our meetings and followed Gorbachev very closely." Lupoi was quoted in *Le Figaro* as saying that the Front "had been set up a long time ago, but it had in fact come to life on the barricades, during the anti-Ceauşescu insurrection."[119] Senior foreign politicians also began to suggest that all was not as it had first seemed in Romania. The French foreign minister, Roland Dumas, stated in a radio interview that he also had known of a plot since the summer because the French ambassador in Bucharest "had done his job."[120] When he visited Romania shortly after the revolution, Dumas tried to play down his remarks, stating categorically that he did not believe there had been a coup.[121] However, the cat had been let out of the bag and Dumas heightened the speculation further through a passing comment that in his opinion the Soviet Union "undoubtedly knew [about the plot] too." Some support for this statement comes from the fact that as early as 6:00 p.m. on

---

stated that the Committee of National Salvation was created in January 1985. Săndulescu (c1996), 95.

117. Săndulescu (c1996), 90–91. Brucan also told Almond (1990b), 42 n. 14, that the conspirators were in contact with the KGB. Vasile Patilineţ was a former minister and alternative member of the PEC.

118. Andrew and Gordievsky (1990), 485–86.

119. *The Times,* January 3, 1990, 1, 6; Shafir (January 19, 1990), 19 n. 7.

120. Quoted in Ratesh (1991), 102; see also *The Times,* January 4, 1990, 8.

121. *Guardian,* January 12, 1990, 10.

December 22 (about the time Militaru was making his statement at the central committee building meeting), Moscow radio's Romanian service reported that the existence of the NSF had been known since the autumn and that this organization had called on the 14th RCP congress not to re-elect Ceauşescu.[122] Again this might just show that Moscow radio had also been listening to RFE, but, as noted previously, Brucan and Militaru had been in contact with Gorbachev and other Soviet officials beforehand, and in an interview in May 1990 Valentin Falin, head of the International Department of the Communist Party of the Soviet Union, suggested that Moscow did indeed have some prior knowledge of a conspiracy when he said, "We knew that a coup was inevitable because the regime was not only rotten but intransigent. . . . When key critics of the regime, like Silviu Brucan came to Moscow in November [1988], we were asked to appreciate that Romania had no other way out. We, therefore, watched the developments within the armed forces of Romania and the growth of resistance to the regime . . . very closely."[123]

The Response of the National Salvation Front to the Allegations

The new regime flatly denied that it had taken power through a coup d'état. As early as December 26, just after the trial of Ceauşescu had been broadcast, Iliescu publicly denied the revolution was "a coup performed by some organised force supported even by abroad," and over the next few weeks a stream of Front spokesmen repeated the same message.[124] The apotheosis of the creed came in a statement from Brucan on January 4, 1990:

> I must tell you frankly how amazed I was that serious newspapers in the West are taken in by the fantastic story of the ploy supposedly set up six months ago to overthrow Ceauşescu. I have never thought that [the] Western media are so vulnerable to such a grossly fabricated story, such a monumental fake. The first thing that should have occurred to them is that if the six-months' ploy involving the Front and the Army were to be true we the leaders of the Front would have boasted about it from the very beginning. To be able to tell the Romanian people that Ceauşescu has been overthrown as a result of a well-thought [out] conspiracy that we planned a long time ago could have constituted a formidable asset and a great historical merit deserving the warmest congratulations of the Romanian people.
>
> In fact . . . the truth is that it [sic] has never been such a plan. The truth is that the making of such a plan in Ceauşescu's totalitarian police state was simply impossible. The repression and surveillance in Romania were so ef-

122. Shafir (January 19, 1990), 17, 19 n. 6.
123. Falin (1990), 24.
124. BBC EE/0649, B/6, December 29, 1989.

fective that no political grouping could possibly take shape either within the party or outside the party. Even less one involving the military, the army. The historcal truth is that the massive social explosion of 22nd December was one hundred per cent spontaneous and it was only during the powerful attack on the former Central Committee building that the leaders of the Front were for the first time together.[125]

The vehemence of the Front's denials that it had mounted a coup was a response to political needs. When it ascended to power the NSF could not draw on any residual legitimacy left from the discredited former regime, nor did it yet have an electoral mandate. The NSF's spokesman, Munteanu, was only stating the obvious when at a press conference on January 8, 1990, he said, "The National Salvation Front is . . . an outcome of the revolution. It only has the legitimacy endowed by the revolution."[126] Any admission that the Front had achieved power other than as the head of a spontaneous popular uprising would have left it vulnerable to challenge from the newly emergent opposition, which had quickly realized the political significance of the revolution.

The apparent refusal of the Front's leaders to tell the truth about the origins of their own movement also seriously undermined their standing with the foreign media. Through satellite relay the Romanian revolution had been transmitted to the four corners of the globe, and the fact that it coincided with Christmas only seems to have heightened its emotional impact. The starkly black and white picture of a victorious people overthrowing the most iniquitous of dictators and then securing a hard-fought victory against his evil henchmen produced worldwide interest in Romania and a tremendous sympathy that was afterward cemented by poignant tales of appalling hardship in children's homes and hospitals. The heroic image of the revolution as it was portrayed on television, and these feelings of condolence for a country that had experienced so much pain, fused to produce perhaps rather excessive expectations of the new regime on the part of the outside world. This seems to have particularly applied to the French, leading Andrei Codrescu to note, "The French had a special interest. France had fallen in love with Romania. In 1989, in the year of the bicentennial of their own revolution, after they had been saturated by ceremonial imagery of *la glorie* and *la patrie,* the Romanian Revolution exploded like a magnificent illustration of all their history. It was the grande finale of all the fireworks shows put on by every *mairie* from Paris

125. BBC EE/0655, B/9:36, January 6, 1990. For a similar statement from Iliescu see Ratesh (1991), 87–88, such statements led Ratesh to talk of a conspiracy to cover up a conspiracy.

126. BBC EE/0658, B/12:21, January 10, 1990; Brucan suggests the same in BBC EE/0675, B/8–9:24, January 30, 1990.

to Strasbourg. Romania gave the French the third dimension of their grand commemoration: reality."[127]

Then, when some of the members of the NSF did not turn out to be quite so pure in background as first thought and the revolution more murky and inconclusive than portrayed, the downside was equally unbalanced. With an agenda driven to a greater or lesser extent by the sizeable Romanian émigré population in Paris, relations between part of the French media and the new regime soon disintegrated into a morass of mutual recriminations.[128] Beginning with Michel Castex, who was head of the Agence France Press team that arrived in Bucharest on December 25, 1989, their doubts about the events were expanded into a series of critical magazine articles and later books. Most of these first appeared in France, but via short-wave radio broadcast and other means they rapidly filtered back into Romania with a number being translated and reprinted in the domestic press.[129]

As the foreign media attempted to pry open the mysteries of the revolution, some confirmation of their suspicions about preexisting conspiracies came in a series of interviews given by figures formerly associated with the new regime who declared they now wished to tell the "real" story behind the events. Often printed in obscure Romanian magazines, these revelations chiefly came from Brucan, Radu, Militaru, and another former army general, Ștefan Kostyal.[130] The various stories about conspiracies against Ceaușescu have to be taken seriously, but also with considerable caution, as they offer a highly selective reading of the past by the plotters themselves, many of whom were discarded after the revolution and had obvious political axes to grind. Michael Shafir, for instance, has clearly shown that Brucan and Militaru's aforementioned August 23, 1990, *Adevărul* article was primarily designed to discredit Iliescu and drive a wedge between him and then prime minister Roman.[131] Indeed, it can be argued that the stories of conspiracy basked under so much attention largely because they were perceived as undermining the revolutionary legitimacy of the NSF and its successors, and, given this background, the extent to which they trade historical veracity for political expediency must always be open to question.

127. Codrescu (1991), 84–85. On French enthusiasm for the Romanian revolution see *Independent,* January 6, 1990, 15.

128. *The Times,* December 28, 1989, 6.

129. The clearest exposition of the various allegations occurred in an article by Weber and Portocala in *Le Point* of May 21, 1990. This appeared in a Romanian translation in *Expres,* July 4–11, 1990, 44–45. The themes were later expanded in several books, extracts of which were widely translated in the Romanian press; see Portocala (1990); Castex (1990); Loupan (1990); Gabanyi (1990). For an attempted autopsy of the French reporting of Romania see Reporters san Frontières (1990).

130. Shafir (May 11, 1990), 24–27; Shafir (October 12, 1990), 29–42; Ratesh (1991), 80–119; Behr (1991), 220–29; Deletant (1995), 342–51.

131. Shafir (October 12, 1990), 29–42.

In terms of their content the revelations raised as many questions as they answered. Plots by their very nature normally work on a need-to-know basis. Few, if any, of the conspirators have an overall picture of the events so personal recollections tend to offer only a fragmentary view, leaving space for further conjecture. There is also a fine line between serious planning for a coup and disgruntled scheming. To be accepted as a dissident, it seems, one must speak openly, but successful plots by their very nature are hidden until sprung. The failings of the Ceaușescu regime were not hidden from many members of the Romanian *nomenklatura,* but when does private dissension and complaint turn to open plotting? And how many of the elaborate imbroglios presented by the conspirators, involving submarines and the like, stretched much further than idle dreams?

The Conspiracies against Ceaușescu

The chief interest of the revelations is that they confirm longstanding rumors that in the 1980s there had been various attempts to mount a coup against Ceaușescu.[132] Most of the sources suggest the most significant of these was set for October 15–17, 1984, although Radu suggests that another coup was also planned for February 1985.[133] The October coup was due to take place when the Ceaușescus were making an official visit to West Germany. Its mechanics are interesting, not so much in terms of their potential feasibility in 1984, but because they appear to prefigure important elements of the 1989 revolution. According to Brucan, the 1984 plot had three main strands: the detention of Ceaușescu's chief aides and the transmission of power within existing Party structures; the support of the Bucharest army garrison and other divisions stationed near Bucharest (these units were supposed to intervene in order to counter any possible challenge from the forces of the *securitate*); and the securing of key strategic objectives, including the national radio and television stations, to call on the people to rise against the leadership so as to ensure the success of the military operation.[134] The details of this plan have been broadly confirmed in a separate interview by Kostyal, who noted the key military objectives were the Ministry of Defense, the airfields around Bucharest, and the television station. The seizure of the latter was deemed necessary to win the support of the population for the coup, which, it was foreseen, might trigger a wider popular uprising. According to Brucan and Radu, the plotters were betrayed in 1984 by figures on the fringes of their group, Lieutenant-Generals Gomoiu and Popa, although it is

132. *The Times,* February 7, 1983, 6; Maier (March 17, 1983), 14–18; Maier (November 17, 1984), 2; Maier (January 10, 1986), 7–10. See also *Independent,* December 22, 1989, 1.
133. Testimony of Radu in Săndulescu (c1996), 90.
134. Brucan (1993), 133–34.

strange, if the planning for a coup was as advanced as Brucan has claimed, that none of the participants received particularly harsh punishment. Militaru, for instance, was merely replaced as a deputy minister before losing his seat on the Central Committee at a Party congress later that year, as did Ioniță.

Two of those said to be key participants in the 1984 conspiracy died shortly afterward. Vasile Patilineț was killed in a car crash in Turkey in October 1986, which Radu has alleged was staged on Ceaușescu's orders, and Ioniță died of cancer in July 1987. The death of these two figures together with increased surveillance by the authorities not only made any further plotting extremely difficult but also strained relations within the group of conspirators. Nevertheless, some activity seems to have continued. By his own admission, in 1987 Militaru contacted the Soviet consulate in Constanța asking for aid and Radu says he drew up anti-Ceaușescu manifestos, but after he failed to meet a fellow conspirator, Virgil Măgureanu, at a Bucharest train station, he was arrested and in September 1987 jailed for ten years. Radu suggests that he was the only one of the conspirators punished because Ceaușescu was unwilling to create political turbulence at the time of the Brașov riots, but in reality the plotters seem to have had problems securing money and arms and, as Shafir has aptly noted, a "conspiracy involving the military that has difficulty in getting hold of guns can hardly be taken very seriously."[135] On his release in February 1988 under a general amnesty, Radu seems to have kept some contact with other conspirators, suggesting that they continued to plan, and indeed both he and Militaru have mentioned that another coup was planned for February 1990. However, the fact that a coup had been planned in 1984 and possibly in 1987 does not mean that something similar was enacted or even proposed by the same conspirators in 1989. It might be true that at first sight the events of December 1989 did bear a passing resemblance to the plans of 1984, although it should perhaps be remembered that the latter were not actually made public until well after the revolution. But any insurrection in Romania, however it was triggered, was likely to take a similar course. Mass mobilization, defections within the security forces, and seizures of radio and television stations are the staples of many revolutions. Subsequent to the events, Militaru did say that the conspirators were taken by surprise by the revolution, and this was inadvertently confirmed by Kostyal when he admitted to the journalist Edward Behr that he only went to the Ministry of Defense on December 22 because he had remembered it was one of the targets in 1984.[136]

However, if it is accepted that some of those involved in planning a coup in 1984 were still meeting after that date, then it immediately raises

135. Shafir (October 12, 1990), 32; Ratesh (1991), 94.
136. Militaru quoted in Ratesh (1991), 91; Behr (1991), 227.

questions as to the extent they influenced the events of 1989. Brucan speaks of a deliberate three-pronged strategy of infiltrating the army, *securitate,* and Party apparatus, to mixed results, but such an organized structure may have been more the product of hopes rather than reality. When links were formed they seem often to have been highly nebulous and racked with mutual suspicion, especially after 1984. Outside the bounds of the military, the figures most frequently mentioned as being part of some form of conspiracy are Brucan, Măgureanu, and Iliescu. The amount of time they had been part of any plot and the weight ascribed to their roles vary depending on the sources consulted, with Radu, for instance, claiming that Măgureanu recruited Iliescu into the ranks of the conspirators as early as 1971, after his demotion and dispatch to Timișoara. Militaru, who says he first met Iliescu in a hospital in 1982, has said that he was regularly in contact with him during the months prior to the revolution, and this has been confirmed by Roman, who added that after one meeting they were called in by the *securitate* for questioning.[137] Iliescu has admitted that he took part in a conspiratorial group, saying that some members of this, such as Militaru, were more enthusiastic, while others, such as Ioniță and Măgureanu, were more circumspect. However, Iliescu has also tended to downplay any plotting, suggesting, probably correctly, that they remained an isolated group and, when he did speak to some more senior members of the Party, he says they met by accident, he was left with the clear impression that any conspiracy had little chance of overthrowing Ceaușescu.[138] In his August 23 interview Brucan claims connection with the conspiracy from 1983, when he began having regular meetings with Ioniță and other military figures, but he features little in the accounts of the others. Iliescu admits knowing Brucan but says they were not close.[139] After the "Letter of the Six" was made public Brucan was placed under house arrest and eventually moved to what he describes as a "shack" in the Dămăroaia suburb of Bucharest. Cut off from contact with the outside world, he arrived at the television station on December 22 only because he was brought by an old friend, Eduard Stan.[140] Brucan was hardly in a position to influence events immediately prior to December 1989, and the same can also be said for Măgureanu. Previously a member of the *securitate,* he had apparently left active service in favor of a post at the Party's Ștefan Gheorghiu Academy. In June 1989 he had been transferred to the relative obscurity of the museum of history in Focșani, and December 22 found him in Zalău, in northern Transylvania, from where he did not leave for Bucharest until late in the afternoon.[141] Unde-

---

137. Ratesh (1991), 92; Shafir (January 19, 1990), 17.
138. Iliescu (1995b), 34.
139. Ibid., 66.
140. Brucan (1993), 169–70.
141. Neacșu (c1999). After the revolution, Măgureanu was appointed head of the SRI.

niably Brucan, Măgureanu, and especially Iliescu played key roles in the revolution. However, this does not mean that they ascended to power through a well-planned conspiracy. There is little evidence for this. Of the three, only Iliescu was in Bucharest and had some freedom of movement in the days prior to the revolution. He and others may have made some preparations to take power. As will be seen below, one source says he tried to contact some senior generals and party officials during this period to sound out their intentions, and at least one list of those about to take office was circulating beforehand, because an American academic living in Bucharest was handed one on the evening of December 21.[142] Still, this all smacks more of a group preparing to take advantage of the emerging situation rather than one actually shaping the events. Similarly, although a number of those who appeared at the television station on December 22 do seem to have known each other, rather than being indicative of serious plotting, this could have been a byproduct of the relative narrowness of the Bucharest elite and the general discussions about conditions in Romania that Iliescu admits to having with a number of people beforehand.[143]

A key determinant in any revolutionary situation is the position adopted by the security forces, but the degree to which any conspiracy had infiltrated the ranks of the security forces remains unclear. Brucan, Militaru, and Kostyal all speak of the existence of a "Military Resistance Committee" in 1989 which, they say, comprised at least twenty senior officers. These names have not been revealed but Shafir, following Radu, has suggested that the eighteen generals officially reactivated from the reserve during the revolution were at its core, and indeed Cheler, Ionel, and Pletos, each named in connection with previous plots, are to be found on this list.[144] However, not included are a number of reserve generals from both the army and the Ministry of the Interior forces who are known to have played a role in the revolution and who might be presumed to have been privy to any conspiracy. These included Tudor, Emil (Cico) Dumitrescu, and Kostyal; from their statements made on tele-

142. My thanks to Paul Michelson for this information.

143. Voiculescu has said that even though many of the new leaders gave the impression that they knew each other, most did not or, if they did, it was only superficially. Marcu (1991), 13.

144. Recalled to active service were Col. Gen. Vasile Ştefan Ionel, Lt. Gen. Paul Romano Cheler, Lt. Gen. Jean Ioan Moldoveanu, Maj. Gen. Marin Gheorghe Bălteanu, Maj. Gen. Ion Bucur Bordei, Maj. Gen. Liviu Traian Ciubăncan, Maj. Gen. Horia Traian Opruţă, Maj. Gen. Dumitru Nicolae Pletos, Maj. Gen. Gheorghe Constantin Popescu, and Rear Admiral Nicolae Gheorghe Hîrjeu, see *Monitorul Oficial al României*, December 29, 1989, 5. Lt. Gen. Gheorghe Lavric, ibid., December 31, 1989, 3. Col. Gen. Gheorghe Petre Ion, Col. Gen. Marin Voinea Nicolescu, Lt. Gen. Ion Aurel Şuţa, Maj. Gen. Grigorie Tudor Drăghici, Maj. Gen. Dumitru Ion Dumitru, and Maj. Gen. Florian Emilian Truţă, ibid., January 5, 1990, 3. Recalled to Ministry of the Interior, Inspectorate General of Police was Maj. Gen. Octavian Gheorghe Pop, ibid., January 9, 1990, 3.

vision Colonel-General Nicolae Doicaru and Colonel-General Stelian Țârcă can probably also be added to this list, together with Major-General Marin Pancea.[145] The extent of contacts the plotters had with the regular army is less clear. In 1984 a key priority had been securing the support of the Bucharest garrison, and it seems probable that the same held true for later plans. Indeed, the commanders of the capital's garrison seem to have been a permanent thorn in the flesh for Ceaușescu. In 1971 the holder of the post, Lieutenant-General Ioan Șerb, was apparently caught passing military secrets to the Soviet military attaché in Bucharest, and later something similar may have happened with another incumbent, Militaru, who is said to have become amorously involved with a Soviet spy, although he has denied the allegations.[146] According to his declaration on the television, in 1989 the garrison was under the command of Chițac, and his still unexplained early arrival at the television station, where he declared himself for the revolution and spoke confidently of the "new democratic socialist political orientation of our country" before the arrival of Iliescu, together with his subsequent appointment to the key post of Minister of the Interior, would suggest that not only did he have access to information but also that he was particularly trusted.[147]

Of the other serving senior army officers, the available evidence does not seem to point to any serious involvement in pre-revolutionary plotting, until perhaps after the demonstrations in Timișoara had begun, when, it seems, within the realms of probability, that some may have been contacted in order to try and ascertain their inclinations, and Brucan has said that Iliescu and Roman at this time discussed together which generals and party figures should be approached to support a move against Ceaușescu.[148] Militaru has said that he was a close friend of Milea, but in a rather woolly statement he appears to rule him out from being part of a conspiracy. He also says he knew Vlad, but nobody has said he was part of

145. Doicaru was a former head of foreign intelligence and deputy minister of the interior. He remained a candidate member of the central committee until 1980, when according to his testimony he was placed under arrest and discharged from his office because he opposed Ceaușescu's method of rule. He died of an alleged shotgun accident in March 1991. Deletant (1994), 47.

146. King (March 6, 1972), 1–11; King (May 17, 1972), 8–10; Bacon (1978), 170–71; Pacepa (1989), 195–97; Crowther (1989), 214–15. Reports reached the West that Șerb had been executed, but in fact, after being sentenced to seven years imprisonment, he was released following a meeting between Ceaușescu and Brezhnev and sent to work on a collective farm; see Deletant (1995), 88–89. For Militaru see Pacepa (1989), 193–97; *The Times*, December 28, 1989; Shafir (January 12, 1990), 36; *Expres*, January 2, 1991, 2; Ratesh (1991), 91–92.

147. For Chițac's statement on television see Televiziunea Română (1990), 35. His rather contradictory account of his journey to the television station can be found in ibid. (1990), 213.

148. *New York Times*, January 3, 1990, A 12.

any conspiracy.[149] The evidence regarding Stănculescu is more ambiguous.[150] His participation in Ceaușescu's execution and subsequent high profile political career would seem to suggest he was in a privileged position, but he was not connected with any plotting according to Kostyal, and, although Radu has said that he approached Stănculescu to sound him out about joining the conspiracy in 1984, further contact was then forbidden by Ioniță. No serious allegations seem to have ever been made that Generals Gușă, Voinea, Eftimescu, or any others were implicated in any conspiracy. This does not mean, however, that they had no knowledge of any coup plans, because Radu has also revealed how some officers, such as Colonel Victor Pângulescu, were aware of the conspiracy without actually being part of the group. Although little information is available, no suggestion has been made that any of the higher ranking officers within the *securitate* were part of any conspiracy. The only exceptions may be Colonel Dumitru Penciuc of the *securitate* troops—Militaru says he secured his cooperation in 1986, although Radu dates it to 1987—and a certain Colonel Bucur who, according to an unidentified former Ministry of the Interior general speaking on television on December 22, "knows how we feel."[151]

If the military officers party to any plotting were mostly reserve generals, it begs the question as to their effectiveness when they returned to duty. There have been claims that they were the decisive factor in determining the fate of the revolution, with Brucan and Militaru declaring, perhaps not unsurprisingly, in their interview, "Once General Militaru took over as Minister of Defense—the whole chain of command shifted into the hands of generals devoted to the revolution."[152] However, most of the reserve officers were already old—Kostyal was seventy-nine, Țârcă seventy-five, and Militaru sixty-five—and given the fact that for all intents and purposes the army had already come to the side of the revolution by the time they appeared, the scope for them to play any major military role was extremely limited. On December 22, Tudor quickly arrived at the television station, closely followed by Militaru and Dumitrescu, while Kostyal went to the Ministry of Defense. Their initial lack of communication with the regular army is evident from the fact that Militaru called on Voinea and Gușă to come to the television station, even though Voinea had already appeared and Gușă was still en route from Timișoara. Militaru, who took over as Minister of Defense during the revolution, was obviously the

149. Televiziunea Română (1990), 208.

150. For Kostyal's verdict on Stănculescu see Behr (1991), 222–23, and for Radu's see Shafir (October 12, 1990), 35.

151. Televiziunea Română (1990), 57. Penciuc had a puzzling post-Ceaușescu career. Initially promoted to major-general, he was subsequently placed in the reserve on a pension before being recalled almost immediately into the police. *Monitorul Oficial al României,* January 20, 1990, 13; ibid. February 22, 1990, 3; ibid. February 28, 1990, 5.

152. *East European Reporter,* 1990, 4:3, 76.

most important of these figures and, presumably, he did have considerable influence on the unfolding events from the early afternoon of December 22, but according to Iliescu his relationship with serving military officers was turbulent and he resigned shortly after the revolution. Of the other reactivated officers, some, like Major-General Gheorghe Popescu, who was placed in command in Timişoara on December 24, and Lieutenant-General Paul Cheler, who became commander of the 4th Army, did ascend to important positions, but others were less influential. On his own admission, Kostyal played little active role. After meeting Stănculescu at the Ministry of Defense, he proceeded to the central committee building but was excluded from any important meetings. Eventually, he made his way to the Băneasa air base, where he remained until December 26, assisting the head of the anti-aircraft unit.[153] Radu played a similarly uneventful role. On the advice of a friend in the military he had left Bucharest on December 21 for Constanţa. Here, apart from calling Stănculescu from the office of Rear Admiral Plăviciosu, he seems to have played no real part in the revolution, before returning to Bucharest by train on the evening of December 22. In the capital he remained a mere "spectator," making no contact with his fellow "conspirators" until a meeting with Militaru on December 30.[154]

The influence of Tudor is more difficult to assess. The overall defense of the television station seems to have been placed in his hands by Stănculescu during the evening of December 22, although actual troop dispositions remained in the hands of the unit commanders.[155] In the pages of *Revoluţia Română în direct* the contributors from the army waste no opportunity to pour scorn on Tudor, painting a picture of a crazed old man suffering from cerebral arteriosclerosis who was prone to wandering around in his stocking feet. It could be that the deliberate downplaying of the roles played by Tudor and Lupoi at the time is merely a symptom of later conflicts within the army and a general reluctance on the part of the authorities to recognize the existence of pre-coup plotting. However, independent witnesses have also reported disagreements between regular army officers and Tudor during the revolution, which in one instance apparently led to the near fatal stabbing of the vice president of the television service, Traian Puşcaşu.[156] In circumstances that are far from clear he was the subject of a knife attack by Lieutenant-Colonel Constantin Vasiliu, although the intended victim seems to have been Tudor. Vasiliu had apparently been held before this incident as a suspected terrorist. It is also notable that Tudor, unlike many of the aforementioned generals, was not recalled for active service nor promoted after the revolution.

153. Behr (1991), 227–33.
154. Testimony of Radu in Săndulescu (c1996), 112–18.
155. Nicolaescu (1999), 197.
156. Televiziunea Română (1990), 135, 144, 148, 164, 265–66.

The generals who were reactivated during this period proved an insurance at a time when the new regime could be absolutely sure of the loyalty of only a few officers from the army and the Ministry of the Interior. Placed within the higher levels of the security forces, while the NSF consolidated its hold on power, most of these generals were soon once more returned to the reserve when it became clear that there was no effective challenge to be faced and rumblings of discontent were heard within the army over blocked channels of promotion. The speed with which they were then removed from office suggests that they held little political strength and certainly not the prestige that would have been accorded to them, if they truly were the very bastions of the revolution.

External Conspiracies

At his trial Ceauşescu had not only suggested that he had been betrayed by traitors but also that they had received foreign help in mounting their coup. This emphasis on external conspiracies has appeared regularly since the revolution, particularly in the literature of those who wish to further a partial rehabilitation of the old regime, which they see as being a flawed but truly Romanian administration.[157] Many of the earlier allegations of foreign involvement occupied the wilder fringes of conspiracy, with stories abounding of masked foreigners wreaking death and havoc on the streets of previously tranquil Romanian towns. There are, however, a number of puzzling incidents that have yet to be explained, and the whole issue deserves discussion not only because it has been the subject of so much attention in Romania but also because it raises interesting subsidiary questions regarding the attitude of the superpowers to the events in Romania and the possibility of external intervention in the country.

Many of the foreign intervention conspiracy theories have their roots in the December 2–3, 1989 Bush–Gorbachev summit in Malta. American sources suggest that Gorbachev was largely preoccupied with domestic affairs at this summit, but he apparently also gave a commitment not to intervene in Eastern Europe.[158] In turn, the Americans promised not to take advantage of the evolving situation, which both superpowers, by mutual recognition, realized they could do little to change.[159] There is no indication that the issue of Romania was specifically broached at the summit, but this has not deterred those who would read external intervention into the events of 1989 from arguing otherwise. They inevitably start by pointing to the fact that the substitution of a single letter can turn Malta

157. For examples of such argumentation see Teodorescu (1992); Saucă (1994); Băcescu (1994).
158. Beschloss and Talbott (1993), 168.
159. *Washington Post*, January 1, 1990, A1.

into Yalta, and, indeed, their argument is that the summit saw a carving up of Eastern Europe similar to the infamous Second World War "percentage agreement" between Churchill and Stalin, which is still very much a running sore on the Romanian body politic. The only variation being that, this time, it was the U.S. president, George Bush, who was selling out Romania and consigning it to remain in the Soviet orbit. It should be noted, however, that this reading of events is not unique to Romania. George Schöpflin was present when the same "alphabetic conundrum" was used by István Csurka, a prominent Hungarian nationalist politician, to suggest that the two superpowers had cheated Hungary out of its revolution, and the formulation was also noted in Bulgaria, Poland, and Czechoslovakia.[160]

Reports from Romanian embassies abroad at this time suggest the leadership was preoccupied with the issue, and certainly these rumors of a superpower carve-up of Eastern Europe fell on fertile ground in Romania.[161] In the past, the Romanian lands have regularly fallen under the rule of powerful neighbors, principally the Ottoman, Habsburg, and Russian Empires. The legacy of this experience has been the creation of a widespread belief that the destiny of the country to a considerable extent lies in the hands of larger foreign powers. It is hardly surprising that many members of a generation that saw the Soviet Union swallow Bessarabia and Northern Bucovina and brutally impose an alien political system on Romania itself should once again discern the hand of Moscow behind the events of 1989. It was also an accepted commonplace within Romania that Ceaușescu's idiosyncratic foreign policy riled Moscow and that the Soviet leadership would be happy to see the last great bastion of neo-Stalinism in the Eastern Bloc deposed. Yet, as was shown in Chapter 1, the relationship between the two countries by the late 1980s had settled into ritualized indifference, and a transcript of the last meeting between Gorbachev and Ceaușescu at a Warsaw Pact meeting on December 4, 1989, reveals it to have been a bland and noncommittal affair. This does not mean Gorbachev was unhappy to see the Romanian leader fall. When he announced Ceaușescu's fall to a session of the Congress of People's Deputies it was met with loud applause and called not only a victory for Romania but also an "example" of Soviet reforms.[162]

By 1989 many Romanians, not just old members of the Party, were looking to the Soviet Union for inspiration. The dissident poet Mircea Dinescu was reported as referring to Gorbachev's reforms as "the miracle of restructuring," and the liberal intellectual Petru Creția obliquely praised *perestroika* when just prior to the revolution he wrote, "the Romanians in

160. Schöpflin (1993), 254; Todorova (1992), 159 n. 32; Rosenberg (1995), 109–117, 235.

161. See the reports reproduced in Sava and Monac (2001).

162. *Washington Post*, December 23, 1989, A14.

Bessarabia [i.e., Moldova, USSR] are our only combative and fearless representatives in any possible fight for national rebirth. Of all Romanians, they alone are positively taking a stand in the irreversible process of emancipation of the Eastern Bloc countries."[163] However, it is also undeniable that the revolution did raise to prominence a group of former senior Party figures who do seem to have looked more favorably on the Soviet Union than the Ceaușescu regime. Some of these were reformers, like Brucan and Iliescu, who naturally turned to Gorbachev and perestroika as a source of ideas, while others, such as Kostyal and Militaru, were conservative military officers who had been educated at Soviet military academies.[164] Indeed, it is interesting to note that both these officers, as well as several others presumed to have been linked to the pre-1989 conspiracies, such as Dumitrescu and Pancea, had previously been accused of spying for the Soviet Union.[165] Sometimes the charge seems to have had as its basis nothing more than having a Russian wife, which Ceaușescu, according to the Czech defector, Jan Sejna, viewed with enormous suspicion.[166] Accusations of being a Soviet spy were not so unusual in the nationalist hysteria of Ceaușescu's Romania and it does not mean that any of the above had any significant contacts with the Soviet military or political leadership. As mentioned previously, Militaru says he made little headway when he contacted a Soviet diplomat in Constanța.[167] Prior to the revolution only Brucan among the future leaders of the NSF seems to have had high-level contact with the Soviet leadership. Through the good offices of his old acquaintance Anatoly Dobrynin, the former Soviet ambassador in Washington, Brucan had a meeting in November 1988 with Gorbachev, but, as noted previously, Brucan has stated that little was achieved.[168]

Much has also been made of the fact that many of the senior members of the NSF, including Iliescu, Marțian, and Király, had received a postgraduate education in the USSR. In particular, it has been alleged that Iliescu was a KGB agent and that during his sojourn in Moscow at the Institute of Energy from 1950 to 1954, when he was secretary of the Union of

163. Shafir (September 16, 1988), 27; *The Times*, December 22, 1989, 7. The Republic of Moldova at that time was part of the USSR.

164. Nicolaescu (1999), 176.

165. Pancea had come under suspicion while working in Paris in the late 1970s. He was recalled to Bucharest, demoted, and dispatched to a provincial posting, but during the revolution he reappeared in Brăila and according to some reports took command of military operations. Some confusion seems to have reigned before Militaru called him to Bucharest on December 26. It has been alleged that during the revolution Pancea ordered the Brăila garrison to facilitate the entry of troops into Romania from the nearby Soviet Union, although this did not occur. Codrescu et al. (1998), 382–83, 456–58; Deletant (1995), 92–93; Alexandru (1998). Pancea eventually was to take up a role of presidential counselor to Iliescu and secretary of the Supreme National Defense Council, although Iliescu denies that he knew him before 1989. Iliescu (1995b), 56.

166. Sejna (1982), 67.

167. *Independent*, December 16, 1994, 21.

168. Brucan (1993), 149–52.

Romanian Students, he became acquainted with Gorbachev.[169] Iliescu has consistently denied this and other stories, but at the time of the revolution the charge surfaced once more in the West alongside the other long-standing rumor that he was Gorbachev's favored candidate to succeed Ceaușescu.[170] Again, such accusations belong to a distinct domestic political agenda, and even if Iliescu had met Gorbachev nearly forty years previously, there is no evidence to suggest that afterward they maintained close contact. Moreover, some tantalizing evidence exists to suggest that it was not Iliescu but Corneliu Mănescu, a former Romanian foreign minister and one of the signatories of the "Letter of the Six," that the USSR expected to head the NSF. Certainly this is the assertion of Valentin Falin, then the head of the International Department of the Communist Party of the Soviet Union, who says Mănescu only declined the offer because of ill health.[171] Mănescu's name appeared on a number of the lists of new leaders read out from the balcony of the central committee building on December 22, and it was also widely reported abroad that he had taken power, even though he does not seem to have appeared in person.[172] The muddle is usually ascribed to a case of mistaken identity, with Sergiu Nicolaescu, when he appeared on television, being confused with Mănescu. Nonetheless it is striking how quickly news that Mănescu had taken power was being broadcast by foreign news agencies, with Agence France Press and Tanjug carrying the story little more than an hour after the flight of Ceaușescu.[173]

Although the Soviet Union may have wished to see the replacement of Ceaușescu, it seems to have fought shy of committing itself to the pre-1989 conspirators, probably because it doubted the viability of their plans. Likewise, although rumors continue to circulate to the contrary, the Soviet Union does not seem to have played any greater role during the days prior to Ceaușescu's flight. The only known official contacts between the outbreak of the disturbances in Timișoara and the overthrow of the regime are a meeting Ceaușescu held on December 19 with the Soviet ambassador to Bucharest, and another on the morning of December 22 between Ilie Ceaușescu and the Soviet military attaché, Rear-Admiral

169. For the story Iliescu was a KGB agent; see BBC EE/2309, B/4:10, May 22, 1995; BBC EE/2330, B/1:3, June 15, 1995; BBC EE/2331, B:4/9, June 16, 1995; BBC EE/2333, B/4:9, June 19, 1995.

170. *Washington Post*, December 23, 1989, A11. For an early example of rumors that Iliescu would be the next leader see Gabanyi (September 21, 1987), 3–6.

171. Falin (1990), 22. For an example of Western press reports that Mănescu had taken power see *The Times*, December 23, 1989, 6. Mănescu reveals little in a book-length interview published after the revolution, Mănescu (2001).

172. Like Brucan, Mănescu had been banished to poor accommodation on the outskirts of Bucharest, in his case in Chitila, Mănescu (2001).

173. Sârcă (1998), 275–81. An article in *The Times* suggested a Western diplomat was the source for these stories and a radio report of the time named the British diplomat Jonathan Lamb. *The Times*, December 23, 1989; Sârcă (1998), 281.

Mihailov, accompanied by the local deputy representative of the commander in chief of the Warsaw Treaty Organization, Major-General Bociaev. This meeting, which was also attended by a number of Romanian officers, including Vice-Admiral Ştefan Dinu and Colonel Dumitru Mircea, like the meeting between Ceauşescu and the ambassador beforehand, aside from the news that a new government was about to be appointed, seems to have produced little other than the usual affirmations of solidarity with the socialist bloc by Lieutenant-General Ceauşescu and charges that Romania was facing an imperialist plot designed to destroy socialism and wrench it away from the Warsaw Pact.[174] In many ways, of all the countries of the Soviet bloc in 1989, the USSR was least equipped to influence events in Romania. Direct intervention was virtually impossible, because there had been no Red Army troops stationed in Romania since 1958. Indeed, it may even be argued that it was this absence of Soviet troops that led to Romania experiencing such a violent revolution, as no outside forces were available within the country to facilitate a smooth transfer of power or to moderate the scale of the explosion once it occurred. However, even if no regular troops of the Red Army played a role in the Romanian revolution, this has not stopped speculation that covert forces were engaged in fomenting the unrest that led to Ceauşescu's downfall.

A belief that the KGB played a crucial role in shaping the events of 1989 in Eastern Europe is not limited to Romania. Similar claims also surfaced elsewhere, especially in Bulgaria, Czechoslovakia, and East Germany, although, as usual, in each case the picture was far from clear. During previous periods of unrest, in Hungary in 1956, Czechoslovakia in 1968, and Poland in 1980, KGB agents, many of whom were stationed in the West, do seem to have been infiltrated into these countries on the assumption that as "Westerners" they would be accorded freer access to information from opposition sources. In the cases of Hungary and Czechoslovakia such agents may also have been ordered to act as agents provocateurs to prepare the way for the Warsaw Pact invasions.[175] It seems possible that similar tactics could have been used in Romania to destabilize the Ceauşescu regime, and both the report on the revolution from the SRI and the post-1989 testimony of former *securitate* officers, such as Vlad, have made much play of the high numbers of Soviet "tourists" present in Romania at the time.[176] Soviet citizens had long crossed Romania on their way to shopping trips in Yugoslavia, but, at the beginning of De-

174. See the transcript in Sava and Monac (2001), 218–22, and Munteanu (n.d.), 8; Codrescu et al. (1998), 120; Săndulescu (c1996), 228, 309–10. A meeting was also arranged with representatives from the Chinese embassy but this failed to take place due to the collapse of the regime.

175. Andrew and Gordievsky (1990), 434, 486–87, 580.

176. *Raportul SRI; Adevărul,* February 16, 1991; Teodorescu (1992), 92–95. In December 1989, 69,022 Soviet citizens entered Romania as against 30,879 in the same period of the year before. Of this figure, 43,201 held transit visas. During the same period 72,875 Soviet

cember 1989, it was claimed that the average number of vehicles making this trip had risen sharply from eighty to over a thousand per day, and that with two to three well-built men in each car they were often traveling in suspicious convoys.[177] Indeed, on the night of December 16–17, when the first major demonstrations were just beginning in Timişoara, it was alleged that one such convoy tried to enter the city.

The suspicions about tourists had first been roused by Ceauşescu, who at the December 17 PEC meeting had suggested they were spies. The next day it was announced that no more would be accepted into the country, supposedly because of a shortage of hotel beds.[178] Soviet citizens returning from Yugoslavia, however, were still allowed passage, although, as a Tanjug correspondent at the Vršac border crossing point reported, the Romanian authorities insisted on organizing their vehicles into convoys before escorting them into Romania, which may at least in part account for stories about suspicious groups of cars.[179] One of these convoys was later to run into a Romanian army roadblock at the village of Brădeşti near Craiova in the early hours of the morning of December 25. When the eight cars failed to halt, the soldiers opened fire, immobilizing five of the vehicles—one of which was totally burned—and injuring at least one of the passengers, a woman. Afterward, in April 1990, when some of members of the convoy returned to try to reclaim the damaged vehicles, it was apparently revealed that one of the women involved in the incident was a major in the Soviet armed forces.[180] If Soviet agents were present in Romania, they were probably sent to gather intelligence and just possibly even attempt to influence the outcome of events.[181] However, whether they had any real impact on the course of events must remain doubtful as, in general, the tide was running so strongly that little could be done to divert or stem the flood of revolution. According to Falin, on the Soviet side they never imagined before December 1989 of "the extent of the bloody bacchanalia that came to pass," and overall, the presence of such agents,

citizens left Romania, as compared with 32,672 in 1988. All figures taken from Nicolaescu (1999), 583–86. For a full discussion of the issue see Hall (2002) and Mioc (2000).

177. The rise in transit visas is proportionate to the total rise in visa numbers at the time.

178. Nicolaescu (1995), 287.

179. Hall (1997), 199.

180. *The Times,* December 28,1989, 6; *Independent,* July 19, 1994, 10; Codrescu et al. (1998), 336, 456 n. 34.

181. An interview with one of these alleged KGB agents by Sorin Roşca-Stănescu appears in *România Liberă,* April 18, 1991, 8. The anonymous agent arrived in Romania on December 14 but, aside from traveling to Timişoara and then to Bucharest, he seems to have done little before leaving the country on December 26. Stănescu was revealed to have been a *securitate* informer in 1992. See ibid., April 30, 1992, 1, 3; and May 9, 1992, 5. Reference might also be made to unsubstantiated reports of the name of Iliescu being heard on the lips of demonstrators in Timişoara since December 19; see *Washington Post,* December 31, 1989, A31; Nicolaescu (1999), 87, notes that it accompanied chants of "Gorbachev" and "Perestroika"; and Pitulescu et al. (1995), 124, say it was heard alongside cries for "King Michael."

if it is true, serves to demonstrate that the USSR had a far greater awareness of the weakness of the Ceaușescu regime than most commentators in the West, but probably little else.[182]

Finally, the role of the Soviet Union after the overthrow of Ceaușescu has also come under scrutiny, with most of the speculation centering on the degree of contact that existed between the new regime and the Soviet Embassy in Bucharest during the revolution. Again the interest seems to have been largely driven by the domestic political agenda inside Romania, with opponents of Iliescu apparently thinking that, if they could show he had close contact with Soviet officials at this time, it would somehow invalidate his and the NSF's right to rule. Iliescu has admitted telephoning the Soviet Embassy from the central committee building on December 22, and he can be heard on the videotape of the meeting held at this time saying he did so to say "who we were and what we want," so they could then tell Moscow.[183] In itself this statement would seem to be most significant because it indicates that the Russians had no forewarning of the takeover and had to be reassured about who had taken power.[184] It had little bearing on the course of the revolution, and more interesting is the question of how close Romania came to seeing the intervention of Soviet troops at this time. In the hours after the overthrow of Ceaușescu, the Romanian army maintained close contact with the Soviet military.[185] In the late afternoon of December 22, Lieutenant-General Eftimescu informed Major-General Bociaev that the NSF had taken control of the revolution with the support of the army and asked him whether Soviet forces were massing on the Romanian border. Shortly afterward Bociaev telephoned to assure him that this was not the case and that the Red Army was not preparing to intervene in Romania but that it was ready to supply any other help that was required. The idea of requesting Soviet troops seems to have first arisen during the night of December 22–23. As heavy fighting raged outside the television studios, Dinu Cornel, who was present at the eleventh floor command center that night, says the new leaders talked about asking for several battalions of elite troops, and the next morning Bucharest radio did report that the Soviet Embassy had promised military assistance to help counter the helicopters full of armed men sent to Romania by foreign agencies.[186] When they received the request in the early

182. Falin (1990), 24. But note the letter from Shevarnadze to Gorbachev reproduced in Sava and Monac (2001), 186, which seems to show that neither of the Soviet leaders had much idea of what was happening in Romania.

183. Pitulescu (1998), 247; see also Iliescu's account in Televiziunea Română (1990), 224, and Iliescu (1995b), 18.

184. Televiziunea Română (1990), 197. Later, it was publicly admitted that Iliescu had first spoken to Gorbachev by telephone in the late afternoon of December 27, 1989; see Iliescu (1996), 479; Adevărul, December 28, 1989, 1.

185. Codrescu et al. (1998), 205. See also Sava and Monac (2001), 222–24.

186. Sârcă (1998), 209; Televiziunea Română (1990), 168.

hours of December 23 the Russians seem to have contacted Guşă in the central committee building to see if assistance really was required.[187] Guşă replied that it was not, but around noon the same day Eftimescu, speaking directly to the Soviet High Command in the presence of Iliescu and many other leaders of the revolution, seems to have raised the issue again, because shortly afterwards, Guşă, with the aid of two translators and again in the presence of the leaders of the NSF, had to repeat the message that no troops were required, this time directly to the Chief of the General Staff of the Red Army.[188] The next day, this was confirmed by Gorbachev, when he told the Congress of People's Deputies that, although requests for help had been made, Guşă had said that Romania did not need assistance for the time being.[189]

Whether there was ever any real likelihood of Red Army troops being sent to Romania remains doubtful. The Soviet Embassy soon emphasized it was just talking about material aid and afterward Gorbachev lowered expectations even further by only mentioning medical assistance. Although the events are still veiled in some confusion, it would seem that the talk about Soviet intervention may have been connected with an incident during the night of December 22–23 that involved Soviet personnel. A detachment of troops from Ploieşti seems to have opened fired on several buildings housing Soviet diplomats after they themselves had come under fire and sustained casualties.[190] It was probably this incident that Gorbachev was referring to when he revealed that a member of a Soviet trade delegation in Romania had been wounded and buildings housing various Soviet missions and employees in Bucharest severely damaged.[191] And a statement, carried by both Pravda and Izvestia on December 24, after giving some details of the events, bears an unmistakable air of warning: "an apartment building in which the families of members of the Soviet trade mission reside is in the shooting zone. Armed individuals have entered the building and are engaged in intensive firing from there. Fires have broken out in the building, and the lives of Soviet people, including women and children, are in serious danger. The Soviet Union cannot remain indifferent to the fates of Soviet citizens, and it demands that those who unleashed the indicated actions jeopardizing the lives of Soviet

187. Ratesh (1991), 111–12.
188. *Adevărul*, February 2, 1991, 2; Săndulescu (c1996), 317.
189. Ratesh (1991), 111; *Washington Post*, December 25, 1989, A1, A41. A slightly different version of the events was given to a reporter from the *Washington Post* by a spokesman of the Soviet embassy in Bucharest. He confirmed that the NSF had asked for military aid but said that it was Moscow that had turned down the request; ibid., December 23, 1989, A22. A Spanish agency who made contact was told that only medical assistance had been offered; Sârcă (1998), 211.
190. Codrescu et al. (1998), 220.
191. *Washington Post*, December 23, 1989, A22. For references to this incident see Televiziunea Română (1990), 164, 166.

people stop them immediately."[192] The trade mission seems to have been abandoned with the personnel finding refugee in the Soviet Embassy, which then organized a more general evacuation of Soviet citizens. On December 24 they were escorted to a train that was eventually to take them out of the country, although at one point a power outage halted their passage.[193] After that date Soviet sources became adamant that military intervention was unnecessary. The Soviet prime minister, Nicolae Ryzhkov, even made a parallel with past invasions when he stated that in the same month the Soviet Union had admitted that the 1968 invasion of Czechoslovakia had been an error, it would hardly make the same mistake twice. And Andrei Grachev, deputy head of the Central Committee International Department, pointedly contrasted the behavior of the two superpowers when he commented that Gorbachev "is certainly not going to intervene [in Romania] as Bush intervened in Panama."[194]

The Soviet Union's decision not to intervene in Romania was not made under pressure from the West; indeed, all the evidence suggests that the West would have accepted the dispatch of Soviet troops at this time. During the shooting after the overthrow of Ceauşescu, the French foreign minister said that his government had contacted the Soviet authorities to say they would support Warsaw Pact intervention, and this position was later backed by the Dutch.[195] Even the Americans came to support such a view. On news of the suppression of the demonstrations in Timişoara, the secretary of state, James Baker, seems to have passed a note to his Soviet counterpart, Eduard Shevardnadze, asking him to press Ceauşescu to call a halt. Ceauşescu fell before this note was delivered, but a meeting between the American ambassador in Moscow, Jack Matlock, and the Soviet deputy foreign minister, Aboimov, went ahead on December 25, although Matlock gives no details in his memoirs.[196] On that day Baker appeared on the NBC television program *Meet the Press* and stated that the Americans would be inclined to follow the lead of France and support any Warsaw Pact intervention in Romania "on behalf of the opposition." Shevardnadze apparently thought the idea "stupid," and the State Department later repudiated Baker's comment, saying it was an off-the-cuff remark made without any forethought.[197] But the fact that an American

192. *The Current Digest of the Soviet Press,* 41:51, 1989, 15, 28; Sârcă (1998), 211–14.

193. *Financial Times,* December 27, 1989; Sava and Monac (2001), 225.

194. *Washington Post,* December 23, 1989, A22; ibid., December 25, 1989, A40. For continuing Russian denials see *Guardian,* January 5, 1990, 9.

195. *Washington Post,* December 25, 1989, A37. Dumas was also reported as backing the deployment of an international brigade of volunteers. Sârcă (1998), 214–15.

196. Matlock (1995), 261–62; Munteanu (n.d.), 1; and for Aboimov's notes of the meeting see Sava and Monac (2001), 337–40.

197. Ratesh (1991), 113; Beschloss and Talbott (1993), 170–71. According to Condoleezza Rice (1997), Romania was peripheral to the Bush administration's interests at this time.

secretary of state could even countenance such a possibility is testament to the extent that the old certainties of the Cold War had already broken down by December 1989.

Apart from the Soviet Union, the only other country that is alleged to have played a role in fomenting the revolution is Hungary. These charges again directly flow from Ceaușescu's claim that the unrest was the work of Hungarian irredentists. This fed on national prejudices and featured prominently in the defense of those implicated in the massacres in Timișoara.[198] The detailed analysis of the events in Timișoara contained in Chapter 2 has revealed the weakness of this argument, and here it remains only to consider the wider role of the Hungarian state during the revolution. One slightly perverse consequence of the breakdown in Romanian–Hungarian relations during the 1980s, outlined in Chapter 1, is that both states seem to have made considerable efforts to make sure that no misunderstandings occurred at this time. When, in the first half of December, the Romanians became aware of Hungarian troop movements close to the Romanian border, Milea ordered his chief of staff to establish direct telephone contact with his Hungarian counterpart, and from these conversations it was decided that the Hungarians were in fact only engaged in routine exercises and that Romania was not under threat of military attack.[199] Then, when tensions increased, following the outbreak of demonstrations in Timișoara, the Hungarian Defense Ministry on December 19 again stated that there were no troops concentrated on the Romanian border.[200] The next day Lieutenant-General Eftimescu was to ask the same question again in a telephone call to the chief of the Hungarian General Staff, but on December 21 roles were to be reversed when it was the turn of the Hungarian minister of defense, Colonel-General Ferenc Karpati, to calm Hungarian fears of a possible Romanian attack.[201] After a meeting with the Romanian military attaché in Budapest, Karpati stated that he had been assured that the Romanian security forces in Timișoara had taken action " 'in the interest of restoring order'; . . . [and that] very careful analysis of reports that the Romanian army was preparing for action against Hungary would be needed before such reports could be believed."[202] By this time, the revolution was in full flow, and the speed of the events meant that neither side could take any further actions until Ceaușescu was overthrown, when Lieutenant-General Eftimescu in the afternoon of December 22 twice made contact with Karpati and mem-

198. BBC EE/1150, B/3:11(a), August 14, 1991.
199. BBC EE/1150, B/3:11(b), August 14, 1991.
200. BBC EE/0645, i, December 21, 1989.
201. Codrescu et al. (1998), 205; Sava and Monac (2001), 217–18.
202. BBC EE/0646 ii, December 22, 1989, and see also *Independent*, December 21, 1989, 11.

bers of the Hungarian General Staff telling them that the NSF had taken power with the backing of the army and asking them to dispel rumors that Hungarian troops were massing on Romania's borders.[203] Karpati duly did so while at the same time offering any help that was required, and subsequently food supplies did arrive, but not troops.[204]

Conclusion

In general, it seems that the importance of any conspiracies should not be overemphasized. That there was deep dissatisfaction within the ranks of the army, the Ministry of the Interior, and the Party is undeniable, and this does seem to have given rise to a certain amount of conspiring against Ceaușescu during the 1980s. The *securitate*, however, always seems to have kept one step ahead of these conspiracies and, even among the prospective plotters, there appears to have been considerable doubts as to the feasibility of any projected coup. By 1989, most of the conspirators had retired from active military service and with few serving officers within their ranks, their plans seemed to have been a mere rehash of the earlier coup model of 1984. However, the coup planned for that year had been betrayed and, although circumstances were greatly changed in 1989, there seems to be no intrinsic reason why such a project would necessarily have been any more successful in that year, or 1990 for that matter. Ceaușescu remained acutely aware of the possibility of a coup and, given the apparent reluctance of the security forces to side with the revolution when it broke out in Timișoara, it seems quite probable that the plotters would have met some opposition from *securitate* and army units loyal to the regime. On the other hand, a popular uprising, such as the one that engulfed Romania after December 15, 1989, would have been very difficult to suppress at any time, whether or not it was backed by any kind of military plot. Prior to the flight of Ceaușescu the plotters seem to have had a minimal influence on the unfolding developments, and, subsequent to that event, their efforts were largely centered on establishing control over the situation and presenting themselves as the only credible alternative leadership.

203. Codrescu et al. (1998), 205.
204. Săndulescu (c1996), 229–328.

CHAPTER FIVE

The Council of the National Salvation Front

> The certitude that there is no salvation is a form of salvation, in fact it *is* salvation. Starting from here, we might organize our own life as well as construct a philosophy of history: the insoluble as solution, as the only way out . . .
>
> EMIL CIORAN, The Trouble with Being Born

The Structure of the New Regime

The formation of the Council of the National Salvation Front on the evening of December 22 merely marked the first step toward the creation of a new structure of power. Within a matter of days, there quickly followed bodies covering all levels of government (fig. 5.1). As the legislative body, the CNSF continued to lie at the heart of the new regime, but real power resided in the smaller Executive Bureau at its head. Below this, the Council was directly supported by two other structures: the government, which was its administrative arm, and a series of NSF commissions, which were to serve in an advisory capacity. Further down there stretched a series of county and communal NSF councils, which again functioned with executive bureaus and whose administrative arms were the local mayors. There also appeared a parallel structure of NSF factory councils, although these were never formally constituted.

The structure of the new NSF administration in many ways mirrored that of the former communist regime. Some bodies such as the Grand National Assembly had disappeared, but equivalents for the various commissions and the government had existed before and the actual Council itself broadly replicated the old RCP Central Committee, with the Executive Bureau filling the role of the PEC. At the lower level, many of these structures were occupied by familiar faces, but instead of being installed through official fiat from above, these former communists now retained their positions by virtue of their own authority within their local communities. Even in the upper tiers of the regime, the new leaders did not

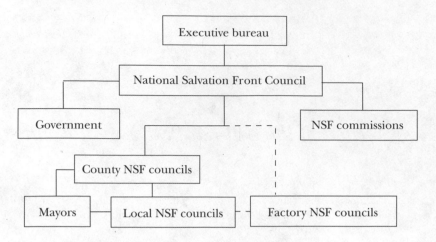

Fig. 5.1 The structure of the National Salvation Front

enjoy an entirely free hand in choosing who would occupy senior positions. When he named several prominent non-Party dissidents at the head of the first list of CNSF members, Iliescu had been, to a certain extent, responding to the expectations of national and international public opinion. Only in the case of the government and, to a slightly lesser extent, the NSF commissions was the process completely under the control of the new leaders.

The formal powers of the CNSF were laid down by the "Decree-Law on the Constitution, Organization and Functioning of the Council of the National Salvation Front and its Local Councils."[1] This Decree-Law was promulgated on the radio by the vice president of the Constitutional, Judicial, and Human Rights Commission, Oliviu Tocaciu, which suggests that this body, initially headed by Mazilu, was chiefly responsible for its form. It gave the CNSF sole legislative power with the right to issue laws and decrees. These were to be adopted by a simple majority vote of Council members and published in the official journal, *Monitorul Oficial al României.*

The original CNSF, as announced by Iliescu on December 22, 1989, comprised just 39 members but by December 30 it had already grown to 145. In composition it does appear to have been a clean break with the immediate past. Only General Guşă, who presumably secured nomination on the first list of Council members due to the military situation, had been a member of the 466 strong Central Committee named at the 14th Congress of the RCP in November 1989. According to Iliescu, the extra members of the Council, apart from the chairmen of the county

1. *Adevărul,* December 29, 1989, 1.

councils of the National Salvation Front, who automatically secured representation, had been chosen largely on a symbolic basis, with the intention of extending coverage both geographically and socially. Proportionate representation for the largest ethnic minority was secured by the nomination of sixteen members from the ranks of the newly established Hungarian Democratic Union of Romania. Many of the members of the Council, and particularly those drafted from outside Bucharest, once more sank back into obscurity after the May 1990 election. From the available names, it seems only about 20 percent ran for and were elected to the Romanian parliament at this time, although a few others were later returned at the 1992 poll. Nearly all of those who ran did so as candidates for the NSF and, subsequent to the split in this party, the vast majority gravitated toward the wing that identified with Iliescu. The bulk of the CNSF was composed of well-educated technocrats. The biggest group were engineers, but their numbers were leavened by a scattering of workers, students, and professors. There was also an important small minority of "liberal" intellectuals including Gabriel Andreescu, Ana Blandiana, Mariana Celac, Doina Cornea, Mircea Dinescu, Radu Filipescu, and Andrei Pleșu. Although they do not appear to have acted as a unified group, their record of dissidence under Ceaușescu gave these figures a strong moral authority which extended well beyond the bounds of Romania. Their pronouncements—especially those of Cornea and Blandiana—received widespread attention, and when doubts were cast about the political orientation of the Front they increasingly became the voice heard in the Western media.

The diverse membership of the CNSF was drawn from the four corners of a large country whose communications were still in a state of revolutionary flux. This made it a difficult and unwieldy body to convene and, in its short history, it does not seem to have met more than two or three times before it effectively voted for its own dissolution by accepting on January 23, 1990, that the NSF would participate in the elections as a political party. Real power throughout this period lay in the hands of the far smaller Bucharest-based Executive Bureau of the Council. This body was not only responsible for determining the composition of the larger CNSF but was also empowered to act on behalf of the Council between its full sessions. The Executive Bureau had a membership of eleven, consisting of the president, Ion Iliescu; first deputy president, Dumitru Mazilu; deputy presidents, Cazimir Ionescu and Károly Király; secretary, Dan Marțian; and six members, Bogdan Teodoriu, Vasile Neacșa, Silviu Brucan, Gheorghe Manole, Ion Caramitru, and Nicolae Radu. The formal powers of the president of the Council, Iliescu, as interim head of state, were ostensibly limited, the most important being the rights to conclude foreign treaties and appoint and recall Romania's ambassadors. But because of the dominant position of the Executive Bureau, which he headed, his powers in reality were considerable. The presence of a number of students and other political tyros within the Executive Bureau also meant that the six senior members, Iliescu, Mazilu, Ionescu, Marțian, Király, and Brucan, were generally dominant. The members of the Executive Bureau also effectively controlled the policy making process, since each of the nine main NSF commissions was headed by one of its members. The two most important commissions responsible for much of the early legislation of the NSF were those concerned with foreign affairs, and constitutional, juridical, and human rights issues.

The government was established as the supreme administrative body of the state. The appointment of the new premier, Petre Roman, was officially announced on December 26. Born in 1946, Roman was the son of Valter Roman, a senior RCP figure, who had occupied a number of important posts. An engineer by profession, between 1970–74 Roman had studied in France before returning to an academic career at the Bucharest Polytechnic. Although he had been a member of the RCP, most accounts agree that prior to the revolution he had not been politically active. Officially he secured the role of prime minister because, after his prominent role during the events, he was seen as being an intelligent and youthful face to front a revolution, which by common consent was the preserve of the young. However, more important, he seems to have personally known Iliescu and the other leaders of the NSF.[2]

The new government was entirely responsible to the CNSF. It was obliged to fulfill the goals laid down in the December 22 NSF program and to apply the measures decreed by the Council. The government adopted its decisions by a simple majority of votes, but the Council retained the right to cancel such decisions when "it believes that they are at variance with the laws and decrees in force or at variance with the interests of the people."[3] All the ministers were officially appointed by presidential decrees signed by Iliescu. Of those selected only the vice premier, Mihai Drăgănescu, and the foreign minister, Sergiu Celac, were at the time considered to be close to Iliescu; the former can be seen as the main representative of the Iliescu group within the administration.[4] Presumably the ministerial candidates were chosen by the inner council of the NSF, and, in keeping with the ideas contained within the ideology of Consensus detailed below, selection was said to have been purely made on the grounds of competence. Indeed, the government did have a strong technocratic base, with most of the new ministers being bureaucrats drawn from the second echelon in their departments or, occasionally, recalled senior figures who had previously served in the same ministry. Several

2. *New York Times,* January 3, 1990, A.12.
3. BBC EE/0653, B/21:70, January 4, 1990.
4. For a discussion of the government see Shafir (January 12, 1990), 35–38.

ministers had previously been members of the RCP Central Committee with one, Ioan Folea, the minister for geology, even being reelected at the November 1989 Party Congress. The only powerful interest group represented was the army, with three members being serving generals: the minister of national economy, Victor Stănculescu, the minister of the interior, Mihai Chiţac, and the minister of defense, Nicolae Militaru—the minister for tourism, Mihai Lupoi, was also a regular army officer. At the time this gave rise to much speculation about the strength of the military within the new regime. However, rather than being the precursor of a significant movement of the military into politics, their appointment was more a recognition of the important role the army had played in the December conflict. As the NSF increased in confidence, and divisions surfaced within the military, their influence in the new regime sharply waned. Few of the new ministers made any lasting impact on the political stage and virtually the whole cabinet slipped back into obscurity after the May 1990 election. Only Roman, Andrei Pleşu, the minister of culture, and, to a lesser extent, Mihai Şora, the minister of education, retained any lasting political influence, although within the ranks of the deputy ministers there were two future prime ministers: Theodor Stolojan and Nicolae Văcăroiu. Some of the more important of the other ministers, such as Celac and the vice premier, Voiculescu, were also to find compensation in diplomatic postings. In general, it was a rather bland and uninspiring government, scarcely chosen to excite and lead. Most charitably, it might be said, it was the stopgap response of a regime without deep reserves of trusted lieutenants to promote. More harshly, it can be viewed as an administrative arm designed not to challenge the leading position of the Executive Bureau of the CNSF. In truth, it just followed the tradition of the governments of the communist period, which were almost solely concerned with the administration of policies decided elsewhere.

The Leaders of the National Salvation Front

Among the more prominent members of the new Front administration it seems possible to identify three groupings roughly based on age. Although, before proceeding, it should be noted that, while shared experience to a certain extent gave rise to common mentalities, diversity within these generations was often as prevalent as commonality. First, there are those who might be considered the "old guard," although they were not necessarily the most conservative voices to be heard. Foremost among this group were three of the signatories of the "Letter of the Six"—Silviu Brucan, Alexandru Bârlădeanu, and Corneliu Mănescu. Born in the first decades of the century, they were the direct contemporaries of Ceauşescu, old *illegalists* (members of the RCP when it was a persecuted underground body) whose past gave them considerable moral authority in the postwar Party. Each had held a string of high posts: Brucan had been Romanian ambassador to the United States and the UN, Mănescu a former foreign minister, and Bârlădeanu a member of the highest RCP body, the Executive Committee. They had all lived through successive changes of policy before each, in turn, had come into conflict with Ceaușescu and been forced into political obscurity. As a group they appear to have retained some sort of belief in the Soviet Union as a guide to events, and were unwilling to unthinkingly jettison a life devoted to the Left. However, this does not mean they shared a common belief system. In particular, Brucan's and Mănescu's extensive contact with the West appears to have marked them out from Bârlădeanu, allowing them to adopt a differing posture in post-Ceaușescu politics. Mănescu became a senator in the May 1990 elections, but both before and after this, on account of his ill health, he played a minor role in public life. Likewise, although Bârlădeanu, as chairman of the Senate, later became identified as one of the staunchest lieutenants of Iliescu and something of a bastion of conservative thinking, his initial influence seems to have been largely confined to behind-the-scenes activities. At first the most active and important of this group was Brucan. He has been called the éminence grise of the revolution, although his fluency in English and evident enthusiasm for granting interviews to the Western press probably played a role in gaining him this accolade. In fact, it remains difficult to determine his real influence on affairs. Elements of the political agenda laid out in one of his books, *World Socialism at the Crossroads: An Insider's View,* published in the West in 1987, can be traced in the program of the NSF, but in the new regime he held no public positions other than his membership of the Executive Bureau and the chairmanship of the Foreign Affairs Commission. Perhaps rather ingeniously, he described the latter post as being purely honorary, even though this body contained many of the Young Turks of the revolution. Immediately after the conflict ended, Brucan seems to have been most concerned with establishing his version of the events and the importance of his role in the dissidence against Ceaușescu. At least in public his view was, therefore, more retrospective than forward looking, and even he makes no claims to be the instigator of any major initiative in the period after the revolutionary violence.

The standard bearers of the second group were Ion Iliescu, Dan Marțian, and Mihai Drăgănescu, with Károly Király and Nicolae S. Dumitru also apparently having some initial influence. Born in the late 1920s or early 1930s, all were long-term members of the RCP, who in the case of Iliescu, Drăgănescu, Marțian, and Király had risen to senior positions in the Party before falling out with Ceaușescu. Iliescu, Marțian, Király, and Dumitru had all studied for a number of years in the Soviet Union, the latter three during the years of the Khrushchev thaw. They were highly educated technocrats, the direct Romanian equivalent of the Gorbachev generation. Their formative political experiences had been gained in the era of post-Stalinist liberalization, a period that in Romania, due to Ceauşescu's opposition to the Warsaw Pact invasion of Czechoslovakia, had stretched beyond 1968 into the early 1970s. Cast aside during the years of Ceauşescu stagnation, they remained untainted by the corruption and venality of his decaying regime and, indeed, came to see its moral degeneracy as one of the root causes of Romania's decline. They had seen the successes of communism in Romania and it was possible for them to ascribe its failures to the mismanagement of Ceauşescu and his clique. Stephen Hanson has suggested that some of their Soviet equivalents were the last uncorrupted believers in Marxism-Leninism, and in Romania this age group also seems to have retained a high regard for the values, if not the doctrines, of communism.[5] In February 1990, Iliescu, in answer to a question by a French journalist about whether he was still a communist, replied:

> Today, you know, it is difficult to set out to establish such a definition. Let's say I was born into a family of militants and I have always remained a political militant. . . . Marxism inspired human thought of the last century. There were scientific reasons for its appearance and therefore it remains an historical stage in the development of ideas. If it is considered as an instrument of analysis, and if we cease to consider it as a rigid dogma, it retains some usefulness. However, in its social, economic, and political practices the ideology that inspired these, in this case, is completely discredited. It is not any more on this ideological base that we can plan the development of modern society. Contemporary thought is much greater, richer, more flexible, and better adapted to the dynamism of today. The simple Marxist model, of the classical type, is no longer sufficient. The modern world can be characterized by a technological and scientific explosion that revolutionizes everything. It is difficult to approach this reality through bygone models.[6]

The third and most numerous group to be considered are those who were born in the late 1940s and 1950s. Among this generation may be numbered Petre Roman, Vasile Secăreş, Dan Mircea Popescu, Ioan Mircea Paşcu, Adrian Severin, Eugen Dijmărescu, Adrian Năstase, Mugur Isărescu, Dorel Şandor, Victor Babiuc, Daniel Dăianu, Vladimir Pasti, Cornel Codiţă, Liviu Mureşan, and Ion Aurel Stoica. The formative years for this generation had been the late 1960s and 1970s. Old enough to remember 1968, they had lived through the hope engendered by the Nixon–Brezhnev détente but also the disasters of late Ceauşescu communism. Far more open to the West, where Roman among others had studied, and not educated in Moscow, they had only known rejection of the

5. Hanson (1991), 33–59.
6. *Le Monde,* February 28, 1990, 1.

USSR. Socialist values were to prove stronger in some than others and the members of this generation were in the coming months to divide between those who almost totally rejected the past in favor of a liberal Western free market model, and those who in varying degrees retained an attachment to some elements of the communist past, while still advocating a broadly similar Western model.

Many of these figures from the third group, at the time of the revolution, were informally gathered into a forum known as the Trocadero Group, so-called because, when members were given directions for meetings at the Institute of World Economy, they were told it was next to the Trocadero Restaurant.[7] The members of this group were mostly drawn from three of the most senior research institutes in Bucharest: the Institute of World Economy, the Party Institute for Political Research (the Ştefan Gheorghiu Academy), and the Association for International Law and International Relations. As is perhaps inevitable, given its association with the last days of communism, the exact composition of the Trocadero Group remains shrouded in some mystery, but among the names most frequently mentioned as possible members are Vasile Secăreş, Dan Mircea Popescu, Ioan Mircea Paşcu, Adrian Severin, Eugen Dijmărescu, Adrian Năstase, Mugur Isărescu, Dorel Şandor, and Victor Babiuc. The members of the group were the intellectual crème de la crème of the younger generation of the RCP. Actively promoted as the acceptable face of Romanian communism, they appeared at international conferences and thus maintained contact with the outside world. Within their prestigious institutes, this young elite seems to have found considerable intellectual latitude in comparison with the closed world of the rest of Ceauşescu's Romania. They had access to external information and computers and were able to study both capitalist economies and the changes occurring in the rest of Eastern Europe. Thus, not only were some of the most talented and technically competent members of the establishment able to monitor the full ramifications of the catastrophic situation unfolding inside Romania and the decline of the country's international standing, but they were also able to gain some idea of what effect the reforms seen elsewhere in the Soviet Bloc would have if they were to be applied to Romania. The exact status of the Trocadero Group continues to be difficult to determine and, indeed, one member of the group has suggested that it is better to see it as representing a spirit rather than a formal body. However, several members have confirmed that the group did gather a number of times in the days shortly after the fall of Ceauşescu and most, if not all, of its members were subsequently drafted onto the Foreign Affairs Commission under Brucan, with Secăreş being named as his deputy. In the chaos of January 1990 there were few available who had the experi-

7. Pasti (1997), 220–21.

ence needed to draft the considerable amount of new legislation required and so it was to members of this group that the new leaders turned for ideas. Adrian Severin, for instance, seems to have been at least partly responsible for two of the most important early decree-laws, one on passports and travel abroad and the other the landmark "Decree-Law for the Organization and Unfolding of Economic Activity on the Basis of Free Initiative."

Reform Coalitions in Communist Romania

To gain some understanding of the foundations underpinning the ideology of the NSF it is necessary first to look at the position of intellectuals in Romanian society. Intellectuals have traditionally enjoyed a high status in Eastern Europe due to the weaknesses of state and society. This was particularly true of Romania, where the bourgeoisie was notably frail and largely non-national in composition. At the same time, the lateness of state formation, with modern Romania only taking something like its present shape after 1918, and the needs of nation building provided the grounds for a particularly fertile interaction between intellectuals and nationalism.[8] Through their scholarship the intellectuals gave the modern nation its form and in the process claimed for themselves an exalted status as the very conscience of the people.[9] This left them endowed not only with considerable cultural significance but also, in the past, with a great deal of political influence, as many intellectuals ascended to high governmental office. Until the 1950s intellectuals in the humanities had predominated, but from that period onward, Romania underwent a massive program of industrial development that fundamentally changed the social profile of the nation. In the years up to 1977, Romania registered one of the highest growth rates in the world, with industrial output increasing by an average of 12.9 percent per annum between 1950 and 1977.[10] The new industries required a vast number of technocratic specialists and this led to important changes in Romania's educational system, which became almost entirely geared to the production of engineers and subengineers, as the natural and especially the applied sciences blossomed at the expense of the humanities, which were decimated. There also appeared a proliferation of advanced scientific and economic research institutes, which by 1989 were recorded as employing staffs totaling nearly 170,000.[11] Indeed, no clearer indication of the prestige endowed to science at this time was Elena Ceaușescu's selection of chemistry as the field in which she would become a "scholar" of international repute.

8. Livezeanu (1995).
9. Schöpflin (1993), 147–48.
10. Shafir (1985), 107.
11. *Anuarul statistic al Romaniei 1991* (n.d.), 190.

The rise of this stratum of scientific-technical specialists coincided with a period of liberalization in Romania, as the Party leadership retreated from the violent excesses of Stalinism and began to pay increasing attention to the demands of society in the hope of building a more consensual base for continuing single party rule. Central to this strategy was a switch away from the old symbolic-ideological legitimation of Stalinism and a move toward a more remuneratively based legitimation founded on the supply of consumer goods. The skills of the technical-scientific elite were to play a key role in this process, and, in recognition of their growing importance, representatives of this group began to gain positions within the upper echelons of the regime.[12] Their position was cemented during the 1960s by a tactical alliance with the new leader Ceaușescu, as he consolidated his hold on power, and through their support for his semiautonomous foreign policy, which was seen as distancing the country from the USSR. The new foreign policy produced changes in trade patterns, as Romania secured openings in the West and began to introduce advanced technology and scientific ideas, most notably in several high-profile projects in aeronautics and nuclear power.[13] In response to these changes, a number of Romanian social scientists, while still closely adhering to Marxist ideology, began to offer a theoretical base for the importation of Western scientific and managerial methods to permit accelerated economic development.[14] Among the most prominent of these ideologues was Valter Roman.[15] Drawing on contacts made with leading Western communists during his time in the International Brigade in the Spanish Civil War, Roman amassed a personal library of social science literature, which was said to be the envy of Bucharest, and his house seems to have become a meeting place linking different generations of like-minded reformers, including Iliescu, Drăgănescu, and, presumably, Valter Roman's young son, Petre.[16]

Valter Roman and his fellow technocratic reformers had argued for a greatly increased role for the technical elite in the policy-making process, but unexpectedly, in the 1970s, this group from the promised land found themselves increasingly cast into the wilderness. The grounds for this change were laid in the "July Theses" of 1971 in which Ceaușescu signaled his intention to abandon his brief flirtation with legitimation by remuner-

12. Crowther (1988), 82–85.
13. Smith (1979), 323–61; Socor (October 29, 1985), 11–17.
14. Socor (January 13, 1984), 1–9.
15. A member of the RCP since the early 1930s, after the communist takeover Valter Roman had served as chief of the general staff of the Romanian army, but, by the 1960s, after a brief ministerial career, he had retreated into academic life as a professor of scientific socialism.
16. Shafir (January 12, 1990), 36; Rady (1992), 128; Calinescu and Tismaneanu (January/April 1991), 53 n. 41. Note that Valter Roman and Drăgănescu also had shared ties within the National Council for Scientific Research.

ation in favor of a return to symbolic-ideological legitimation and the reimposition of ideological conformity.[17] In fact, the fall from grace was a rather haphazard and patchy affair. It was not until the onset of the economic crisis of the 1980s that the scientific-technical elite seems to have become totally alienated from the regime, and for much of the 1970s, while the economy continued to grow and a succession of new economic ministries were founded, they appeared to be still consolidating their position within the political bureaucracy. However, from the early 1970s there was an unmistakable shift back from "expert" to "red" and, although this does appear to have often overlapped and overlaid pre-existing patterns of factional infighting within the Party, the result, nonetheless, was the eventual exclusion from power of a segment of the scientific-technical elite who had pioneered the previous industrial expansion. Iliescu's career mirrored this process. After achieving some prominence within the communist youth movement, he had quickly risen up the RCP ladder, becoming an alternative member of the Central Committee in 1968 and then occupying a series of senior party positions, including minister of youth affairs (1967–71) and secretary for propaganda and education of the Central Committee (February–September 1971). But following disagreements with Ceauşescu, he had commenced a lengthy fall from grace, being dispatched from Bucharest to be first secretary of the county RCP committees of Timiş (1972–76) and then Iaşi (1976–79). Although these moves were demotions, his disgrace does not seem to have been total, and in the late 1970s he even made something of a comeback when he was made chairman of the National Water Council. It was only in 1984 with his dismissal from the Central Committee and his appointment as director of the Editura Tehnică publishing house that his RCP political career was brought to an end.

However, despite the sidelining of many of those associated with the 1960s reform movement, even in the 1980s, occasional signs of reformist thinking still broke to the surface, as in a couple of articles that appeared in 1984 and 1985 by two young economists, Daniel Dăianu and Vasile Pilat.[18] In their writings they pressed for the abandonment of autarky in favor of the rational development of selected fields, decentralization, greater managerial autonomy, increased competition, and a partial reversion to a market pricing system. Written in English in a dense and highly specialist language and published in an official journal, which had a very restricted circulation, probably the articles made little impact. However, they do suggest a degree of reform economic thinking within some institutions in Romania, which appears to have been on a par with elsewhere

17. Verdery (1991), 107.
18. Pilat and Dăianu (1984), 245–61; Pilat and Dăianu (1985), 33–48. For an analysis see Maier and Ionescu (October 5, 1984), 1–4. The two economists were then at the Institute of Socialist Economics in Bucharest.

in Eastern Europe; more important, at various times during the late 1970s and 1980s even elements of official policy, such as the New Economic and Financial Mechanism, began to reflect these ideas. This sought to instill some degree of market mechanism into the system through concepts such as "self-financing," by which enterprises were expected to generate sufficient income to sustain themselves without recourse to subsidies from the state. Like so much else in late Ceaușescu Romania, the NEFM remained an empty formula with little real content. Nevertheless, it does indicate the presence of a degree of reformism within late Ceaușescu policy formation, at least until the mid-1980s, which is often overlooked. This is significant, because not only did such ideas offer one possible avenue of reform, once Ceaușescu was deposed, but also because the search for reasons to explain the failure of the 1980s measures seems to have produced two important assumptions among reformers within the Party. The first was a belief that the disastrous position of the Romanian economy in the late 1980s was primarily due to a combination of the policies pursued by Ceaușescu and the actions of an obstructive central bureaucracy, which in protecting their own interests had moved to block any redistribution of resources. This belief appears to have generated something of a myth of a lost opportunity of creating a technocratically based, modern, industrial, and socialist Romania, preventing the formation of an appreciation on anything but a limited scale that it might in fact be impossible to reform the system. Second, the obstructive nature of the bureaucracy and an understanding among some reformers that the RCP, despite its allegedly high membership, was nothing more than a hollow shell with an unsupported elite held up by an administrative superstructure seems to have bred a feeling that any economic reforms would have to be matched by political changes. Some, including Brucan, even began to argue for the primacy of political reform.

In his 1971 speeches Ceaușescu had also spoken out against the slavish imitation of foreign forms and this was to presage over the coming years an intensified use of nationalist symbolism and a gradual cutting of links with the outside world in favor of an indigenist and autarkic pattern of development. Katherine Verdery has plausibly argued that the concept of the nation has been such a potent "master symbol" in Romania that, historically, it has subsumed under a debate couched in terms of national identity (or, as she terms it, "national essence") nearly all other issues, including key questions relating to the suitability of differing political models to Romania, relations between state and society, and, in particular, the appropriate path for modernization. Historically, this debate has created the space for intellectual endeavors and served to distinguish the intellectual stratum from the peasant masses, and it is Verdery's contention that it has become so embedded within the Romanian intellectual discourse, even taking physical form through the various institutions established in its wake that eventually it was even able to subvert the official ideology of Marxism-Leninism. Her argument is that it was not just the Party which turned to a nationalist ideology as a source of legitimation but also that "to a considerable extent . . . the Party was *forced* onto the terrain of national values (not unwillingly) under pressure from others, especially intellectuals, whom it could fully engage in no other manner."[19]

Behind the rhetoric, the debate on national identity has often served as an idiom for intra-elite conflict and this was to be the case again during the 1980s, when the Roman/Dacian dichotomy, which lies at the heart of the question of the origins of the Romanian people, was once more played upon, this time to produce legitimation for an indigenous model of development.[20] This paved the way for the rise of a relatively small group of artistic-literary intellectuals who were encouraged to produce the appropriate nationalist symbolism required to support the change in policy. Often termed the protochronists, due to the stress they laid on the pseudo-supremacy of Romanian (Dacian) thinking in all fields from political economy to sociology, their argument that a strong indigenous culture could only grow through isolation from contaminating foreign values fully reflected the autarkic policies of Ceauşescu and the cult mythology that emphasized his providential role in Romanian history.[21] However, while the protochronists were rising in official esteem, another larger group of cultural intellectuals, many of whom had been associated with the brief window of reform in the late 1960s, were being eclipsed. As in the case of the technical intelligentsia, their displacement from positions of influence was a gradual and uneven affair, stretching throughout most of the 1970s. They even retained control of the Writers' Union until the early 1980s, when the regime, apparently tiring of ever bringing it back under full control, moved to effectively render the organization impotent.[22]

While bearing in mind that many intellectuals occupied an intermediate position, it is nonetheless possible for heuristic purposes to divide Romanian cultural politics in the late 1980s into two opposing groups: one relatively small, indigenist, or protochronist group in close alignment with Ceauşescu and the ruling Party apparat, and the other larger and often more liberal in orientation deprived of any power and influence. Also largely excluded from power and increasingly chafing at their forced impotence were leading members of the scientific-technical elite. During

19. Verdery (1991), 122 (emphasis in original). The conceptual framework for this section draws heavily upon this excellent study of intellectuals in Romania in the 1980s, and to prevent repetition only direct quotes will be noted in the future.

20. Deletant (1988), 77–91. The Dacians were the inhabitants of the lands conquered by the Roman emperor Trajan in 106 and that today constitute Romania.

21. For the protochronists see Verdery (1991), 167–214; Marga (1993), 14–32; Tismaneanu (1994), 404–5; Gabanyi (2000), 155–62.

22. Verdery (1991), 184–88, 345–46 n. 26.

1987, two potential leaders of this elite, Iliescu and Brucan, published works in which they appeared to be proposing a potential reform coalition between their group and the displaced cultural intellectuals. In an article in *România Literară*, which was effectively a hymn of praise for technocrats, Iliescu suggested that the defining characteristic of the twentieth century had been technological development. As the century had progressed, he argued, the introduction of automation and advanced production techniques also had important social consequences, as the demand for manual labor declined in relation to a corresponding rise in the need for technical expertise.[23] On the basis of these changes, Iliescu suggested that society could now be broadly divided into noncreative and creative forces, the former roughly identified with the working class, the latter with intellectuals—defined at their widest extent. In making such a division, in the context of Ceaușescu's Romania, Iliescu might have been aiming to reassert the importance of intellectuals vis-à-vis the working class, but, more immediately, he appears to have been making a plea for the equality of technical creativity with cultural creativity; indeed, he even suggests that the former may be accorded greater status on account of its less ephemeral nature. Then, by identifying bureaucratic inertia as the common foe of both technical and cultural intellectuals, Iliescu suggests that these two forces should make common cause in the interests of reform. In a book published in the West in the same year, Brucan also voiced a similar argument, when he suggested that the only revolutionary group capable of challenging the entrenched power of the apparat was the scientific and technical elite in alliance with cultural intellectuals.[24]

It seems possible that both these analyses owe something to the New Class theory of György Konrád and Iván Szelényi, first propagated during the 1970s. Broadly, this held that with the scientific-technical revolution in Eastern Europe, a fused humanistic and technical intelligentsia by virtue of its knowledge would, as a class, displace the old-line bureaucrats and ascend to power.[25] Brucan was aware of Konrád and Szelényi's work and the whole tenor of his pre-revolutionary writings suggests that he broadly accepted their formulation, although from a theoretical point of view it is not entirely clear whether he saw the intellectuals as a separate class.[26] Brucan termed intellectuals the "most advanced and important part of socialist society," and, during the events of December 1989, he was emphatically to state, "In the revolution it is the intellectuals who are in command."[27] Thus, within the framework of a strong domestic tradition

23. *România Literară*, September 3, 1987, 19; Gabanyi (September 21, 1987). For some details about how this article came to be published see *România Literară*, July 5, 1990, 15.
24. Brucan (1987), 111–21.
25. Konrád and Szelényi (1979); see also Szelényi (1986–87), 103–44.
26. Brucan (1990), 114–15.
27. *Financial Times*, December 29, 1989, 11.

of intellectuals holding a preeminent place in society, it can be construed that some elements of the NSF leadership, as they ascended to power, were thinking in terms of the New Class project. Indeed, Michael Shafir did equate the postcommunist reality in Romania with the nightmare-come-true of Konrád and Szelényi's rule of the intelligentsia, and the idea surfaces again in a controversial remark made by Brucan during an interview in January 1990 when he noted, "Everywhere in the world, the intellectuals are marching to power. . . . They are the only social category which can cope with the information revolution."[28] In this brave new world it seems only intellectuals would be qualified to rule.

Within the writings of Iliescu, Brucan, and some of the younger members of the technocratic elite it is possible, with an eye to a subtext that has become more apparent with hindsight, to read support for an alternative set of values to those championed by the regime. Broadly, these were centered on a concern about the growing "information gap" between Romania and the outside world, the necessity of adopting realistic and not utopian policies, the value of both professional expertise and accrued knowledge, and the need for Romania to reconnect with the European mainstream. This latter sentiment, which was by far the most important in defining their position, was strikingly caught in the "Letter of the Six" in which the writers lecture Ceauşescu: "Romania is and remains a European country and as such must advance along with the Helsinki process and not turn against it. You started changing the geography of the countryside, but you cannot remove Romania to Africa."[29] Later, during the revolution, the same message was to reappear in Front communiqués which asserted that "Romania was and remains an European country," and in a January campaign to reverse the decision to hold a referendum on the death penalty, the NSF argued that through its abolition of capital punishment Romania was conforming to the norms of civilized Europe.[30]

By defining their position through reference to Romania's relations with the remainder of Europe, the 1980s reformers were adopting a stance close to that previously occupied by the interwar literary critic Eugen Lovinescu, who sought through "synchronism" with the outside world to encourage the growth and development of Romanian culture to internationally accepted norms. They were, thus, again recycling the longstanding debate on "national essence" and using it as an idiom to express intra-elite conflict. In the works of the philosophers, adherence to this European agenda meant stressing the inheritance of Plato and Hegel in preference to the Geto-Dacian cult of Zalmoxis, while for political scientists, such as Ioan Mircea Paşcu, it meant emphasizing the universality

28. *Independent,* January 29, 1990, 8; Shafir (February 15, 1991), 33.
29. Brucan (1993), 155.
30. *Adevărul,* January 16, 1990, 1, 5; "Statement of the Ministry of Foreign Affairs" (1989), 413.

of international relations and reminding the reader of the rich heritage of Plato, Thucydides, Hobbes, Rousseau, and Kant, among others.[31] In the context of the fall of communism, Jadwiga Staniszkis has suggested that similar lines of confrontation could be identified elsewhere in the communist world with the main axis of conflict being "the choice between an *ontological opening*, followed by Westernization, or the *reinforcement of specificity*."[32] Staniszkis labeled those who supported the process of reform "globalists," and this term has been adopted in this study to describe those who wanted to see Romania reorient itself toward the European mainstream. However, beyond the embracing of new technology and entry into global markets, what this actually meant for the likes of Brucan and Iliescu is more difficult to fathom. In particular, its implications for domestic political reform were left uncharted. This may have been because the globalists were unable to shape a full political program in the coercive atmosphere of the late Ceauşescu regime, but it could also be because they always meant the concept to be empty of content. The globalists needed to define themselves in relation to the indigenist Ceauşescu and his protochronist allies and to build the broadest possible reform coalition. To do this they adopted an emotive idea with great historical resonance that they knew would be attractive to the broadest possible spectrum of the Romanian intelligentsia.

Consensus

The creation of a broad reform coalition needed a wide-ranging consensus and this was the initial defining goal of the revolution as perceived by the NSF. During the first days after the overthrow of Ceauşescu, the new leaders peppered their speeches time and again with references to consensus; such was the importance of the concept that some of the chief political actors of the time have chosen to describe the initial ideology of the NSF through this word.[33] As they were closely involved with the political scene, it seems reasonable to follow their lead, but with the caveat that the original use of the name may have served an ulterior political motive. Not only did the rather bland sounding appellation "Consensus" shroud any links with perestroika and reform socialism but, by stating that Con-

31. Paşcu (1987). In fact, the Romanian debate is merely part of a wider regional discourse that draws upon the supposed tensions that exist between "oriental" Eastern and "enlightened" Western traditions; Hayden and Bakić-Hayden (1992), 1–15; Todorova (1997).

32. Staniszkis (1990), 95, identifies two other factions beside the "globalists"; one is the "populists" and the other the "bureaucratic." The "populists" of Staniszkis' model can be equated with the protochronists but, since in Romania "populism," as identified with Constantin Stere, has historically adopted a qualified pro-Western stance, I have preferred to keep the term "protochronist," even though, strictly speaking, this should be used to refer to a literary group.

33. A Future for Romania Foundation (1993), 17.

sensus was abandoned in January 1990, they were also probably trying to draw a clean divide between the NSF and its earliest ideological roots. To circumvent this problem, a distinction will be made in this work between the ideology of Consensus and the political project that it spawned, because, while the latter was rapidly abandoned in January 1990, the ideal of building a consensual, as opposed to a competitive, political arena continued long afterward to have vitality within Romanian politics.[34] At the time of the revolution, the new leaders saw both Consensus and the Front as permanent fixtures on the Romanian political scene. On December 26 Iliescu spoke of building an enduring consensus on the foundations of the revolution and explicitly stated, "Our front is organized as a permanent structure."[35] Then, returning to the same theme several days later he added: "We intend that the general consensus, which was the determining idea in the struggle, should continue to play a dominant role in all structures which we will create."[36] Clearly, to the new leadership, the Front and the ideology it championed were indivisible. Consensus, as expressed through the near universal support for the overthrow of Ceaușescu, was the ideal of the revolution, with this unity of purpose legitimizing both the bearers of the message—the Front—and the message itself, which became the ideology of the people. Consensus was thus presented as the will of the people, the ideological equivalent of the popular slogan "We are the people."[37]

The roots of Consensus were diverse. Indeed, it may be argued that within Southeastern Europe there is a tendency to believe that society should be organized on a consensual rather than a confrontational basis. Ultimately, this has its foundations in the abiding influence of integral nationalism in the region and a persisting attachment to rather idealized peasant values that are underlined by Orthodox preaching on conformity and universality.[38] However, the immediate line of descent stretched to the communist reformers of the 1960s and their desire to accommodate the changes in society wrought by the scientific-technological revolution. By the 1980s, the emphasis had shifted to the information technology revolution, but many of the concerns remained the same as reformers, such as Iliescu and Brucan, sought to embrace technological change and harness it to the cause of political reform.[39] In the era of perestroika Soviet ideologists spoke of the Party taking on a new role as "an instrument to

34. To differentiate between the two, when indicating the ideology "Consensus" will bear a capital "C."

35. BBC EE/0649, B/6, December 29, 1989.

36. BBC EE/0651, B/6:12, January 1, 1990.

37. Ibid.

38. McNeill (1978), 120–21.

39. Indeed, the link between the two reform periods is evident in the title of Brucan's *World Socialism at the Crossroads: An Insider's View,* which is clearly modeled on a book that, according to Szelényi (1986–87), 112, was something of a bible for members of the Eastern

achieve consensus not an end of power in itself."[40] In its new guise the Party would make some concessions to pluralism by renouncing its claim to a monopoly of power and allowing new political movements to emerge, including political parties, but this did not mean that it would abdicate control of the political process. The Party was still expected to retain something akin to its leading role, at least temporarily, as "an essential factor ensuring broad consensus in the transition towards democratic and humane socialism."[41] In their writings prior to the revolution, the future leaders of the Front had advocated similar ideas, but once they entered power they seemed to distance themselves from such thinking. Brucan vehemently declared that "there is none of this reform communism nonsense in Romania," and Iliescu was equally adamant when he stated that the new leaders were "not the slaves of any ideology, of any preconceived ideas, of any prefabricated models."[42] Yet despite these assertions, within the often ambiguous rhetoric of the early speeches of the NSF leaders there can be glimpsed the shadowy outline of something close to the Soviet model. The first point of the NSF program may have committed the new regime to abandoning the leading role of a single party and to establishing a democratic and pluralist form of government, but in the mind of Iliescu this seems to have more closely resembled the one-party pluralism of reform communism than a recognizably West European pluralist model.[43] In his New Year's speech at the close of 1989 the new Romanian leader gave some hint of this political vision:

A guideline in everything the National Salvation Front undertakes has to be the promotion of democracy in all spheres of social life, a genuine participation of the masses in decision making and their control of the leading factors. We will also promote the Front's programme-like ideas regarding the achievement of a large, novel political pluralism, relying not only upon the existence of several parties, but also upon a genuine assertion of a broad democratic framework in which all tendencies, all interests and all values may be manifest, and all creative forces of the country may be involved in constructive work.[44]

European new class during the late 1960s: Radovan Richta's *Civilisation at the Crossroads: Social and Human Implications of the Scientific and Technological Revolution.*

40. Falin (1990), 23.

41. Lebedev (1990), 24. Although they often claimed to be innovative, these formulations were in practice remarkably similar to models first floated in the 1960s, which had subsequently been dubbed "one-party pluralism." For a review of reform currents in Eastern Europe toward the close of the 1980s see Schöpflin (1988), 1–5.

42. *Financial Times,* December 29, 1989, 11; BBC EE/0652, B/9–11:14, December 31, 1989.

43. Schöpflin (1988).

44. BBC EE/0652, B/9–11:14, January 3, 1990.

The "novel political pluralism" of which Iliescu spoke was never to be fully revealed, but a careful reading of this and other speeches discloses, through keywords such as "participation," "representation," and "pluralism," a distinct vision of democracy that was often shaped in terms of goals rather than process.

Earlier in his 1987 book, Brucan had argued that a one-party system could only be seen as being truly legitimate and representative if it embraced the idea of pluralism, by which he implied the acceptance of groups and factions within the party. Not only would these permit debate, thus breaking the stultifying monologue that had pervaded the latter years of communism in Romania, but the existence of such groups would also ensure greater accountability.[45] Once it entered office, the NSF moved rapidly to put such ideas into practice, permitting the formation not only of factions but also of other political groupings. On December 31, 1989, a "Decree on Registration and Operation of Political Parties and of Public Organizations in Romania" was announced, which placed few restrictions on political formations other than the banning of fascist parties.[46] In response a number of political groupings swiftly emerged but, at the same time, considerable efforts were made by the new leaders to ensure that they did not become too independent. Thus, Iliescu stressed that, while the main Hungarian grouping, the Hungarian Democratic Union of Romania, had its own program, this was fully in keeping with the spirit of the NSF platform, and similarly the Democratic Federation of Magyars in Cluj was also described as being one of the "grass-root branches of the National Salvation Front . . . subordinated to the NSF."[47] In an early television debate, Cazimir Ionescu of the NSF Executive Bureau also made strenuous efforts to win Adrian Ştefanescu and his newly formed Romanian Democratic Party over to the side of the Front by stressing the similarities between their two political programs, before finally ending by grudgingly admitting, "If you really want to remain as a separate *faction,* we have nothing against it."[48] When the Front spoke of parties it clearly did not see them in traditional Western terms, as Iliescu was to underline when he addressed a gathering of students on January 20. "There are many who reduce democracy to the existence of several parties, as if the political confrontation among these different parties

---

45. Brucan (1987), xiv.
46. To register at the Bucharest Municipal Court each party had to present its statutes and political program, declare its headquarters and financial resources, and prove it had at least 251 members. Military cadre and civilian staff of the Ministry of National Defense and the Ministry of Interior, judges, prosecutors, diplomats, and personnel of the radio and television stations were prohibited from joining political parties. Otherwise, the only restriction was that nobody might participate in more than one party.
47. BBC EE/0653, B/26:87, January 4, 1990.
48. BBC EE/0649, B/4, December 29, 1989 (emphasis added).

would be a guarantee of democracy. I think that this is an obsolete historical model. . . . Parties which, inevitably, represent sectarian interests—interests of groups or social categories. . . . In this sense, the notion of 'party'—as a narrow concept—represents an old-fashioned concept."[49]

It seems that the Front was prepared to allow discrete voices to exist but these were clearly expected to subscribe to the basic tenets of the Front's program and to operate within a restricted remit. The definitive statement stressing the all-encompassing nature of the Front was issued by Rompres on January 4, 1990, on the eve of Shevardnadze's visit to Romania. "In connection with the National Salvation Front, we are in a position to specify that it is not and will not become a party. The Front will take part in the April elections as a broad political organization gathering *all* the personalities and groups that rouse [*sic*] courageously in defense of freedom and dignity in the years of totalitarian tyranny."[50] The new leaders seem to have seen the NSF acting as some kind of guiding umbrella institution within the Romanian body politic—in the words of Aurel Dragoş Munteanu, it was to be a "moral platform."[51] Encompassing various factions or parties and individuals of talent, the Front would provide a forum for debate and a wing under which they could shelter. Ostensibly, this was to be until they reached political maturity, but the assumption seems to have been that under this arrangement they would become so persuaded of the benefits of the Front that they would willingly choose to remain under its tutelage. If the Front had been able to fulfill this political vision, its powers would have been considerable, as it would have been the goal setter, universal arbitrator in all debate, and the executor of decisions reached. Undoubtedly it would have retained a leading role in society, and this was clearly within the plans of the new leaders, because Brucan warned in an interview that the CNSF was to "be so powerful there will be little room outside of it."[52] Thus, from the outset the new leadership saw the Front not as a temporary stopgap on the road to Western-style pluralism but as the leading player in the construction of a new type of politics. Consensus had been shaped under communism and, willingly or not, its ideologues had accepted the constraints imposed by that system, particularly the need to maintain the predominance of a socialist party. According to Brucan, when he met Gorbachev in 1988 he was told that reform must be based on the continuation of communist party rule and all his writings prior to 1989 were founded on this assumption. However, the revolution had swept away not only the RCP but with it the single-party system, creating an effective tabula rasa for Romanian politics, allowing the possibility of a choice of models for the future. In this atmosphere,

49. Quoted in Haşeganu (1998), 93 n. 10.
50. BBC EE/0654, B/14:23, January 5, 1990 (emphasis added).
51. BBC EE/0658, B/12:21, January 10, 1990.
52. *Financial Times*, December 29, 1989, 11.

those who retained a belief in the idea that one-party rule continued to hold legitimacy seem to have been culpable of an unreasonable optimism. They were guilty of overestimating the ease with which a popular consensus might be forged for the continuation of single-party rule in a society largely alienated from such a concept, and also the ease with which pluralism and increased institutional autonomy, once it was unleashed, could be squared with such a system. In an opinion poll conducted at the end of December 1989, largely among the inhabitants of Bucharest, 62 percent of the 1,231 respondents stated that they favored a multiparty system, with only 6 percent wishing to see a continuation of single-party rule.[53] It might be true that the ideal of rule by a rationalizing and modernizing single party has deep roots in Romania, and Mary Ellen Fischer has pointed out similarities between the language employed by Iliescu and the interwar neoliberal and champion of corporatism Mihail Manoilescu.[54] However, in reality, the excesses of Ceauşescu and his predecessor had stripped legitimacy not only from the RCP but also from the whole concept of single-party rule.

Dialogue

Frequently linked with Consensus in speeches during the revolution was the concept of dialogue. Iliescu spoke of the NSF engaging in a permanent dialogue with society and, at one point, he even referred to Consensus in terms of a "vivid dialogue."[55] Yet dialogue was not the same as Consensus. It had different roots and embraced another constituency, because primarily it seems to have been seen as a strategy for intellectual inclusion.

The emphasis on dialogue also stemmed in part from thinking on the consequences of the information technology revolution. In the future, access to information was seen as being not only difficult to curtail but also detrimental, as the free flow of knowledge and ideas was deemed to lie at the root of development and progress. This belief was at the bottom of Brucan's desire to promote the emergence of factions and debate under the umbrella of a single party. Beyond this, however, there was also to be a dialogue with and within society through the establishment of a free press, and soon after the overthrow of Ceauşescu publications such as *România Liberă* did begin to openly display a line critical to the thinking

53. This was carried out between December 26–30 by the Center of Sociological Research of Bucharest University. Eighty-four percent of the respondents lived in Bucharest, 11 percent in other towns, and 5 percent in rural areas. Seventy percent of men supported a multiparty system but only 49 percent of women. Nearly 33 percent of those polled professed themselves uncertain about democratic political practices; *Adevărul,* January 12, 1990, 3.

54. Fischer (1992), 51.

55. BBC EE/0649, B/6, December 29, 1989.

of the regime—presumably with some official approval, since Brucan used the pages of the newspaper to engage in a public polemic with Gheorghe Apostol over the "Letter of the Six."[56] This spirit of openness to the press, which of course bears many similarities with glasnost in the Soviet Union, was also initially discernible in the new regime's dealings with the international arena, as the leaders of the NSF gave numerous interviews to foreign journalists.[57]

As well as looking to the future, dialogue was also shaped by the past, with Brucan arguing that its absence had been a root cause of stagnation in communist societies. As with earlier absolute monarchies, it is possible to see the public space under Ceauşescu as providing little more than the room for him to flaunt his authority. In the term of Jürgen Habermas, it was a "representative public sphere," which functioned not as a social entity but as an arena for spectacle and display. In such circumstances, the populace could only to a limited degree assert itself on an individual rather than a collective basis, and the only source of information outside the control of the state was gossip and rumor. Brucan and the other globalists were aware of the ideas of Habermas and through their stress on dialogue they seem to have been advocating the creation of what Habermas terms a "critical reasoning public sphere." In this, alternative channels of information would exist and, to the extent that legislation reflected public opinion, authority would cease to base itself on the capricious whims of one man and instead would derive from consensus.

Expanded in terms of practical politics, in what it must be remembered was a concept shaped within the confines of a one-party state, dialogue was seen as being something like a halfway house on the road to full pluralism. Through dialogue, regime and public would embark on a mutual apprenticeship: the authorities would learn to take the needs of the population into greater account when making decisions, while at the same time public opinion would reemerge as a social factor. However, since the technical problems associated with running a modern state were clearly beyond the ken of most, the real beneficiaries would be those who were qualified to enter the debate, and these were largely the specialists and technicians who held the necessary knowledge. The raising in status and general emancipation of intellectuals would therefore be the prime consequence of such a strategy, because they would have the duties of both explaining decisions that had been made to the general population and articulating the demands of society to the authorities. In the process they would assure for themselves a pivotal position as the transmission belt between society and state. This open consultation process, in which repre-

---

56. *România Liberă*, January 10, 1990, 1, 5; for Brucan's response see ibid., January 11, 1990, 1, 5. Brucan was to accuse Apostol of betraying him to the *securitate*.

57. Devlin (February 9, 1990), 26–30.

sentatives of all major interest groups and even individuals could be heard, would guarantee the widest possible social support for any decisions taken, avoiding confrontation and instead ensuring its antithesis— consensus.[58] Dialogue, therefore, held out the prospect of bridging the chasm between the individual and the general, which earlier reformers during the 1960s had found impossible to surpass.

Dialogue as both a social goal and a political strategy found its fullest expression during the revolution in the ideals of the Group for Social Dialogue. It has even been suggested that it was Silviu Brucan who named the group, although others have pointed to Mihnea Berindei, an exiled dissident who returned from Paris immediately after the overthrow of Ceaușescu.[59] Under its wing the GSD assembled some of Romania's most prominent intellectuals, many of whom had been known dissidents. Among the early members were Doina Cornea, Petru Creția, Mircea Dinescu, Ștefan Augustin Doinaș, Gabriel Liiceanu, Alexandru Paleologu, Dan Petrescu, Andrei Pleșu, Mihai Șora, Călin Anastasiu, Thomas Kleininger, Andrei Pippidi, Radu Bercea, Pavel Câmpeanu, and Stelian Tănase. Formed on December 31, 1989, the GSD published its declaration of principles in Romanian, English, German, and French on January 20, 1990, in the first edition of its influential journal, 22. This was named after the date of Ceaușescu's overthrow, although curiously the GSD seems first to have thought of calling it *Azi* (Today), the name later adopted by the chief NSF newspaper.[60]

Like the NSF, the GSD was established as an umbrella grouping, but in this case with the express aim of representing Romania's intellectuals and moving them from the margins to the center of the national stage. Members were expected to be independent of all political affiliations, and as a group the GSD professed a neutral political stance, seeing itself as a purely intellectual forum for the airing of divergent views. Its strength was to come not from the exertion of actual power but from the elevated position it adopted above the political fray as "the moral conscience of our humiliated and destroyed society."[61] In this guise, and in line with the concept of dialogue, the GSD sought to establish itself as the voice of society and as a mediator between it and the new regime, as well as to represent intellectuals, many of whom were acutely aware of the great divide that had opened between themselves and the workers in communist Romania. Indeed, they considered that Ceaușescu's manipulation of this cleavage was one of the chief reasons for his ability to maintain his hold on power. Now, they sought to bridge this chasm, partly, it seems, by tak-

58. These ideas were most clearly articulated by Mihai Botez; a report on various interviews he gave to the Western press can be found in Socor (March 6, 1987), 13–16.
59. Mungiu (1996), 351.
60. *România Liberă*, January 6, 1990, 5.
61. 22, January 20, 1990, 1.

ing the Polish Workers' Defense Committee (KOR) as a model.[62] However, all the earliest overtures by GSD members to the workers seem to have been rebuffed and the first real attempts at dialogue were instead made with more friendly groupings. A meeting was arranged with actors and directors from the world of theater and film at the Nottara Theater in Bucharest, and this was later followed by discussions with the leaders of the "traditional" parties and the HDUR. The GSD also had early meetings with representatives of the ruling regime, including Cazimir Ionescu and Silviu Brucan, suggesting that there was some official recognition, at least among part of the NSF, for the role it sought to play.

The declaration of principles of the GSD highlighted not so much the practical economic problems facing Romania, but the diseased mentality which it perceived was crippling the nation. In the first editorial of the journal 22, communism was presented as having eroded the positive values of dignity, honor, truth, freedom, and even beauty, leaving only a false life, suffocated by fear, terror, and vulgarity. In the face of such degeneration, the regaining of positive moral values was seen as the greatest of national imperatives. Intellectuals were urged to embark on a crusade to reassert dignity and spiritual purity that was frequently expressed in almost apocalyptic biblical terms, often revolving around the word salvation.[63] This emphasis on moral values within the GSD may partly be explained by the fact that many of the group were grounded in the humanities, but it also finds an echo in the teachings of Constantin Noica, the last philosopher to remain in Romania from the influential interwar generation, which had included Emil Cioran and Mircea Eliade. In 1974 Noica had retreated into an ascetic existence in a small cabin at Păltiniș, high in the Carpathian Mountains near Sibiu, but he remained a preeminent figure in Romanian cultural life, largely through the activities of a small group of disciples, the most prominent of whom were Gabriel Liiceanu and Andrei Pleșu. In particular, in the 1980s, Liiceanu had propagated Noica's ideas to a wider public through two books, *Jurnalul de la Păltiniș* and *Epistolar.*[64] The impact of these on Bucharest cultural circles had been, by all accounts, considerable, with Vladimir Tismaneanu suggesting that Noican thinking "more or less visibly irrigated" all major recent cultural controversies in Romania.[65] For Noica the remedy for man's ills was not politics but the ending of his internal spiritual alienation: "If there is misery, then this is to be found in yourselves, in your inner limitations."[66] This stress on the inner world and the spiritual seems to have fueled an initial tendency among many intellectuals to eschew direct involvement

---

62. Ibid., March 9, 1990.
63. Verdery (1991), 278.
64. For an English translation of *Jurnalul de la Păltiniș,* see Liiceanu (2000).
65. Tismaneanu (1994), 411.
66. Liiceanu, *Jurnalul de la Păltiniș* quoted in Marga (1993), 22.

in politics. In what may be described, perhaps a little harshly, as the politics of naïveté, after years of being silenced, it was believed by some that the mere production of the journal 22 would suffice to lead to the general acceptance of their elevated values and prescriptions for recovery.

At first sight, from this discussion it might seem there was a certain commonality of language and ideals between the GSD and the NSF. However, from the outset the Group adopted a stance firmly outside the Front. Indeed, by claiming alongside the Front to be the authentic voice and representative of those who had fought on the streets, it rapidly became a competitor for the symbols of the revolution, which, in contrast to some within the NSF, the Group saw as being driven by liberal values. Its distinctive position was also reinforced by its emphatic rejection of cooperation with anybody connected with the previous regime, its frequent and serious consideration of human rights questions, and a genuine belief in the necessity of fostering a liberal civil society in Romania. In the pressurized atmosphere of the revolution, perhaps inevitably, disagreements arose within the Group. At their heart these divides were not primarily over goals, nor over the idea that the pursuit of freedom required affirmative action, but rather over whether the group should abandon its medial role and directly enter the political arena. As January progressed, and new cleavages appeared within the Romanian body politic, many of the members of the GSD moved toward a more proactive stance, arguing that the building of a civil society in Romania necessitated an entry into the political fray. The moralizing discourse used against Ceaușescu was increasingly transferred to his successors, as in the pages of 22, members of the group asked how, with so many former RCP members within its ranks, the Front could be trusted not to adopt the "mask of communism."[67] During the elections of May 1990 several of the more prominent members of the group, including Gabriel Liiceanu, Stelian Tănase, Petru Creția, and Alexandru Paleologu, were to stand as independent candidates for parliament. The bulk of the GSD had begun the process of transforming itself into an intellectual opposition, a path that was eventually to lead to the formation of the Civic Alliance in November 1990.

Competence

Alongside dialogue, another important concept within the matrix of ideas taken up by the Front was competence. Immediately after the overthrow of Ceaușescu, the new leaders began to offer an analysis of Romania's ills that concentrated almost solely on the human failings of the previous regime. In the words of Roman, the deficiencies of the system were entirely due to the fact that Ceaușescu's appointees "were never selected

67. 22, January 27, 1990, 1.

on the basis of competence but only on the basis of blind submission."[68] The bitter attacks launched on Ceauşescu and his clique were therefore more than political mudslinging; they underlined a conceptual view of the Romanian situation that saw its misfortune rooted in the mismanagement of a gerontocracy. Only through the better utilization of human resources and knowledge could a brighter future be assured, but such a strategy also had significant political consequences. By focusing on technical skills the new leadership were not only side-stepping the issue of past political affiliations, but they were also, as with dialogue, redefining boundary markers so as to exclude opponents and raise their own social status. Indeed, in this regard, adherence to competence extended far beyond reform communist circles to encompass the writings of many displaced cultural intellectuals during this period, with, for example, Noica propounding an intellectual strategy and language of discourse that stressed the accumulation of knowledge and its use by specialists, that is, competent people.[69]

Beyond professional expertise, competence also had an important moral dimension, although this was not shaped, as many revolutionaries may have preferred, in terms of the sins of the past. Competence alone was not sufficient to guarantee the selection of the right candidate for a job; moral rectitude was also required, with the two virtues constantly referred together as a pair. The stress on moral cleanliness was, in part, another attempt to erect a barrier between the new regime and the venality and corruption of the late Ceauşescu era, but it also carried a deeper ideological resonance that tapped into the egalitarianism of communism. When Iliescu called for "more modesty in everyone's private life, the limitation of everybody's incomes to decent dimensions, without neglecting the incentives for the promotion of true values," he was effectively seeking to lay the foundations of a value system in which national salvation would be achieved through hard work and moderate and abstemious behavior.[70] Imbued with these "true" values, society, freed from all political impositions and offering real rewards for its labor, would work with fresh vigor toward the goal of national renewal. This vision appears remarkably similar to the ideas current in perestroika at the time, usually labeled the "human factor" and identified with the Russian sociologist Tatiana Zaslavskaia. Indeed, Brucan includes Zaslavskaia's work in the bibliography of *Pluralism and Social Conflict* and mentions the "human factor" within the text, although he seems to suggest that these ideas derived from the work of Radovan Richta.[71] The advocates of the "human factor" held that the solution to the widespread problem of poor workforce discipline and

68. BBC EE/0649, B/9, December 29, 1989.
69. Verdery (1991), 272.
70. BBC EE/0649, B/6–7, December 29, 1989.
71. There are references throughout Brucan (1990), 112–13.

economic stagnation was not a return to coercion, with its obvious long-term motivational difficulties, nor recourse to the sanction of unemployment. Instead, what was required was a cultural transformation that would bring about an increased professionalism in working practices and a widespread enthusiasm for labor.[72] Within Romania the popular mobilization effected by the revolution appeared to offer an exceptional opportunity for achieving such a goal, and an opinion poll carried out at the end of December 1989 by the Center for Research into Youth Problems clearly mirrors this agenda. When it asked its respondents whether in the future they believe people will work harder, 97 percent replied yes and only 1 percent no.[73]

Increased motivation for work would come through the provision of decent civilized conditions for the labor force. Repeatedly the leaders of the new regime stressed its "profoundly popular and humanistic character" and, when Iliescu promised that bread and edible oil would be available for all without queuing, he was not only removing a potential cause of social unrest but also seeking to end popular alienation from the system.[74] Moves to lower the prices of electricity and gas and remove restrictions on their domestic usage as well as a string of decrees abolishing the worst excesses of the Ceaușescu regime can all also be seen in the same light. So can the new government's quick promise to cut the working week to five days, although this raised fears in some quarters that, since wages were linked to productivity, it would lead to a fall in pay. The minister responsible, Mihnea Marmeliuc, quashed such concerns by arguing that a reduction in the work week from forty-six to forty hours would have no effect on levels of production.[75] This is an argument that can only be grounded in an assumption that a reinvigorated labor force would be prepared to work harder. The regime was effectively offering the country a new social contract in which, in return for a renewal of labor enthusiasm, it was prepared to guarantee the availability of basic commodities and full employment. Roman declared that "we have pledged ourselves to ensure that each citizen of this country should have a secure job and conditions for a decent, civilised life" and a decree law was enacted promising that all those who asked for work before February 15, 1990, would be found employment by the new Directorate for Work and Social Protection.[76] This was potentially a highly controversial law, because, in a move that appeared to completely override the market-oriented criteria of efficiency

72. This analysis of the "human factor" leans heavily on Hanson (1991), 33–59.

73. *Adevărul*, December 30, 1989, 4. The Center for Research into Youth Problems polled 232 members of "patriotic organizations" on guard duty around Bucharest; the remaining 2 percent were "don't knows."

74. BBC EE/0652, B/9:14, January 3, 1990; BBC EE/0651, B/4(b), January 1, 1990.

75. *Adevărul*, January 10, 1990, 1.

76. BBC EE/0664, B/13:14, January 17, 1990.

and profitability enshrined in point four of the NSF program and in other laws of the period, the new jobs were to be allocated in direct proportion to those already employed, with each unit being held responsible for creating the necessary places.[77] Although the future was to cruelly strip bare the false illusions of the new leaders' hopes, at first it did seem that the proposed "contract" might be generally accepted by the population. In the middle of January, Roman confidently asserted, "Now . . . the people work far better because they work in normal conditions: normal technological discipline, normal management, correct technical-material supply, free of any arbitrariness and voluntarism."[78] Front leaders also spoke optimistically of generating among the workforce a feeling that "they are acquiring a specialization and become useful to society" and even of introducing some form of popular participation into the decision-making process.[79]

The idea that the Western model of democracy could be improved through the adoption of new participatory forms, which would bring "the voice of the ordinary citizen into the political process," has been a recurring theme in both academic and popular literature in the West.[80] In the late 1980s, these ideas were enthusiastically taken up by reformers in Romania, with Iliescu and Brucan arguing that, as the post-industrial world emerged, by embracing radical reforms the socialist societies had a unique chance to leapfrog the representative model of democracy associated with industrial capitalism and move straight to a more advanced participatory form.[81] Despite their ambitious words, none of the Romanian reformers ever seem to have clearly spelled out what they implied by participatory democracy nor how it might be applied in such a technologically backward country. It is possible that their schemes might have entailed little more than the ideas embedded in dialogue, but during the revolution Iliescu hinted at a more radical construct through the concept of eligibility. This appears to have implied a real transfer of power to the grass roots of society, with Iliescu promising, "The constitution will consecrate the principles of compulsory eligibility of all managerial bodies and factors from central to local level" before adding that the question of eligibility was even discussed in relation to the militia, "which should be held responsible to the masses and not the reverse."[82] This appears to suggest that some form of popular democracy would be instituted at the local and workplace level, the obvious forum for which was the grassroots NSF enterprise councils, not least because the introduction of popular democ-

77. *Monitorul Oficial al României,* January 20, 1990, 1.
78. BBC EE/0666, B/11:52, January 19, 1990.
79. BBC EE/0664, B/13:14, January 17, 1990.
80. See, for instance, *Independent,* November 10, 1994, 18.
81. *România Literară,* September 3, 1987, 19; Brucan (1990), 138.
82. BBC EE/0649, B/6, December 29, 1989.

racy might also be expected to offer the best chance of the hoped-for re-motivation of the labor force, and, indeed, according to Mihai Montanu, the chief task of the NSF councils was to "mobilise all Romanians to real work, to intelligent activity."[83]

Enterprise Councils of the National Salvation Front

During the Ceaușescu era, and especially under the NEFM, considerable emphasis had been placed on enterprise "self-management," with workers' councils being established within factories. Superficially, in creating these councils Romania appeared to be adopting a model similar to that found in Yugoslavia, Hungary, or Czechoslovakia in 1968. In reality, however, any similarities were purely semantic, as the councils were just another facet of "simulated change" with few real powers.[84] Headed by the Party first-secretary of the enterprise and with worker representation kept to a minimum, they were little more than a conduit for regime propaganda and an additional tool for mobilizing the workforce.[85] Now, following the downfall of Ceaușescu, these relics of the old regime aligned themselves with the incoming order by transforming themselves into NSF enterprise councils.[86] Often the changes stopped with the new name, but in other cases there do seem to have been serious attempts to fill the councils with fresh life and give the old forms real content. The composition of the new NSF councils depended to a large extent on the prevailing circumstances within each factory. Much rested on the status and strength of personality of the individual, but, as a general rule, it seems that the larger enterprises in the bigger cities saw more radical changes.[87]

For years the workers had received poor rewards under an often corrupt and bullying factory regime, which had frequently achieved power through political loyalty rather than managerial ability, and now, during the revolution, their resentment boiled over. Across Romania the workers sought the power long promised by communist propaganda, but never achieved in reality. They began to seize control of *their* factories and as they did so, in some cases they moved to remove their previous bugbears and install their own management. Sometimes this merely led to the reinstatement of somebody from the ranks of the previous bosses, but occasionally it led to complete outsiders being chosen, as was the case with Dan Antal in Bacău. Long considered a complete wastrel by the commu-

83. BBC EE/0651, B/8:19, January 1, 1990.
84. Shafir (1985), 58.
85. Nelson (1981), 174–97; Linden (1989), 303.
86. *România Liberă,* January 16, 1990, 2.
87. For a general analysis of the NSF factory councils see ibid., January 18, 1990, 1, 2.

nist regime, Antal suddenly found himself catapulted into office as president of a large city center service cooperative. Initially, the authorities declared his election void, but after protests from the workers and a strike they had to back down and accept his elevation.[88] In appointing someone such as Antal, the workers may have been genuinely seeking a competent replacement untainted by the past, but the search for such figures was seldom easy and, with few candidates to choose from, the new leadership was usually drawn from any members of the second tier of management who had been held in popular esteem within the factory.

The revolutionary mood at this time is caught in a dispatch by the journalist, Harvey Morris, from the Tractorul factory in Braşov, where the former director was forced to resign. At the plant Morris found "a tangible atmosphere of workers' rule. Conscripts with ancient bolt-action rifles guard the gates, and work has been disrupted by a series of crisis meetings. Sergiu Nicolaescu . . . has twice flown up from Bucharest to try to resolve the workers' challenge to the prevailing government line that, in the name of economic reality, the old Party apparatchiks should remain at their desks."[89] Such a situation was not unique and elsewhere there were also reports of enterprise councils voting out of office their existing management or at least the boss.[90] In the absence of detailed statistics it is difficult to gauge the scale of the changes at this time, but on the basis of some figures from Harghita and Covasna, where it is possible that some of the dismissals might have been made on ethnic grounds, it seems that in some areas of the country the changes may have been quite considerable. In Harghita, twenty out of the forty biggest republican and local enterprises experienced a change of director at this time, as did twenty-three out of eighty state institutions and enterprises in neighboring Covasna.[91] Elsewhere, however, the changes were less drastic and in many cases the members of the old council merely met behind closed doors and recast themselves in a NSF guise. This is what the journalist Jonathan Randal discovered at a margarine factory in Bragadiru near Bucharest, although here, by the middle of January, there were rumblings of discontent and calls for new elections to the NSF enterprise council, which was composed entirely of members of the old workers' council minus only the chief RCP secretary.[92] Occasionally, this battle between management and workers was aired in the pages of the press, as was the case with a factory at Lehliu-Gară, just outside Bucharest. According to the complaints of a delegation

---

88. Antal (1994), 175–76. Without any formal management training, Antal was to remain at his new post until September 1990, when his anti-regime views made his position untenable. My thanks to Dan Antal for clarifying some points.
89. *Independent,* January 13, 1990, 13.
90. See for instance *România Liberă,* January 16, 1990, 2; and ibid., January 18, 1990, 2.
91. Parlamentul României (1991), 25–31.
92. *Washington Post,* January 13, 1990, A17.

of twenty workers, who arrived at the offices of *Adevărul,* in this factory of 1,300 employees the old leadership had ignored calls for a vote and instead elected themselves to the new NSF council. The head of the works had become the president of the council and had promptly ejected the newly elected leader of the free-trade union.[93]

The revolution brought chaos to many of the factories of Romania and sometimes the upheavals seem merely to have served as a mask for private vendettas and the settling of scores, amid a general atmosphere of disruption verging on anarchy. The ethos of worker ownership, as propagated by the communists, had placed intangible boundaries around the concept of property, and now the chaos and uncertainty of the revolution seems to have provided the cover for a considerable amount of theft. The actual extent of this is totally unknown, but management and workers seem to have been as guilty as each other, and, while undoubtedly hampering state production, the flow of goods out of the public sector at this time did much to energize the private black economy. A general effect of the collapse of discipline in the workplace, however, was a dramatic fall in output, and so an early imperative for the regime was the restoration of order in the factories. In particular, there were repeatedly pleas from members of the leadership for the reestablishment of dismissal from above instead of from below, with Iliescu, at the beginning of January, stressing that the dismissal of management that did not reach the desired level of "quality, competence, and moral authority" could only come through the councils of the NSF appealing to higher authorities.[94]

Although in many factories the incoming regime was presented with the de facto creation of the councils, this does not mean such structures did not generally fit within the new leaders' plans as regards labor mobilization and worker participation. Before the revolution Brucan had written of the "*direct* participation of the working class in both economic management and political government," and, in the first flush of the revolution, Iliescu voiced his support for the councils, seeing them as a way in which the "representatives of the masses really contribute to finding solutions to problems."[95] However, he added the telling proviso that this must only be as "a collective body in which the administrative management, manager, deputy manager, chief engineer, and chief accountant should be represented, as well as the representatives of the Front committee, and that they should co-operate for the success of the overall activity."[96] Confronted with the desire of many workers to become actively engaged in the running of their enterprises, the NSF struggled to define

93. *Adevărul,* January 27, 1990, 1.
94. BBC EE/0657, B/6:8, January 9, 1990.
95. Brucan (1987), xvi (emphasis in original); BBC EE/0651, B/4:9(b), January 1, 1990.
96. BBC EE/0651, B/4:9(b), January 1, 1990.

the exact role of the councils and the nature of their relationship with management.[97]

As the chaos in the workplace continued, Iliescu began to openly express doubts about the value of the enterprise councils. Noting that the NSF in general had "criticized the tendency of taking over the role of the former party organizations in enterprises," he stressed that the new councils could never become political organizations.[98] The role of the councils was further clarified in a series of regulations published in the press, with a commentary on the radio stressing that they " 'do not have political ambitions of management and control over the technical-administrative apparatus.' Their role, the new regulations show, is to represent the interests of the collectivities that elected them, giving assistance in the technical-administrative management, in the settlement of all issues. . . . These councils debate and advance proposals to the administrative executives regarding the working conditions, organization and conduct of the activity, the elimination of the administrative-bureaucratic methods, social assistance, etc."[99] In other words, their duties were to be broadly similar to trade unions that, according to the statement, would "be set up in enterprises" and "take over the attributions of the Councils of the National Salvation Front."[100]

Thus, while the existence of NSF factory councils probably fitted well within the overall goals of the new regime, they were becoming in many cases unruly subordinates. The Front tried to distinguish between the organizational role of the councils and the more representative duties of the trade unions, but by the middle of January, the situation was still so chaotic that the Front started to view the latter as a more amenable alternative, although this expectation largely seems to have been prompted by a belief that the many new unions created during the revolution would willingly place themselves under the umbrella of the National Provisional Committee for Organizing Free Trade Unions. This body, which was soon to rename itself the Confederation of Free Trade Unions in Romania, had emerged within days of the downfall of Ceaușescu and sought, like the old communist General Trade Union Federation of Romania, to be the voice of the country's workers. It also claimed control of the considerable assets of the GTUFR and even occupied the same offices in a wing of the Ministry of Labor. Some of the CFTUR leaders had also occupied

97. BBC EE/0655, B/8:35(ii), January 6, 1990. The intricate web of connections that frequently bound factory NSF councils with local administrative councils only served to complicate matters further. In Timișoara and Brașov, among other cities, representatives of the NSF enterprise councils had been directly involved in electing the local county councils and in many other towns and cities factory managers also sat on the other councils as well; see *România Liberă*, January 19, 1990, 2.

98. BBC EE/0664, B/13:14, January 17, 1990.

99. *Adevărul*, January 12, 1990, 3; BBC EE/0663, B/10:41, January 16, 1990.

100. BBC EE/0663, B/10:41, January 16, 1990.

prominent positions in the former trade union and, when the new union started making effusive pledges of support to the NSF regime, to many Romanians it looked as though it also thought it had a similar political role. The new union claimed a membership of 2.5 million, but this was only about 33 percent of the membership of the former GTUFR, and in reality any hopes the new rulers may have harbored of inheriting a compliant trade union movement had been dashed with the appearance of hundreds of independent unions during the revolution. By mid-February, it was reported that 2,084 of these had been established with a claimed membership of more than 1.5 million.[101] These new unions in many cases were the spontaneous creation of the workers and, as such, they were another sign of their desire to take greater control over their own lives. Indeed, in some factories it seems to have been the new independent union that took the initiative in ousting the existing management.[102] However, in other cases, as with many of the NSF enterprise councils, the new unions seem to have been nothing more than an arm of a management that was dominated by former communist appointees, and certainly this was the situation Randal found at the margarine factory in Bragadiru.

Most of the new unions were relatively small, being based on individual plants, but by the end of January they were already beginning to come together in larger groupings, with the chief early formation being the Fraţia confederation established in January 1990.[103] Most of the trade unions that joined Fraţia were based on individual factories, such as Policolor and IMGB in Bucharest, but others had wider constituencies, including an oil workers' union from Ploieşti and a drivers' union from Bucharest led by Miron Mitrea. Fraţia quickly came into conflict with the CFTUR, particularly as it also staked a claim to the funds of the old GTUFR. The dispute was couched in terms of the main postcommunist political divide, with an article in a Fraţia publication, *Argument,* claiming that the CFTUR was nothing but a "confederation of official, communist trade unions linked to the National [Salvation] Front, which is the former communist party."[104] This conflict at the top was sometimes reflected in individual factories, as the various unions and NSF councils sought predominance. Indeed, at the Policolor works in Bucharest, Fraţia claims to have been responsible for expelling the NSF council from the factory.[105]

With the new unions also proving hopelessly unruly, in the middle of January, as the Front reoriented itself as a political party drawing on

101. Sturdza (July 27, 1990), 36, 41 n. 4.
102. *Washington Post,* February 4, 1990, A32.
103. Early signs of union activity can be found in *România Liberă,* January 6, 1990, 5; *Washington Post,* January 13, 1990, A17; *România Liberă,* January 19, 1990, 3; *East European Newsletter,* 4:54, March 1990, 4; see also Bush (1993), 382–87.
104. Sturdza (July 27, 1990), 37.
105. Bush (1993), 384.

working-class support, its leaders again turned their attention to the NSF councils. Iliescu and Roman held a series of meetings with workers' groups, including, on January 19, representatives of the Jiu Valley miners, and, when Iliescu spoke again about the NSF councils, he placed renewed emphasis on their central place in Front thinking.[106] Now, instead of calling for their amalgamation with the trade unions, he suggested that they could be the dominant partners in an alliance that would lay the foundations for a "participational democracy and of a framework of co-participating of workers and labourers in the management of enterprises."[107] However, the respite was only to be temporary and, by the end of January, the tide had again begun to turn against the NSF councils, as they increasingly became identified with some of the more unsavory aspects of the new regime. At times of adversity, and most recently in response to the demonstrations in Timișoara, Ceaușescu had mobilized workers in support of his cause, and the potential effectiveness of such cohorts had not been lost on the leaders of the Front. Faced with unrest in Bucharest, they were not slow to follow this "traditional" pattern and call the workers onto the streets, apparently through the agency of the NSF enterprise councils. In many places the NSF councils had always been viewed with suspicion as relics of the communist past, and now that it became apparent that they might become an important arm of NSF power, the NPP, NLP, and other parties of the opposition began to call for their dissolution.

Thus, at the beginning of February, with the foundation of the PCNU, although they never appear to have been formally disbanded, the councils were allowed to fade from the political scene. They were even disavowed by Iliescu, who pointed out that they had never been officially constituted by the NSF through a normative act. In some cases, as at the massive August 23 Factory in Bucharest, they were reconstituted as a trade union, while elsewhere they just disappeared.[108] The continued existence of the NSF councils was incompatible with Western norms and their eclipse was probably sped by pressure from both the opposition and the outside world. By the time of their demise, they were also proving to be of doubtful utility to the NSF, since, once they became institutionalized and were effectively shorn of their popular legitimacy, they appear to have proved a less than effective mobilizing force. The heavy reliance of the NSF on the miners during subsequent demonstrations would seem to indicate that they were less than sure that the rest of the workforce would rally to their cause, and indeed there are reports of workers from the August 23 works in Bucharest and the May 1 oil refinery at Ploiești refusing to heed calls

106. *România Liberă,* January 17, 1990, 5; ibid., January 20, 1990, 3; *Adevărul,* January 20, 1990, 5; ibid., January 24, 1990, 3.
107. BBC EE/0671, B/12:54(ii), January 25, 1990.
108. *New York Times,* February 5, 1990, A9.

from their local NSF branches to join the February 19 pro-Front rally in Bucharest.[109]

The new trade unions and NSF enterprise councils in some cases were a grassroots manifestation of the revolution. For a few weeks in some factories they mounted a direct challenge to the ruling bureaucratic techno-administrative elite and the established hierarchy, and through them, to a limited extent, power did start to flow from the bottom upward. However, they never had any real impact on the upper levels of the pyramid of power, and slowly, as management and the bureaucracy gained control, at least one avenue of development for the revolution was closed, which some have suggested could have been a radical worker-based movement.[110]

The Failure of Consensus

References to consensus suddenly disappear from Iliescu's speeches on January 7, 1990, and do not reappear after that date. After the optimistic and visionary word of his New Year's address of only a week before, in which he had laid out the bare bones of a "novel" political pluralism, the sobriety of the January 7 speech provides a stark contrast. Invoking realism Iliescu called for national unity, hard work, and perseverance in the face of the multitude of problems that confronted the country. In searching for reasons for this abrupt change of tone, it is interesting to speculate what effect the visit of the Soviet foreign minister, Eduard Shevardnadze, which ended on the same day of January 7, may have had on Iliescu's apparent change of direction. Unfortunately no detailed report of their talks has ever emerged, but it is inconceivable that the future political direction of Romania was not on the agenda. Following the lead of Iliescu, the term "consensus" seems to have disappeared from the speeches of the other leaders of the Front after this date as well, although traces of the ideology continued to appear. Many of the forms of Consensus, if not the word itself, featured prominently in a television appearance of Iliescu, Mazilu, and Roman on January 13 and also in a speech Iliescu made to students on January 20, 1990.[111] Even as late as January 25, the term itself appeared in a front page editorial in *Adevărul*, but in this it was conspicuously linked to the new keyword of "unity." Previously on January 23, 1990, consensus, as a political project, had been effectively laid to rest, when a meeting of the CNSF had decided that the NSF would participate in the coming elections as a full-fledged political party.[112]

---

109. *East European Newsletter,* 4:54, March 1990, 4.
110. *Expres,* February 13, 1990, 3.
111. BBC EE/0664, B/13–17:14, January 17, 1990; Haşeganu (1998), 93.
112. *Adevărul,* January 25, 1990, 1.

The reasons for the failure of Consensus are varied, with one of the most important being the political pressures brought to bear on the NSF, which are discussed at greater length in the next chapter. Deep-rooted structural contradictions, though, also played a part, including the unexpected intensity and persistence of the crisis in the economy. When they initially entered office, the new leaders had generally spoken optimistically about the economy, with Iliescu confidently stating that "provided work is well organized and efficient . . . units . . . have real chances to obtain as early as the current year results clearly superior to those obtained during Ceauşescu's time."[113] Just as Consensus was a "novel" form of political pluralism, so under the NSF the economy was to be organized on the entirely new basis of a "socialist market economy," a structure for which the leading NSF economist, Bârlădeanu, freely admitted they had no model to follow—the Yugoslav experience being ruled out as too confusing.[114] In line with the ideas inherent in competence, instead of major structural adjustments, the key to unlocking the productive forces of the Romanian economy was to be the removal of political controls, especially the burden of an excessive centralization, which, according to Roman, was the most extreme in Eastern Europe. This had stifled managerial enterprise and made nearly all economic decision making subject to political criteria. The new regime through decentralization would lessen bureaucratic and political control in favor of managerial autonomy, thereby liberating the rich human resources ignored by Ceauşescu.

However, instead of the revolution and the economic concessions made by the NSF galvanizing the workforce to greater productivity, as the ideologues of the "human factor" had preached, industrial production began to plunge sharply from December 1989 onward. Outmoded machinery and production techniques can only be partly blamed for this, as can the withdrawal of military labor previously deployed in the industrial sector, although this undoubtedly had a serious effect in the coal mines. A more intractable problem was the fact that the ingrained workplace culture of minimal work for low rewards easily overrode what little carrot was offered by the small improvements in living conditions granted by the new regime. At the same time, the ideological rejection of the sanction of unemployment effectively removed any stick that could be wielded. Many factories were plagued by incessant labor troubles and strikes and so, rather than the workers rediscovering their enthusiasm for work, January 1990 was to see constant but largely ineffective exhortations by the new leaders for a greater commitment to work.

The much-vaunted decentralization also ran into similar problems. Almost immediately from when it entered power, the NSF moved, at least

113. BBC EE/0657, B/5:8, January 9, 1990.
114. Alexandru Bârlădeanu interviewed in *Adevărul*, January 7, 1990, 1, 2.

superficially, to restructure the central bureaucracy. In a flurry of decrees names were changed and ministries reorganized, some being dissolved, others divided or merged, and yet more created. The extent of these changes would seem to indicate that, at least in part, they had been planned in advance, but, while new faces appeared at the top, it must be doubted if they brought any great transformations in personnel lower down the chain or any real innovations in bureaucratic practices. The Front's concept of decentralization seems to have rested more on imposing different criteria for decision making, rather than on any large-scale redistribution of resources. The only law to be enacted tackling the question during January 1990, the "Decree-Law on Investment," while paying lip service to the principle that all future investment was to be subject to the criteria of "profitability and efficiency," showed little divergence from communist economic orthodoxy. Investment would still occur according to plan, with decision making being delegated to differing levels depending on the sum involved. In most industries only investments up to 20 million lei could be sanctioned at the enterprise level, investments between 20 and 60 million lei could be decided by local industrial centers, but nearly everything over this figure had to be directed by the central authorities in Bucharest.[115]

Well into the new year, the language of the NSF leaders, when they spoke of bureaucratic reform, indicated that their vision was one of adjustment rather than radical change. In part, this may be because, when they spoke of bureaucracy, they seem to have been implying not the enormous central and provincial administration nor technical-managerial groups but rather the relatively narrow band that constituted the ranks of the late Ceauşescu *nomenklatura*. Many members of this latter group do seem to have been ousted from political office during the revolution, often to find a ready consolation in newly acquired economic power, but whether any greater onslaught on the bureaucratic structure of the state was ever intended must remain an open question. As the pressure for market-led reforms increased, the natural constituency of the NSF, the technocratic-managerial bureaucracy, who were often saddled with running totally nonviable enterprises, were more and more drawn toward the position of the administrative bureaucracy, who appear to have rejected all attempts to redistribute their considerable powers.[116] In response, the leadership of the NSF, faced with the emergence of an effective opposition and increasingly needing to cement its own political position, began to align itself with the interests of the bureaucracy in all its guises. Whether such a strategy was embarked upon willingly or not is unclear,

115. *Monitorul Oficial al României,* January 15, 1990, 4–5.
116. In distinguishing between the technical-managerial bureaucracy and the administrative bureaucracy I am following the division of the bureaucracy into producers and nonproducers as suggested by Pavel Câmpeanu (1988), 145.

but soon the NSF was passing legislation that appeared to be deliberately aimed at gaining the administrative bureaucracy's support, such as a decree committing the state to find jobs for officials threatened with unemployment by the reforms.[117] The limits to the decentralization of power had clearly been revealed. It could neither be allowed to unleash uncontrollable political forces, as in the trade unions and NSF enterprise councils, nor could it alienate bureaucratic support.

The NSF's initial stress on the need to assess the real condition of an economy, so distorted by false statistics that it was "based on a gross lie," may be understandable but, as talk continued of reviewing the next year's plan so as to set it on a more realistic basis in tune with the country's requirements, the limits of many of the ruling group's vision of reform became clear.[118] This reluctance to embrace more deeply rooted changes led to the creation of a political paradox that was to undermine both the standing of the new regime and the ideology and political project of consensus. From almost the moment they entered power the new leaders had called for stabilization and continuity; Iliescu had stressed that the Front did "not want to demolish the present central organs, as we must rely on the existing structures."[119] However, the events of December 1989 had been acclaimed by many, including the new leaders, as a revolution and, since such a word carried connotations of radical change, it bred an expectation among a significant segment of society that there would be a fundamental transformation. The resulting discrepancy between the regime's ideology and these expectations drew the leaders of the Front into acrobatic feats of verbal gymnastics, as calls for stability and change were frequently paired in the same sentence. As early as December 26, Iliescu had spoken of "ensuring the continuity of a normal life by reorganising it on new bases," and afterward he continued to stress the newness of the NSF and its institutions and speak of radical renewal while simultaneously advocating a return to normalcy.[120] But what was normality in a Romanian context? Clearly it could not refer to the late Ceaușescu era. But did it refer to the early Ceaușescu period? Or was it a normality as understood in West European terms?

The stressing of an absence of any firm ideological commitments, either to the "right" or to the "left," would seem natural for a regime attempting to build an organic solidarity, since few are likely to be alienated by the adoption of a truly central position in the political spectrum. However, the stress in the NSF was not on political centrality but on political neutrality, which has a totally different basis. Through Consensus the

117. *Monitorul Oficial al României,* January 3, 1990, 4.
118. BBC EE/0651, B/4(b), January 1, 1990; BBC EE/0651, B/6–7:14, January 1, 1990; BBC EE/0651, B/3(ii), January 1, 1990.
119. BBC EE/0649, B/6, December 29, 1989; BBC EE/0651, 4(b), January 1, 1990.
120. BBC EE/0649, B/6, December 29, 1989.

NSF regime seems to have been warily treading toward a new ideological base that might be termed "the end of politics." Indeed, if politics is understood as a competitive bargaining process, then consensus, as the antithesis of competition, has its root in the diminution of politics. In the vision of the Front, the postindustrial information technology age would usher in a new political era in which such outmoded structures as parties and labels such as "left" and "right" would be banished. This idea that politics could be minimized was strengthened by both the technocratic base of Consensus—science and technology are by their very nature relatively value-neutral—and through specific conditions appertaining in Romania, where the common aim of the technocrats and the artistic intellectuals was the removal of political criteria from their specialist spheres and the reassertion of competence and expertise. Embedded in the idea was the assumption that politics was to be a mere support act, with its primary role being the creation of the social and administrative framework necessary to promote technical expertise and professionalism. The cynical might presuppose that the ideology of the NSF was merely a strategy for maintaining the Front's hold on power and, indeed, there is much truth in this; however, it also does seem to have contained some elements of thought that were a genuine attempt to move beyond the confines of an economically derived socialism toward a new agenda of the "left." In this, it might be said that the NSF was only embarking on a similar quest to other European socialist and social democratic parties at this time.

However, the minimization of politics was only one strand of Consensus, because like its progenitor, Marxism-Leninism, the ideology was also characterized by what Ken Jowitt has termed "charismatic impersonalism."[121] By this he meant that the ideology imbibed both rational-legal norms and a charismatic revolutionary emphasis on transcending the existing order. In the immediate post-revolution ideology of the NSF, technocratic competence was united with a utopian vision of a reinvigorated society working together toward the goal of national renewal. However, by the first weeks of January, this dream already lay in ruins, when it became clear that the workers were not going to respond to the prospective social contract on offer. Instead of finding common cause, a deeply atomized Romanian society had merely divided into a host of competing groups. Then, as the situation in the factories began to fall out of control, threatening to undermine the very basis of the existing order, the Front had responded by reining in the NSF enterprise councils and trade unions, thereby effectively killing not only hopes of a radical mobilization of the workforce but also all chances of a charismatic driven Consensus.

The abandonment of Consensus and, thus, radical reform socialism left the NSF leaders adrift in a sea of ideological confusion. At the end of Jan-

121. Jowitt (1978), 34–44.

uary, Iliescu publicly admitted that as of that moment he had no vision of the future.[122] The various members of the NSF leadership were to respond to this situation in differing ways, but, in their search to develop credible political strategies, most adopted an eclectic mixture of the concepts already discussed, combined with elements from Western political ideologies and varying degrees of belief in free market economics. Later, it was the nuances between these various formulations that formed the basis of the divisions which were to split the NSF asunder. The failure of the leaders of the NSF in January 1990 to clearly enunciate their ideology had been both a weakness and a strength. Hidden behind impenetrable and largely meaningless slogans, Consensus was unable to act as an effective mobilization tool, but at the same time this very imprecision gave the Front the leeway necessary to shape new strategies, once the original ideology had been abandoned.

Of the concepts discussed in this chapter, it is competence that retained the most lasting significance. In a limited marketplace of ideas, it remained one of the chief bases for political legitimation, broadly understood as "we are capable of doing things better." Ostensibly competence merely indicated the placing of trust in professional expertise. However, the retrogression of the Romanian economy and the influence of a political culture marked by relatively low levels of political socialization meant that inherent within its bounds there was also an assumption of social backwardness and the need for intellectuals to lead society toward modernity. Competence, thus, reinforced the traditional role sought by Romanian intellectuals. However, in the face of the political realities of the revolution, most accepted that the embracing of democracy effectively ruled out such rarefied elitism. Instead, they were forced to enter a highly competitive political arena in which the NSF was challenged by several new opposition groupings, and it is within these events that the real causes for the downfall of consensus as a political project can be traced.

122. BBC EE/0676, B/8, January 31, 1990.

CHAPTER SIX

A Marked Lack of Consensus

With the dawn of the new year, as the swirl of battle dimmed and the worst of the fighting ebbed from the streets of Bucharest and the other cities, the people of Romania emerged to contemplate a new but uncertain future. The scent of victory was sweet and a feeling of excitement and expectation hung in the air, but with the return of a semblance of normality even this began to pall, as the drudgery of everyday existence reasserted itself with a painful jolt. During the revolution hidden stockpiles of food had been broken open, bringing scarcely remembered quantities of provisions to the shops. Unexpected luxuries, such as oranges, had also appeared. But now, with the exhaustion of these stocks, the exotic fare disappeared from the shelves and the daily grind of standing in line began anew.[1] Disappointment and doubts started to surface, as many of the dreams of the revolution began to crumble, and older, more sinister habits reappeared. Foreign journalists noted that Romanians were once again "resorting to whispering lest their views are noted by the Securitate men they are convinced are working for the ruling National Salvation Front in another guise," and, despite the appearance of a markedly more open media, people were still reported to be subsisting "from hour to hour on a diet of rumours," many of which were fixed on the tantalizing questions that remained unanswered after the revolution.[2] How many

1. *Adevărul,* January 12, 1990. On January 6 rationing seems to have been reintroduced in some areas, see Jackson (February 2, 1990), 30.
2. *The Times,* January 15, 1990, 8; *New York Times,* January 4, 1990, A14.

had really died? Who had been responsible for the shooting? When would they be brought to trial?

However, even if the material condition of everyday life quickly returned to something close to former levels and old fears and suspicions remained far from banished, there were also considerable changes. Most obviously, the people of Romania began to take the first tentative steps toward reclaiming the public sphere previously appropriated entirely by the Party-state. The monolithic world vision rigidly imposed from above during the Ceauşescu years had been shattered. In its place diversity returned. In the capital people thronged streets lined with makeshift shrines honoring the dead of the revolution. Most strikingly after the fearful public silence of the Ceauşescu era everywhere there was discussion and debate. In Gail Kligman's evocative words: "Talk—energetic, angry, fearful, hopeful—talk about the past, present, and future constantly filled the air in the city, as well as in remote villages."[3] In Bucharest, Timişoara, Braşov, Cluj, and the other major centers, where the revolution had been a mass experience drawing vast crowds onto the streets, the politicization of the population was tangible. Politics became a passion, as informal groups began to gather in public places, such as an underground concourse in Bucharest. Here they debated the issues of the day amid graffiti-adorned walls, where painted slogans battled for space with posters announcing public meetings called by freshly emerged political groupings.[4] This explosion of popular expression was one facet of a powerful and dynamic radicalism, which somewhere during the dust of battle had transformed what for the protesters had begun as an anti-Ceauşescu uprising into a full-blown anticommunist revolution. The roots of the opposition movement that arose to challenge the NSF can be traced not so much in any political leader or grouping, but rather in the raw energy of the streets. It grew out of a deep anger that was chiefly focused on the abuses of the past. This gave the movement an essentially negative edge, as it was driven largely by a desire to erase the past rather than by any unified vision of the future. In a personalized political arena, in which ideology was often minimized, the targets of the protesters' wrath were not only their oppressors of old, the Ceauşescus, the *nomenklatura* and the *securitate,* but also increasingly those who were seen as being tarred with the same brush: Iliescu and his fellow leaders of the NSF. Many of the most pointed slogans of the time drew the two strands together: "Ceauşescu, don't be sad, Iliescu is a communist," "NSF=RCP," and "NSF, NSF, go to the Soviet Union." The hostility of the crowd was drawn not only from skepticism at the sight of so many former communists professing Damascene conversions, as they struggled to take the helm of what—from the perspective of

3. Kligman (1990), 397.
4. For examples of graffiti see Nicolau et al. (1990).

the streets—was an avowedly anticommunist revolution. It also derived from a bitter sense of deceit. With the first doubts about the true nature of the revolution, each of the individuals who had participated on the streets and carried their own personal vision of the events, usually expressed in terms of heroism and bravery, was required to equate this with a growing perception of falsification. The consequence was a paradoxical situation in which many of those who claimed status as revolutionaries actually came to deny that the events should be termed as such.[5] This produced a particularly strong sense of betrayal that drove much of the political dynamic of this period, as those who felt they had been dispossessed of power rose to challenge the newly promoted elite.

These feelings seem to have been particularly strong among sections of the country's youth. Assured an Olympian status through their bravery in the revolution, the young people of Romania were lionized by the new leaders of the NSF, who declared it was their participation that had given a unique character to the events. Iliescu spoke of "our wonderful youth, whose blood has restored our sense of national dignity," and Bârlădeanu affirmed, "What is unique about it [the revolution] is that it was made by the youth, the working, learning and military youth, a youth that had been robbed of its future."[6] With words such as these ringing in their ears the young demonstrators on the streets readily came to believe that they had been given a legitimate right to pass judgment on the new rulers. Most vocal were the students, who even during the shooting began to organize themselves into bodies such as the Students' League and the Students' Union, which was also known as the Free Trade Union of Students. Of the two the League was reported as being the more radical, although rather than being an overtly political grouping, it appears to have considered itself akin to a trade union with individual members being free to decide their own political affiliations.[7] The League, which soon claimed a membership of 10,000, had a five-man council, the most prominent members of which were Marian Munteanu, Vlad Niculescu, and Radu Ghesaru.

From the earliest days of the revolution in Timişoara the crowd had chanted "Down with communism," but most of their anger and slogans had been directed at Ceauşescu and his clan. Now, with his departure from the scene, the scope of the slogans broadened to take on a sharper anticommunist edge and encompass more of the old regime.[8] On Decem-

---

5. A 1992 opinion poll showed participants in the revolution were much more likely to view the events as a plot than those who had not taken part; see Câmpeanu (1993), 182.

6. Pompey (March 2, 1990), 26; BBC EE/0655, B/12:48, January 6, 1990.

7. *East European Newsletter,* January 8, 1990, 2; Pompey (March 2, 1990), 27.

8. On December 25 a delegation of young people arrived at the newspaper *Adevărul* to ask that "in the memory of the victims [of the revolution] . . . the word 'communism' no longer appears in the free press," quoted in Pompey (March 2, 1990), 28.

ber 26, the discontent crystallized in a public demonstration in front of the old central committee building. Chanting "Without communism" the few hundred protesters expressed their disquiet at the rapid execution of Ceauşescu and called for a more thorough cleansing of the Augean stables of the previous regime. The same evening, Adrian Ştefanescu, one of the leaders of the newly formed Romanian Democratic Party, appeared on television as a spokesman for the protesters in a discussion with Cazimir Ionescu of the Front.[9] This encounter was important because it marked the first public acceptance by the new rulers that there was popular discontent with their regime. It also showed that "dialogue" could encompass public disputation, although in this instance it would be something of a misnomer to term the encounter a "debate," given the rather patronizing manner in which Ionescu brusquely dealt with the inexperienced Ştefanescu.[10] Nevertheless, the precedent was set, and over the coming months many other political groups were to demand television airtime to voice their opinions and "dialogue" with the leaders of the Front.

The return of political diversity thrust the media to the forefront of the debate, and this was particularly true of television. Despite the sharp rise in the circulation of newspapers at this time, the relatively high levels of radio and television ownership meant that they remained the chief sources of information for much of the population. This was particularly true outside Bucharest, where newspapers usually arrived several days late, because of the poor distribution system. The new Free Romanian Television found an avid audience. Freed from the constraints of the Ceauşescu era, the time on air rose sharply from a mere twenty-two hours a week to more than a hundred, as drab reports on industrialization and the doings of the Ceauşescus were replaced by a diet of news, cartoons, films, and programs imported from the West.[11] Many of the presenters, however, were the same as those who for years had mouthed the banalities of the old regime and, although they protested that "physically we are the same people, but mentally we are completely different," their continued presence only served to undermine the message they purveyed. Soon demonstrators were calling for greater changes, and on January 31, 1990, in a presage of what was to become a familiar form of protest, a twenty-

9. Whether the RDP ever represented the real voice of the protesters is questionable. When it made no bones about its broad social democratic orientation and its willingness to accept former communists who had a "clear conscience" into its ranks, it quickly aroused public suspicions. On January 3, 1990, another of its leaders, Nicolae Costel, felt the need at a press conference to categorically state that he had not been a member of the RCP and that his party was not a façade for the Front. By the May 1990 elections the party had virtually dropped off the political map. BBC EE/0654, B/14–15:26, January 5, 1990.

10. BBC EE/0649, B/4, December 29, 1989; see *Washington Post*, December 27, 1989, A14.

11. The hours broadcast on television increased from 1,795 in 1989 to 8,135 in 1990, and those on radio from 30,148 hours in 1989 to 52,309 in 1990; see *Anuarul statistic al României, 1992* (n.d.), 236–38. On the avid viewing of television see Kligman (1990), 413.

five-year-old engineer was reported to have begun a hunger strike outside the Intercontinental Hotel in Bucharest to protest the bias present within television reports.[12] The chief target of the protesters' wrath appears to have been Aurel Dragoş Munteanu, whose combined roles as head of the television service and spokesman of the NSF seemed to epitomize the Front's domination of the media. Eventually, under mounting pressure he was forced to step down, first as the regime's spokesman on January 29 and then from his post at the television on February 9.

During 1990, the state television service was to maintain its monopoly over broadcasting, but elsewhere, from the start of the year, there were considerable changes. Several private radio stations were established, often amid considerable political controversy, but most striking of all, there were the first tentative signs of a reemergence of diversity in the printed word as a few publications moved away from the "official line" and started to publish investigative and polemical articles critical of some aspects of the new regime. Later in the year, there was to be a tremendous explosion in the number of publications, but initially the field was still dominated by the traditional titles, although in keeping with the political events, some of these felt it prudent to adopt a change of name.[13] Thus, *Scînteia* (The Spark), after appearing for one day under the name *Scînteia Poporului* (The Spark of the People), dropped the tainted "Spark" in favor of the "Truth" (*Adevărul*) and *Informaţiă Bucureştiului* (Bucharest's Information), which had heralded the revolution on December 22 under the name *Libertatea* (Freedom), continued to bear that appellation. The titles *Tineretul Liber* (The Free Youth) and *România Liberă* (Free Romania) were deemed sufficiently neutral to remain unaltered and, ironically, in the coming months, the latter was to change far more than many of the other newspapers where the transformation was largely confined to the masthead.[14] Immediately after they reappeared on the news stands, the daily newspapers claimed large rises in circulation. During the period January 3–5 it was reported that 439,000 subscriptions had been taken out for *Adevărul*, raising daily sales to 1,848,629. In the process, such a strain was placed on the antiquated presses that the paper had to shrink to four pages. Not to be outdone, *România Liberă* was soon also boasting a rise in circulation to 1,000,000.[15] Long lines were reported for some publications, and a number less identified with the regime, such as 22 and *România Liberă*, seem not to have received sufficient newsprint from state sup-

12. Stefanescu (March 23, 1990), 26.

13. The numbers of newspapers, magazines, and other periodicals produced increased sharply rising from 495 in 1989 to 1,444 in 1990, see *Anuarul statistic al României 1991* (n.d.), 210. The figures given cover only those entered into the holdings of the National Library and, as many of the magazines lasted no more than a handful of issues, it seems likely that the true number of publications was even higher.

14. For these titular changes see BBC EE/0648, B/13, December 28, 1989.

15. *Adevărul,* January 10, 1990, 1.

pliers to meet demand, giving rise to accusations that the shortages were being politically manipulated to curb the opposition press.[16]

A deputation of youths that visited the offices of *Adevărul* on December 25 demanded that in the future all reporting should be accurate and impartial but, with little experience to draw upon, it soon became clear that there was no consensus as to what constituted such journalism. Differing interpretations can be observed by contrasting reports of the students' meeting of January 7. The Western press the next day was full of stories about the expression of anti-Front sentiments, but these were totally ignored by *Adevărul*, which chose to focus exclusively on the academic demands of the students.[17] This position also seems to have been followed by the television, judging from a lengthy letter that appeared shortly afterward in *România Liberă*, denouncing the "censored" television report of the event.[18] While *Adevărul* was slow to change and appears to have remained to a large extent the mouthpiece of the regime, *România Liberă*, through the publication of letters such as this and a number of other articles, was already moving toward a more independent position by the beginning of January. Under the editorship of Petre Mihai Băcanu, Anton Uncu, and Mihai Creangă the paper increasingly began to reflect the anticommunist tone of the revolution of the streets.[19] On December 31 an article implored all those who "remind us of the nightmare" of the Ceaușescu period "not to show themselves anymore" and, shortly afterward, Băcanu launched a series of articles, in which he publicly denounced a string of senior officials and ministers for their past activities.[20] Among his first targets were Virgil Cazacu, a former secretary of the RCP Central Committee and deputy prime minister, who had been appointed head of Uniunii Centrale a Cooperativelor Meșteșugărești (UCECOM) after the revolution; and Paul Niculescu-Mizil, the only member of the former PEC who seems to have still retained some degree of influence, because, according to Brucan, he knew the whereabouts of strategic food reserves.[21] Then, shifting his target to the new administration, the charges Băcanu leveled against the vice president, Dumitru Mazilu, and the minister for foreign trade, Nicolae M. Nicolae, were so damaging that they appear in both cases to have directly contributed to their resignation from

16. Kligman (1990), 412.

17. *Washington Post*, January 8, 1990, A17; *Guardian*, January 8, 1990, 1; *Adevărul*, January 9, 1990, 1.

18. *România Liberă*, January 11, 1990, 2.

19. Băcanu had served on the staff of the paper but was arrested by the *securitate* in 1989 for trying to publish an independent newspaper and only released after the revolution. *Nouvel Observateur*, February 15–21, 1990, 4–10.

20. *România Liberă*, December 31, 1989, 2.

21. For Cazacu see ibid., January 10, 1990, 5; ibid., January 12, 1990, 5; and for Niculescu-Mizil see ibid., January 12, 1990, 1, 2; ibid., January 16, 1990, 3; Brucan (1993), 177–78.

office. Two other ministers, Stelian Pintelie, minister for post and telecommunications, and Mircea Angelescu, minister for sport, were also seriously embarrassed but clung onto office, with the latter reportedly having his offer of resignation rejected.[22] These attacks seem to have been concentrated not so much on those who had been members of the former regime but rather those suspected of belonging to the *securitate*. Mazilu and Pintelie were both said to have been colonels in the organization and Nicolae a major-general. Băcanu's sources of information were obviously good and his intentions may have been noble, but nonetheless, his methods bore unsettling similarities to tactics used by the communists beforehand. Despite his alleged links to the *securitate*, Mazilu seems to have been on the reform wing of the NSF, and the same was sometimes said of Nicolae, who claims that he ran foul of the NSF council in his ministry when he tried to institute changes. The clash came to a head when the members of the council demanded he sack a list of supposed *securitate* agents they had produced. Nicolae refused, he says because he wanted dismissals to occur on professional grounds only and he felt the slated names were only a tiny fraction of the *securitate* officers employed within the ministry. When the issue could not be resolved, Nicolae resigned.[23] To a certain extent, the campaign in *România Liberă* was merely an extension of a phenomenon sweeping Romania at that time, with scores of people being denounced as either former members of the *securitate* or their informers. However, by apparently confirming suspicions that the new government contained a whole barrel-full of rotten apples, it could only weaken the NSF, while at the same time legitimizing *România Liberă* as a crusading newspaper of the opposition.

The growing plurality in the media was mirrored in the political arena, where nineteen political groupings had already been registered by January 25. Following patterns seen elsewhere in Eastern Europe, several of these new groups chose not to call themselves "parties," although they were primarily political groupings. Principal among these was the NSF, but they also included various ethnic groupings, of which only the Hungarians under the banner of the Hungarian Democratic Union of Romania were numerous enough to be a serious political force, as well as the Ecological Movement of Romania. The Group for Social Dialogue, a section of which was eventually to transmute into the Civic Alliance, might also be added to the list, although it was not registered as a political

22. For Nicolae Nicolae see *România Liberă*, January 11, 1990, 1, 5; ibid., January 13, 1990, 5; Nicolae (2000). For Pintelie see *România Liberă*, January 14, 1990, 7; ibid., January 19, 1990, 5, and note the use of the respectful plural form in the title as Băcanu is forced to backtrack on his allegations, ostensibly in the face of a stream of letters and telexes arriving at the offices of *România Liberă* in support of the minister. For Angelescu see ibid., January 23, 1990, 1, 2; ibid., January 31, 1990, 5. In the same series see also ibid., January 24, 1990, 1, 5.

23. Nicolae (2000), 256–61.

group. In each case, the rationale behind the decision to eschew the use of the title "party" stemmed not so much from a desire to avoid the use of a word tainted by past associations with The Party, but rather from a quest to establish new broader movements that represented the interests of one particular group or addressed an issue of such importance that a stance had to be adopted above the party-political fray. Thus, the EMR claimed to be speaking on behalf of the devastated natural environment, the GSD for Romania's intellectuals, the HDUR for the Hungarian community, and the NSF for the nation as a whole. The existence of these broader movements appears to have dovetailed with the Front's idea that it would form a political umbrella under which various representative groups could shelter, and generally these groupings seem to have initially been more generously received by the new authorities than those organizations that preferred to see themselves in more traditional political terms as parties.

These broader organizations, however, were the exception rather than the rule, and the vast majority of the new political formations did readily adopted the epithet "party." With few members and no organization, these early groupings were frequently little more than platforms for their often vociferous leaders who were in the most part totally untutored in the art of politics. The leaders of the RDP, initially the most prominent of these proto-parties, were reported to be an actor and a Sanskrit scholar. References to the RDP regularly appeared in the Western press, perhaps largely because one of its leaders, Nicolae Costel, seems to have operated most of the time from a sofa in the hall of the Intercontinental Hotel, the established residence of the foreign press corps.[24] By January 15 the Romanian Democratic Party claimed to have one thousand members, but its real capabilities were perhaps more accurately divined by a Western journalist when he remarked that the party "would have difficulty running a village in the Carpathian mountains, let alone a crisis-ridden country of 23 million."[25] In the subsequent months, many of these first political groupings collapsed, while others entered into a frenzied game of musical chairs, in which acronyms and partners were changed with bewildering frequency.

In general, it might be said that the rapid emergence of so many political parties, even if it did not directly force the Front to abandon the one party pluralism of consensus, did cement the return to political pluralism and help raise levels of social politicization. The many frailties of the new political parties, however, together with a widespread popular distrust of those unknowns who sought to proclaim themselves as new leaders, combined to throw the spotlight firmly onto three more recognizable political entities, which now reappeared after a long forced absence. These were

24. *The Times,* January 4, 1990, 8.
25. Ibid., January 15, 1990, 8.

the "traditional" or "historic" parties that had dominated Romanian politics before the communist takeover: the National Peasant Party, the National Liberal Party, and the Social Democratic Party of Romania.[26] All these parties, as a legacy of their long heritage, possessed a defined identity and leaders unequivocally accepted as being untainted by the past. By a twist of fate, however, this same history that thrust them to the fore was to often weigh heavily, circumscribing their horizons and preventing them from fully seizing the opportunities on offer.

The Traditional Political Parties

The first of the traditional parties to appear in Romania after the flight of Ceaușescu was the National Peasant Party. As early as December 22, the very day of Ceaușescu's overthrow, survivors of the old prewar party, including Corneliu Coposu, Ion Puiu, and Ion Diaconescu, had met in Bucharest to reactivate its organization and draw up a draft proclamation, which was printed later that night and distributed the next morning.[27] During the following days, the old party seems to have rapidly merged with two new groups that had appeared during the revolution with similar political inclinations: the predominantly youth-based Christian Democratic Party and the Christian National Peasant Party.[28] After these mergers, the National Peasant Party added the epithet Christian Democratic to its historic name and took up temporary residence in the old villa of Nicolae Titulescu on Șoseaua Kiseleff.[29] The party was formally reestablished on December 26, 1989, at a meeting of more than one hundred veteran and younger supporters, and a provisional leadership elected with Coposu at its head.[30] In these early days the ranks of the party were also boosted by the return of a number of influential exiles, the most important of whom was to be Ion Rațiu.[31] One claim is that the party inscribed

26. Throughout this study the term "traditional" has been preferred to the frequently en countered "historic" when describing these parties, since this is the term used by the parties themselves at the time and because there has been a tendency for the word "historic," when used in reference to the parties, to become invested with slightly derogatory overtones.

27. Interview with Corneliu Coposu, September 1993.

28. *Financial Times,* January 3, 1990, 2; Socor (February 16, 1990), 30–31, quoting from the NPP journal *Renasterea.*

29. For the sake of convenience and because of historic convention the abbreviation NPP has been retained instead of the more cumbersome NPP-CD.

30. *Adevărul,* December 29, 1989, 3; *Financial Times,* January 3, 1990, 2. It was officially registered on January 8, 1990.

31. Posted to the Romanian embassy in Great Britain during the Second World War, Rațiu had remained in exile after the communist takeover. Subsequently, he combined an extremely successful business career with a public role as one of the most trenchant critics of the RCP regime; see the brief biographical note in Datculescu and Liepelt (1991), 197, Rațiu (1975), and Rațiu (1999).

over 30,000 new recruits within these first weeks and, inside a month, this had allegedly leapt to 260,000.[32] The veracity of this figure may be doubted, but the degree of support the party received at this time seems to have been sufficient to produce a self-confident posture in the talks that were to take place with the NSF over the formation of the PCNU.

After the Second World War, the NPP had been at the heart of the resistance to the communist takeover. As a consequence, following the arrest of the party's leader, Iuliu Maniu, in 1947, it had been officially dissolved and banned. This tradition of resolute anticommunism and refusal to compromise was to be fully embraced by the "new" leaders of the party, many of the more elderly of whom, like Coposu, a former secretary to Maniu, had endured long terms in jail and great suffering during the preceding forty years.[33] Their position was also buoyed by the myth that the party had been the real victor of the 1946 election, only to be robbed of power when the communists reversed the vote.[34] This not only produced a belief that the party had a legitimate right to accede to power, once the communist regime fell, but it also cast the last forty years of Romanian history as an illegal and disastrous interregnum. These traits of anticommunism and opposition were perhaps reinforced by the experience of the party during the revolution, when Coposu had responded to Iliescu's call for responsible people to come to the central committee building in the afternoon of December 22 only to be excluded from the discussions.[35]

The anticommunist stance of the NPP, however, while proving undeniably popular with the more implacable foes of the past regime, was also to prove something of a double-edged sword for the party. For most Romanians everyday existence under communism had entailed some degree of compromise, however small this might have been, and this made few so free of sin as to be able to cast the first stone. The edge was also taken off the NPP's anticommunist rhetoric—especially as regards its attempts to tar its NSF opponents—by the fact that within Romania the dominant public perception of the previous regime was that it had been Ceaușescu's personal dictatorship. The view that it was a communist dictatorship appears to have been only secondary, and so for many the death of Ceaușescu had been equated with the death of the previous regime. Despite their links with the RCP, the leaders of the Front, capitalizing on their performance during the revolution, were able to build on this perception to slough off the stigma of their past in the eyes of most of the

32. *Financial Times,* February 1, 1990, 2.
33. Coposu (1998).
34. Hitchins (1994), 533.
35. Roman (1994), 120; Coposu (1998), 163. Coposu also seems to have gone to the television station during the evening of December 22 and, according to Bârlădeanu, he was not invited to take part in the discussions because nobody knew who he was. Ivan (1998), 186–87.

population. Also, although the role Coposu and many of the other senior leaders of the NPP had played in opposing the post–Second World War communist takeover gave them considerable moral legitimacy, it meant that by 1989 they were old men and this did not aid their party's cause in what was, fundamentally, a youthful society.

After so many years of interdiction, the provisional manifesto of the NPP, as might be expected, bore all the hallmarks of a leadership long cut off from the political mainstream and was a disparate mixture of a search for traditional roots and an attempt to come to terms with the realities of postcommunism. For instance, although the NPP envisaged a far larger private sector within a mixed economy, certain key sectors, such as energy and transportation, were still to remain under state control, and privatization was to be spread over a period of ten years with, significantly, the form of ownership most favored being worker-joint stock companies. In the countryside, the policy was to reverse the legacy of communism through the breaking up of collective and state farms in favor of individual farmers and peasant associations, but, as with industrial privatization, this was to be a gradual process spread over three years. Further pledges were also made that resources would be redistributed to the countryside and that agriculture would continue to receive state assistance. These last promises suggest that values rather than economics were central to NPP policy. Privatization was primarily seen as a step toward the recreation of a property-owning bourgeoisie, especially in the countryside, because only through the regeneration of the peasantry and Christian teachings—the party promised to reintroduce religion into schools—would the moral renewal of Romania be secured by the reassertion of the old precommunist value system. Finally, in what can best be interpreted as an act of realism, the party, while committing itself to the reintegration of Romania into Europe and promising a warm welcome for any investment from the West, gave assurances that it would maintain existing external commitments, including the Warsaw Treaty.[36]

At first sight, in their mutual stress on a mixed economy and continued state assistance, there appears to be a considerable amount of convergence in the political programs of the NSF and the NPP, but in reality they were looking at the same problem from entirely opposite viewpoints. For the NPP, reforms were the first steps toward the recreation of precommunist social structures, while for the NSF they were the means for broadly maintaining the existing structure. Overriding all, and preventing any possibility of compromise, was the ever-present shadow of the past. Many of the leaders of the NPP saw the NSF as being nothing other than a continuation of the RCP under another name, and Grigore Brancuși, a seventy-nine-year-old nephew of the famous sculptor and member

36. *Adevărul,* January 10, 1990, 3; Socor (February 16, 1990), 30–31.

of the NPP leadership, who had spent thirteen years in jail, was not offering an isolated opinion when he baldly stated in an interview with a Western journalist, "We want . . . compensation for the thousands of political prisoners and justice."[37]

In the first days after the overthrow of Ceaușescu the pace was set by the NPP but, as January progressed, the other great political party of Romanian politics, the National Liberal Party, was also revived. Following two earlier meetings, one of which seems to have designated Mihnea Marmeliuc as chairman, a committee of initiative was formed on January 6, 1990, with eleven members and an executive of five.[38] Power was placed in the hands of a group of former "Young Liberals," chief among whom was Radu Câmpeanu, who was made general secretary of the party. The first program was broadly similar to that of the NPP, with the subtle difference that less emphasis was placed on restoration, so that, for instance, under decollectivization land was to pass to those who would work it rather than to past owners. The Liberals also championed the idea of dual speed privatization, seeking a rapid return of the retail, service, and light industrial sectors to private ownership but a slower transition for heavier industry.

The NLP had a history and traditions markedly different from the NPP. It had been in office for much of Romania's history as an independent state, breeding an expectation of power and a feeling that it was the natural party of government. This belief appears to have often prompted a greater readiness to compromise and participate in governments of various political hues, in an impulse that can most charitably be interpreted as a desire to serve the nation. The most recent and significant example of this practice was the participation by the senior NLP politician and former prime minister, Gheorghe Tătărescu, in the postwar communist dominated Groza government. These natural tendencies toward compromise were perhaps reinforced in 1990 by the fact that the party had fared badly in the 1946 elections—older members of the party can remember the NLP leader of the time, Constantin Brătianu, being ashen faced when he heard the result—and so had possessed no myth of victory to sustain themselves through the long years of communism. During this time the NLP had disappeared as a political entity, with many of its members suffering equally as much as those of the NPP, but it was never formally dissolved and banned; rather it appears to have just faded away, giving it overall a more ambiguous relationship with the communist past than the clean cut experienced by the NPP. All this seems to have combined to give the NLP a slightly less belligerently anticommunist air than the NPP.

37. *Financial Times,* January 3, 1990, 2.
38. The party was officially registered on January 10, 1990.

In particular Radu Câmpeanu seems to have favored the idea that the party should occupy a distinct position in the center of Romanian politics between the former communists and the peasant party. The NLP's tradition of alliance building coincided with the NSF's desire to build the broadest of coalitions, and, shortly after the revolution, a number of party members did enter the NSF administration. Most prominently, Marmeliuc became minister for labor and social security, but Nicolae Grigorescu was also appointed an advisor to the prime minister and, significantly, Câmpeanu himself was later to be one of the NSF's nominees for the Executive Bureau of the PCNU.[39] Contradictions, however, were inherent in the NLP's attempt to maintain an intermediary position within the political arena. Even as it was forging these often personal links with the NSF, the party was also joining the NPP to form the core of the opposition to the Front. It always remained, however, slightly wary of its old rival, and in the 1990 election conspicuously failed to establish a formal electoral alliance, preferring instead to rely on a joint communiqué and a nonaggression pact.

The third of the traditional parties, the Romanian Social Democratic Party, has historically played a relatively minor role in a country that, until the advent of communism, had a limited industrial base and a largely nonunionized workforce. After the Second World War, the left-leaning RSDP was placed in a more ambiguous position vis-à-vis the RCP than the other traditional parties. Many members joined the communists in the National Democratic Front, before the two parties formally merged in February 1948. An important remnant, however, under the most distinguished RSDP leader, Constantin Titel Petrescu, remained outside the communist dominated bloc and, instead, aligned themselves against the communists with the NPP and NLP. It was as heirs to this heritage that some veteran members of the party gathered in Bucharest, after the fall of Ceaușescu, to resurrect the RSDP. Adrian Dimitru, a former RSDP minister, was declared honorary president, and Sergiu Cunescu active president. The party was to have less impact than the other traditional parties, garnering a lower vote in the May 1990 elections than either the NPP and the NLP, although all three only attracted a small fraction of the support enjoyed by the Front at this time. In reality, in January 1990 all the revived parties were weak and hollow structures, notwithstanding an illusory appearance of strength based on the uncertainties of the revolution and their often vociferous supporters.[40]

39. But note the disclaimer from the NLP stating that Marmeliuc and Grigorescu took office in a personal capacity and not as representatives of the party; see BBC EE/0675, B/7–8:18, January 30, 1990.

40. For a fuller analysis of the fortunes of the traditional parties in the first months of 1990 see Siani-Davies (1998), 125–46.

The Roots of Conflict: January in Bucharest

Peace seems to have more or less descended on Bucharest by the end of December, although there were reports of isolated outbreaks of shooting well into the new year. Immediately after the fighting had died down, the crowds on the streets thinned markedly, as the onset of much colder weather seems to have been sufficient to curb the enthusiasm of all but the most ardent of revolutionaries. There may still have been occasional sporadic protests, but the first major demonstrations of the new year did not take place until January 7. On that day, gatherings of students took place in a number of cities, including Bucharest, Timișoara, Galați, and Bacău, and the NPP youth section held a demonstration in the center of the capital.[41] At the student meetings an eleven-point program was presented. Most of these were concerned with education, with calls for the granting of autonomy to all academic institutions and student representation on bodies at all levels. However, some of the other demands, such as calls for an end to compulsory job assignment after graduation and an ending or reduction of conscription, also carried political ramifications. Underlying the meetings there was a bitter sense of betrayal. The students felt empowered by the revolution but sidelined by the new leaders. They openly distrusted their "representatives" who had been co-opted onto the Front Council, although, whether a change in personnel would have made much difference is debatable, since at the Bucharest meeting one of the students sitting on the CNSF, Marian Mierlă, declared that they were in fact little more than "marionettes," whose participation in the discussions had no more relevance than a "piece of furniture."[42] Still, calls were made for the election of new representatives to the CNSF, as a more radical note entered the gathering, with speakers voicing the fear that the NSF had hijacked the revolution and was monopolizing power "like another form of communist party."[43]

The growing tension was eventually to come to a head a few days later on January 12, on what had been officially declared a day of national mourning for the victims of the revolution. After thousands had thronged the churches and streets of Bucharest paying homage to the fallen, a crowd gathered outside the Front headquarters in a building overlooking the huge open expanse of Piața Victoriei. The size of the crowd seems to have ebbed and flowed, making it difficult to gauge its strength—official figures put the number at no more than 1,000, while Western journalists

41. For the NPP demonstrations see *România Liberă,* January 18, 1990, 2.

42. Pompey (March 2, 1990), 27, quoting *Der Spiegel,* January 8, 1990. Mierlă was to quit the CNSF on January 24.

43. *Washington Post,* January 8, 1990, A17; *Guardian,* January 8, 1990, 1; Pompey (March 2, 1990), 27, 30; *The Times,* January 8, 1990, 8, and for the NPP demonstrations *România Liberă,* January 18, 1990, 2.

speak of 7,000–10,000. As the day passed, the waiting throng became more restive. A tank posted to guard the building was transformed into an impromptu rostrum, with members of the crowd scrambling on top to harangue the assembled mass. The demands they voiced, although they were often confused and inarticulate, seem to have encapsulated many of the wider fears and doubts that beset the country. They wanted a more accurate and honest picture of the revolution that was to include the publication of official casualty figures and detailed information about the terrorists. How many were held in detention and when would they be brought to trial? Clarification was also demanded about the exact relationship between the new Front councils and the former RCP, both at an institutional level and as regards the political orientation of individual members. Unsatisfied by previous assurances, the crowd also demanded the legal dissolution of the RCP and the distribution of its assets among the new political parties. And, showing the degree to which the Front had already become compromised in the eyes of some sections of the population, there were also calls for the freedom of the forthcoming elections to be guaranteed by the presence of impartial UN observers.

Seeking a response to their grievances, the crowd chanted for the leaders of the Front to come and address them in person, and in the late afternoon, they were rewarded by the appearance of the prime minister, Roman. Under constant barracking Roman parried questions relating to the democratic credentials of the Front, but reassured the crowd that the NSF was a transitional body that would only hold power until the elections. Pressed by persistent questioning about the future of the Communist Party he apparently pledged that the RCP—which he described as a manifestation of the Ceauşescu dictatorship—would be abolished by law. When he withdrew, Roman was replaced by Dumitru Mazilu, who, amid chaotic scenes in which he could barely make himself heard, reassured those assembled that the Communist Party was outside the bounds of legal election and that its assets would be redistributed equally among other parties.[44] Despite Mazilu's promises, the crowd remained restless, with its members bickering among themselves and openly unhappy because Iliescu had not appeared. Eventually, shortly before 7 o'clock, the president of the CNSF himself emerged and among boos and constant interruptions began to speak. At first, he tried to defuse the situation by reiterating that the Front was only a temporary structure and that its sole political task was the organization of elections. Then, directly addressing the demands of the protesters, he promised that the trials of all those accused of crimes during the revolution would be broadcast live on television. This reassurance, however, did little to satisfy the more vocal of the crowd, and the meeting rapidly degenerated into something of an inter-

44. BBC EE/0662, B/14–15:54, January 15, 1990.

rogation, with Iliescu fending off a number of hostile questions relating to his past and current political beliefs. At one point, he was specifically asked that each party should have three representatives in the Front. Significantly, Iliescu replied that he had "nothing against this," an indication that even at this early stage, well before the formation of the PCNU, the possibility of widening political representation in the ruling body was under serious consideration. Iliescu, then, withdrew inside to open negotiations with a delegation drawn from the ranks of the protesters, while the proceedings were relayed to the waiting crowd outside by loudspeaker. At 9:45 the members of the leadership emerged for a second time to announce to the waiting throng, who in the biting night air had dwindled to a few thousands in number, that as a result of their deliberations a number of decrees would be issued to outlaw the RCP, sanction a national referendum on the reintroduction of the death penalty, and establish a national commission to address the grievances of those who had suffered under the dictatorship.[45] This declaration seems to have more or less satisfied the crowd and brought the long proceedings to a close, although the negotiations between the two delegations seem to have continued for a while longer, and, in a pointer to the future, as midnight approached, large numbers of workers mixed with a few students began to arrive in the square to stage a counter demonstration in support of the Front.[46]

The demonstration of January 12, 1990, offered confirmation of several important trends in the development of the revolution. Before the whole nation watching excerpts from the proceedings live on television, the weakness of the Front had been clearly revealed, as its leaders apparently capitulated to the demands of a small number of rowdy demonstrators. The fact that this had been able to occur so easily without intervention from any of the security forces underlined the isolation of the new regime to the watching public. The army had been present in the square but had made no attempt to disperse the demonstrators. In fact the experience of the revolution seems to have so traumatized the various branches of the security forces that none felt able or willing to intervene in the political struggle. Having finally come on the side of "the people" during the revolution, the army seems to have been loath to jeopardize its newly exalted status—it gained a 97 percent approval rating in an opinion poll of the time—by springing to the defense of an apparently unpopular and visibly weak political regime. Moreover, even if trained forces could have been mustered for crowd control, which seems unlikely, any large-scale deployment of army units would have placed enormous strains

45. BBC EE/0662, B/17–18:57, January 15, 1990; *Independent*, January 13, 1990, 1. The abolition of the death penalty had been announced on January 7, BBC EE/0658, B/14:24, January 10, 1990.
46. *Adevărul*, January 13, 1990, 1, 5; ibid., January 14, 1990, 1, 2.

upon an institution that was already simmering with discontent. This had already surfaced in the so-called officers' rebellion of January 6–7 and continued during a series of mutinous demonstrations by military personnel on the streets of Bucharest.[47] The militia was also totally demoralized and remained under such a cloud of suspicion, that, throughout this period, it appears to have been unable to conduct all but the simplest policing duties. This left only units of the *securitate,* now absorbed into the army, but even if their deployment was feasible, given the extensive restructuring then taking place and persisting doubts as to the loyalty of some units, it would have been tantamount to political suicide on the part of the new leaders.[48]

Unable to rely upon the regular security forces for support the new regime had to turn to more unorthodox forces. After the January 12 demonstration Brucan gave an explicit warning: "We were taken by surprise then. . . . We will no longer be taken by surprise I can assure you," and now, in the long tradition of Romanian communism, and directly following in the footsteps of Ceaușescu during the revolution, the new regime began to mobilize workers and especially miners in its defense.[49] The lessons drawn by the opposition from the demonstrations were to be equally important in shaping the immediate future of Romanian politics. The apparent reluctance of the security forces to intervene to keep public order, and the ease with which concessions had been wrung from the Front, led the opposition to conclude that a policy of direct confrontation on the streets might pay political dividends. After January 12, the stage was set for six months of clashes, which reached its culmination with the bloody rampage of the miners through Bucharest in June 1990.

The live television broadcast of the scenes from Piața Victoriei closed with the words: "I think we will all agree that we have all regretfully noted that we still do not know what to do with this freedom, won with the blood of all those who were killed only a few weeks ago."[50] In voicing these sentiments of disapproval, the television commentary probably fairly accurately reflected the general mood of the country, especially outside the capital. The ugly scenes from Bucharest appear to have heightened distrust in the new political process and merely served to confirm support

47. *The Times,* January 18, 1990, 6. Out of these protests grew CADA, the Action Committee for the Democratization of the Army, which continued to campaign for changes in the army. In particular, it sought a full investigation of crimes committed during the revolution and a swift return to the reserve for the reactivated generals who threatened to block channels of promotion. The two demands, however, were not entirely complementary, as the struggle for the latter brought CADA into alignment with Stănculescu, who was implicated in the massacres in Timișoara. Hall (1997), 373–76; Watts (1992), 95–126; Blackwell (2002).

48. Some branches of the *securitate* do, however, seem to have been secretly reactivated at this time; see Ionescu (July 29, 1994), 27–30.

49. BBC EE/0663, B/11:46, January 16, 1990.

50. BBC EE/0662, B/16:55, January 15, 1990.

for the established authorities. Certainly, the Front's propagandists leapt at the opportunity to extract maximum benefit from the incident. The next day, *Adevărul* carried a large number of telephone messages from "concerned citizens" voicing their disgust at the scenes from the square and their unwavering support for the NSF. The tone is best caught in a contribution from one Speranţa Spiloaca, a medical assistant from Galaţi: "I have been without a father since the age of four. I have never felt parental warmth. I look on Mr. Iliescu as a father. His smile inspires belief. We must not harm him. He is a good man."[51]

The capricious manner in which the Front's leaders had capitulated to the demands of the crowds also drew criticism from within the NSF. Brucan stated that it would be a practical impossibility to organize a referendum before the planned date of January 28 and described the whole affair as a "monumental mistake."[52] This brought a harsh reprimand from Adrian Sârbu who, after objecting to such a public airing of feelings without authorization, continued, "Brucan is a senile old man who got carried away." It may be, however, that Brucan's angry comment only reflected other tensions simmering within the Front. During the demonstration, Roman is popularly supposed to have made a gesture toward supporting demands by the crowd that Brucan be removed from the NSF, and Mazilu is also widely believed to have tried to use the occasion for his own political purposes.[53] According to Iliescu, the first vice president had originally been sent to address the crowd because he knew some of those present and, presumably, it was these same supporters, who later, while Iliescu was speaking, had begun to loudly chant Mazilu's name. Mazilu was afterward to publicly recant and to admit that he had been asked to take sides and that, having made the "wrong" decision in a "facile manner," he had repeated over the microphone some of the slogans chanted by the crowd—including, it seems, "death to the *securitate*."[54] In fact, the demonstration was to prove Mazilu's nemesis, because during the tumult a woman can be heard giving voice to accusations that he had previously been a member of the *securitate*. The next morning the charge was taken up by *România Liberă,* which carried a front page article demanding his immediate resignation, as he had "prepared and led a serious attempt at the policy of national consensus" and used "as personal political capital the day of national mourning trying to take over power."[55] The article reproduced

51. *Adevărul,* January 14, 1990, 1, 2. It would seem likely that the campaign was highly orchestrated but it should be noted that *Adevărul* had been publicizing a telephone number through which readers could give their opinions, as had *România Liberă.*

52. *Independent,* January 22, 1990, 9.

53. *Cotidianul,* January 17–18, 1994.

54. BBC EE/o667, B/8:30, January 20, 1990. See also Mazilu (1999), 293–97.

55. BBC EE/o663, B/12–13:54, January 16, 1990; *România Liberă,* January 13, 1990 1, 5.

Mazilu's résumé, and, on an inside page there appeared a clutch of letters and telegrams from "concerned citizens," all of whom seem to have a remarkably similar knowledge of his past. Similar messages appeared in *Adevărul*, and over the coming weeks *România Liberă* was to keep up the pressure with a string of articles denouncing Mazilu, until he was eventually forced to resign on January 26.[56]

The day after the demonstration, January 13, the leaders of the Front began the tricky process of extracting themselves from the pledges of the previous night. Firstly, they announced that the measure to outlaw the RCP would also be subject to a referendum on January 28, at the same time as the proposed vote on the death penalty. Then, later in the same evening, Iliescu, Roman, and Mazilu appeared on television for a lengthy exercise in damage limitation.[57] Repeatedly stressing the unity of the Front, they sought to reassure the nation over contentious issues such as trials, enterprise councils, and the freedom of the forthcoming elections. Then, engaging in self-criticism, they chided themselves for yielding to the pressure of a small minority and pledged they would draw heart from the large number of messages, telephone calls, and letters they had received urging them to stand firm against such unrepresentative groups. The retreat was completed four days later, on January 17, when at a meeting of the CNSF the decrees of January 12 were annulled by 117 votes to none, with four abstentions, on the basis that they were an "unprincipled capitulation to pressure that ran counter to our democratic principles."[58]

Participation in the Elections

On January 23, 1990, after a lengthy debate, the CNSF formally decided by a 128–8 vote, with five abstentions, to participate in the forthcoming elections in all but name as a political party. At the same time, by 139 votes to none with two abstentions, it was decided to postpone the elections until May 10, a fraction of the delay requested by the opposition, but probably sufficient to allow the Front to put in place the rudiments of a national organization. Finally, perhaps, as something of a sop

56. *Adevărul*, January 14, 1990, 1, 2; see also *România Liberă*, January 14, 1990, 3; ibid., January 23, 1990, 3; and the front-page editorial in ibid., January 18, 1990, 1. ibid., January 24, 1990, 3, pours scorn on Mazilu's story that he had been detained under Ceaușescu. Mazilu's response to the allegations can be found in ibid., January 27, 1990, 1, 2.

57. BBC EE/0663, B/8:32, January 16, 1990; BBC EE/0664, B/13–17:14, January 17, 1990. Iliescu (1995a), 69–74.

58. *Independent*, January 15, 1990, 1; *Financial Times*, January 19, 1990, 2; Iliescu (1995a), 74–81. Diplomatic sources reported pressure from the USSR to reverse the decision over the Communist Party, and, in an interview, Brucan, noting that there were communist parties in all neighboring countries, stated that by "taking such a measure they were offending those parties and posing them problems." BBC EE/0666, B/14:65, January 19, 1990.

to the opposition, in a bid to gain international credibility, the CNSF also voted to accept outside observers at the polls by a vote of 135–4, with two abstentions.[59]

The decision of the Front to participate in the elections was the keystone around which the immediate postcommunist history of Romania was built. As has already been stressed, from the outset under Consensus the NSF, on the basis of the legitimacy gained from the revolution, visualized the CNSF playing a permanent role in Romanian politics as an umbrella body. The abandonment of the political project of consensus and the tacit acceptance of a Western pluralist model necessarily brought an end to this idea, with the CNSF instead becoming a temporary body awaiting replacement by a parliament legitimized through popular elections. To retain power, the NSF would have to contest the elections as a political party, but initially Iliescu and the other leaders of the Front seem to have done little to clarify what these changes meant and, in particular, the crucial differences that now existed between the roles of the CNSF and the NSF. Instead, as they came under increasing attack, the tendency grew for them to deflect criticism by stressing the transitional nature of the Front, by which they implied the CNSF, without making clear the long-term ambitions of the NSF. This gave the impression in some quarters that the Front, as an entity, was about to withdraw from the political arena, and, when this was revealed not to be the case, it brought charges of duplicity against the new leaders and a perceptible rise in the political temperature.

The decision of the Front to stand in the elections was initially broadly welcomed by the traditional parties, presumably because it clarified the political landscape and provided an issue around which they could unify. They qualified their acceptance, however, by demanding that the coming electoral contest must take place on a level playing field. For this to occur, they argued that the Front had to renounce the levers of power, giving up its acquired assets and replacing the current administration with a more neutral body. They also wanted guarantees of equal media coverage for all parties, especially on television and radio, and curbs placed on the activities of local Front councils in the workplace. At the same time, the traditional parties also moved to wrest from the Front the legitimacy endowed by the revolution by exploiting to the full growing doubts about the true nature of the events of December. In a communiqué dated January 24 they conspicuously avoided the word "revolution" in preference to the more neutral "anticommunist insurrection" and, directly challenging the Front's claim to be the very embodiment of the revolutionary movement, they stressed that victory belonged to the whole

59. Iliescu (1995a), 84–85.

people and that "nobody can appropriate it in order to claim legitimacy or monopolize political power."[60]

In order to achieve their aims, the opposition parties began to harness the radicalism of the streets, and in Bucharest and elsewhere there now followed a wave of protests that brought an immediate response from the authorities in the shape of a much tighter ruling on public demonstrations.[61] This seems to have been little heeded, and on January 24 hundreds were reported to be marching on the Front headquarters in Piaţa Victoriei, with a dozen representatives of the crowd being allowed to enter the building to air their grievances.[62] Behind the scenes negotiations seem to have continued throughout the period but, perhaps, to keep the pressure on the Front, on January 25, the NPP, NLP, and RSDP nonetheless announced that they were forming a "resistance front" against the NSF and called for massive demonstrations on January 28, 1990, to protest at its decision to run in the elections.[63] The stakes the opposition parties were playing for were high, with one member of the NPP even being quoted as saying that they could mount a second revolution.[64] Any demonstration would technically be illegal, since it would not conform to the stipulations of the new law on public demonstrations, but, as last ditch attempts at compromise failed, the NSF appears to have accepted that a protest march would occur and to have made some efforts to reroute it away from the seat of government in Piaţa Victoriei.[65]

The Demonstrations of January 28–29, 1990

As the morning of January 28 dawned, people began to gather outside the headquarters of the traditional parties hours before the planned demonstration. They remained there until shortly before midday, when they began to march towards Piaţa Victoriei. Some reports speak of them numbering as many as 40,000, while others give a more conservative figure of 15,000. The official tally was a modest 8,000.[66] Chanting "Down with Communism," "Down with Iliescu," and other anti-NSF slogans, the supporters of the traditional parties poured into

---

60. BBC EE/0672, B/3:2, January 26, 1990.
61. *Monitorul Oficial al României,* January 25, 1990, 3; see also BBC EE/0672, B/3:3, January 26, 1990.
62. *Financial Times,* January 25, 1990, 2.
63. Iliescu (1995a), 100; BBC EE/0675, B/3:11, January 30, 1990.
64. *Financial Times,* January 26, 1990, 2.
65. BBC EE/0675, B/5–6:16, January 30, 1990.
66. Nearby, outside the Town Hall of Sector 1 on Banu Manta, a much smaller crowd of mostly workers had also gathered but this time to hear a number of speeches in favor of the Front. For these speeches see *Adevărul,* January 30, 1990, 1, 3.

Piața Victoriei. At one end of the square the government building was cordoned off by a large contingent of troops, supported by a number of armored vehicles with their machine guns symbolically turned skyward to reassure the gathering throng that they would not be used in anger. As the crowd began to assemble, shortly after 1:00 p.m., a delegation from the three traditional parties headed by Coposu, Câmpeanu, and Cunescu entered the Front headquarters to begin talks with a NSF team headed by Iliescu, Roman, and Ionescu. The discussions were protracted and, as time passed, the tension began to rise before, in the late afternoon, the representatives of the Front and the traditional parties appeared first on a balcony in the square and then on television to announce the commencement of detailed negotiations between the two sides.[67] However, despite this apparent successful conclusion to the day's events, it seems that some within the NSF had decided that the time was ripe for the regime to mount a telling counterblow against its opponents. With both the radio and television carrying appeals for people to rally to the Front's support, it was announced that 200,000 workers were approaching the square to mount a pro-Front demonstration.[68] The workers seem to have been told that "foreign elements" and "bands of hooligans" were trying to destroy the Front and destabilize Romania. Chanting slogans such as "We are with the Front," "The Front is with us," and "We are the people" they roughly pushed and shoved the opposition demonstrators to the further limits of the square, so that, by the time Iliescu appeared on the balcony in the early evening, the supporters of the Front were in the ascendant and he was warmly received by the crowd. The scenes around the square were uglier. Opposition demonstrators were seen fleeing with "bruised limbs and bleeding faces" and Western journalists began to report that Bucharest had passed under mob rule.[69]

The next morning, January 29, 1990, found the streets under the control of the partisans of the Front, as thousands of workers were bused into Bucharest from as far afield as Iași and Constanța. In Piața Victoriei large crowds chanting "We are with the Front" and "They provoked, we won" were addressed by the leaders of the NSF, including Roman and Iliescu. Others gathered outside the offices of the traditional parties shouting hostile slogans. The NLP offices were stormed and occupied, while at the NPP headquarters only the arrival of Roman with a detachment of soldiers secured the safety of Coposu, who was escorted away in an armored

67. A transcript can be found in Iliescu (1995a), 102–22.
68. Mazilu was later to say (after he had lost office) that the leaders of the Front had discussed the possibility of mounting a counter demonstration on January 25, 1990; see Shafir (March 2, 1990), 21.
69. *Independent,* January 29, 1990, 1; *Washington Post,* January 29, 1990, A20; *New York Times,* January 29, 1990, A1, A9; *The Times,* January 29, 1990, 9.

car.[70] Among the ranks of the protesters outside the NPP building, there seems to have been some miners and, later that evening, 5,000 more were reported as arriving in the capital fresh from their shifts at the coalface.[71] Following three hours of "talks" with Roman and Iliescu, they eventually left for home but not before they had made the chilling promise that, if the Front was ever to be threatened again, they would descend in their thousands on the capital in its defense.[72]

Following hard on the heels of the disturbances of January 12, the demonstrations of January 28–29 can be seen as a turning point of the revolution. Even if they were not the catalysts of the change, alongside the formation of the PCNU they symbolically marked the conclusion of one phase of the revolutionary process and the beginning of another. The already fast fading honeymoon was at an end. The anti-Ceauşescu coalition had irreversibly fractured and for the next few years the political scene in Romania was to remain deeply polarized between the NSF and its opponents. The bloody pro-Front counterdemonstrations were merely a foretaste of more violent conflicts to follow, as the opposing sides battled for political supremacy. At the same time, in a pattern which was to become familiar during the coming months, violence was also to be the immediate precursor to compromise, since, within a matter of days after the strife, the NSF announced the official dissolution of the CNSF and its replacement by the all party PCNU.

The Formation of the Provisional Council of National Unity

From the beginning of their negotiations with the NSF, the principal demand of the traditional parties was for representation on the new governing bodies. Now, following the demonstrations at the end of January, on February 1, 1990, at a meeting between representatives of the Front and twenty-eight political groupings it was announced that a new supreme body with full legislative powers was to be established. Called the Provisional Council of National Unity this would include representatives from all registered political groupings. Although this declaration marked the formal acceptance by all parties that the long rumored PCNU would be established, there still remained some confusion as to the size and structure of the new body.[73] At first, it appears that the Front proposed to esta-

70. *New York Times,* January 30, 1990, A12; *Independent,* January 30, 1990, 1; *Financial Times,* January 30, 1990, 2; *The Times,* January 30, 1990, 9; BBC EE/0676, B/7:6, January 31, 1990.
71. *Adevărul,* January 30, 1990, 2.
72. Ibid., January 31, 1990, 2.
73. Articles in the Western press indicate some of the various formulations suggested; see, for instance, *Financial Times,* February 10, 1990.

blish two forums, but after further talks this plan was dropped in favor of the straight replacement of the CNSF by the PCNU.[74] Fifty percent of the members of the new council were to be nominated by the CNSF, while the other fifty percent were to come from registered political groupings, with each, irrespective of its strength or standing, being allowed three representatives. Nine organizations, representing national minorities, were also each allowed to nominate members as was the Association of Former Political Prisoners.[75]

While the basic fifty-fifty division seems to have been readily conceded by the opposition parties, the main bone of contention was the number of political groups that would be allowed to nominate representatives. The traditional parties wanted to restrict representation to those that had participated in the February 1 negotiations, while the Front argued that those established afterward should also be included; a position that may, in part, have been shaped by the fact that the Front itself was not officially registered as a political grouping until February 6.[76] The argument was eventually decided in favor of the Front, and the number of political groupings subsequently admitted into the PCNU was thirty-seven, together with the Association of Former Political Prisoners. The rapidity with which many of these had been formed, once the foundation of the PCNU became widely mooted, led members of the opposition parties to charge that a number of "front" parties had been deliberately established by the NSF in order to assure its control over the new body.[77] Given the close relationship several of these new groupings subsequently developed with the Front, and the fact that a suspiciously large number failed to field candidates at the coming election, there may be a grain of truth in these allegations. If so, the Front probably adopted the strategy with the aim of not only creating a number of reliable allies but also of maximizing the size of the CNSF delegation under the prevailing fifty-fifty rule. This was necessary, because the Front delegation was neither a homogeneous block nor entirely dominated by those who can be considered adherents to the Iliescu line. It included a number of figures from what may be considered the liberal wing of the CNSF: Gabriel Andreescu, Ion Caramitru, Mariana Celac, Mircea Dinescu, Dan Petrescu, and Andrei Pleşu, among others. The presence of the presidents of the forty-one county councils of the National Salvation Front within the CNSF delegation also seems to have been considered mandatory and, as these ranged from a former

74. BBC EE/0679, B/8:20, February 3, 1990.
75. *Financial Times*, February 12, 1990, 4.
76. BBC EE/0681, B/11, February 6, 1990.
77. See the open letter to Iliescu from Alfred Neagu in *România Liberă*, February 1, 1990, 1, where he terms these new groupings "satellite" parties and the discussion in Shafir (March 2, 1990), 19.

Ceaușescu minister to inexperienced young technocrats, it seems probable that in most cases they remained an unknown quantity. Indeed, it is striking how few were seen as worthy of being nominated to stand for the NSF at the May 1990 elections. It therefore seems likely that the NSF was trying to boost the size of the CNSF delegation in the PCNU because it wanted to create space for its core supporters, as well as a number of representatives from large industrial plants so as to cement its alliance with the industrial workforce.

The first meeting of the PCNU, mainly devoted to procedural matters, was held on February 9.[78] The new body had an Executive Bureau of twenty-one, which was to be responsible for day-to-day decision making when the council was not in session.[79] In line with the main council, the Executive Bureau was also chosen on a fifty-fifty basis, with half being nominated by the CNSF and the rest being selected through an election in which each party, including the NSF, was allowed to nominate up to ten candidates. Alongside Iliescu the eleven NSF members selected for the Bureau included Cazimir Ionescu, Ion Caramitru, Károly Király, Corneliu Mănescu, Mircea Dinescu, Alexandru Bârlădeanu, and Nicolae S. Dumitru. No other grouping had more than one representative. Ion Diaconescu gained a place on behalf of the NPP and Radu Câmpeanu for the NLP. The PCNU like its predecessor, the CNSF, was also supported by a number of specialist commissions. Broadly these were the same as before, although a number of them were subdivided and two new commissions added to consider abuses under the communist regime. The replacement of the CNSF by the PCNU was mirrored at the county and local levels by similar transformations, as representatives of the other political parties were introduced into the local councils. This was meant to be in the same proportions as at the national level, and in the county councils and larger town councils this does seem to have happened, but at the lowest level, where representatives of other political parties were not so easy to find, it seems that in many instances the old councils simply recast themselves once again, this time in the guise of the local PCNU.

Through the creation of the PCNU Romania had at last gained a proto-parliament that reflected most of the political currents present in the country. The wider foundation of the new body conferred upon it greater legitimacy and it was to remain largely unchallenged until replaced by an elected parliament in May 1990. This first step toward parliamentary democracy, however, was not without problems. The lack of a parliamentary culture and the inexperience of most of the new politicians made the Provisional Councils of National Unity both at a national and a local level

78. Iliescu (1995a), 137–77.
79. *Monitorul Oficial al României,* February 14, 1990, 1.

somewhat rowdy. Frequently the proceedings degenerated into a chaotic shouting match in which the various factions traded mutual accusations.[80] Iliescu was correct in saying that December might have brought momentary genuine national consensus, but January brought differentiation and acute political confrontation.[81] Moreover, although the formation of the PCNU gave the traditional parties and the new political groupings their first postcommunist taste of power, it was probably most beneficial to the NSF. Through the PCNU the Front was able to retain control of the political mechanism, while at the same time distancing itself from the deteriorating economic situation, thus preserving its electoral appeal.

So far this chapter has focused almost exclusively on the demonstrations that shook Bucharest during the first weeks after the fall of communism, but, while the pressure exerted by the opposition was important in spurring the NSF to replace the CNSF with the PCNU, international factors also played a role. The revolution had placed Romania firmly under the spotlight of world scrutiny. After years of diplomatic isolation, the month after the fall of Ceauşescu had seen a steady stream of Western visitors to Bucharest, including such senior figures as the German and French foreign ministers, Hans-Dietrich Genscher and Roland Dumas, as well as Frans Andriessen, the European Community commissioner for foreign affairs, and William Waldegrave, minister of state at the British Foreign and Commonwealth Office. The presence of so many foreign dignitaries bolstered the domestic standing of the NSF and gave it a useful seal of international respectability. At the same time, however, these visiting statesmen presumably left the leaders of the Front in no doubt about the political system Western Europe expected to see put in place in Romania and the steps the country would have to take if it was to fully return to the European fold and establish a sound trading position with the European Community. Romania was expected to establish a recognizably Western model of democracy and, as a step toward this, at least one of the visitors, Waldegrave, seems to have pressed the Front to give the opposition parties a greater political role.[82]

From the middle of January, the Front seems to have accepted that it would have to participate in a competitive political arena and that, before then, it would have to enter into some form of a power-sharing agreement with the other political parties. Such a major shift in strategy required a new political message, and so, grafted on to the old themes of the NSF being the embodiment of the revolution and the savior of the nation, there now appeared a new stress on the Front as the only practical alterna-

---

80. For the transcript of the first meeting of the PCNU see Iliescu (1995a), 137–72.
81. BBC EE/0678, B/6:30, February 2, 1990.
82. *Independent,* January 17, 1990, 9.

tive to chaos, anarchy, and a return to dictatorship.[83] Front spokesmen increasingly argued that, if it gave way to the traditional parties, greedy for power, it would only put the gains of the revolution at risk. To the NSF its participation in the elections was not only justified, but a veritable moral obligation, because only through the long-term vision of renewal that was its program could the best interests of the nation be assured. To make sure it secured its position at the helm after these elections the Front had to both identify its natural electoral base and develop a clear strategy to mobilize this constituency in its support. Having apparently given up on the intellectuals and the peasants, whom initially they seem to have mistakenly abandoned to the NPP, the leaders of the Front increasingly came to focus their attention on the industrial workforce and the technical intelligentsia. In the communiqué that announced the Front's participation in the elections, Iliescu placed special emphasis on the fact that the decision had been made only after talks with "numerous workers . . . with miners in the Jiu Valley, in Maramureș, with workers in large works in the capital, with representatives of local organisations of the Front, of free trade unions," and now, as January turned to February, he made the first of several visits to factories to speak directly to the assembled workforce.[84] The ending of the need to cater to the eclectic tastes of a broad coalition of intellectuals also permitted the leaders of the Front to turn to the tried and trusted methods of the past to mobilize the workforce. At the simplest level, this involved little more than reinforcing crude stereotypes from the communist past and playing on fears of change through often vicious caricatures of the traditional parties. At the Front meeting of January 28, one speaker, after declaring that the leaders of the traditional parties had done great damage to the country in the past, accused them of being only interested in grasping power for its own sake. In the traditions of the Romanian political discourse, accusations of foreignness were also used to try and delegitimize opponents. At the same meeting, it was mischievously charged that the leaders of the traditional parties had never suffered the hunger and cold of the Ceaușescu years, a sentiment later echoed in the NSF slogan "While we were suffering here under Ceaușescu, they had coffee and croissants in Paris."[85]

83. Many pronouncements of the Front at this time pick up this theme; see *Monitorul Oficial al României*, January 27, 1990, 1–3, and *Adevărul*, January 25, 1990, 1, where the Front is described as a symbol of normality in a world of chaos.

84. *Monitorul Oficial al României*, January 25, 1990, 1–3; see also BBC EE/0671, B/14:55, January 25, 1990; *Adevărul*, January 27, 1990, 5.

85. For a report on the meeting see *Adevărul*, January 30, 1990, 1, 3; for the later slogan see Shafir (February 15, 1991), 35. The sentiments of this meeting were graphically and crudely shown in a front-page cartoon in *Adevărul* of January 28, 1990. The cartoon depicted a blindfolded "ordinary" citizen, surrounded by caricatures of the other parties (the NLP is represented in crown and ermine, the ecologists as innocent babies, and the NPP as

As the NSF redefined its constituency from the general to the particular, there was also an important ideological shift as, in place of "consensus," there appeared a new keyword, "unity." The semantic difference between the two might appear slight but their bases were entirely different. Consensus was essentially voluntary and inclusive in concept, while unity was more coercive and exclusive. The Front still claimed to be the embodiment of the revolution and therefore the voice of the people, but the people from being the whole population who rose against Ceauşescu were now subtly redefined to more selective bounds. The theme was fully enunciated by Iliescu in the passionate speech he made to Front supporters gathered in Piaţa Victoriei on January 29. "The Front has gained the trust of the people through everything it has proposed to do in order to promote a true democracy, the people's democracy! The Front holds nothing more sacred than serving the interests of the Romanian people! . . . Our force lies only in people and the *unity* of the people around the Front is the guarantee of our victory!"[86] The people had become those who unified around the Front, leaving those who chose to escape its embrace beyond the political pale, and ominously the NSF leader warned that "anybody who detaches himself from the people will represent nothing in this country."[87] The return to a more nationalist rhetoric inherent in "unity" also had the effect of further alienating the Hungarian community, heightening the sense of unease already evident in Transylvania, and beginning a process that would eventually see the Hungarians desert the NSF en masse and solidly back Radu Câmpeanu for the presidency in the coming elections.[88]

The reversion to the language of Ceauşescu also seems to have heralded the return of elements of the old protochronist school, with a prominent front page editorial in *Adevărul* presenting the NSF and the revolution itself in terms of Romanian exclusivity.[89] Starting from the premise that the revolution was a unique event unmatched in world history, the article argued that it derived its singularity from the fact that it embodied the unique historical experience of the Romanian people. Then, molding this idea to the familiar theme that the NSF was the embodiment of the revolution, it declared that the Front had become the "model of our life," a creation from "our" life embodying "our" own expe-

---

old peasants and grasping capitalists), desperately searching for the isolated and gagged figure of the Front (dressed in the suit of a technocrat).

86. BBC EE/0676, B/5–6:5, January 31, 1990 (emphasis added).

87. Ibid.

88. Câmpeanu polled 76.58 percent in Hungarian-dominated Harghita against 19.56 percent to Iliescu, and 65.69 percent in neighboring Covasna, where Iliescu managed a more respectable 32.12 percent. These were the only two counties where Câmpeanu secured a higher proportion of the votes than Iliescu.

89. *Adevărul,* January 25, 1990, 1.

rience. According to the editorial this made it impossible for the Romanian revolution to follow any model; it had to take its own exclusive, national path into the future. Reform socialism had been wedded with the nationalist language of the protochronists to produce a creed with an important political subtext, both as regards the past and the future. The revolution was unique and only a novel solution would heal Romania's ills. This effectively ruled out as illegitimate the programs of those parties that would resurrect old forms of government, and these were principally the chief opponents of the NSF, the traditional parties.

With its acceptance of a competitive political arena and the creation of the PCNU, the NSF seems to have abandoned all attempts to preserve its own party unity. Contemporary reports often divide the CNSF into reform and anti-reform wings and such a division would appear to have some basis, although the composition of these factions seems to have varied with viewpoint. For instance, in the Western press Mazilu and Lupoi were often painted as being standard bearers of reform, championing the proposed electoral law and the legislation on passports, which was seen as something of a benchmark by which to judge the intentions of the new regime.[90] Yet this law appears to have been largely drafted by Adrian Severin, who remained a prominent member of the Front long after Mazilu and Lupoi had departed.[91] There were splits within the Front, but whether ideological considerations or other criteria were to the fore remains unknown. What is certain is that now, with the need to forge tighter party discipline before the election campaign, two of the four political figures who publicly fronted the revolution, Brucan and Mazilu, disappeared from the limelight, leaving Iliescu supported by the young and inexperienced Roman as unchallenged leader.

As previously noted, Mazilu's public standing had already been badly eroded by the campaign in *România Liberă* and, at the time of his departure, some Western journalists even argued that his continued presence had become such a liability to the Front that he was purged to restore the regime's increasingly battered image. The roots of the rift were probably deeper, and in his resignation communiqué Mazilu tried to present himself as the victim of communist hard-liners, caustically commenting, "It is with profound pain and deep bitterness that I have noticed [that] Stalinist methods . . . based on Securitate files are still in use."[92] The motivations behind Brucan's decision to resign from the Executive Bureau of the NSF on February 4, 1990, and withdraw from politics have long been shrouded in mystery, although, perhaps significantly, he too was being

90. *Financial Times,* January 8, 1990, 2.
91. The law guaranteed a ten-year passport within twenty days of application; *Financial Times,* January 10, 1990, 2; BBC EE/0658, B/13:23, January 10, 1990.
92. *Financial Times,* January 27, 1990, 3.

openly castigated in the pages of *România Liberă* at this time.[93] Over the years, he has suggested a number of reasons for his decision, ranging from a wish to return to more academic pursuits to altruistic desires to let the revolution be fronted by more youthful figures. Neither of these rings particularly true, and, at the time, Brucan hinted at a greater sense of resentment when he said he was withdrawing because "The honest people stay at home . . . leaving the political arena to be dominated by personal ambitions, careerism and political opportunism."[94] Brucan's harsh words may well relate to his ongoing public polemic with Octavian Paler, but he does also seem to have had his differences with other members of the regime and, if his departure was not because of policy differences, it may be because his authoritarian and ill-disciplined views were seen as an electoral liability.

Mazilu and Brucan were not the only prominent figures to leave the NSF stage at this time. The resignation of Mihai Lupoi on February 6 from his post of minister of tourism, allegedly because of the "dictatorial practices" of Roman, received some attention in the Western press, but he appears to have only been thrust into the limelight by the revolution and his departure made little long-term impact on the Romanian political scene.[95] Considerably more significant was the resignation from the CNSF of Doina Cornea, the most widely known Romanian dissident under communism. From early in the month she had been voicing sharp criticisms of the prominent position taken by former communists within the Front, and the declaration at the time of her eventual departure, in which she spoke of a revolution betrayed, seriously dented the moral authority of the new regime both on the international stage and inside Romania. Detailed reports of her departure were carried in most leading Western newspapers and she also gave a series of interviews to *România Liberă*.[96] Following the bloody clashes of January 29, Cornea was joined by a second dissenting voice, the poet Ana Blandiana. On her resignation from

93. The paper had reprinted a controversial interview Brucan gave to the London-based *Independent*, and two hostile articles appeared in *România Liberă*, January 26, 1990, 1, 2, and ibid., January 31, 1990, 1, 2; for Brucan's response see ibid., January 27, 1990, 1, 2.

94. *Independent*, February 5, 1990, 8; BBC EE/0681, B/11:51, February 6, 1990. It may be significant that the Front's election program was presented two days after Brucan announced his intention to withdraw from politics and it seems he did not play a great role in drawing up this document.

95. Roman had apparently ordered the Ministry of Tourism to hand twenty-one hotels back to the army and a restaurant to the Academy of Sciences. For one interpretation of the circumstances surrounding Lupoi's resignation see Sturdza (April 13, 1990), 31. The official degree removing him from office was issued on January 7.

96. BBC EE/0672, B/5:5, January 26, 1990. From the beginning of the month Cornea had been voicing concerns that the revolution was "in danger" and that the leadership included too many former communists; see *Washington Post*, January 10, 1990, A15; also *Independent*, January 15, 1990, 12. In an interview in *Libération* on January 24, 1990 Cornea was to state that the revolution was "in the process of being betrayed"; cited in Devlin (February 9, 1990), 28.

the CNSF she told *Româniă Liberă,* "My presence in the Council has become incompatible for a writer who has always been against the aggressiveness, hate and intolerance generated by power struggle."[97] The demonstrations of late January and the resignations of Cornea and Blandiana from the CNSF brought a sharp change in international perceptions of the Front. Under heavy criticism from a number of countries, including the United States, the leaders of the NSF were transformed from dashing heroes of the revolution into malevolent relics of the communist past. The revolutionary honeymoon with the outside world was over and the climb back to international political respectability for the Front and Romania was to be both protracted and painful.

Local Councils of the National Salvation Front

So far this chapter has concentrated on developments in Bucharest, but equally fierce political battles were also being fought elsewhere in the country. By and large the events at a local level seem to have mirrored the national picture, although in places there were significant variations. In general, the revolution seems to have been more marked in certain geographical regions—principally in Transylvania and the Banat—and in the larger cities and towns. Here, the politicization engendered by the violence of December spilled over into a bitter political struggle that persisted long after the shooting had ceased. As in the capital, during January there was a tendency for these conflicts to become slowly subsumed under a narrower contest that matched the NSF against the traditional parties. By the end of the month, from cities as distant as Bacău there came reports of authorized demonstrations organized by the three traditional parties being broken up by busloads of workers from local factories who were shouting slogans in favor of the NSF and against the opposition.[98]

At the heart of these confrontations were the local Front councils. Following the departure of Ceaușescu, in many of Romania's urban centers groups of excited protesters had stormed and occupied local municipal and county council offices—26 percent of the respondents in a later opinion poll reported such actions taking place within their neighborhoods.[99] In the face of this influx many office holders of the previous regime seem to have fled their posts, leaving a vacuum of power that some protesters tried to fill by establishing their own local administrative councils. With their members chosen from those who had been at the van of the demonstrations these councils can justifiably be said to have been a genuine expression of the revolutionary enthusiasm of the crowd. However, despite

97. *Financial Times,* February 1, 1990, 2.
98. *Românià Liberă,* January 31, 1990, 5.
99. Câmpeanu (1993), 187.

the independent basis of their creation, on the lead given by the television, within hours of their formation, most seem to have adopted the name National Salvation Front, implying that they were willing to subordinate themselves to the new central authorities.

Inside a week of the overthrow of Ceaușescu, at the same time as it established its national organization, the central NSF laid down a framework for local government.[100] As at the national level, the overwhelming impulse of the new regime was to broadly replicate the previous order, and the articles establishing local administrations even prescribed continuity when they stated, "The apparatus of the executive committees and bureaus of the former people's councils, the apparatus of the local specialised bodies of state administration and the apparatus of local social and cultural institutions will carry on their activity in their current structure."[101] The new councils were to have variable memberships, depending on the size of the community served, with county and Bucharest municipality councils having thirty-five to fifty-one members, municipal councils fifteen to twenty-seven, town and Bucharest sector councils eleven to twenty-one, and communal councils between nine and fifteen. For everyday business each council was to elect an executive bureau consisting of a chairman, two deputy chairmen, a secretary, and three to five members. All decisions were to be made by a simple majority, and on paper the councils were to have broad areas of responsibility, including medical care, education, cultural and administrative activities, defense of civic rights, and maintenance of public order.[102]

The new law stressed continuity, but in many cases at the county level and in the larger urban centers the sheer force of the revolution made this impossible. In the absence of any detailed statistics, some gauge of the extent of the change of personnel at this time comes from a 1992 poll that asked respondents whether three prominent officials from the old regime still held posts in their locality (Table 6.1).[103] While bearing in mind the survey reflects perceptions rather than reality, the picture presented is one of considerable change, with the only group showing any resilience being those who held the less politically sensitive post of mayor, with 14 percent of respondents saying that they were still in office against 59 percent who thought they had departed. Most higher local party secretaries and *securitate* chiefs do appear to have disappeared from the scene, with only 6 percent of the respondents thinking that the former were still in office as against 50 percent who thought they had departed, although in all cases the large number of "don't knows"—43 percent in the case of the head of the local *securitate*—suggests a high degree of ignorance.

100. *Adevărul*, December 29, 1989, 1.
101. BBC, EE/0650, B/7, December 30, 1989.
102. *Adevărul*, December 29, 1989, 1.
103. Câmpeanu (1993), 187.

Table 6.1. Local officials still holding power after the revolution

Are local officials still in power after the revolution?	Yes	No	Don't know
Local Party secretary	6%	50%	35%
Mayor	14	59	26
Head of local *securitate*	5	45	43

Source: Câmpeanu (1993), 187.
Note: No explanation given for figures failing to amount to 100 percent.

Many of the local NSF councils had been formed on a completely ad hoc basis and this was later underlined by Iliescu, when he stated that they had been created "spontaneously" and that there had been "a lot of improvisation in the way they were set up."[104] Drawing on the popular legitimacy of the revolution, the right to lead the new local regime was frequently claimed by those who had first entered municipal and county council buildings, but these "new men" were often largely unknown, even within their own native localities. Soon rumors were rife about murky pasts and doubtful presents. The result was that the legitimacy of many of the new leaders came under sustained challenge from both above and below, as political forces of all hues struggled for control of the new councils. On one side were the central authorities who sought to remove the more uncontrollable elements. Iliescu in a speech stressed the new leaders must have "moral authority" and the need "to avoid the infiltration of accidental elements such as upstarts, careerists and demagogues, who in moments of confusion and haste try to sneak into leading positions."[105] Within days the state controlled media were reflecting these strictures in a series of articles challenging selected local council members over their lack of competence or moral probity. The head of the Craiova council was said to be "locally renowned for his immorality" and a member of the council in Focşani was forced to resign, after having apparently played a prominent role in the revolution in that town, because he was said to have been a *securitate* informer.[106] In Sector 6 of Bucharest the head of the council was alleged to be nothing more than a common criminal with ten convictions to his name, who had secured his position only through his early entry into the building and the skillful cultivation of the persona of

104. BBC, EE/0655, 8:35ii, January 6, 1990. The first NSF council in Sibiu of thirty members was headed by a writer and musicologist and included professors, journalists, students, an economist, a lawyer, seven engineers, seven workers, an orthodox priest, and two army officers, including the head of the Sibiu garrison. Nicolaescu (1999), 331.

105. BBC, EE/0657, B/5:8, January 9, 1990.

106. For Craiova see *România Liberă*, January 12, 1990, 5; for Focşani see *New York Times*, January 2, 1990, A1, A12; *The Times*, January 3, 1990, 6, and for similar accusations from Târgovişte see *Adevărul*, January 12, 1990, 2.

a "hero of the revolution."[107] This pressure from above for change, in many instances, was more than matched by the activities of the crowd on the streets, among whom other concerns usually predominated, with doubts centering on lurking fears that many of the new local leaders had deeply compromised pasts within the RCP and often links with the *securitate*.[108] The overall result of this pressure from above and below was that, although nearly everywhere the new NSF councils were readily accepted as being legitimate, their membership was often not; and over the coming month a series of often bitter political contests were to give them a highly fluid composition, as many were reshuffled, frequently several times. Sometimes the struggle for power remained within the new body, as in the case of Sector 6 in Bucharest, where the council seems to have submitted itself to new internal "elections" in order to secure a more "acceptable" composition, but elsewhere the process all too readily boiled over into open demonstrations, public unrest, and occasionally wider consultative exercises, as occurred in both Brașov and Timișoara.[109] Members of the new leadership were often forced to make repeated visits to county towns to try and instill order with Mazilu being called to Târgoviște twice in one day to try to sort things out.[110] As late as the middle of January, the situation still seems to have been chaotic, with Roman admitting in an interview that no firm links had yet been established between the government and the local NSF councils, because the latter were in a state of constant flux.[111]

The storming of state institutions and the establishment of popular councils did not just occur at the higher levels. In many smaller towns and commune centers, where the local institutions of state power, such as peoples' councils, collective farms, and militia stations, were located, the fall of Ceaușescu also seems to have been marked by the departure of local officials and an explosion of popular political activity. Following procedures that often conformed to older traditions of communal democracy, in many villages ad hoc assemblies gathered to discuss and vote on decollectivization and press for government action on local issues, such as the breaking up of multi-village communes established during the communist era in favor of more organic units. In some places these assem-

107. *Adevărul*, January 10, 1990, 2.

108. In Baia Mare it was reported by Cornea that, when the chief figures of the old regime tried to reform themselves as the local council of the NSF, they had been opposed by local miners. A sympathetic lawyer had been encouraged to read out a list of the proposed membership of the council from the balcony of the county council building, asking the assembled crowd to pass judgment on each name. Of the forty-five names on the list only two were said to have withstood this test of popular democracy, with the other places being filled by representatives of "the people." *Independent*, January 15, 1990, 12.

109. Siani-Davies (1995), 296–303.

110. *Adevărul*, January 12, 1990, 2.

111. Ibid., January 17, 1990, 1, 3.

blies elected Front councils to run the local administration but elsewhere the transfer of power was to be more chaotic. In his study of the revolution in Hârseni commune, near Făgăraş, David Kideckel relates how a factory engineer assumed the mantle of leader of the local Front on apparently no authority other than his own. The incumbent mayor was dismissed from his post with his place eventually being filled after a few days of confusion by the former deputy mayor. The new Front leader initially won some support in the village but, when he failed to keep his early extravagant promises, he was largely ignored and lapsed back into obscurity once the local PCNU was established in early February 1990.[112] The case of Hârseni may not altogether be typical, as in other instances the revolution seems to have brought less change with self-appointed local Front leaderships (who may or may not have included representatives from the old regime) meeting secretly to reinstate previous officer holders, as Robert Fox apparently found in Sânmihaiu Român just outside Timişoara.[113] Indeed, with the passing of the first months of the revolution this increasingly became the pattern, as the early enthusiasm dissipated, to be replaced by disillusion with the national political scene, as the NSF moved to reestablish order in the local councils, arranging for the "reelection" of new leaders when necessary.

The lack of any clear channel of authority between the national CNSF and county councils appears to have been fully replicated in relations between these intermediate bodies and the lower strata of local administration, which also remained ill-defined throughout this period. The main task of the county NSF councils was the establishment of local administrations throughout the area under their jurisdiction and, especially, the replacement of mayors and deputy mayors. All candidates for these posts were supposed to be nominated by the local NSF council with names being passed to the center for approval, but the chief problem appears to have been that the new county councils frequently had no idea who might be suitable to occupy these posts. Thus, while candidates were supposedly selected on the basis of professionalism, youth, and not having a deeply compromised past, all too often being acquainted with those who had come to power was the main determinant. While this does not necessarily mean that they were unsuitable for the job, selection by such a criterion did leave the new office holders open to challenge and heightened the unrest during this period.

Eventually, as was the case at the national level, with the creation of local Provisional Councils of National Unity and the absorption of representatives from the other political parties, the county councils appear to have become more stable. The best available indication of the final form

112. Kideckel (1993), 215.
113. *Daily Telegraph,* December 28, 1989, 9.

taken by these councils comes from a study of the details of the incumbent presidents at the time of the formation of the county Provisional Councils of National Unity. As might be expected, since they were created under the fifty-fifty rule, after their formation the NSF continued to dominate, but what is particularly striking is the similarities in profile of many of the office holders.[114] First, nearly all in political terms appear to have been previously unknown, with the only two exceptions being the writer Mircea Tomus, who came to head the council in Sibiu, and Barbu Popescu, president of Tulcea council. The latter had enjoyed a prominent career in the RCP during which, among other posts, he had been deputy minister of agriculture, a full member of the Central Committee and, significantly, also first secretary of Tulcea county's RCP committee and chairman of the county's peoples' council. Second, most of them were relatively youthful, with eleven out of the fourteen whose age is known being between thirty-four and forty-one when they took office. All these subsequently enjoyed national political careers underlining the generational shift at the heart of the revolution. Third, nearly all the presidents were members of the creative or technical intelligentsia (stretched to include military officers), with no fewer than fifteen describing themselves as engineers, while most of the remainder were university or polytechnic professors, actors, artists, writers, or lawyers, the most important of whom was to be the head of the Călăraşi council, Doru Ioan Tărăcilă, a later minister of the interior. Finally, the strong presence of the army is noticeable. More than 120 serving officers and NCOs sat on Front councils, with members of the military at one time or another heading the county councils in Braşov, Buzău, Călăraşi, Dâmboviţa, Ialomiţa, Maramureş, Mureş, Neamţ, Prahova, Sălaj, Satu Mare, Timiş, and Vâlcea and serving as vice presidents in Botoşani, Constanţa, Neamţ, Teleorman, and Vaslui.[115] However, it seems that this temporary prominence was mostly a consequence of the instability brought about by the revolution and did not prefigure any general move by the army into the corridors of power, although it is striking that all but one of those army officers who came to head the county Provisional Councils of National Unity subsequently secured places in the new parliament.

114. For the domination of the Front within the local Provisional Councils of National Unity see Kideckel (1992), 74.
115. Codrescu et al. (1998), 460–61.

CHAPTER SEVEN

The Myths and Realities of Revolution

In the year 1821, on the 18th day of January, it came to pass that Prince Alexander Soutzos, who was the ruler here in this Romanian land, died; and suddenly we saw a rebellion break out; but, in an extremely strange way, and very dissimilar, I might say, to other rebellions that we see in history.

Revolutions resting on mass mobilization and state breakdown tend to encompass both the swirl of battle and the chaos of defeat. This gives them an intensity and complexity that eludes easy analysis, and the Romanian revolution, as this book has shown, is no exception to this rule. Thus, rather than trying to summarize the narrative within a few short pages, this conclusion will return instead to issues raised in the introduction, notably the name that should be given to the events of December 1989 and the popular narratives that have been constructed about them. As noted at the beginning of the book, aside from being called a "revolution," the events of December 1989 have also often been termed a "coup d'état" and sometimes even a "popular uprising."[1] So, before finishing, it

I am indebted to Alex Drace-Francis for this opening quotation, which comes from an 1823 text entitled *Zilot Romanul. Jalnica cintare a lui Zilot, intru care sa cuprind revulutiia romanilor supt Tudor sluger Vladimirescu, i zuvera, supt Alecu beizadea Ipsilanti, i stapinirea turceasca, supt Kehaia Bey, si oaresice din domniia romaneasca, intoarsa iar la romani de la grecii fanarioti, supt domnul Grigorie Ghica voevod, alcatuita de un patriot romani si afierosita fratilor sai patrioti, spre stiinta si spre povatuire, la anul de la Hristos 1823.*

1. Treated here as being synonymous with "revolt," "rebellion," and "insurrection." At this point it might be appropriate to add a few words about why this book avoids measuring the events of December 1989 against any of the many available definitions of revolution. The reasons for this are more fully explored in Siani-Davies (1996) but broadly they fall into two categories. First, it is difficult to justify the privileging of any one definition above the others. Second, all definitions of revolution, by their very nature, are tautologies drawn from the events they seek to describe. In the past the tendency was to base such definitions upon the so-called great revolutions but this led them to be unduly restrictive. A more recent trend toward inclusion, while allowing more events to join the select club of revolutions, has been accompanied by a shift towards variability that at times has left some definitions looking like multiple choice questions, as, for instance, Goodwin (1994), 577, 597 n. 3. Each rev-

would seem worthwhile to make some comparisons between the events in Romania and frequently held meanings of these terms. The introduction also intimated that this process of name formation could only be fully understood if it is placed within the appropriate domestic cultural context, and this conclusion will not only expand on this idea but will also suggest that in a complex interaction the view of the outside world also played a role.

Revolution, Coup d'État, or Popular Uprising?

Coups d'état are generally seen as simpler affairs than revolutions. They involve a sudden attack on a government and are usually restricted in their objectives.[2] Lacking connotations of mass mobilization, they often pass with minimal bloodshed to be followed by a relatively quick return to what is perceived as normality, with only a limited amount of change. Various types of coup may be distinguished, but the one usually said to have occurred in Romania is a palace coup.[3] In this an all powerful leader is directly replaced by one or more conspirators drawn from the ranks of the ruling regime. Other than death, this was the traditional form of leadership change in East European communist states. During 1989, Erich Honecker in East Germany, Todor Zhivkov in Bulgaria, and Miloš Jakeš in Czechoslovakia all fell victim to palace coups. Can the same be said of Ceaușescu? If the other members of the RCP leadership had taken the opportunity to remove the Romanian leader prior to December 22, it would have been fitting to speak of such a coup, but his departure from the central committee building on that day, in front of a vengeful crowd, and subsequent flight to Târgoviște seems to accord more with the imagery of revolution than coup d'état. Likewise, the mass mobilization, widespread violence, spontaneous creation of local revolutionary councils, breakdown of the revolutionary coalition, and subsequent fierce struggle between the revolutionary contenders on the streets of Romania's cities all would seem to belong to the repertoire of revolution rather than coup d'état. Moreover, even if Ceaușescu had fallen in a coup, this need not have prevented the events in Romania bearing the name revolution. The military coup that launched the Portuguese revolution in April 1974 did not place in question the revolutionary experience of that country, and the same may also be said about the various coups that removed the other East European leaders in 1989. It seems that within a revolution a coup can just be the "surface manifestation of much deeper currents of

---

olution is historically and culturally specific and rather than tying itself to any one definition this study has instead preferred to rely on broad descriptors which encompass popular expectations of such events.

2. Krejčí (1994), 15.
3. Hagopian (1974), 3–9.

change."[4] The events of December 1989 do not readily fit the image of coup d'état; even if they did this would not necessarily nullify the idea of revolution. Many questions still remain unresolved about Ceauşescu's overthrow, but those who charge that it was by coup seem to have in mind not so much the mechanics of the Romanian leader's removal but rather the nature of the political succession after his departure.

Popular uprisings too can be seen as relatively simple affairs that do not lead to any major transfer of state power. However, this notion all too easily relegates them to being little more than revolutions that fail. It may, therefore, be better to consider them as being distinct entities in their own right, with three possible indicators distinguishing revolutions from popular uprisings being (a) that they rapidly move from the rectification of grievances, which are the prime aim of uprisings, to a wide scale redistribution of political and economic power, leading to major shifts in social structure; (b) that normally discernible at all times within a revolution is an overall sense of purpose, which can take the form of a steady ideological commitment, but is more likely to lie within a broader future orientated trajectory. This enables a revolution, once power is gained, to rapidly pass beyond the largely destructive urges associated with the identification of scapegoats (which characterizes uprisings) and, instead, move to exit state breakdown (which in itself appears to belong to revolutions rather than uprisings) through a considered political strategy; (c) that in order to effect these aims a revolution is more likely to draw some of its leaders from within the ranks of the established elite, while uprisings tend to be headed by "natural" but inexperienced leaders thrown up by the crowd.[5]

Taking the last of these points first, the Party background of the NSF leadership would suggest that the events in Romania were more characteristic of a revolution than an uprising, but as already noted the same fact can also be used to argue that they were a coup. Common to both palace coups and revolutions is the idea of an often violent transfer of power, although in the latter the expectation is that the resulting change of personnel will somehow be deeper and draw in figures from outside the previous ruling group.[6] This, however, does not mean that all figures from the ancien régime will be excluded, because after initial periods of radicalism, many revolutions do seem to close in some form of Thermidorian reaction.[7] Revolutions seldom bring as clean a break with the past as their protagonists would like to suggest or hope and, indeed, all questions relating to political succession are liable to be highly subjective and necessarily politically charged. Aside from the obvious problems of deciding

4. Ibid., 4.
5. Siani-Davies (1996), 459–61.
6. Tilly (1991), 4.
7. Tilly (1993), 14; Calvert (1990), 46; Krejčí (1994), 250–51.

the time frame of any comparison and the number and type of posts to be compared (direct equivalents not being easily established after the changes instituted by a revolution), the thorny question of what constituted the old regime also has to be tackled. In Romania, at its broadest this has been extended to encompass all former members of the RCP but, since this numbered nearly four million, it was judged to be an unacceptable measure by all but the most obdurate of anticommunists. An intermediary measure, more widely promoted by opponents of the NSF regime, was membership of the estimated 200,000-strong *nomenklatura*.[8] However, the bounds of this body were imprecise and, even if they could be ascertained, many within the new leadership would have argued that the concentration of power in the hands of Ceauşescu and his cronies made those who held sufficient power to influence in some way policy decisions the only useful measure. This limited the bounds of the old regime to members of the Central Committee and a few others within the upper echelons of the RCP, all of whom do seem to have been ousted from power during the revolution. Only Guşă was a member of both the first CNSF and the last RCP Central Committee. It seems possible to say that there was a degree of political succession in Romania in December 1989, and this was deeper than that usually associated with a palace coup, as the old communist bosses were replaced by a younger generation of technocrats. Nearly all of these were from the second and third echelons of the Party, but few had been able to wield as much influences as they wished during the later Ceauşescu years.

Still, the new leaders who actually took power were hardly the fresh faces that were seen elsewhere in Eastern Europe. Romania had no equivalent of Václav Havel or Lech Walesa, and at the time this often led to invidious comparisons with other former communist states. Instead, the reins of power were taken by a group of apparatchiks, many of whom had previously held high political office. By the time of the revolution, however, Iliescu, Brucan, Bârlădeanu, Marţian, Drăgănescu, and the others were far enough beyond the circle of power that they were able to take on something of the mantle of dissidents, since under the exclusionary Ceauşescu regime even reform socialism was outside the bounds of the accepted political discourse. From their unique insider–outsider position the new leaders were able to both place sufficient distance between themselves and the previous regime to permit their acceptance as legitimate political successors by most Romanians during the revolution, and to use their old roots within the Party to exert their authority over the remnants of the RCP regime once they took power. Many state employees at all lev-

8. Gafton (August 14, 1987). This figure applies to the whole leadership, including middle-level and local officials and suggests the *nomenklatura* compromised some 6 percent of the Party. If the count is restricted to high central officials, what Gafton terms the "RCP Central Committee *nomenklatura*," the figure shrinks to just 10,700.

els saw in the Front a promise of stability and continuity, and the endless telegrams of support for the new leaders that were read out on the television and radio during the first days after Ceaușescu's overthrow helped cement the impression that these sentiments were shared by the whole country.[9]

Turning to the second possible distinction, revolutions are often presented as having an overall sense of purpose that is lacking in uprisings. Usually, this purposefulness is presented as a vision of the future that remains constant from the ideological stirrings of the first revolutionaries through to the "successful" outcome. Brucan later subtitled his autobiography "Memoirs of the Romanian Journey from Capitalism to Socialism and Back," but it is difficult to find much evidence to suggest that many of the new leaders at the time of the revolution saw the future of Romania as a free-market democracy.[10] Instead, the idea of return seems at first to have been the dominant motif. Reflecting the main cleavage in the anti-Ceaușescu coalition, this centered on two contrasting "golden age" myths. One, which belonged to the traditional parties, might be termed restorative, since it sought to expunge the trauma of communism by returning to the ideals of a precommunist Eden.[11] The other, identified with the NSF, was more rectifying, since, by focusing on the successes of the late 1960s and early 1970s, it portrayed the revolution as essentially a corrective to Ceaușescu's 1980s neo-Stalinist model, thereby opening up the possibility of a democratic socialist middle way. Both of these "golden age" myths were based on utopian and rather rose-tinted visions of the past. During the interwar years, levels of democracy in Romania had at best been debatable, with capitalism heavily circumscribed by paternalism, while the communism of the 1960s was founded on the same structural deficiencies that were eventually to bring systemic collapse in 1989. Instead of being prescriptions for the future, in the months after the revolution, these myths of return served more as markers for shaping political identity. As time progressed and their emptiness become more apparent, they faded, with both positions tending to wither toward a pragmatic neo-liberalism.

Does the absence of a coherent, clearly presented ideological path from the outset mean that the events should not be considered a revolution? The idea that revolutions follow such a pattern is itself a Jacobin myth, and interpretations that cast the revolution solely in terms of the inevitable victory of the triumphant ideology over its vanquished opponents are usually teleological metanarratives.[12] Revolutions in reality are

9. Neacșu (c1999).
10. Brucan (1993).
11. Tismaneanu (1993), 314, has stressed the dominance of restorative motifs within the discourse of the opposition. See also Habermas (1990), 4.
12. Doyle (1991), 106.

far more messy affairs, yet within the process it is often possible to trace a consistent broader general trajectory.[13] In Romania traces of such a trajectory based on a globalist viewpoint could be found within both the embryonic elite revolutionary coalition and the broader popular movement, although it was little articulated before the revolution, due to the difficulties of communication within a coercive regime. The image of Ceaușescu as scapegoat was also such a dominant mobilizing issue that it allowed little space for other views, as groups harboring very different grievances, such as workers, cultural intellectuals, and ethnic Hungarians, buried the hatchet in an inverted cult of personality. When it did emerge, the globalist trajectory encompassed a program of moderate change based on competence, rationality, and moral renewal. Autarky and isolation were rejected in favor of an opening to the outside world and the hesitant embrace of elements of the European political mainstream, including a commitment to human rights and ideals such as the separation of powers within the state and the free and open exercise of a universal franchise. This globalist trajectory often articulated as a "return to Europe" has remained dominant in post-1989 Romania. Initially, however, it was shaped not through a positive attachment to these ideals but in negative reference to the Ceaușescu regime, to which it was seen as a corrective. This made it open and imprecise, providing sufficient political space for a number of ideological strands to initially cohabit, ranging from the perestroika-influenced Consensus to free-market liberalism.

In truth, as Tocqueville noted, revolutions often bring about far less change than revolutionaries claim and revolutionary intentions are rarely clearly discerned during the early stages of the process.[14] At this time, moving to the third of the differences between revolution and uprisings outlined above, it is the rectification of existing grievances rather than a widespread redistribution of power that is usually first on the agenda of most of the revolutionaries.[15] This was the case in Romania, where the NSF moved quickly to rescind the most draconian and disliked of Ceaușescu's legislation, expel the most compromised members of the previous leadership from office, and stem corruptive practices by reintroducing notions of legality. Such were the extremes of the Ceaușescu state, however, that it was both expected by the population and accepted by the incoming leaders that rectification would necessarily also require some degree of political and economic redistribution. The problem was that the parameters of this process were far from agreed, and initially within the bounds of Consensus the NSF seems to have seen it as being limited. Within the agricultural sector some degree of land reform was envisaged, although the extent re-

13. Krejčí (1994), 12.
14. Halliday (1991), 131.
15. Goldstone (1991), 45.

mained unclear, and, it seems likely, the Front's hand was pushed by private seizures. In industry, it was to be limited to the extremities of the service sector that were to be freed from central control. Any wider reform involving the moribund heavy industrial sector would have created widespread unemployment, which would have cut across rectifying promises and alienated both the bureaucracy and the workers. This initial stance of the Front was to prove untenable, and slowly it was pushed to a wider redistribution of economic resources, partly because of the depth of the economic crisis but also because of political pressures.

It may be that social polarization and the creation of two confrontational blocs is an inevitable consequence of the radical/conservative dichotomy that lies at the heart of all revolutions.[16] In Romania, the anti-Ceauşescu coalition that arose during the events, due to its breadth and the largely spontaneous nature of its birth, was a loose and uncoordinated body. It contained a welter of potential lines of fracture along such axes as elite or mass movement, passive or active revolutionaries, radical or moderate reformers, former members of the RCP or those who had steadfastly remained outside the Party. It was, therefore, not surprising that the stresses and strains imparted by the revolution were soon sufficient to pull the coalition apart. In Romania the honeymoon period, to use Crane Brinton's term, when euphoria and hope are dominant, was to prove conspicuously short-lived. Instead, against a backdrop of socioeconomic collapse, Romania slipped into a protracted period of political turmoil.

When they took control, the leaders of the NSF seem to have wanted to restrict power to a relatively narrow ruling coalition. The revolution, however, had empowered broad swaths of the population and, throughout January 1990 and beyond, as the Front struggled to restore order, it was forced to meet challenges from both "left" and "right." From the "left" the threat came from the scores of ad hoc NSF councils and free trade unions that had sprung up in the wake of the events. A disparate and unruly bunch, in the weeks after the revolution, they were often convulsed by paralyzing strife. Nonetheless, especially in the large cities, they seem to have contained the germ of a more radical revolution with, for instance, factory workers in some enterprises usurping control over managerial appointments. During January, the Front, in alliance with the managerial and increasingly the state bureaucracy, moved to stamp its authority on the situation and roll back the power taken by this revolution of the "left." By the end of that month, the NSF enterprise councils had disappeared, traditional hierarchies of control had been re-established in the factories, and a series of "reelections" held to give many of the local administrative councils a more desirable composition.

16. Stone (1966), 165–66; Rosenberg and Koenker (1987), 296–326.

The challenge from the "right" was better organized and much more difficult for the NSF to weather, since it was spearheaded by the newly reemerged traditional parties, especially the NPP and the NLP. They boasted a credible alternative legitimacy and derived considerable support from many of the country's students, who also claimed authority from the revolution and possessed, perhaps, the most radical agenda of all the various groupings at this time. To deal with the challenge from the "right," the NSF adopted a dual policy mirroring the two often contradictory tendencies within its own makeup. A pluralist strand sought to institutionalize the revolutionary struggle within a "normal" political framework. At the beginning of February, this policy was to result in a more formal redistribution of power, when the creation of the PCNU provided the political space for representatives of the pre–Second World War elite and a handful of figures who had gained prominence in the revolution to join the current holders of power. The other Leninist strand within the Front was far less tolerant. It sought to dominate the revolution by mobilizing its supporters, especially the miners, to crush all opposition. This made for a rough and sometimes explosive political scene, which did Romania little credit, and placed the NSF in the worst possible political light, especially after the merciless attack by the miners to crush the occupation of Piaţa Universităţii in Bucharest in June 1990.

There are as many similarities between the events in Romania and other revolutions as there are differences with coups d'état and popular uprisings. The events in Romania were violent and involved widespread mass mobilization, which led to the storming of institutions of the old regime at both the national and local level, followed by the establishment of revolutionary councils. Some of these were more radical than others, but the collapse of the RCP and the installation of the CNSF did mark a major transfer of power and a degree of political succession, with higher members of the old regime either executed or removed from office. Into their place moved new leaders, a number of whom had previously occupied offices in the higher reaches of RCP. However, they had long been alienated from the center of power and they were joined in 1989 by a significant influx of figures from the second and third tiers of the old regime. This produced a pronounced power shift, as a previously excluded younger generation took office, and was part of a wider redistribution of political and economic power, which, in a hesitant and fitful manner, since 1989, has brought major changes to Romanian society, including the slow (re)construction of a middle class. This process took place within an overall globalist trajectory broadly based on the idea of a "return to Europe." No ideology was initially particularly dominant in this process, which was embraced more willingly by some political actors than others, but it did see the broad acceptance of West European models. In many ways, therefore, the events in Romania do resemble a revolution, and this is why the term has been employed throughout this book. However, descriptors in themselves cannot determine what the events should be called. Many still question whether December 1989 should be considered a revolution because of the political symbolism that lies within the event.

The Narratives of Revolution

One of the main arguments of this work has been that the Romanian revolution can only be understood in terms of popular narratives. The Ceauşescu regime had carefully cultivated the myth of the *securitate* as an omnipresent and omnipotent force in order to instill mass obedience. Among Romanians this myth fostered what Mariana Celac has termed an "intra-uterine" personality, "withdrawn, fearful and suspicious of the outside world."[17] The revolution released the country from this dark confinement, but in the process an equally nocuous myth was born: that the downfall of Ceauşescu was certain to be accompanied by a vicious backlash from the forces that had for so long underpinned the foundations of his regime. This myth of *securitate*-generated violence introduced a powerful new dynamic into the second phase of the revolution, causing much of the fighting and most of the deaths. The reality behind this myth remains opaque and, in all probability, will do so for the foreseeable future. However, by producing the fury and unbridled passion usually associated with revolution, it helped define the events in the eyes of the participants and a watching world. What, until then, had been the violent overthrow of a tyrannous leader was transformed into a "true" revolution replete with new images and symbols—from the tumult in the television station to the dead Ceauşescus. Out of a violence largely rooted in myth, there thus sprang a new reality, as the bravery of the young people on the streets fueled calls for a new world to be constructed fit for such heroes.

The first demonstrators stepped to the microphone at the radio station in Bucharest at 1:05 p.m. on December 22 and announced "Brother Romanians! We come from the center of our capital, from the center of the capital of Romania! Brother Romanians, it has been a peaceful revolution, a revolution of all of us, not only of the children, not only of the young, but ours, of our parents, of our grandparents, of all of us!"[18] From these words it is clear that for many of the protesters the events they were witnessing were a revolution, and throughout the rest of the day this word was regularly used both on radio and on television.[19] As with the term

---

17. Feffer (1992), 202. The chapter on Romania in Feffer is a good example of the strength of the *securitate* myth. Myths in this work are understood as established popular narratives that may or may not be true.
18. Sârcă (1998), 76; BBC EE/0649, B/1, December 29, 1989.
19. Sârcă (1998), 76, 82, 102, 107, 188, 200, 206, 207, 230, 286.

"terrorists," in choosing to call the events a "revolution" the protesters were again borrowing a word frequently used in the lexicon of socialism. Indeed, prior to December 1989, Brucan and some of the other leaders of the revolution had conceived of revolutionary change within the existing socialist framework by recasting the antagonistic social groupings of Marxist analysis. Working outside the familiar class model, Brucan placed on one side a technical and cultural elite that wanted reform, while on the other was a centralized bureaucracy that sought to preserve the status quo. The working class were ascribed an ambiguous role, being fundamentally conservative, but with the possibility that they could be won to the side of the "progressive" forces. Brucan's book is not specifically concerned with the situation in Romania but it can be argued that by conceiving of the overthrow of Ceaușescu in these terms, those conspiring against him, most of whom were members of the Party, were able to invest their plans with an intellectual legitimacy that aided this self-belief. It allowed them to justify their actions to their peers within the customary ideological framework, and opened up the possibility of an ideological continuum beyond the revolution, since the motive forces prompting the overthrow of the old regime could be seen as conforming to the inexorable passage of the wheel of history. Gorbachev referred to his proposed changes within the Soviet Union as a "revolution within a revolution," and it seems possible to see Consensus, its Romanian equivalent, also in such terms.[20]

Yet when they ascended to power, the new leaders of the NSF seem initially to have been a little reluctant to fully embrace the term "revolution." During their first broadcasts on television, Iliescu, Brucan, and the others assiduously avoided the word in favor of terms such as "change" and "transformation."[21] But as the RCP collapsed and firing began anew, amid rumors that the Front was losing its grasp on power, the new leaders had no alternative, either in practical or ideological terms, but to adopt the term of the street and place themselves at the head of the revolution as the voice of the people. In a radio broadcast on December 23 Iliescu referred to the existence of a "revolutionary moment," and the following morning Virgil Măgureanu, reading a communiqué of the National Salvation Front, was to triumphantly embrace the term when he declared, "The revolution has won!"[22] Whether or not they had done it willingly, the new leaders had recognized they were heading a revolution and, once this term was adopted, it at least raised the possibility of a clean break with the past and placed on the agenda the prospect of radical wholesale, rather than limited evolutionary, change.

20. Bruz (1991), 185.
21. Televiziunea Română (1990), 46.
22. BBC EE/0648, B/11, December 28, 1989; BBC EE/0648, B/13, December 28, 1989.

However, while the new leaders were embracing the revolution, some of the crowd on the streets were, beginning to have their doubts about the term. After years of Marxist-Leninist indoctrination, as elsewhere in Eastern Europe, many could only equate the word with the post–Second World War communist takeover.[23] To them the concept was fundamentally illegitimate, as it implied the carefully planned seizure of power by a small secretive Leninist vanguard grouping backed by a foreign power.[24] The NSF realized such a model no longer held any legitimacy, and so the new leaders repeatedly stressed the non-Leninist attributes of their own revolution. According to Iliescu, it was "a special, sudden and violent event which has eliminated the despotic power. . . . In the process of structuring the new element of power, the Front, which emerged spontaneously at the moment of the explosion and which represents the soul of this process, assumed the responsibility of taking over power."[25] By emphasizing that the revolution was a spontaneous mass movement, the NSF was attempting to equate the events of December 1989 with an older and (supposedly) more national pre-Leninist revolutionary tradition, which portrayed revolution as a legitimate political corrective against unjust rule. The Balkans are even said to have a special revolutionary tradition, although in the Romanian case this image of revolution largely arose through a mythologized view of the French revolution of 1789, refracted through the local liberal event of 1848.[26] The politically inspired reductionism, which resulted from this rejection of the Leninist model of revolution in favor of an idealized reading of the liberal variant, imposed an impossibly narrow definition of revolution onto the political debate in Romania. Not only did the revolution have to be an entirely spontaneous mass uprising untainted by previous plotting or the meddling of foreign powers, but also the new leadership had to derive from the crowd and be totally unconnected with the previous ruling group.

Meeting such criteria would be difficult for any revolution, but the myth propagated by the NSF that the leadership had been thrust upon it through popular acclaim, as it rose like a phoenix from the ashes of the Ceaușescu regime, was so porous as to leave it open to attack on several levels. Its opponents, however, did not just point to the inconsistencies in the Front's story; they drew upon them and the many unanswered questions surrounding the events to create their own myths of revolution. Following the lead given by the psephological studies of Pavel Câmpeanu, it is possible to suggest that these took two forms: the myths of "stolen" and "false" revolutions. The myth of the stolen revolution rested on the assumption that the revolution really had been a popular liberal movement

23. *Guardian*, August 13, 1992, 19.
24. For the Leninist interpretation of revolution see Kimmel (1990), 120.
25. BBC EE/0651, B/4, January 1, 1990.
26. Djordjevic and Fisher-Galați (1981); Tilly (1993), 89–100.

seeking the complete overthrow of the communist system. This had then been hijacked by a group of plotters, all former members of the old regime, who wanted to limit the amount of reform. The implication was that a neo-communist group had used conspiratorial communist means to seize power by what was effectively a coup d'état. The second, false revolution, myth held that the events should not even be graced by the term "revolution." Instead, they had been nothing more than a carefully staged political charade completely manipulated by foreign interests, principally the KGB working in conjunction with the Hungarian security forces. The new leaders were the puppets of these foreign forces, who had orchestrated the events from above, with the masses below following in dumb anger. In a December 1992 opinion poll Câmpeanu found that only 46 percent of his respondents believed that they had witnessed a true revolution in December 1989. Of the rest, 31 percent said it had been a stolen revolution, while 23 percent saw it as a false revolution.[27]

As in all opinion polls, it can be argued that the questions largely mirrored the agenda of the pollster, who to a certain extent was guilty of imposing his own typology on his respondents. Indeed, such a stark categorization of the events of December 1989 must be viewed largely as a heuristic exercise, since in reality the various interpretations have intermeshed into a complex pattern of beliefs giving each Romanian a discrete interpretation of the revolution. In particular, the scission into stolen and false revolutions is highly artificial, as over the years the two have become increasingly intertwined. At times this has produced strange alliances, with members of the anticommunist opposition making common cause with Ceauşescu nostalgics.[28] The fundamental divisions, however, remains valid, because of the underlying assumptions behind the various interpretations, which, according to Câmpeanu, initially conformed to different political agendas.

Having established his three basic categories founded on interpretations of the revolution, Câmpeanu then went on to ask each group their opinions about a number of often controversial post-Ceauşescu political events. The three groups generally responded to the questions in a similar fashion but in some cases, such as whether the NSF should have participated in the May 1990 elections and whether the police should have used violence to clear Piaţa Universităţii of protesters in June 1990, there were substantial differences.[29] These results led Câmpeanu to sug-

---

27. Câmpeanu (1993), 181. Verdery and Kligman (1992), 119, also note that virtually every Romanian seemed to interpret the events of December 1989 as a plot of one kind or another.

28. See the comments in Hall (1998), 264, about Angela Băcescu and Pavel Coruţ and note the declaration by the NPP senator Şerban Săndulescu alongside the preface by the Ceauşescu-era poet and publisher of journals such as *Totuşi Iubirea* and *Vremea*, Adrian Păunescu, in Bunea (2000). For Coruţ see Shafir (November 12, 1993).

29. Câmpeanu (1993) 178–204.

gest that the three broad political mentalities which developed in Romania after 1989 bore a direct relationship to perceptions of the revolution and, if his work is taken in conjunction with the statements made by various political parties during the revolution and since, especially at the time of the December anniversary, it is possible to suggest that a certain degree of alignment came to exist between interpretations of the revolution and political orientations. Broadly, as might be expected, the spontaneous revolution scenario seems to have found greatest favor with supporters of the NSF and its pro-Iliescu successors, the DNSF and the PSDR. The stolen revolution scenario echoed particularly strongly with many of the sansculottes on the street, and during 1990 it was to fuel another myth, that of the "second revolution," which held that the only solution to Romania's woes was the immediate catharsis of a new and "real" revolution.[30] It also came to be embraced by the traditional parties, especially elements within the NPP, and later the DCR. Finally, the false revolution scenario, the most Leninist and nationalist of interpretations, which emerged slightly later than the other two, proved to be particularly attractive to many linked to the old regime and those who followed more nationalist political groupings, such as the Greater Romania Party.

It was not just the Romanians who created myths of revolution; so did the outside world. The foreign media shaped their own narrative of the events, which was in turn based partly upon yet more myths. The Romanian revolution, due to the television coverage it received, to a certain extent, became a shared experience for the outside world. Some indication of the level of popular identification with Romania at this time comes from the extraordinary number of charities established in Great Britain after 1989 to channel aid to a country that previously had been on the periphery of public awareness. In the process, the West, and especially the French, who in 1989 were celebrating the two hundredth anniversary of their own revolution of liberty, equality, and fraternity, projected their own expectations of revolution onto Romania. Then, when these high expectations were not met and the country was sorely found wanting, as it was, especially after the brutal June 1990 excursion of the miners onto the streets of Bucharest, Romania was transformed from being a damsel in distress to the unacceptable face of postcommunist Eastern Europe.

The first image of the Romanian revolution that reached the outside world through the international media was a starkly black and white picture of horrifying slaughter, as unarmed revolutionaries laid down their lives battling against Ceaușescu and his evil henchmen. Then, almost as soon as foreign journalists entered the country and began sifting through a morass of often conflicting gossip, rumors, and conspiracy stories, this

30. Tismaneanu (1994), 417, 436; *Washington Post,* January 3 1990, A28.

image became blurred and confused. The dominant motifs of the revolution rapidly turned from heroism and selfless sacrifice to suspicion, deceit, and recrimination. This rather negative appreciation eventually rested on a number of strands, but initially it seems to have arisen from confusion over the death toll. At first it was reported that enormous numbers of people had died in the most horrific circumstances but, when it later became clear that the figure was a gross exaggeration and there had not been the widespread slaughter initially reported, it was somehow held as being symptomatic of greater duplicities.

Estimates of death tolls are notoriously difficult to produce, especially when news coverage is limited and a political advantage can be gained from maintaining confusion. The true death count after the crushing of the Tiananmen Square protests in 1989 remains unknown, and Iraqi casualties during the first Gulf War also seem to have been initially grossly exaggerated. Still, the numbers produced during the Romanian revolution were particularly farfetched, with Radio Budapest on December 23 reporting, on the basis of a "level-headed" source, a figure of 70,000–80,000 dead and 300,000 wounded.[31] The most commonly cited figure of 60,000 dead seems to have derived from the first incomplete details of Ceaușescu's trial. The full transcript, which was soon produced, was more ambiguous about the causes of the genocide, yet the idea persisted that large numbers had died during the revolution.[32]

The apparent near universal acceptance of the inflated casualty figure may in part be explained by a necessary reliance on unconfirmed reports. After the outbreak of disturbances in Timișoara, the borders of Romania were effectively sealed to western correspondents. The first did not arrive in the country until the evening of December 22, and after this date their movements were necessarily curtailed by the ferocity of the firing. Yet throughout the revolution a parallel, more or less accurate, casualty count does seem to have been available, as careful scrutiny of Western newspaper articles often reveals more realistic estimates buried within the text below the headlines. Prior to the overthrow of Ceaușescu, East European correspondents had been present in Romania and their reporting of the events was often reasonably accurate. Both Budapest and Warsaw radios reported a death toll of around twenty in Bucharest on the night of the December 22–23, with the Hungarians also noting thirty-two had died in Cluj.[33] After December 22, when Bernard Kouchner, the French junior minister for humanitarian aid, visited Romania, it was reported that he had been told on December 25 that 364 dead had been recorded in the hospitals of Bucharest with a further 850 receiving treatment, while na-

31. Sârcă (1998), 331.
32. Ibid., 335.
33. BBC EE/0647, i, December 23, 1989.

tionwide the estimate was of 746 dead and 1,800 wounded.[34] The day before a slightly higher estimate of 2,500 dead had already been made by European Community ambassadors, a figure also produced by the Hungarian army and the International Committee of the Red Cross.[35] In a news conference on January 3, 1990, Ionel, while giving no figures for deaths, said that 450 army personnel had been wounded, thus indicating that the death toll would be far smaller than first suspected, and at the end of that month, during the trial of Bobu, Dincă, Postelnicu, and Mănescu, a figure of 689 dead and 1,200 wounded was mentioned.[36]

Only in the case of Timișoara were the figures exaggerated from an early stage. From early on December 19, Radio Budapest and other sources had been suggesting that 300–400 had died in the city, but in the evening a figure of 2,000 was carried by German radio stations and the Yugoslav agency, Tanjug. The next day, new sources, including some Greek students leaving Romania, led to the death toll initially being lowered to 600–1,000, but by the evening the East German agency, ADN, was broadcasting a figure of 3,000–4,000. The Bulgarian BTA raised this figure to 4,700, which generally held for the period of the revolution, although at one point Tanjug raised it to 12,000.[37] In fact, prior to December 22, around 70 people died in Timișoara. The death toll reported by the news agencies was able to climb to such heights partly because of the uncertainty following the massacre of December 17. The bodies of some of the victims had been spirited away to Bucharest to be burnt and, when this was coupled with the fact that many others were unaccounted for, because after being arrested they had been unable to notify their families, speculation was able to run rife. But above all, the exaggerated death toll in Timișoara was accepted because it was believed that the Ceaușescu regime was capable of such brutality. One of the most famous photographs of the revolution appeared to testify to this, as it showed a dead baby lying on the corpse of its supposed mother amidst other bodies in a Timișoara graveyard.[38] At first, it was claimed that all the corpses were victims of the massacre of December 17, but after the revolution it was revealed that the women had in fact perished from alcohol poisoning on November 8, 1989, while the child, a young girl, had died on December 9. The bodies had been excavated during the first frenzied search for those who were missing after the massacre of December 17 and, presumably because it

34. *Sunday Times,* December 31, 1989, A13.
35. Ibid.; *Washington Post,* December 28, 1989, A1.
36. *The Times,* January 4, 1990, 8; Sturdza (April 13, 1990), 29.
37. Sârcă (1998), 308–33; BBC EE/0647, i, December 23, 1989.
38. An example can be found in the Greek newspaper *Eleftheros Typos,* December 27, 1989, 48, under the headline "Over 60,000 victims of the Communists." The caption under the picture reads, "Document of massacre: mass graves dug by communist dictator Ceaușescu's murderers in Timișoara, among the victims a pregnant women whose unborn baby did not have the chance to see the light of day."

made a striking picture, the baby had been placed on the woman and the image filmed by Novi Sad Television and MTV of Hungary.[39] Despite the fact that the corpse of the woman was badly decomposed and had obviously been in the ground for several weeks, the image was accepted and widely reproduced, presumably because such horrors were only to be expected from Romania.

It is therefore not just a matter of the exaggerated death toll, although it is salutary to recognize that if it had approached the levels suggested it would have equaled American losses during the whole of the Vietnam War, but rather how such wild stories about bloodthirsty assassins slaughtering thousands of victims in a cataclysmic Götterdämmerung came to be so readily accepted. Michel Castex, who was among the first of foreign journalists to cast doubt on the authenticity of the revolution, has suggested the blame can partly be laid on the presence of the international media en masse, most of whom lacked any experience of Romania. Under pressure for sensational stories they readily took refuge in an uncritical consensus and, in the absence of any hard evidence to the contrary, this created a uniformity of opinion that no news editor was willing to challenge.[40]

For most of these foreign journalists and their readers, Romania was a strange and distant country ruled by a savage and cruel dictator. An editorial in *The Times* of December 19, 1989, equated the Romanian leader with the Roman emperor Caligula, asserting that he ruled by the same dictum of "let them hate as long as they fear."[41] The primary cultural reference points for this bizarre land were Transylvania and the Dracula legend and, as Gail Kligman, drawing on Bram Stoker notes, "Transylvania is conceived of as a rather uncivilized boundary of European civilization.... Only in the chaos of 'one of the wildest and least known portions of Europe' could Dracula thrive. Only in the 'horseshoe' of the Carpathian Mountains where 'every known superstition in the world is gathered' could the objectivity of scientific rationalism be suspended."[42] It is a little ironic that a revolution which sought to reassert rationality in Romania created an apparent collective loss of the same faculty in the outside world. In a triumphal blending of myths, Ceaușescu, who had often equated himself with Vlad Țepeș, the fifteenth-century prince of Wallachia on whom the Dracula legend is said to be based, was transmogrified into Bram Stoker's famous character.[43] The *Guardian* correspon-

39. Suciu (1990), 249–50; Armanca (1997), 167–71; *Washington Post*, December 28, 1989, A1, A26; *The Times*, February 7, 1990, 8.
40. For Castex's views see *Independent*, April 23, 1991, 15. For similar conclusions from a different conflict see Pedelty (1995).
41. *The Times*, December 19, 1989, 15.
42. Kligman (1988), 2. Although Kligman attributes them to another source, her quotes are in fact from Stoker's famous novel; see Stoker (1993), 8.
43. *Independent*, January 6, 1990, 15. See also *The Times*, January 10, 1990, 6.

dent Michael Simmons wrote of Țepeș having a personal security force, the *sluji,* which bore an uncanny resemblance to the *securitate,* while in *Le Monde* Claude Fischler coined the term "draculization" when he spoke of Ceaușescu as a "paranoic dracula," "tyrant of the Balkans," and "proletarian despot."[44] But it was not just the outside world that embraced the image. Inside Romania an anti-Ceaușescu montage mounted on the side of a tank in Timișoara pictured the Romanian leader "the most renowned among vampires" with fangs and horns, and the point was also graphically made in a conversation Codrescu had with a family from Timișoara:[45]

> I could see that Ceaușescu had already become a creature of legend, a monster of the past, linked to other figures of dread in a history rich in them. Maria's husband, Dincu, said that Ceaușescu often needed blood transfusions. To this purpose he selected healthy young boys from villages, had blood taken from them, and then had them killed. . . . In Bucharest and in other cities the demonstrators shouted, "Down with the vampire!"
>
> "And you heard about the blood banks?" one of the children, a twelve-year-old boy, asked gravely. I had, but I let him tell it anyway.
>
> "Ceaușescu ordered his men to smash the blood banks during the fighting so that the wounded would not get emergency aid," the boy said.
>
> "They poisoned the water!" added Maria.
>
> "He's Dracula!" they said, almost at once.
>
> They compared Vlad Dracula . . . and Ceaușescu for a long time. "Dracula was better. He was a just man who helped the peasants!" They agreed that Dracula was by far the better man. They crossed themselves.[46]

The internal and external myths became mutually supporting because both were based on ignorance. Under Ceaușescu all reliable news had effectively disappeared from official channels of communication. Instead informal oral networks of gossip and rumor had predominated. These had deformed reality to such an extent that the bounds of the lie became practically unlimited, because, if nothing is believable, everything is plausible.[47] At the same time the language of the lie, the ritualized wooden words of official pronouncements and often absurd laws, had been semantically stripped bare. This encouraged linguistic elasticity, as ambiguities were played upon to escape the embrace of crass or coercive impositions. In such circumstances exaggeration became easy, and many of the rumors circulating prior to the revolution were as outlandish as the tales of horror that emerged from the events. Stories that human flesh was on sale in restaurants were the direct progenitors of the canard that the *secu-*

44. *Guardian,* August 6, 1990, 19; *Le Monde,* January 3, 1990, 2.
45. Aside from this chapter, this picture also appears on the cover of Wagner (1990).
46. Codrescu (1991), 71.
47. Sampson (1981–1983), 174–75.

Nicolae Ceaușescu, "the most renowned among vampires, criminals and dictators," is adorned with a swastika and horns in a montage photographed in Timișoara on December 24, 1989. © Owen Franken/CORBIS

ritate blew up blood banks in Bucharest and other cities to prevent the treatment of the wounded.

The stories of atrocities provided good copy for the western journalists but, for the Romanians and especially the army and the new leaders of the NSF, they fulfilled other needs. For the Romanian people the terrorists, who were popularly equated with the *securitate*, became the embodiment of the evils of the Ceauşescu regime. By making them guilty of the most inhuman behavior during the revolution, the ordinary citizens of Romania thrust these figures beyond the pale of their society, and thereby began the process of cleansing themselves from the nocuous residue of the past. Indeed, sometimes the terrorists even passed beyond the bounds of the Romanian nation, becoming Arabs, Russians, or, in an apparent blending of the Ottoman practice of the *devershime* and the Jewish golem myth, orphaned automata raised in isolation to obey the dictates of an evil leader. The myth of the terrorists and the stories of atrocities were widely accepted because, after the long years of tyranny in which the *securitate* had terrorized the Romanian people, they seemed credible. However, once the more nebulous realities of the revolution became apparent and blame more difficult to apportion, the persistence of the myth of the *securitate* as the avatar of all evil made coming to terms with the day-to-day existence of such men within their midst a painful process for many Romanians. There was also a sense in which exaggeration served as a means of excusing past inaction. Only through turning the old myth of the *securitate* as brutal supermen into a "reality" could previous acquiescence be explained and condoned. However, as this new "reality" was not only a myth but a false myth, it only led to a damaging hunt for a terrorist chimera, a search rooted in a malign reality, but nonetheless one that was destined to bear little fruit.[48]

For the leaders of the NSF the terrorists may have served other purposes. Stories that the new leaders were living in fear of their lives, moving around Bucharest in tanks and regularly changing homes to avoid assassination, continued to flourish long after the worst of the fighting had diminished.[49] It may be that by dwelling on the security danger while they consolidated their hold on power the new leaders sought to slough off their communist past and cement their newly found identification with the people.[50] However, even if the NSF can be accused of massaging the image of the fighting to suit its own requirements and, in particular, using the terrorist threat to secure its hold on power, it still takes a considerable leap to arrive at charges that it actually organized the violence in an elab-

48. The myth of the *securitate* is cut down to size by Eyal (1990), 150. Feelings of shame and guilt at prior acquiescence are noted in the *Guardian*, January 12, 1990, 23.

49. For such stories see the *Independent*, December 30, 1989, 1.

50. Octavian Paler cited in Calinescu and Tismaneanu (January–April 1991), 45 n. 12.

orate diversion, as some have suggested.[51] There is as little evidence to support this as there is the idea that the outcome of the events was determined beforehand by foreign intelligence agencies. The army also had a vested interest in painting the war against the terrorists in the strongest possible light. The heroic posture it adopted during the second phase of the revolution allowed it to consolidate its position as the guardian of the nation and effectively gain absolution from the sins incurred during the brutal suppression of the first street demonstrations. In the process it also brought some degree of protection from prosecution for the commanders who had been responsible for the massacres in Timișoara and elsewhere prior to December 22.

The sum of the revolution is far more than the terrorists and the National Salvation Front, and any study that fails to recognize this runs the risk of diminishing the role of the thousands who courageously took to the streets to defy Ceaușescu. It was these protesters who made the Romanian revolution of December 1989 and, ultimately, it was an important section of this crowd who imparted much of the radicalism to the event. As they chanted "Freedom" before the mass ranks of the security forces in Timișoara, Bucharest, and elsewhere, it would seem that in their conception of revolution the protesters were closest to Hannah Arendt, who saw revolution as a search for freedom and the revolutionaries as those who fought for freedom in the face of tyranny.[52] And, notwithstanding the ills of postcommunist Romania and the manifold doubts that still persist over the events of December 1989, the undeniable fact remains that at that time the Romanian people did overturn a particularly unpleasant regime. One of the greatest of Romanian historians, Alexandru Xenopol, earlier last century, perceptively wrote that Romania had traditionally experienced constitutional settlements that "taught us freedom, rather than constitutional contracts born out of the exercise of freedom."[53] During the Romanian revolution of December 1989 the citizens of Romania, rising in search of freedom, played their part in determining the eventual constitutional settlement of the revolution. In the process, they gave their country the opportunity to break from the past and to set forth on a differing and more propitious path to the future.

51. Ratesh (1991), 61–64.
52. Arendt (1973), 28–35. This is a simplification of Arendt's argument in which she distinguishes between a quest for liberty (the removal of oppression), and one for freedom (a desire to constitute these liberties). The Romanian language does not distinguish between the two words, but this study would argue that while "liberation" may have been initially to the fore, "freedom" became the ultimate goal for most of the revolutionaries.
53. Cited in Eyal (1990), 142.

Bibliography

Books and articles

Adler, Nanci, Gerard O. W. Mueller, and Mohammed Ayat. 1993. "Psychiatry under Tyranny: A Report on the Political Abuse of Romanian Psychiatry during the Ceaușescu Years." *Current Psychology* 12:1, 3–17.

A Future for Romania Foundation. 1993. "The End of Transition." *Sfera Politicii* 1:3, 17–18.

Alexandru, Ionel Ștefan. 1998. *Revoluția din decembrie 1989: momentul Brăila.* Brăila.

Alexiev, Alex. 1982. "The Romanian Army." In *Communist Armies in Politics,* edited by Jonathan R. Adelman, 149–66. Boulder, Colo.

Almond, Mark. 1990a. "Romania since the Revolution." *Government and Opposition* 25:4, 484–96.

———. 1990b. *Retreat to Moscow: Gorbachev and the Eastern European Revolution.* London.

———. 1991. "Decline without Fall: Romania under Ceaușescu." In *Europe in Turmoil: The Struggle for Pluralism,* edited by Gerald Frost, 279–329. London.

———. 1992. *The Rise and Fall of Nicolae and Elena Ceaușescu.* London.

Andrew, Christopher, and Oleg Gordievsky. 1990. *KGB: The Inside Story of Its Foreign Operations from Lenin to Gorbachev.* London.

Angelescu, Ioana. July 17, 1985. "Foreign Students Creating Problems." *Radio Free Europe Research,* Romanian Situation Report/11 19–21.

Anon. [Câmpeanu, Pavel]. October 23, 1986. "Birth and Death in Romania." *New York Review of Books* 33:16, 10–18.

Antal, Dan. 1994. *Out of Romania.* London.

Anuarul statistic al României 1991. n.d. Bucharest.

Anuarul statistic al României 1992. n.d. Bucharest.

Appleby, Joyce, Lynn Hunt, and Margaret Jacob. 1994. *Telling the Truth about History.* New York.

Ardeleanu, Tana, Răzvan Savaliuc, and Ion Baiu. 1996. *Procesul Ceaușescu.* Bucharest.

Arendt, Hannah. 1973. *On Revolution.* Harmondsworth, England.

Arjomand, Said Amir. 1995. "Plea for an Alternative View of Revolution." In *Debating Revolutions*, edited by Nikki R. Keddie, 142–54. New York.

Armanca, Brîndusa. 1997. "Morţii din cimitirul săracilor: un caz de jurnalism emoţional." In *O enigmă care împlineşte şapte ani: Timişoara, 1989–1996*, edited by Romulus Rusan, 167–71. Bucharest.

Atanaskovici, Mirko. 1997. "Revoluţia a făcut-o popurul român." In *O enigmă care împlineşte şapte ani: Timişoara, 1989–1996*, edited by Romulus Rusan, 183–85. Bucharest.

Avram, Vasile. 1992. *Zeul din labirint: Sibiu, decembrie 1989.* Sibiu.

Aya, Rod. 1990. *Rethinking Revolutions and Collective Violence: Studies on Concept, Theory and Method.* Amsterdam.

Băcescu, Angela. 1994. *România 1989: din nou în calea navalirilor barbare.* Cluj-Napoca.

Bacon, Walter M., Jr. 1978. "The Military and the Party in Romania." In *Civil-Military Relations in Communist Systems*, edited by Dale R. Herspring and Ivan Volgyes, 165–80. Boulder, Colo.

Banc, C., and Alan Dundes. 1990. *You Call This a Living? A Collection of East European Political Jokes.* Athens, Ga.

Barsan, Vasile, trans. 1975. "Mioriţa: Romanian Folk Ballad." *Romanian Sources* 1:1, 35–37.

Beck, Sam. 1984–85. "Changing States of Drinking: Alcohol Use in the Balkans." *East European Quarterly* 18:4, 395–413.

Behr, Edward. 1991. *Kiss the Hand You Cannot Bite: The Rise and Fall of the Ceauşescus.* London.

Berkhofer, Robert F., Jr. 1995. *Beyond the Great Story: History as Text and Discourse.* Cambridge, Mass.

Beschloss, Michael R., and Strobe Talbott. 1993. *At the Highest Levels: The Inside Story of the End of the Cold War.* New York.

Betea, Lavinia. 1998. *Alexandru Bârlădeanu despre Dej, Ceauşescu şi Iliescu, convorbiri.* Bucharest.

Birăescu, Traian Liviu. 1990. "De ce Timişoara?" In *Timişoara 16–22 decembrie 1989*, edited by Ion Anghel. 11–15. Timişoara.

Bishop, Robert, and E. S. Crayfield. 1949. *Russia astride the Balkans.* London.

Blackwell, Stephen. 2002. "Reform and Institutional Cooperation: Romanian Civil-Military Relations and the Accession Process to NATO and the European Union." In *South-Eastern Europe, the Stability Pact and EU Enlargement*, edited by David Phinnemore and Peter Siani-Davies, 228–51. Cluj-Napoca.

Boia, Lucian. 2001. *History and Myth in Romanian Consciousness.* Budapest.

Bradu, Mircea, and Gabriel Moisa. 2000. *O minune de trei zile: Oradea, decembrie '89.* Oradea.

Brateş, Teodor. 1992. *Explozia unei clipe: 22 decembrie 1989 — o zi în studioul 4.* Bucharest.

Brezinski, Horst, and Paul Petersen. 1990. "The Second Economy in Romania." In *The Second Economy in Marxist States*, edited by Maria Los, 79–80. London.

Brucan, Silviu. 1987. *World Socialism at the Crossroads: An Insider's View.* New York.

———. 1990. *Pluralism and Social Conflict: A Social Analysis of the Communist World.* New York.

———. 1993. *The Wasted Generation: Memoirs of the Romanian Journey from Capitalism to Socialism and Back.* Boulder, Colo.

Bruszt, László. 1990. "1989: The Negotiated Revolution in Hungary." *Social Research* 57:2, 365–87.

Bruz, Wlodzimierz. 1991. " 'Perestroika': Advance or Retreat of a Revolution?" In *Revolution and Counter–Revolution*, edited by E. E. Rice, 171–87. Oxford.

Brzoska, Michael, and Thomas Ohlson. 1987. *Arms Transfers to the Third World, 1971–1985.* Oxford.

Bunea, Mircea. 2000. *Agonia generalilor.* Bucharest.

Bush, Larry S. 1993. "Collective Labor Disputes in Post-Ceauşescu Romania." *Cornell International Law Journal* 26:2, 382–87.

Buzura, Augustin. 1994. *Refuges.* Translated by Ancuţa Vultur and Fred Nadaban. Boulder, Colo.

Calhoun, Craig Jackson. 1988. "The Radicalism of Tradition and the Question of Class Struggle." In *Rationality and Revolution,* edited by Michael Taylor, 129–75. Cambridge.

Calinescu, Matei, and Vladimir Tismaneanu. January/April 1991. "The 1989 Revolution and Romania's Future." *Problems of Communism* 60, 42–59.

Calvert, Peter. 1990. *Revolution and Counter–Revolution.* Milton Keynes, England.

Câmpeanu, Pavel. February 1, 1990. "The Revolt of the Romanians." *New York Review of Books* 37:1, 30.

——. 1988. *The Genesis of the Stalinist Social Order.* Armonk, N.Y.

——. 1993. *De patru ori în faţa urnelor.* Bucharest.

——. 2002. *Ceauşescu, anii numărătorii inverse.* Bucharest.

Câmpeanu, Pavel, and Ştefana Steriade. 1993. "The Revolution: The Beginning of the Transition." *Social Research* 60:4, 915–32.

Castex, Michel. 1990. *Un mensonge gros comme le siecle: Roumanie, histoire d'une manipulation.* Paris.

Chamberlain, Lesley. 1990. *In the Communist Mirror: Journeys in Eastern Europe.* London.

Chaplin, Ari. 1983. "The 'Popular War' Doctrine in Romanian Defense Policy." *East European Quarterly* 17:3, 267–82.

Chehabi, H. E., and Juan J. Linz, eds. 1988. *Sultanistic Regimes.* Baltimore.

Chirot, Daniel. 1991. "What Happened in Eastern Europe in 1989?" In *The Crisis of Leninism and the Decline of the left: The Revolutions of 1989,* edited by Daniel Chirot, 3–32. Seattle.

——. 1994. *Modern Tyrants: The Power and Prevalence of Evil in Our Age.* New York.

——. 1995. "After Socialism, What?: The Global Implications of the Revolutions of 1989 in Eastern Europe." In *Debating Revolutions,* edited by Nikki R. Keddie, 254–74. New York.

Cocan, Aurel Ioan Laurenţiu. 1999. *Trădare la nivel înalt.* Cluj-Napoca.

Codrescu, Andrei. 1991. *The Hole in the Flag: A Romanian Exile's Story of Return and Revolution.* New York.

Codrescu, Costache, Radu Olaru, Mircea Seteanu, and Constantin Monac. 1998. *Armata română în revoluţia din decembrie 1989.* Bucharest.

Cole, John W., and Judith A. Nydon. 1990. "Class, Gender and Fertility: Contradictions of Social Life in Contemporary Romania." *East European Quarterly* 23:4, 469–76.

Coposu, Corneliu. 1998. *Confessions: Dialogues with Doina Alexandru.* Translated by Elena Popescu. Boulder, Colo.

Corley, Felix, and John Eibner. 1990. *In the Eye of the Romanian Storm: The Heroic Story of Pastor Laszlo Tokes.* Old Tappan, N.J.

Cornea, Doina. 1991. *Scrisori deschise şi alte texte.* Bucharest.

——. 1997. "Cluj—21 decembrie 1989: cine a tras în noi?" In *O enigmă care împlineşte şapte ani: Timişoara, 1989–1996,* edited by Romulus Rusan, 239–44. Bucharest.

Cornis-Pop, Marcel. 1989. "Narration across the Totalistic Gap: On Recent Romanian Fiction." *Symposium* 43:1, 3–19.

Coruţ, Pavel. 1993. *Să te naşti sub steaua noastră.* Bucharest.

Costello, Michael. September 6, 1968. "Rumania and Her Allies: August 21 and After." *Radio Free Europe Research,* Rumanian Situation Report/12, 1–11.

Cronica însingerata a Bucureştiului în revoluţie. 1990. Bucharest.

Crowther, William E. 1988. *The Political Economy of Romanian Socialism.* New York.

——. 1989. "'Ceauşescuism' and Civil-Military Relations in Romania." *Armed Forces and Society* 15:2, 207–25.

Csalog, Zsolt. 1989. "Ceauşescu and the Miners: István Husszú's Story." *New Hungarian Quarterly* 30:116, 5–11.

Danta, Darrick. 1993. "Ceauşescu's Bucharest." *Geographical Review* 83:2, 170–82.

Datculescu, Petre, and Klaus Liepelt, eds. 1991. *Renaşterea unei Democraţii: alegerile din România de la 20 mai 1990.* Bucharest.

David, Gheorghe. 1990. "21–22 decembrie 1989: secvenţe Braşovene." *Magazin istoric* 24:9, 3–5.

Davies, James C. 1962. "Towards a Theory of Revolution." *American Sociological Review* 27:1, 5–19.

Dawisha, Karen. 1990. *Eastern Europe, Gorbachev, and Reform: The Great Challenge.* Cambridge.

Deletant, Dennis. 1988. "The Past in Contemporary Romania: Some Reflections on Current Romanian Historiography." *Slovo* 1:2, 77–91.

——. 1989. "Literature and Society in Romania since 1945." In *Perspectives on Literature and Society in Eastern and Western Europe,* edited by Geoffrey Hosking and George Cushing, 121–61. Basingstoke, England.

——. 1993. "Social Engineering in Romania: Ceauşescu's Systematization Program, 1965–1989." *Romanian Civilization* 2:1, 53–74.

——. 1994. "The *Securitate* and the Police State in Romania, 1964–89." *Intelligence and National Security* 9:1, 22–49.

——. 1995. *Ceauşescu and the Securitate: Coercion and Dissent in Romania, 1965–1989.* London.

——. 1998. *Romania under Communist Rule.* Bucharest.

Devlin, Kevin. February 9, 1990. "Romanians use Foreign Interviews to Debate Country's Future." *Report on Eastern Europe* 1:6, 26–30.

Dinescu, Mircea. 1985. *Exile on a Peppercorn.* Translated by Andrea Deletant and Brenda Walker. London.

Djordjević, Dimitrije, and Stephen Fisher-Galaţi. 1981. *The Balkan Revolutionary Tradition.* New York.

Dobrynin, Anatoly. 1995. *In Confidence: Moscow's Ambassador to America's Six Cold War Presidents 1962–1986.* New York.

Dolghin, Florentina, Ioan Lăcustă, Dorin Matei, Marian Ştefan, and Ioana Ursu. 1990. "Ei, tinerii, au făcut revoluţia. Ei, tinerii, scriu istoria." *Magazin Istoric* 24:2, 3–7.

Domenico, Viorel. 1992. *După execuţie a nins.* Bucharest.

——. 1999. *Ceauşescu la Târgovişte 22–25 decembrie 1989.* Bucharest.

Doyle, William. 1991. "Revolution and Counter–Revolution in France." In *Revolution and Counter–Revolution,* edited by E. E. Rice, 95–108. Oxford.

Dragoş, Z. c1995. *Marturii tragice. Harghita, Covasna, Târgu Mureş: decembrie 1989–martie 1990.* Bucharest.

Dragostea noastră fierbinte pentru-al tării preşedinte. 1988. Bucharest.

Dumitriu, Petru. 1964. *Incognito.* London.

Durac, Nicolae. 1997. "Implicarea armatei în decembrie 1989, la Timişoara." In *O enigmă care împlineşte şapte ani: Timişoara, 1989–1996,* edited by Romulus Rusan, 115–19. Bucharest.

Eisenstadt, S. N. 1978. *Revolution and the Transformation of Societies: A Comparative Study of Civilizations.* New York.

———. 1992. "The Breakdown of Communist Regimes and the Vicissitudes of Modernity." *Daedalus* 121:2, 21–41.

Eyal, Jonathan. 1988. "Transylvanian Disorders." *World Today* 44:8–9, 130–32.

———. 1989. "Romania: Between Appearances and Realities." In *The Warsaw Pact and the Balkans: Moscow's Southern Flank,* edited by Jonathan Eyal. Basingstoke, England.

———. 1990. "Why Romania Could Not Avoid Bloodshed." In *Spring in Winter: The 1989 Revolutions,* edited by Gwyn Prins, 139–60. Manchester.

———. 1992. "Romanian-Soviet Relations." In *The End of the Outer Empire: Soviet-East European Relations in Transition, 1985–90,* edited by Alex Pravda, 185–204. London.

Eyal, Jonathan, and Ian Anthony. 1988. *Warsaw Pact Military Expenditure.* London.

Falin, Valentin. 1990. "The Collapse of Eastern Europe: Moscow's View." *New Perspectives Quarterly* 7:2, 22–26.

Feffer, John. 1992. *Shock Waves: Eastern Europe after the Revolutions.* Boston.

Filip, Teodor. 1999. *Secretele U.S.L.A.* Craiova.

Fischer, Mary Ellen. 1981. "Idol or Leader? The Origins and Future of the Ceauşescu Cult." In *Romania in the 1980s,* edited by Daniel Nelson, 117–41. Boulder, Colo.

———. 1985. "Women in Romanian Politics: Elena Ceauşescu, Pronatalism, and the Promotion of Women." In *Women, States and Party in Eastern Europe,* edited by Sharon L. Wolchik and Alfred G. Meyer, 121–37. Durham, N.C.

———. 1989. *Nicolae Ceauşescu: A Study in Political Leadership.* Boulder, Colo.

———. 1992. "The New Leaders and the Opposition." In *Romania after Tyranny,* edited by Daniel N. Nelson, 45–65. Boulder, Colo.

———. 1993. "Stalinism in Romania: A Preliminary Discussion of Stalin, Ceauşescu, and Totalitarianism." Conference Paper Prepared for the Second International Congress of Romanian Studies, July 6–10, 1993. Iaşi.

Fleurs, René de. 1984. "Socialism in One Family." *Survey* 8:4, 165–74.

Fortuna, Lorin. 1997. "Semnificaţia zilei de 20 decembrie 1989." In *O enigmă care împlineşte şapte ani: Timişoara, 1989–1996,* edited by Romulus Rusan, 162–66. Bucharest.

Freund, Emil. 1983. "Nascent Dissent in Romania." In *Dissent in Eastern Europe,* edited by Jane Leftwich Curry, 60–68. New York.

Gabanyi, Anneli Ute. April 22, 1987. "A Chronology of the Romanian-Hungarian Minority Dispute." *Radio Free Europe Research,* Romanian Situation Report/3, 11–15.

———. September 21, 1987. "Disgraced Romanian Leader Calls for Changes." *Radio Free Europe Research,* Romanian Situation Report/10, 3–6.

———. November 6, 1987. "Nicu Ceauşescu on the Way Up?" *Radio Free Europe Research,* Romanian Situation Report/12, 9–12.

———. 1990. *Die Unvollendete Revolution: Rümanien zwischen Diktatur und Demokratie.* Munich.

———. 2000. *The Ceauşescu Cult: Propaganda and Power in Communist Romania.* Bucharest.

Gafton, Paul. May 17, 1984. "Heavy Drinking and Alcoholism." *Radio Free Europe Research,* Romanian Situation Report/8, 13–16.

———. November 14, 1985. "The State of Emergency and the Militarization of the Power Industry." *Radio Free Europe Research,* Romanian Situation Report/16, 7–11.

———. December 17, 1985. "The Electricity Crisis." *Radio Free Europe Research,* Romanian Situation report/17, 27–32.

———. July 3, 1987. "Ceauşescu Increases Power for Himself and His Family." *Radio Free Europe Research,* Romanian Situation Report/6, 3–5.

———. August 14, 1987. "Ceauşescu's Strained Relationship with the *Nomenklatura.*" *Radio Free Europe Research,* Romanian Situation Report/9, 3–5.

———. October 15, 1987. "Officials in Charge of Energy Dismissed." *Radio Free Europe Research,* Romanian Situation Report/11, 7–9.

———. March 4, 1988. "Romania Renounces MFN Trade Status with the USA." *Radio Free Europe Research*, Romanian Situation Report/4, 3–5.

———. April 29, 1988. "The Romanian Communist Party Today." *Radio Free Europe Research*, Romanian Situation Report/6, 9–10.

———. June 23, 1988. "Wage Increase of 10% Approved." *Radio Free Europe Research*, Romanian Situation Report/8, 21–23.

———. December 29, 1988a. "The 1989 Plan and Budget." *Radio Free Europe Research*, Romanian Situation Report/15, 3–5.

———. December 29, 1988b. "The Foreign Debt." *Radio Free Europe Research*, Romanian Situation Report/15, 7–9.

Gallagher, Tom. 1995. *Romania after Ceauşescu: The Politics of Intolerance*. Edinburgh.

Galloway, George, and Bob Wylie. 1991. *Downfall: The Ceauşescus and the Romanian Revolution*. London.

Georgescu, Vlad. 1983a. "Politics, History and Nationalism: The Origins of Romania's Socialist Personality Cult." In *The Cult of Power: Dictators in the Twentieth Century*, edited by Joseph Held, 129–42. Boulder, Colo.

———. 1983b. "Romanian Dissent: Its Ideas." In *Dissent in Eastern Europe*, edited by Jane Leftwich Curry, 182–94. New York.

———. 1988. "Romania in the 1980s: The Legacy of Dynastic Socialism." *Eastern European Politics and Societies* 2:1, 69–93.

Gilberg, Trond. 1990. *Nationalism and Communism in Romania: The Rise and Fall of Ceauşescu's Personal Dictatorship*. Boulder, Colo.

Giurchescu, Anca. 1987. "The National Festival 'Song to Romania': Manipulation of Symbols in the Political Discourse." In *Symbols of Power: The Aesthetics of Political Legitimation in the Soviet Union and Eastern Europe*, edited by Claes Arvidsson and Lars Erik Blomqvist, 163–71. Stockholm.

Giurescu, Dinu C. 1990. *The Razing of Romania's Past*. New York.

Goldstone, Jack A. 1986. "Revolutions and Superpowers." In *Superpowers and Revolution*, edited by Jonathan R. Adelman, 38–48. New York.

———. 1991. "An Analytical Framework." In *Revolutions of the Late Twentieth Century*, edited by Jack A. Goldstone, Ted Robert Gurr, and Farrokh Moshiri, 37–51. Boulder, Colo.

———. 1995. "Analyzing Revolutions and Rebellions: A Reply to the Critics." In *Debating Revolutions*, edited by Nikki R. Keddie, 178–99. New York.

Goldstone, Jack A., Ted Robert Gurr, and Farrokh Moshiri, eds. 1991. *Revolutions of the Late Twentieth Century*. Boulder, Colo.

Goodwin, Jeff. 1994. "Old Regimes and Revolutions in the Second and Third Worlds." *Social Science History* 18:4, 575–604.

———. 1997. "State-Centred Approaches to Social Revolutions: Strengths and Limitations of a Theoretical Tradition." In *Theorizing Revolutions*, edited by John Foran, 11–37. London.

Goodwin, Jeff, and Theda Skocpol. 1989. "Explaining Revolutions in the Contemporary Third World." *Politics and Society* 17:4, 489–509.

Gorbachev, Mikhail. 1996. *Memoirs*. London.

Govender, Robert. 1982. *Nicolae Ceauşescu and the Romanian Road to Socialism*. London.

Graham, Lawrence S. 1982. *Romania: A Developing Socialist State*. Boulder, Colo.

Granqvist, Raoul. 1999. *Revolution's Urban Landscape: Bucharest Culture and Postcommunist Change*. Frankfurt am Main.

Gross, Peter. 1996. *Mass Media in Revolution and National Development: The Romanian Laboratory*. Ames, Ia.

Gurr, Ted Robert. 1970. *Why Men Rebel*. Princeton, N.J.

Gurr, Ted Robert, and Jack A. Goldstone. 1991. "Comparisons and Policy Implications." In *Revolutions of the Late Twentieth Century*, edited by Jack A. Goldstone, Ted Robert Gurr, and Farrokh Moshiri, 325–52. Boulder, Colo.

Habermas, Jürgen. 1990. "What Does Socialism Mean Today? The Rectifying Revolution and the Need for New Thinking on the Left." *New Left Review* 183, 3–21.

Hagopian, Mark N. 1974. *The Phenomenon of Revolution*. New York.

Haidău, Mihai. 1997. "Telecomunicații, conexiuni, secvențe." In *O enigmă care împlinește șapte ani: Timișoara, 1989–1996*, edited by Romulus Rusan, 158–61. Bucharest.

Hall, Brian. 1988. *Stealing from a Deep Place: Travels in South-Eastern Europe*. London.

Hall, Richard Andrew. 1997. "Rewriting the Revolution: Authoritarian Regime-State Relations and the Triumphs of Securitate Revisionism in Post-Ceaușescu Romania." Ph.D. diss., Indiana University.

———. 1999. "The Uses of Absurdity: The Staged War Theory and the Romanian Revolution of December 1989." *Eastern European Politics and Societies* 13:3, 501–42.

Halliday, Fred. 1991. "Revolution in the Third World: 1945 and After." In *Revolution and Counter–Revolution*, edited by E. E. Rice, 129–52. Oxford.

Hanson, Stephen E. 1991. "Gorbachev: The Last True Leninist Believer." In *The Crisis of Leninism and the Decline of the Left: The Revolutions of 1989*, edited by Daniel Chirot. 33–59. Seattle.

Harding, Georgina. 1990. *In Another Europe: A Journey to Romania*. London.

Harrington, Joseph F., and Scott D. Karns. 1988. "MFN and Human Rights: Romanian-American Relations, 1975–1988." *Southeastern Europe* 15:1–2, 71–97.

Harrington, Joseph F., and Bruce J. Courtney. 1991. *Tweaking the Nose of the Russians: Fifty Years of American-Romanian Relations, 1940–1990*. Boulder, Colo.

Hașeganu, Carmina. 1998. "Transition to Democracy in Romania: Political Developments, 1990–1997." MPhil. diss., School of Slavonic and East European Studies, University of London.

Hayden, Robert, and Milica Bakić-Hayden. 1992. "Orientalist Variations on the Theme "Balkans": Symbolic Geography in Recent Yugoslav Cultural Politics." *Slavic Review* 51:1, 1–15.

Hersh, Bradley S., Florin Popovici, Roxana C. Apetrei, Laurentiu Zolotusca, and Nicolae Beldescu. 1991. "Acquired Immunodeficiency Syndrome in Romania." *The Lancet* 338:8768, 645–49.

Hitchins, Keith. 1994. *Rumania 1866–1947*. Oxford.

Holloway, David. 1988–89. "Gorbachev's New Thinking." *Foreign Affairs* 68:1, 66–81.

Hord, Charlotte, Henry P. David, France Donnay, and Merill Wolf. 1991. "Reproductive Health in Romania: Reversing the Ceaușescu Legacy." *Studies in Family Planning* 22:4, 231–40.

Hunya, Gábor. 1989. "Village Systematisation in Romania: Historical, Economic and Ideological Background." *Communist Economies* 1:3, 327–41.

Iliescu, Ion. 1994. *Revoluție si reformă*. Bucharest.

———. 1995a. *Momente de istorie I—documente, interviuri, comentarii—decembrie 1989–iunie 1990*. Bucharest.

———. 1995b. *Revoluția trăită*. Bucharest

———. 1996. *Momente de istorie II—documente, alocuțiuni, comentarii—iunie 1990–septembrie 1991*. Bucharest.

———. 2001. *Revoluția română*. Bucharest.

The International Institute for Strategic Studies. *The Military Balance, 1989–1990*. 1989. London.

Ionescu, Dan. January 22, 1985. "A Touch of Royalty." *Radio Free Europe Research*, Romanian Situation Report/2, 13–19.

———. November 14, 1985. "The Black Market Flourishes." *Radio Free Europe Research*, Romanian Situation Report/16, 13–16.

——. April 18, 1986. "New Developments in the Harassment of Ethnic German Writers." *Radio Free Europe Research,* Situation Report Romania/5, 7–9.

——. January 28, 1988a. "Religious Elements in the Glorification of Ceauşescu." *Radio Free Europe Research,* Romanian Situation Report/2, 7–10.

——. January 28, 1988b. "Poems for Elena Ceauşescu." *Radio Free Europe Research,* Romanian Situation Report/2, 11–14.

——. March 4,1988. "Food Rationing in Brasov." *Radio Free Europe Research,* Romanian Situation Report/4, 9–12.

——. October 20, 1988. "A Chronology of Western Protests against Romania's Rural Resettlement Plan." *Radio Free Europe Research,* RAD Background Report/212. (Romania), 1–12.

——. December 2, 1988. "Acute Food Shortages." *Radio Free Europe Research,* Romanian Situation Report/14, 12–14.

——. March 9, 1990. "Old Practices Persist in Romanian Justice." *Report on Eastern Europe* 1:10, 44–48.

——. July 29, 1994. "UM 0215: A Controversial Intelligence Service in Romania." *Radio Free Europe/Radio Liberty Research Report* 3:30, 27–30.

Ioniţă, Gheorghe. n.d. "Bucureşti: revoluţia ceas cu ceas." In *România 16–22 decembrie: sînge, durere, speranţă 1989–1990,* 16–18. Bucharest.

Ioniţoiu, Cicerone. 1998. *Album al eroilor: România decembrie 1989.* Sibiu.

Ivan, Sabin. 1998. *Radiografii parlamentare de vorba cu Alexandru Bârlădeanu.* Constanţa.

Jackson, Marvin R. 1986. "Romania's Debt Crisis: Its Causes and Consequences." In *U.S. Congress Joint Economic Committee, East European Economies: Slow Growth in the 1980s.* 3 vols., 489–542. Washington, D.C.

——. 1989. "Statistics and Political Economy in Romania: What Comes Next—Relief or More Exploitation?" In *Pressures for Reform in the East European Economies: Study Papers Submitted to the Joint Economic Committee, Congress of the United States,* 2 vols., 307–27. Washington, D.C.

——. February 2, 1990. "The Economy in the Wake of the Revolution." *Report on Eastern Europe* 1:5, 29–32.

Johnson, Alice K., Richard L. Edwards, and Hildegard Puwak. 1993. "Foster Care and Adoption Policy in Romania: Suggestions for International Intervention." *Child Welfare* 72:5, 489–506.

Johnson, Brooke R., Mihai Horga, and Laurentia Andronache. 1993. "Contraception and Abortion in Romania." *The Lancet* 341:8849, 875–78.

Jones, Christopher D. 1984. "Romania." In *Warsaw Pact: The Question of Cohesion. Phase II—Volume 2: Poland, German Democratic Republic, and Romania,* edited by Teresa Rakowska-Harmstone, Christopher D. Jones, and Ivan Sylvain, 348–411. Ottawa.

Joó, Rudolf. 1994. *The Hungarian Minority's Situation in Ceauşescu's Romania.* Boulder, Colo.

Jowitt, Kenneth. 1971. *Revolutionary Breakthroughs and National Development: The Case of Romania, 1944–1965.* Berkeley, Calif.

——. 1978. *The Leninist Response to National Dependency.* Berkeley, Calif.

——. 1991. "The Leninist Extinction." In *The Crisis of Leninism and the Decline of the Left: The Revolutions of 1989,* edited by Daniel Chirot, 74–99. Seattle.

Karatnycky, Adrian, Alexander J. Motyl, and Adolph Sturmthal. 1980. *Workers' Rights East and West: A Comparative Study of Trade Union and Workers' Rights in Western Democracies and Eastern Europe.* New Bruswick, N.J.

Kideckel, David A. 1984–85. "Drinking Up: Alcohol, Class and Social Change in Rural Romania." *East European Quarterly* 18:4, 431–46.

——. 1992. "Peasants and Authority in the New Romania." In *Romania after Tyranny,* edited by Daniel N. Nelson, 67–81. Boulder, Colo.

———. 1993. *The Solitude of Collectivism: Romanian Villagers to the Revolution and Beyond.* Ithaca, N.Y.

Kimmel, Michael S. 1990. *Revolution: A Sociological Interpretation.* Cambridge.

Kincses, Előd. 1992. *Black Spring.* Munich. Also available at http://www.net.hu/corvinus/lib/kincses.

King, Robert R. March 6, 1972. "Romanian Difficulties in Military and Security Affairs." *Radio Free Europe Research,* Rumania Situation Report/6, 1–11.

———. May 17, 1972. "Reorganisation of the Ministry of the Interior." *Radio Free Europe Research,* Rumania Situation Report/17, 8–10.

Kirk, Roger E., and Mircea Raceanu. 1994. *Romania versus the United States: The Diplomacy of the Absurd, 1985–1989.* New York.

Kligman, Gail. 1988. *The Wedding of the Dead: Ritual Poetics and Popular Culture in Transylvania.* Berkeley, Calif.

———. 1990. "Reclaiming the Public: A Reflection on Creating Civil Society in Romania." *Eastern European Politics and Societies* 4:3, 393–427.

———. 1992. "The Politics of Reproduction in Ceauşescu's Romania: A Case Study in Political Culture." *Eastern European Politics and Societies* 6:3, 364–418.

———. 1998. *The Politics of Duplicity: Controlling Reproduction in Ceauşescu's Romania.* Berkeley, Calif.

Konrád, György, and Ivan Szelényi. 1979. *The Intellectuals on the Road to Class Power: A Sociological Interpretation of the Role of the Intelligentsia in Socialism.* New York.

Koppany S. March 21, 1989. "New Hungarian Minority Publication Appears in Transylvania." *Radio Free Europe Research,* Romanian Background Report/53, 1–3.

Krejčí, Jaroslav (assisted by Anna Krejčová). 1983. *Great Revolutions Compared: The Search for a Theory.* Brighton, England.

———. 1994. *Great Revolutions Compared: The Outline of a Theory.* Hemel Hempstead, England.

Lachmann, Richard. 1997. "Agents of Revolution: Elite Conflicts and Mass Mobilization from the Medici to Yeltsin." In *Theorizing Revolutions,* edited by John Foran, 73–101. London.

Lampe, John R., and Marvin R. Jackson. 1982. *Balkan Economic History 1550–1950: From Imperial Borderlands to Developing Nations.* Bloomington, Ind.

Lebedev, Alexander. 1990. "It Is Wrong to Prod Us On." *New Perspectives Quarterly* 7:2, 24.

Leicànd, Aurelia. July 20, 1988. "What Is Going On in Romanian Soccer?" *Radio Free Europe Research,* Romanian Situation Report/9, 41–43.

Lévesque, Jacques. 1997. *The Enigma of 1989: The USSR and the Liberation of Eastern Europe.* Berkeley, Calif.

Liiceanu, Gabriel. 2000. *The Păltiniş Diary: A Paideic Model in Humanist Culture.* Budapest.

Linden, Ronald. 1986. "Socialist Patrimonialism and the Global Economy: The Case of Romania." *International Organization* 40:2, 347–80.

———. 1989. "Romania: The Search for Economic Sovereignty." In *Pressures for Reform in the East European Economies: Study Papers Submitted to the Joint Economic Committee, Congress of the United States,* 2. vols., 291–306. Washington, D.C.

———. February 2, 1990. "Reaction to the Revolution, Part II: The Ceauşescu's Overthrow and Execution." *Report on Eastern Europe* 1:5, 36–40.

Livezeanu, Irina. 1995. *Cultural Politics in Greater Romania: Regionalism, Nation Building and Ethnic Struggle, 1918–1930.* Ithaca, N.Y.

Lorenz, Chris. 1994. "Historical Knowledge and Historical Reality: A Plea for 'Internal Realism.' " *History and Theory* 33:4, 297–327.

Loupan, Victor. 1990. *La révolution n'a pas eu lieu . . . : Roumanie l'histoire d'un coup d'état.* Paris.

Lungu, Victor. 1997. "La Cluj, după şapte ani." In *O enigmă care împlineşte şapte ani: Timişoara, 1989–1996,* edited by Romulus Rusan, 245–58. Bucharest.

Maier, Anneli. March 17, 1983. "Ceauşescu Defends His Military Doctrine." *Radio Free Europe Research,* Romanian Situation Report/5, 14–18.

———. November 17, 1984. "The RCP on the Eve of Its 13th Congress." *Radio Free Europe Research,* Romanian Situation Report/17, 2–7.

———. January 10, 1986. "Defense Minister Replaced." *Radio Free Europe Research,* Romanian Situation Report/1, 7–10.

———. September 11, 1986. "Growing Job Insecurity for Romanian Nomenklatura?" *Radio Free Europe Research,* Romanian Situation Report/10, 13–18.

Maier, Anneli, and Dan Ionescu. October 5, 1984. "Romanian Economists Criticize Extensive Growth Model." *Radio Free Europe Research,* Romanian Situation Report/14, 1–4.

Mănescu, Corneliu, in conversation with Lavina Betea. 2001. *Convorbiri neterminate.* Bucharest.

Marcu, Dorian. 1991. *Moartea Ceauşeştilor. Romanul imposibilei tăceri: revelaţii şi documente istorice.* Bucharest.

Marga, Andrei. 1993. "Cultural and Political Trends in Romania before and after 1989." *Eastern European Politics and Societies* 7:1, 14–32.

Matlock, Jack F., Jr. 1995. *Autopsy on an Empire: The American Ambassador's Account of the Collapse of the Soviet Union.* New York.

Mazilu, Dumitru. 1991. *De la totalitarism spre libertate: revoluţia furată—memoriu pentru ţara mea.* Bucharest.

———. 1999. *Proclamaţia revoluţiei române: 10 ani de la speranţ din 1989.* Bucharest.

McNeill, William H. 1978. *The Metamorphosis of Greece since World War II.* Oxford.

Meyer, Alfred G. 1972. "Legitimacy of Power in East Central Europe." In *Eastern Europe in the 1970s,* edited by Sylva Sinanian, Istvan Deak, and Peter C. Ludz., 45–68. New York.

Milin, Miodrag. 1990. *Timişoara: 15–21 decembrie '89.* Timişoara.

Moshiri, Farrokh. 1991. "Iran: Islamic Revolution against Westernisation." In *Revolutions of the Late Twentieth Century,* edited by Jack A. Goldstone, Ted Robert Gurr, and Farrokh Moshiri, 116–35. Boulder, Colo.

Müller, Herta. 1989. *The Passport.* London.

Mungiu, Alina. 1996. "Correspondence from Bucharest. Intellectuals as Political Actors in Eastern Europe: The Romanian Case." *East European Politics and Societies* 10:2, 333–64.

Nastase, Adrian. 2001. *Battle for the Future.* Translated by Ilinca Anghelescu, Fabiola Hosu, and Roxana Petcu. Boulder, Colo.

Neacşu, Costel. c1999. "Radioteleviziunea română—regizori şi figuranţi. 22–31 decembrie 1989." Unpublished manuscript.

Nelson, Daniel N. 1981. "Workers in a Workers' State." In *Romania in the 1980s,* edited by Daniel N. Nelson, 174–97. Boulder, Colo.

———. 1988. *Romanian Politics in the Ceauşescu era.* New York.

———. 1989. "Ceauşescu and the Romanian Army." *International Defense Review* 22:6, 737–41.

———. 1990. *Watching the Pact Unravel: The Transformation of East European Political-Military Policies,* Berichte des Bundesinstituts für ostwissenschaftliche und internationale Studien 32, Cologne.

Nicolae, Nicolae M. 2000. *O lume aşa cum am cunoscut-o: amintirile unui fost ambasador al României.* Bucharest.

Nicolaescu, Sergiu. 1995. *Revoluţia, începutul adevărului: un raport personal.* Bucharest.

———. 1999. *Cartea revoluţiei române decembrie '89.* Bucharest.

Nicolau, Irina, Speranța Rădulescu, Ioana Popescu, Aina Blidaru, Șerban Anghelescu, Ioan Pînzaru, Monica Lovinescu, and Daniel Barbu. 1990. *Vom muri și vom fi liberi.* Bucharest.

Oprea, Marius, and Stejărel Olaru. 2002. *Ziua care nu se uită: 15 noiembrie 1987, Brașov.* Bucharest.

Pacepa, Ion Mihai. 1989. *Red Horizons: The Extraordinary Memoirs of an East European Spy Chief.* London.

Parlamentul României. 1991. *Raportul. Comisiei parlamentare de audiere a persoanelor care, după 22 Decembrie 1989, au fost nevoite să-și părăsească locul de muncă și domiciliul din județele Harghita și Covasna.* Bucharest.

Pașcu, Ioan Mircea. 1987. "Theory and Practice in International Relations as a Subject of Study." *Revue roumaine d'études internationales* 21:4, 337–45.

Pasti, Vladimir. 1997. *The Challenges of Transition: Romania in Transition.* Boulder, Colo.

Patapievici, Horia-Roman. 2003. *Flying against the Arrow: An Intellectual in Ceaușescu's Romania.* Budapest.

Pedelty, Mark. 1995. *War Stories: The Culture of Foreign Correspondents.* London.

Personalități publice–politice 1989–92. 1993. Bucharest.

Perva, Aurel, and Roman, Carol. n.d. *Misterele revoluției române.* Bucharest.

Pilat, Vasile, and Dăianu, Daniel. 1984. "Some Problems of the Development of European Socialist Economies." *Revue roumaine d'études internationales* 18:3, 245–61.

———. 1985. "The Crisis of the World Economy—Content and Implications." *Revue roumaine d'études internationales* 19:1, 33–48.

Pitulescu, Ioan, Marin Lazăr, Ion Constantin, Vasile Lăpăduși, and Vladimir Alexandrescu. 1998. *Anul nou se naște în sânge! Ministerul de Interne în decembrie '89. Pledoarie pentru istorie. Volumul II.* Bucharest.

Pitulescu, Ion, Gheorghe Florea, Ion Constantin, Marin Lazăr, Vasile Lăpăduși, and Vladimir Alexandrescu. 1995. *Șase zile care au zguduit România. Ministerul de Interne în decembrie 1989. Pledoarie pentru istorie. Volumul I.* Bucharest.

Pleșu, Andrei. 1995. "Intellectual Life under Dictatorship." *Representations* 49, 61–71.

Pompei-Cojocaru, Carmen. March 25, 1985. "Temperatures (and the Public's Mood) Below Zero." *Radio Free Europe Research Report,* Romanian Situation Report/6, 3–6.

———. October 29, 1985. "The Harassment of Ethnic German Writers." *Radio Free Europe Research Report,* Romanian Situation Report/15, 27–30.

Pompey, Carmen. March 2, 1990. "Students and the Revolution." *Report on Eastern Europe* 1:9, 25–31.

Popa, Petre, and Ilie Ștefan. n.d. "Ieri la Timișoara, azi în toată țara!" In *România 16–22 decembrie: sînge, durere, speranță 1989–1990.* 22–28. Bucharest.

Popplewell, Richard. 1992. "The Stasi and the East German Revolution of 1989." *Contemporary European History* 1:1, 37–63.

Portocala, Radu. 1990. *Autopsie du coup d'état roumain: au pays du mensonge triomphant.* Paris.

Postelnicu, Tudor, interviewed by Sergiu Andon and G. Roveli. n.d. "Tudor Postelnicu martor ocular." In *România 16–22 decembrie: sînge, durere, speranță 1989–1990.* Bucharest.

Pravda, Alex, ed. 1992. *The End of the Outer Empire: Soviet-East European Relations in Transition, 1985–90.* London.

Quinlan, Paul. 1994. "Lupescu: Romania's Gray Eminence." *East European Quarterly* 28:1, 95–104.

Răceanu, Mircea. 2000. *Infern '89: Povestea unui condamnat la moarte.* Bucharest.

Rady, Martyn. 1992. *Romania in Turmoil: A Contemporary History.* London.

Ratesh, Nestor. 1991. *Romania: The Entangled Revolution.* New York.

Rațiu, Ion. 1975. *Contemporary Romania: Her Place in World Affairs.* Richmond, England.

——. 1999. *În fine acasa: note zilnice, decembrie 1989–decembrie 1990.* Bucharest.

Reich, Diana. 1990. "Children of the Nightmare." *Adoption and Fostering* 14:3, 9–14.

Reporters san Frontières, Le Nouvel Observateur and Médecins du Monde. 1990. *Roumanie: Qui a menti?* Montpellier.

Roman, Petre. 1994. *Libertatea ca datorie.* Cluj-Napoca.

Romania: Human Rights Abuses in the Eighties. 1987. London.

Romania: A Case of Dynastic Communism. 1989. New York.

Ronnås, Per. 1989. "Turning the Romanian Peasant into a New Socialist Man: An Assessment of Rural Development Policy in Romania." *Soviet Studies* 41:4, 543–59.

Rosenberg, Tina. 1995. *The Haunted Land: Facing Europe's Ghosts after Communism.* New York.

Rosenberg, William G., and Diane P Koenker. 1987. "The Limits of Formal Protest: Worker Activism and Social Polarization in Petrograd and Moscow, March to October, 1917." *American Historical Review* 92:2, 296–326.

Rupnick, Jacques. 1989. *The Other Europe.* London.

The RUSI Soviet-Warsaw Pact Yearbook 1989. 1989–90. Coulsdon, England.

Sampson, Steven L. 1981–83. "Muddling through in Rumania (Or: Why the Mamaliga Doesn't Explode)." *International Journal of Rumanian Studies* 3:1–2, 165–85.

——. 1983. "Is Romania the Next Poland?" *Critique* 16, 139–44.

——. 1984. "Rumours in Socialist Romania." *Survey* 8:123, 142–64.

——. 1984–86. "Regime and Society in Rumania." *International Journal of Rumanian Studies* 4:1, 41–51.

——. 1985–86. "The Informal Sector in Eastern Europe." *Telos* 66, 44–66.

——. 1989. "Romania: House of Cards." *Telos* 79, 217–24.

Săndulescu, Șerban. c1996. *Decembrie '89, lovitura de stat a confiscat revoluția română.* Bucharest.

Sârcă, Sebastian, ed. 1998. *E un început în tot sfârșitul: culegere selectivă din programele radiodifuzate în zilele de 17–25 decembrie 1989.* Bucharest.

Saucă, Alexandru. 1994. *KGB-ul și revoluția română: intensificarea ofensivei forțelor antiromânești.* Second edition. Bucharest.

Sava, Constantin, and Constantin Monac. 2001. *Revoluția română din Decembrie 1989 retrăită prin documente și mărturii.* Bucharest.

Schöpflin, George. 1988. "Reform in Eastern Europe." *Slovo* 1:2, 1–5.

——. 1993. *Politics in Eastern Europe 1945–1992.* Oxford.

Schöpflin, George, and Hugh Poulton. 1990. *Romania's Ethnic Hungarians.* London.

Schwerthoeffer, Simona. 1985. "The Nationalities Policy: Theory and Practice." In *Romania: 40 Years. 1944–1984,* edited by Vlad Georgescu, 79–92. New York.

Scurtu, Ioan, Ecaterina Mazilu, Ștefania Dinu, and Șeban Pavelescu, et al. 1990. *Sfîrșitul dictaturii.* Bucharest.

Sejna, Jan. 1982. *We Will Bury You.* London.

Selbin, Eric. 1997. "Revolution in the Real World: Bringing Agency Back In." In *Theorizing Revolutions,* edited by John Foran, 123–36. London.

Shafir, Michael. 1985. *Romania: Politics, Economics and Society; Political Stagnation and Simulated Change.* London.

——. July 2, 1986. "Far From the Eyes of Justice, Close to the Party's Heart." *Radio Free Europe Research,* Romanian Situation Report/7, 33–37.

——. 1986a. "Romanian Foreign Policy under Dej and Ceaușescu." In *The Soviet Union and Eastern Europe,* edited by George Schöpflin, 364–77. New York.

——. 1986b. "Romania." In *Leadership and Succession in the Soviet Union, Eastern Europe and China,* edited by Martin McCauley and Stephen Carter, 124–27. Armonk, N.Y.

——. 1987. "The Future of the Rumanian Leadership." *International Journal of Rumanian Studies* 5:1, 33–40.

——. January 28, 1988. "The Dispute with Hungary over Transylvania." *Radio Free Europe Research,* Romanian Situation Report/2, 15–19.

——. June 29, 1988. "Romania: Explosive." *East European Reporter* 2:13, 1–3.

——. July 20, 1988. "Senior Officials Dismissed in Environmental Scandal." *Radio Free Europe Research* Romanian Situation Report/9, 17–21.

——. August 23, 1988a. "The Historical Background to Rural Resettlement." *Radio Free Europe Research,* Romanian Situation Report/10, 3–8.

——. August 23, 1988b. "The Mazilu Riddle: Romanian Official Fails to Appear before UN Body." *Radio Free Europe Research,* Romanian Situation Report/10, 23–26.

——. August 23, 1988c. "A Renewal of Stalinism?" *Radio Free Europe Research Report,* Romania Situation Report/10, 33–34.

——. August 23, 1988d. "West Germany Condemns Village Demolition Plans." *Radio Free Europe Research,* Romanian Situation Report/10, 17–22.

——. September 16, 1988. "A Light from the East: A Romanian Writer Hails *Perestroika* on Radio Moscow." *Radio Free Europe Research,* Romanian Situation Report/11, 27–31.

——. January 5, 1990. "The Isolation of Romania and the Fall of Nicolae Ceaușescu." *Report on Eastern Europe* 1:1, 28–32.

——. January 12, 1990. "The New Romanian Government." *Report on Eastern Europe* 1:2, 35–38.

——. January 19, 1990. "Ceaușescu's Overthrow: Popular Uprising or Moscow-Guided Conspiracy?" *Report on Eastern Europe* 1:3, 15–19.

——. January 26, 1990. "The Revolution: An Initial Assessment." *Report on Eastern Europe* 1:4, 34–42.

——. March 2, 1990. "The Provisional Council of National Unity: Is History Repeating Itself?" *Report on Eastern Europe* 1:9, 18–24.

——. May 11, 1990. "New Revelations of the Military's Role in Ceaușescu's Ouster." *Report on Eastern Europe* 1:19, 24–42.

——. October 12, 1990. "Preparing for the Future by Revising the Past." *Report on Eastern Europe* 1:41, 29–42.

——. February 15, 1991. "Schöpflinian Realism and Romanian Reality." *Report on Eastern Europe* 2:7, 32–40.

——. November 12, 1993. "Best-Selling Spy Novels Seek to Rehabilitate Romanian *Securitate.*" *Radio Free Europe/Radio Liberty Research Report* 2:45, 14–18.

Sharman, T. 1983. "Canal on the Danube Delta." *Geographical Magazine* 55, 317–21.

Shevardnadze, Eduard. 1991. *The Future Belongs to Freedom.* London.

Shotter, John. 1990. "The Social Construction of Remembering and Forgetting." In *Collective Remembering,* edited by David Middleton and Derek Edwards, 120–36. London.

Siani-Davies, Peter. 1995. "The Romanian Revolution of December 1989: Myth and Reality—Myth or Reality?" Ph.D. diss., School of Slavonic and East European Studies, University of London.

——. 1996. "Romanian Revolution or Coup d'État? A Theoretical View of the Events of December 1989." *Communist and Post-Communist Studies* 19:4, 453–65.

——. 1998. " The Traditional Parties and the Romanian Elections of May 1990." In *Occasional Papers in Romanian Studies II,* edited by Rebecca Haynes, 125–46. London.

——. 2001. "The Revolution after the Revolution." in *Post-Communist Romania: Coming to Terms with Transition,* edited by Duncan Light and David Phinnemore, 15–34. Basingstoke, England.

Șimăndan, Emil. 1999. *Întrebătorul din agora: zece ani de la revoluția română din decembrie '89 de la Arad.* Arad.

Simpson, John. 1992. *The Darkness Crumbles: Despatches from the Barricades.* Revised and updated. London.

Skocpol, Theda. 1979. *States and Social Revolutions: A Comparative Analysis of France, Russia, and China.* Cambridge.

——. 1982. "Rentier State and Shi'a Islam in the Iranian Revolution." *Theory and Society* 11:3, 265–83.

——. 1994. *Social Revolutions in the Modern World.* Cambridge.

Slater, Wendy. September 24, 1993. "Russia's National Salvation Front 'On the Offensive.' " *Radio Free Europe/Radio Liberty Research Report* 2:38, 1–6.

Smith, Alan H. 1979. "Romanian Economic Relations with the EEC." *Jahrbuch der Wirtschaft Osteuropas* 8, 323–61, Munich.

Snyder, Richard. 1992. "Explaining Transitions from Neopatrimonial Dictatorships." *Comparative Politics* 24:4, 379–99.

——. 1998. "Paths out of Sultanistic Regimes: Combining Structural and Voluntarist Perspectives." In *Sultanistic Regimes,* edited by H.E. Chehabi and Juan J. Linz, 49–81. Baltimore.

Socor, Vladimir. January 13, 1984. "Valter Roman: Reform Communist Who Failed." *Radio Free Europe Research,* RAD Background Report/4. (Romania), 1–9.

——. October 5, 1984. "The Danube-Black Sea Canal: Anatomy of a White Elephant." *Radio Free Europe Research,* Romanian Situation Report/14, 7–14.

——. July 22, 1985. "Are the old Political Parties Stirring in Romania?" *Radio Free Europe Research,* RAD Background Report/69. (Romania), 1–7.

——. October 29, 1985. "Romanian-Canadian Nuclear Power Project." *Radio Free Europe Research,* Romanian Situation Report/15, 11–17.

——. August 13, 1986. "Eyewitness on the 1977 Miners' Strike in Romania's Jiu Valley." *Radio Free Europe Research,* RAD Background Report/110. (Romania), 1–5.

——. November 6, 1986. "Three Romanians Reported to Have Endorsed Joint Dissident Statement." *Radio Free Europe Research,* Romanian Situation Report/12, 33–34.

——. December 23, 1986. "Exports of Armaments." *Radio Free Europe Research,* Romanian Situation Report/14, 17–21.

——. February 6, 1987. "National Peasant Group Silenced after Human Rights Initiative." *Radio Free Europe Research,* Romanian Situation Report/1, 23–26.

——. March 6, 1987. "Mihai Botez on Romania's Problems." *Radio Free Europe Research,* Romanian Situation Report/2, 13–16.

——. August 7, 1987. "Known Prisoners of Conscience in Romania: An Annotated Checklist." *Radio Free Europe Research,* RAD Background Report/134. (Romania), 1–6.

——. November 6, 1987. "Scanning the High Seas for Clients for the Danube-Black Sea Canal." *Radio Free Europe Research,* Romanian Situation Report/12, 21–24.

——. November 25, 1987. "Recurring Workers' Protests." *Radio Free Europe Research,* Romanian Situation Report/13, 5–9.

——. December 4, 1987. "The Workers' Protest in Braşov: Assessment and Aftermath." *Radio Free Europe Research,* RAD Background Report/231. Romania, 1–6.

——. January 13, 1988a. "Károly Király's Letter to Ceauşescu." *Radio Free Europe Research,* Romanian Situation Report SR/1, 29–31.

——. January 13, 1988b. "Social Protests Continue." *Radio Free Europe Research,* Romanian Situation Report/1, 21–23.

——. March 2, 1988. "Romanian Democratic Action." *Radio Free Europe Research,* RAD Background Report/34. (Romania), 1–3.

——. September 16, 1988. "Group Protests Rural Resettlement and Calls for Referendum on the Matter." *Radio Free Europe Research,* Romanian Situation Report/11, 19–20.

——. November 9, 1988. "Nicolae and Elena Ceaușescu Visit the USSR." *Radio Free Europe Research Report,* Romanian Situation Report/13, 3–8.

——. February 2, 1990. "Pastor Toekes and the Outbreak of the Revolution in Timișoara." *Report on Eastern Europe,* 1:5, 19–26.

——. February 16, 1990. "Political Parties Emerging." *Radio Free Europe Research,* 1:7, 28–35.

Sorkin, Adam J. 1991. "Hard Lines: Romanian Poetry, Truth, and Heroic Irony under the Ceaușescu Dictatorship." *Literary Review* 35:1, 26–38.

Spiridon, Cassian Maria. 1994. *Iași, 14 decembrie 1989, începutul revoluției romăne.* Iași.

Stan, Valerian. 1997. "Armata română în revoluția din decembrie 1989—nevoia de adevăr." In *O enigmă care împlinește șapte ani: Timișoara, 1989–1996,* edited by Romulus Rusan, 193–99. Bucharest.

Staniszkis, Jadwiga. 1990. "Patterns of Change in Eastern Europe." *East European Politics and Societies* 4:1, 77–97.

"Statement of the Ministry of Foreign Affairs, Bucharest 6 January 1990." 1989. *Revue roumaine d'études internationales* 23:5–6, 413.

Stefanescu, Crisula. March 2, 1984. "Increase in Juvenile Delinquency." *Radio Free Europe Research,* Romanian Situation Report/4, 21–24.

——. April 9, 1985. "Where There's a Will There's a Way." *Radio Free Europe,* Romanian Situation Report/7, 19–21.

——. October 1, 1985. "Tuning into Romanian Television." *Radio Free Europe Research,* Romanian Situation Report/14, 15–17.

——. October 14, 1988. "Poem by Ana Blandiana Censored." *Radio Free Europe Research,* Romanian Situation Report/12, 13–16.

——. November 9, 1988. "A Romanian Writer's Letter of Protest." *Radio Free Europe Research ,* Romanian Situation Report/13, 29–30.

——. March 23, 1990. "'Free Romanian Television' Losing Its Credibility." *Report on Eastern Europe* 1:12, 24–28.

Ștefănescu, Domnița. 1995. *Cinci ani din istoria României: o cronologie a evenimentelor decembrie 1989–decembrie 1994.* Bucharest.

Stockholm International Peace Research Institute, *SIPRI yearbook 1990: World Armaments and Disarmament.* 1990. Oxford.

Stone, Lawrence. 1966. "Theories of Revolution." *World Politics* 18:2, 159–76.

Stoker, Bram. 1993. *Dracula.* London.

Stork, Coen, in conversation with Gabriel Andreescu, *Cel mai iubit dintre ambasadori.* 1993. Bucharest.

Stroynowski, Juliusz, ed. 1989. *Who's Who in the Socialist Countries of Europe.* 3 vols. Munich.

Sturdza, Mihai. April 13, 1990. "How Dead Is Ceaușescu's Secret Police Force?" *Report on Eastern Europe* 1:15, 28–36.

——. July 27, 1990. "The Labor Movement." *Report on Eastern Europe* 1:30 36–42.

Suciu, Titus. 1990. *Reportaj cu sufletul la gură: traseele revoluției.* Timișoara.

Sweeny, John. 1991. *The Life and Evil Times of Nicolae Ceaușescu.* London.

Szelényi, Ivan. 1986–87. "The Prospects and Limits of the East European New Class Project: An Auto-Critical Reflection on *The Intellectuals on the Road to Class Power.*" *Politics and Society* 15:2, 103–44.

Tănase, Stelian, 1999. *Miracolul revoluției.* Bucharest.

Tatomirescu, Ion Pachia. 1990. "Nopțile și zilele revoluției romăne din decembrie 1989, la Timișoara." In *Timișoara 16–22 decembrie 1989.* edited by Ion Anghel, 152–64. Timișoara.

Televiziunea Română. *Revoluția romănă în direct.* 1990. Bucharest.

Teodorescu, Alin. 1991. "The Future of a Failure: The Romanian Economy." In *Eco-*

nomic Change in the Balkan States: Albania, Bulgaria, Romania, and Yugoslavia, edited by Örjan Sjöberg and Michael L. Wyzan, 69–82. London.

Teodorescu, Filip. 1992. *Un risc asumat: Timişoara decembrie 1989*. Bucharest.

Tien–lung, Liu Michael. 1988. "States and Urban Revolutions: Explaining the Revolutionary Outcomes in Iran and Poland." *Theory and Society* 17:2, 179–209.

Tilly, Charles. 1991. "Changing Forms of Revolution." In *Revolution and Counter–Revolution*, edited by E. E. Rice, 1–25. Oxford.

——. 1993. *European Revolutions, 1492–1992*. Oxford.

——. 1995. "The Bourgeois Gentilshommes of Revolutionary Theory." In *Debating Revolutions*, edited by Nikki R. Keddie, 136–41. New York.

Tismaneanu, Vladimir. 1986. "Byzantine Rites, Stalinist Follies: The Twilight of Dynastic Socialism in Romania." *Orbis* 30:1, 65–90.

——. 1988. "New Underground Union." *East European Reporter* 3:3, 57–58.

——. 1989a. "The Rebellion of the Old Guard." *East European Reporter* 3:4, 23–24.

——. 1989b. "The Tragicomedy of Romanian Communism." *Eastern European Politics and Societies* 3:2, 329–76.

——. 1992. "From Arrogance to Irrelevance: Avatars of Marxism in Romania." In *The Road to Disillusion: From Critical Marxism to Postcommunism in Eastern Europe*, edited by Raymond Taras. Armonk, N.Y.

——. 1993. "The Quasi–Revolution and Its Discontents: Emerging Political Pluralism in Post–Ceauşescu Romania." *Eastern European Politics and Societies* 7:2, 309–48.

——. 1998. *Fantasies of Salvation: Democracy, Nationalism and Myth in Post-Communist Europe*. Princeton. NJ.

——. 2003. *Stalinism for All Seasons: A Political History of Romanian Communism*. Berkeley. Calif.

Tismaneanu, Vladimir, and Dan Pavel. 1994. "Romania's Mystical Revolutionaries: The Generation of Angst and Adventure Revisited." *Eastern European Politics and Societies* 8:3, 402–38.

Todorova, Maria. 1992. "Improbable Maverick or Typical Conformist? Seven Thoughts on the New Bulgaria." In *Eastern Europe in Revolution*, edited by Ivo Banac, 148–67. Ithaca, N.Y.

——. 1997. *Imagining the Balkans*. Oxford.

Tőkés, László. 1990. *With God, for the People: The Autobiography of László Tőkés*. London.

Tucker, Robert C., ed. 1977. *Stalinism: Essays in Historical Interpretation*. New York.

Turnock, David. 1986a. *The Romanian Economy in the Twentieth Century*. New York.

——. 1986b. "The Danube Black-Sea Canal and Its Impact on Southern Romania." *GeoJournal* 12:2, 65–79.

——. 1991. "Romanian Villages: Rural Planning under Communism." *Rural History* 2:1, 77–107.

Urdăreanu, Tiberiu. 1996. *1989, martor şi participant*. Bucharest.

Ursu, Ioana, Florentina Dolghin, and Ioan Lăcustă. 1990. "Ei, tinerii, au făcut revoluţia. Ei, tinerii, scriu istoria." *Magazin Istoric*. 24:3, 3–7.

Verdery, Katherine. 1991. *National Ideology under Socialism: Identity and Cultural Politics in Ceauşescu's Romania*. Berkeley, Calif.

——. 1994. "The Elasticity of Land: Problems of Property Restitution in Transylvania." *Slavic Review* 53:4, 1071–1109.

——. 1995. "What Was Socialism and Why Did It Fail?" In *Debating Revolutions*, edited by Nikki R. Keddie, 221–43. New York.

Verdery, Katherine, and Gail Kligman. 1992. "Romania after Ceauşescu: Post–Communist Communism?" In *Eastern Europe in Revolution*, edited by Ivo Banac, 117–47. Ithaca, N.Y.

Volgyes, Ivan. 1982. *The Political Reliability of the Warsaw Pact Armies: The Southern Tier.* Durham, N.C.

Wagner, Richard. 1990. *Exit: A Romanian Story.* London.

Watts, Larry L. 1992. "The Romanian Army in the December Revolution and Beyond." In *Romania after Tyranny*, edited by Daniel N. Nelson, 95–126. Boulder, Colo.

Wilder, Bryant Jessie. 1995. "History on the Cutting-Room Floor." *Literature Film Quarterly* 23:4, 243–46.

Witnesses to Cultural Genocide: First-Hand Reports on Rumania's Minority Policies Today. 1979. New York.

Film, television, and the Internet

Blanton, Thomas. March 1998. "When Did the Cold War End?" *Cold War International History Project Bulletin,* no. 10, 184–88. Available from http://cwihp.si.edu/bulletin -pdf.htm.

Dornhelm, Robert, dir. 1990. *Requiem for Dominic.* Austria.

Hall, Richard Andrew. 2002. "The Securitate Roots of a Modern Romanian Fairy Tale: The Press, the Former Securitate and the Historiography of December 1989." *Radio Free Europe/Radio Liberty East European Perspectives* 4:7–9. Available at http://www.rferl.org/eepreport/2002/04/7-030402.html, http://www.rferl.org/eepreport/2002/04/8-170402.html, and http://www.rferl.org/eepreport/2002/05/9-010502.html.

Mioc, Marius. 2000a. *Istoria unei comisii.* Available at http://www.timisoara.com/newmioc/46.htm.

——. 2000b. *Turişti straini în timpul revoluţiei.* Available: http://www.timisoara.com/newmioc/54.htm.

Munteanu, Mircea. n.d. "New Evidence on the 1989 Crisis in Romania." *Cold War International History Project e-dossier,* no.5, available from http://cwihp.si.edu/pdf/Rom-Dossier.pdf.

Raportul SRI asupra evenimentelor din decembrie 1989. n.d. Available from http://www.timisoara.com/timisoara/r.html.

Rice, Condoleezza. December 17, 1997. Interview in the National Security Archive, available from http://www.gwu.edu/nsarchiv/coldwar/interviews/episode-24/rice2.html.

Simpson, John. December 16, 1994. *Newsnight,* BBC2.

Transcript of the closed trial of Nicolae and Elena Ceauşescu. n.d. Available from http://www.timisoara.com/timisoara/rev/trialscript.html.

Transcriptul "procesului" Nicolae şi Elena Ceauşescu. n.d. Available from http://www.timisoara.com/timisoara/rev/proces.txt.

Index

Note: Locators in italics denote illustrations.